ROADMAP TO ENTREPRENEURIAL SUCCESS

Powerful Strategies for Building a High-Profit Business

Robert W. Price

AMACOM

American Management Association

New York • Atlanta • Brussels • Chicago • Mexico City • San Francisco
Shanghai • Tokyo • Toronto • Washington, D. C.

This publication is designed to provide accurate and authoritative information in regard to the subject matter covered. It is sold with the understanding that the publisher is not engaged in rendering legal, accounting, or other professional service. If legal advice or other expert assistance is required, the services of a competent professional person should be sought.

Library of Congress Cataloging-in-Publication Data

Price, Robert W.
    Roadmap to entrepreneurial success : powerful strategies for building
a high-profit business / Robert W. Price.
        p.   cm.
    Includes bibliographical references and index.
    ISBN 0–8144–7190–0
    1. New business enterprises—Management.   2. Entrepreneurship.   I.
Title.
    HD62.5.P66   2004
    658.4'21—dc22

                                                                                2003020905

Printing number

10   9   8   7   6   5   4   3   2   1

Contents

Foreword

A new day has come for entrepreneurs. The torrid and unsustainable pace of investment into start-ups that took place in the late 1990s is history. The rules have changed, and those navigating the waters of starting and managing a new business venture will find a fresh set of value drivers. Gone are the days of plenty of hype and little substance. Businesses today must put forth sustainable value propositions and establish a roadmap for achieving sound objectives.

Today we are welcoming a "back-to-basics" mentality from entrepreneurs and investors alike. This shift is a much-needed response to the economic conditions we are currently experiencing. There is no bear market on good ideas and no bear market for innovations and creative entrepreneurs. So regardless of where we are in the inevitable business cycle, this much is true: To effectively build an organization, you need a clear vision as to where you want to go and a solid business plan that gets you there.

Operating in an economy that is emerging from a recession requires entrepreneurs to enter the market with their eyes wide open. The landscape isn't pretty; but there are plenty of opportunities for those with rational expectations. For instance, the time horizon for a company to "exit," either through an initial public offering or acquisition, has returned to a minimum period of five to seven years from inception. For many, this journey to a successful harvest will be much longer; therefore commitment and persistence is the name of the game. Entrepreneurs who are focused solely on the potential windfall at the end of the day will not only be disappointed when it doesn't arrive on time, but they are also more likely to make operating mistakes at a critical time in their venture's evolution.

The ability to manage effectively in uncertain times and when problems arise will help entrepreneurs and business executives keep their strategic heading. Such maneuvering requires flexibility and an aptitude for seeing beyond the crisis *du jour* to the ultimate objective, building a company with sustainable value. These challenges aside, we must not forget that some of the most successful start-ups began during a recession. Those companies that can survive this environment, make difficult but deliberate decisions, and remain focused will emerge stronger than most.

Whether or not you are searching for outside investors, understanding what successful venture capitalists look for in a start-up company will help set you on the right path. The first, and perhaps most obvious, criterion is strong management. Having a great idea is not enough: Your team needs to be in a position to execute differently. Each executive should bring a level of expertise to the table. That goes for the Board of Directors as well. Corporate directors are now presumed accountable for certain company operations including audit and compensation. They can also be indispensable in other areas, such as the sales process.

Today, sound management is when both the Board and the management team set milestones for the company and often review progress against those goals. Knowing that you are on the right track is important; realizing that you may be on the wrong one is crucial.

Entrepreneurs embody the American dream. Fired with ideas, they have been the engine to our economic growth and subsequently have set our economy apart from all other nations. Entrepreneurship is the vehicle for creating new jobs, generating revenue, advancing innovation, enhancing productivity, and improving business models and processes. Despite the challenges, entrepreneurship has never before been more vital to our economy than it is today. It is our best offense for economic progress and our finest defense against the status quo. Promoting entrepreneurship is in everyone's best interest.

Roadmap to Entrepreneurial Success promotes entrepreneurship and provides the necessary tools for both the new and experienced entrepreneur to stay on course and succeed. It facilitates the strategic focus required to win in the game of business. Launching a new business venture is risky, and nothing is ever guaranteed. *Roadmap* shares good management practices, offers thoughtful insights, and will serve you well throughout the life of your venture. Regardless of your role at your organization, you will find that the decision-making process is subject to a higher level of scrutiny all around. Entrepreneurship is not for the weak at heart. As we say, the risks are plentiful, but so are the rewards for those who make it. Enjoy the journey.

MARK HEESEN
PRESIDENT
NATIONAL VENTURE CAPITAL ASSOCIATION

Preface

Entrepreneurship is the cornerstone of the free enterprise system. In fact, research has found that more than 460 million adults around the globe were engaged in some form of entrepreneurial activity in 2002. Good entrepreneurial management is therefore vitally important to the economic health not only of American businesses, but also of businesses in the rest of the world. Because of its importance, entrepreneurial management should be thoroughly understood, but this is easier said than done. The field is relatively complex, and it is undergoing constant change in response to shifts in economic conditions. In addition, there is a substantial body of knowledge, concepts, and tools that entrepreneurs need to know in order to launch and grow a company successfully. All of this makes entrepreneurship stimulating and exciting but also challenging and sometimes discouraging.

The Purpose of This Book

Are you thinking about starting a new business? Are you in charge of an entrepreneurial activity at work? Do you have a business plan and need to focus on getting your venture financed quickly? *Roadmap* is a strategy book that includes guidelines, instructions, and explanations for creating and leading emerging growth ventures in uncertain times. It will lead you through the actual process of getting a new business venture funded and launched, growing the venture, successfully harvesting it, and perhaps starting the process all over again. It is targeted at all entrepreneurs, at those who invest in them, and also at those who support them.

My objective in writing this book is to provide a comprehensive toolkit that delivers the entrepreneurial discipline and knowledge to stimulate successful new business venturing in our economy. New business venturing is now about focusing on creating value. The key objective of a growth plan is to nail down the elements that drive growth for your venture. But which elements of your venture are capable of creating value? And which elements, if not properly managed, are capable of destroying value? *Roadmap* guides you in the process of uncovering and knowing what creates and drives value in your business. It also helps you prepare and present a winning business plan that communicates your "value drivers" to your venture team and potential investors.

How This Book Is Organized

The book aims at creating knowledge, skills, and awareness in the critical aspects of funding, launching, and growing a new business venture and then leading it to a successful harvest. Each chapter presents key concepts and practical insights on an important management topic. The approach is straightforward, the message is practical, and the information comes directly from the "front-lines" of business battles. The concepts and ideas are tested and ready for you to use today.

Roadmap is divided into five major sections, each dealing with one aspect of understanding and managing entrepreneurial activities.

❖ **Part I: Charting a Course in New Business Venturing Today.** This section opens with a discussion of how the rules of entrepreneurship have changed, and it introduces entrepreneurial management practices and how the business plan guides you through uncertainty. It provides the historical background of entrepreneurship as well as the high-tech revolution we experienced in the late 1990s, and it closes with a discussion of the risk capital industry.

❖ **Part II: Creating and Engineering Your Vision.** This section focuses on opportunity analysis, industry analysis, and crafting a winning business strategy based on a sustainable competitive advantage. It also presents guidelines on assembling a winning venture team and the importance of critical capital resources.

❖ **Part III: Launching and Getting Traction.** This section presents market entry strategies, focuses on creating viable marketing and sales strategies, and introduces concepts for managing a rapidly growing venture. It closes with discussions of creating and leading the networked enterprise.

❖ **Part IV: Reaching Escape Velocity.** This section reviews winning strategies for financing the emerging growth venture and the financials required for investors. It provides the groundwork for creating an exit strategy.

❖ **Part V: Getting Your Venture into Orbit.** This section addresses how all the elements of the business are put together in a business plan. It also discusses presenting before investors and negotiating the best deal. The section closes with a discussion of deal killers and other practices used by entrepreneurs that can sabotage an otherwise winning business plan.

❖ **Case in Point.** To make *Roadmap* as interesting as possible, each chapter begins with a "Case in Point" about an entrepreneur whose activities are especially relevant to the chapter's subject matter.

❖ **Appendixes: Roadmap's Toolkit.** The five appendixes at the end of the book contain practical information for your journey, including outlines for a business plan and a PowerPoint presentation, sample financials, and even a real-world term sheet from a leading venture capital firm.

Why Should You Buy This Book?

Roadmap to Entrepreneurial Success is a strategy book for entrepreneurs. Each step of the entrepreneurial life cycle, from start-up phase to harvest, is succinctly detailed, providing you with the key steps that are vital to your success. Colorful stories bring the strategies and important business concepts to life, helping you internalize key learning points and quickly implement these key points into action. *Roadmap* is a rich and detailed source of guidelines, instructions, and explanations for creating and managing emerging growth ventures in uncertain times. It provides the necessary tools for both the new and the experienced entrepreneur to stay on course and succeed.

This book is a must read for anyone who stands to benefit and profit from the confluence of entrepreneurial activities, including entrepreneurial leaders of start-ups and spinouts; corporate executives in charge of leading new business development and new product innovation; scientists and technology transfer specialists from academic and research institutions; venture capitalists, investment bankers, and angel investors; and professional service providers from major law, accounting, and financial firms.

As the rate of technology development and the pace of competitive pressures accelerate, the flying-by-the-seats-of-the-pants approach to leading a venture is just not cutting it. In order to survive, entrepreneurs must now learn to launch and operate their ventures in a highly unpredictable environment. *Roadmap to Entrepreneurial Success* will be the one book you refer to time and time again on your journey to success.

Acknowledgments

This book reflects the efforts of a great many people over a number of years. First to thank are Jacqueline Flynn and her excellent team at AMACOM, and Niels Buessem at Andover Publishing Services, who performed the final editing. Together, they helped put this book into your hands. It is also a great privilege to thank Mark Heesen and his colleagues at the National Venture Capital Association.

Although the work of writing is a very solitary experience, in reality the process of creating a book is much like new business venturing. It is the result of innumerable interactions and discussions with many significant people. I am very grateful to all the entrepreneurs and professionals who have helped me along our journey. It was through their patience and helpfulness that I gained whatever insights this book may contain. Ultimately, it is through their experience that we all can learn.

I wish to express my deep appreciation to Nichole, for your constant encouragement and inspiration from the first day that I thought of this project. Finally, I wish to thank my parents, who have long supported my ride, for your loving patience and understanding.

ROBERT W. PRICE

In loving memory of my Grandma Sarah,
who always encouraged me to follow my dream

Introduction

Creating Your Start-Up Strategy

The beginning is the most important part of the work.
—Plato

The time to prepare isn't after you have been given the opportunity. It's long before that opportunity arises. Once the opportunity arrives, it's too late to prepare.
—**John Wooden, basketball coach of ten championships teams at UCLA**

Competition for the future is competition to create and dominate emerging opportunities—to stake out new competitive space. Creating the future is more challenging than playing catch up, in that you have to create your own roadmap.
—**Gary Hamel and C.K. Prahalad,** *Competing for the Future*

Identifying the Problem and the Solution

The greatest challenge a new business venture faces is getting the right things done in the right order. Knowing what to do, and in what sequence, is critical, especially since the entrepreneur has very limited time and resources. Craig W. Johnson, chairman of the Venture Law Group, once said that starting companies is much like launching a rocket: If at launch you're just a fraction of a degree off, you could end up a thousand miles off course downrange.

The pressures on the entrepreneur leading a new venture are relentless. The obstacles and challenges are formidable. Everything takes longer than planned. Gaining traction through market credibility and respect is very difficult. Forecasts are rarely accurate, and just making more sales does not always solve a cash crunch. Relationships with suppliers and buyers are more demanding, and just getting paid on time is not always easy. Competitors seemingly come out of nowhere at the worst times. Building a good venture team is difficult and time consuming, and leading and managing the team is the biggest challenge as there will be numerous conflicts among partners and investors.

The problem is entrepreneurship has been rebooted and the rules of launching and financing a venture have changed. The global economy has been struggling along and there is no shortage of geopolitical tensions. Diane Swonk, chief economist and senior vice president at Bank One Corporation, explained that the drivers of uncertainty in the financial world are both numerous and diverse. In fact, she states that the most uncertain times in global financial history started during the past decade. These events were:

1997: Thai bhat devalued
1998: Russian default
1999: Brazilian real devalued
2000: NASDAQ tech wreck
2001: Terrorist attacks on World Trade Center and Pentagon
2002–2003: Corporate governance crisis[1]

The landscape of business is now integrated with the threat of global terrorism on our soil and the impact on the U.S. economy is only beginning to be understood. This threat of terrorism is slowly being incorporated into business planning and operations. Alexis D. Gutzman, writing in *Unforeseen Circumstances: Strategies and Technologies for Protecting Your Business and People in a Less Secure World*, tells us that "September 11, 2001 was a wake up call for businesses. Many standard business practices were suddenly identified as risky behavior." As for business planning, she notes that "any book that was published before January 2002 on the topic of business planning is probably obsolete."[2]

According to Steve Forbes, editor-in-chief at *Forbes* magazine, all these events have put investing on hold in the United States. Forbes says that more than $2 trillion was on the sidelines in the cash markets.[3] These stark tales of uncertainty underscore a new reality confronting companies everywhere. Bill Gartner, a professor of entrepreneurship at the University of Southern California's Marshall School of Business, looks at these problems through the eyes of entrepreneurs. Gartner says, "It's not that there's not money out there, it's just that the money doesn't meet up with the ideas." Entrepreneurs need to focus on the real problem. He adds, "They don't know the right people, they don't understand the industry well enough. That's what they really need to concentrate on."[4]

Successful ventures coming from today's challenging and uncertain times will be built on value. For the past twenty-five years Venrock Associates, based in Menlo Park, California, has managed the Rockefeller family's money. The firm made money on start-ups like Apple Computer and Intel. According to Tony Sun, a Venrock partner, "Historically, the best companies are started in the down times, because during those periods entrepreneurs are very focused on creating core value and building enduring businesses."[5]

Solution: Back-to-Basics Approach

As we stated, knowing what to do today, and in what sequence, is the problem. Our book helps you identify and analyze the right strategic steps, and leads you through in the right sequence. As the rate of technology development and the pace of competitive pressures accelerate, the flying-by-the-seats-of-the-pants approach to management just is not cutting it. Entrepreneurs must now launch and operate their ventures into a highly unpredictable environment.

Our solution is based on a "back-to-basics" approach to entrepreneurial discipline. Discipline is the act of encouraging a desired pattern of behavior. George Washington said that discipline "is the soul of the army. It makes small numbers formidable, procures success to the weak, and esteem to all." We say that entrepreneurial discipline is the orderly conduct that holds a new business venture all together. Karen Griffith Gryga, a principal at Liberty Venture Partners, says that "it may feel like tough medicine, but it is aligning the risk-reward profile of today."[6]

Ironically, the phrase "back to basics" entered the mainstream business management world following the recession of the late 1970s. First prescribed as a solution in 1982, *In Search of Excellence* by Tom Peters and Robert Waterman went on to become a classic. It is still found in bookstores today. Jim Collins, co-author of *Built to Last,* provides sound advice to entrepreneurs in these uncertain times. According to Collins, we don't need to throw out the fundamentals but just do a better job of applying the fundamentals. The rebooting of entrepreneurship leaves entrepreneurs running a business today with some vexing questions: What has changed? What is the next milestone? Are we jumping ahead too fast or taking too long? How do we manage this process? How does entrepreneurial management and practices differ from the management practices we know in the corporate world?

Entrepreneurial Management Practices

The adjective "entrepreneurial" is used in a host of varying contexts and embodies a wide variety of meanings and implications. For instance, "entrepreneurial knowledge," as J.J. Kao points out in *The Entrepreneurial Organization*, can be referred to the concepts, skills, and mindset associated with operating large corporations with greater flexibility, innovation, and responsiveness. However, for this book, entrepreneurial knowledge is restricted to the concepts, skills, and mindset that individual business owners *must* employ in the process of starting and operating high-growth-potential ventures.

In their book, *Entrepreneurship*, Robert Hisrich and Michael Peters say that managing a new venture differs from managing an existing operation along five key management issues: strategic orientation, commitment to opportunity, commitment of resources, control of resources, and management structure.[7] The entrepreneurs born with these management skills come from a rare breed of people with intelligence, great heart, and creative skills. They are visionary and self-confident, good communicators with unlimited energy, and have a strong passion for what they do. Fortunately for those of you who were not born blessed with these skills running through your blood, we know that the most critical skills in launching and running a new venture can be learned. We will teach you some of the most important ones.

Entrepreneurs are directly involved in the dynamic, and very complex, interrelationship between financial management and business strategy. This is the significant difference that sets entrepreneurial management apart from all business management practices. In almost all cases, the person making the decisions has personal risk at stake. The worst-case scenario for folks "at work" is getting fired. The worst case for entrepreneurs is losing their home, personal credit, and lifestyle, as well as the destruction of family relationships.

Peter Drucker remarked that for the existing large company, the controlling word in the phrase "entrepreneurial management" is "entrepreneurial." In any new business venture, the controlling word is "management."[8] Therefore, for the purposes of our book we lean toward "management" as a discipline for entrepreneurs. We define entrepreneurial management as the practice of taking entrepreneurial knowledge and utilizing it for increasing the effectiveness of new business venturing as well as small- and medium-sized businesses. The heart of entrepreneurial management is continually juggling these vital management issues:

- ❖ What is this venture about? (*mission and values statement*)
- ❖ Where should it go? (*goals and objectives*)
- ❖ How will it get there? (*growth strategy*)
- ❖ What does it need to get there? (*people and resources*)
- ❖ What structure is best? (*organizational capabilities*)
- ❖ How much money does it need and when? (*financing strategy*)
- ❖ How will it recognize the final destination? (*vision of success*)

The Entrepreneurial Life Cycle

These vital management issues and activities play out in what we call the *entrepreneurial life cycle*. The entrepreneurial life cycle repeats itself in businesses of all sizes, from start-ups in a garage to corporate entrepreneurship activities in global Fortune 500 companies. It starts with an entrepreneur who perceives an opportunity, creates an organization to pursue it, assembles the required resources, implements a practical plan, assumes the risks and the rewards, all in a timely manner for all involved. It was once said that entrepreneurship is a lot like driving fast on an icy road. We prefer to think of entrepreneurship as less reckless and more methodical. Entrepreneurship is a continual problem-solving process. It is like putting together a huge jigsaw puzzle; at first pieces will seem to be "missing," obscure, or not clearly recognizable. Not all entrepreneurial life cycles follow a single process, but our research suggests that the stages we present below are common in the most successful emerging growth ventures. Size, profitability, commitment, complexity, scale of organizational structure, decrease in risk, increase in value, and decrease in founders' involvement characterize each stage. We believe that by knowing and understanding these stages entrepreneurs, business managers, investors, and consultants will be able to make more informed decisions, and most of all, be prepared themselves for challenges that lie ahead. We present the seven stages in the entrepreneurial life cycle, as follows.

Stage 1. Opportunity Recognition

This "gestation" period is quite literally the "pre-start" analysis. It often occurs over a considerable period of time ranging from one month to ten years. At this stage it is important to research and understand the dimensions of the opportunity, the concept itself, and determine how to decide whether it is attractive or unattractive. The individuals need to look internally and see if they are truly ready for entrepreneurship. The vast majority of people, including almost all inventors, never move off of this stage and remain just "considering" entrepreneurship.

Stage 2. Opportunity Focusing

This is a "sanity check," a go/no-go stage gate for part-time entrepreneurs because it fleshes out shaky ideas and exposes gaping holes. Venture capitalist Eugene Kleiner, of Kleiner Perkins Caufield & Byers, says, "Focus is essential; there can be the possibility of the business branching out later, but the first phase of a company should be quite narrowly defined."[9] It is important to include objective, outside viewpoints because different people can investigate the same opportunity and come to opposite conclusions.

Stage 3. Commitment of Resources

Most entrepreneurs see commitment as incorporating their business or quitting their day job. But this stage actually starts with developing the business plan. There is a huge difference between screening an opportunity and researching and writing a business plan. Writing an effective business plan requires a new level of understanding and intense commitment. The process will take between 200 to 300 hours, so squeezing that amount of time into evenings and weekends can make this stage stretch over three to twelve months. A common mistake entrepreneurs make is skipping the business plan; commit other resources, start the venture, then follow up and try to determine exactly what the focus will be for the venture.

Stage 4. Market Entry

Profitability and success define this stage. The entrepreneur is committed with a very simple organization, the resources were correctly allocated according to the business plan, and the first sales were made. This is what defines success in the very early stages. If the business model was profitable, reasonable objectives were met, and the venture is on track for attaining true economic health, then the entrepreneur can chose between a capital infusion for growth or remaining small with self-financing.

Stage 5. Full Launch and Growth

At this stage, the entrepreneur needs to choose a particular high-growth strategy. Upon considering such alternatives, quite often the entrepreneur chooses to remain a small business and never passes this stage or perhaps opts to remain operating as a sole proprietor. Or the venture could remain small for the simple fact that not all small ventures can or will become big companies. They are not fast growth potential because there is not enough room in the market for growth, their production and management systems are not scalable, or they will not scale because the rate is too great of a challenge to the management.

Stage 6. Maturity and Expansion

Now the venture is a market leader at cruising altitude. The growth becomes a natural extension of the venture through professional management practices. This professional management team is implementing the venture's growth strategy through global expansion, acquisitions, and mergers as cash is plentiful and inefficiencies are completely flushed out.

Stage 7. Liquidity Event

This harvesting stage is focused on capturing the value created in the previous stages through a business exit. Typical exits are an initial public offering or being acquired by a larger publicly traded corporation. Unfortunately, most of the literature in entrepreneurship has concentrated on the earlier stages. Little attention has been given to exits. We know from experience that the opportunity to exit successfully from a venture is a significant factor in the entrepreneurial life cycle, both for the entrepreneur and for any investors providing investment capital along the way.

Your Business Plan: The Roadmap That Guides You to Success

Most people hear "business plan" and think only "start-ups." Yet this is not always true because ongoing companies create business plans, project plans, new product plans, and plans for acquiring and integrating other ventures. General Dwight D. Eisenhower once said, "Plans are nothing. Planning is everything." Planning is a great exercise to help you think through all the business aspects and forces you to know your business. Our book is not about *whether* you should plan. *Roadmap* is about planning *effectively*. As Drucker says, "Entrepreneurship is risky mainly because so few of the so-called entrepreneurs know what they are doing. They lack the methodology. They violate elementary and well-known rules."[10] Entrepreneurs, Drucker argues, need a systematic approach for putting all the pieces of the puzzle together. Business planning helps entrepreneurs work smarter, stay alert for roadblocks, test new ideas, stay motivated, help align expectations with stakeholders and investors, and even reduce stress. Ted Clark, the director of Northeastern University's business planning contest, comments on the importance of business planning, "If you're starting a company, you must have a business plan. If nothing else, it's an educational exercise to learn what you'll need to develop your business."[11] As Eugene Kleiner says, "A plan shows how you'll run your business. Without a plan, you don't know where you're going, and you can't measure your progress."[12] So business planning, as it turns out, is really no more than another good management practice.

Critical Elements of a Business Plan

The business plan is perhaps the most important written document an entrepreneur can ever create. It describes all critical internal and external elements and strategies for guiding the direction of the venture's first several years as well as giving potential investors an idea of the venture's structure, objectives, and future plans. It communicates important entrepreneurial management practices, such as how the venture will mitigate risk, and how the venture will manage uncertainty. Most importantly, new business venturing is now about focusing on creating sustainable value. But which elements of your venture are capable of creating value? And which elements, if not properly managed, are capable of destroying value? Business planning is the process of uncovering and identifying what creates and drives value in your business; the business plan is the document that communicates your Value Drivers. The Ten Value Drivers we discuss in *Roadmap*, and their corresponding chapters, are listed here:

1. Solid Opportunity and Industry Analysis (*Chapter 4*)
2. Business Strategy and Sustainable Competitive Advantage (*Chapter 5*)
3. Proven Venture Team and Sound Organization (*Chapter 6*)
4. Control of Critical Capital Resources (*Chapter 7*)
5. Strategy for Market Entry and Traction with Customers (*Chapter 8*)
6. Strategy for Marketing and Sales (*Chapter 9*)
7. Strategy for Managing Rapid Growth (*Chapter 10*)
8. Strategy for Managing a Networked Enterprise (*Chapter 11*)
9. Sound Financing Strategy (*Chapter 12*)
10. Viable Exit Strategy (*Chapter 13*)

For an element to create value it has to affect one of four inputs into the total business venturing process. It has to:

- ❖ Increase the cash flows generating from existing activities
- ❖ Increase the expected growth rate in earnings
- ❖ Extend the period for which the venture can sustain above-normal growth based on its competitive advantage
- ❖ Curb the aggressiveness of its working capital policies, meaning a reduction for the cost of capital and/or a reduction of burn rate

Internal Uses of a Business Plan

Business planning helps you become the "value manager." A value manager focuses on "long-run cash flow returns" while having the perspective of an "outsider's view of the business" and "a willingness to act on opportunities to create incremental value."[13] The first opportunity to create incremental value is through selling. Entrepreneurship is about selling your ideas, your mind, your labor, your skills, and your teams. Your business plan will help you develop immediate "sales momentum," or what we call traction.

Most entrepreneurs are first "technologists," engineers, or are too deeply involved with their products and need help in selling and communicating the benefits of their products, their ideas, and their ventures. The business plan helps in focusing and communicating what the product does, who are the key customers, and what the milestones are and what are the timelines. Other internal uses of a business plan include: helping you set objectives, managing risk and uncertainty, establishing performance metrics, motivating and focusing venture team, attracting key employees, analyzing capital budgeting decisions, facilitating new product development projects, leading internal projects, integrating new acquisitions, and facilitating and leading restructuring, turnarounds, and restarts. So once a formal business plan is prepared, sections can be pulled out and updated or shared as needed.

External Uses: The Venture Drill

It is very hard to have a dialog about financing without a business plan. As Kleiner states, "In today's business environment, a business plan is an entrepreneurs' most crucial business document. No company can expect to articulate its goals or to secure financing without a well-conceived and well-presented business plan. Without a convincing business plan, no one will seriously consider your business idea."[14] Over the last couple of years business plans have taken many shapes and forms. However, they are still the preferred mode of communication between entrepreneurs and potential investors.

Andreas Stavropoulos, a venture capital partner with Redwood City, California-based Draper Fisher Jurvetson, says they receive some 10,000 to 12,000 business plans from entrepreneurs each year. They might meet with 250 to 300 entrepreneurs, and make a deal with twelve to fifteen of them. He says, "You need more than a great idea. You need a great business plan."[15]

Mark Gorenberg, a partner at San Francisco-based Hummer Winblad Venture Partners, says that a sound business plan will help you convince others that you are a less of a risk than the last or the next business plan.

Against the wishes and hopes of many entrepreneurs, there's no such thing as the "immaculate venture" where the stages in the entrepreneurial life cycle are skipped over from idea to harvest. The venture drill is the formal process that all entrepreneurs must address when raising money from outside investors. The three steps to the venture drill are packaging, placing, and presenting. *Packaging* is researching and writing an effective business plan. *Placing* is skillfully introducing the opportunity before the best investors. *Presenting* is communicating and making the deal in a formal meeting. Entrepreneurs tell us that starting a company, raising money, and making deals is a constant battle and business planning helps them sort issues out. Other external uses of a business plan include communication memorandum with existing investors, arrange strategic alliances, obtain large contracts with marquee customers, facilitate mergers and acquisitions, and secure key executives.

Mastering the Business Planning Process

Your business plan acts as a reflection of you, showing that you have really thought things through. It requires advance preparation, delegation, refinement, and, most importantly, a disciplined approach. Kleiner shares sage advice, "Writing a business plan forces you into disciplined thinking if you do an intellectually honest job. An idea may sound great in your mind, but when you put down the details and numbers, it may fall apart."[16]

Many entrepreneurs begin business planning by incorrectly estimating the length of time and effort it takes to prepare an effective business plan. It cannot be completed in one attempt. A business plan is a living document, and business planning is a process that never ends. The plan changes, especially with most high-tech ventures, where it may change in the early stages on a weekly if not a daily basis. These are not huge changes but iterations, and the business plan becomes "someplace" where modifications are noted as the venture takes shape and more information is collected. The overall business planning effort is based on the degree of uncertainty, the degree of complexity, and the potential threat from competitors.

It Starts with Storytelling

According to David Berkus, a past-president of the Tech Coast Angels, one of the largest angel investment groups in the United States, the first step to writing a business plan is fleshing out your "talking points" and weaving them into a storyline.[17] Storytelling is having the ability to communicate succinctly and precisely what you do, what you want to do, and what you need to do it. Bill Joos at Garage Technology Ventures, who has heard some 100,000 pitches from entrepreneurs, agrees that there is a "big problem with entrepreneurs who have the inability to talk about what they do."[18]

A story conveys not only information, but also meaning and knowledge in a certain context that can be easily remembered. Peter Orton of the IBM Story Project says that "one of the most important yet least appreciated facts about storytelling is that perceivers tend to remember a story in terms of categories of information states such as propositions, interpretations, and summaries rather than remembering the way the story is actually presented or its surface features."[19]

The Writing Process

Crafting an excellent business plan is a very arduous task that involves hundreds of fully committed, heads-down hours, and seemingly endless periods of researching, drafting, discussion, writing, editing, and rewriting. Before beginning, it is important to understand the entrepreneurial life cycle and the venture drill process if you are attempting to raise money from investors. You need to have in mind the purpose of the business plan, the intended audience, and the orientation of your approach to writing it. Set an overall schedule and then start work on writing the plan following the action steps we provide here.

Step 1. Brainstorming

This is the creative and uninhibited step in the writing process. You need to be free and non-critical. Lightly read through our book and begin writing your business plan by jotting down the related ideas, good or bad, in a journal or in a simple Microsoft Word document. Collect information like articles, industry studies, press releases, and Web resources.

Step 2. Organizing

This is the time to be critical. Looking at the random collection of ideas, sketches, and articles that have come from brainstorming, make an attempt to edit them. Look for some common patterns of thought. Examine the Value Drivers in this book in more detail. We suggest that you create ten folders, one for each Value Driver, for segmenting all this information.

Step 3. Outlining and Storyboarding

In addition to creating an outline in Word, we recommend that you work with Microsoft's PowerPoint to storyboard your concept into slides that consist of simple bulleted talking points and diagrams. Print them out as you change or edit them, tape them on a wall or flipchart, and then discuss them with your partners. Storyboarding is effective because it breaks critical thinking into smaller, more manageable parts. Storyboarding goes back to the days when Walt Disney's animators were creating very brief, quickly completed sketches and then posted them on the wall. In 1934, Disney, well overextended on his latest film, *Snow White and the Seven Dwarfs,* used a storyboard presentation to keep Bank of America from calling the studio into bankruptcy. Perfected today, the storyboarding process is described by Disney Imagineers: "Layer upon layer, we create a patchwork of sketches and words that color the original idea. Funny, fantastic, diverting, enhancing, persuasive, serious or not, our visualized thoughts begin to chisel away and uncover the diamond in the rough."[20]

Step 4. Drafting an Executive Summary

Looking up at your top ten or fifteen slides from your storyboard efforts (if they are above your desk in your war room), attempt to write a very tight three- to five-page summary. First segment your slides into the ten Value Drivers. Then write a few talking points for each slide, adding some content to make complete sentences, and review for spelling errors. Then discuss it with your partners, close friends, and your advisors. Avoid the mistake made by entrepreneurs we know who spent as much as $25,000 on preparing a full business plan without the benefit of any feedback.

Step 5. Flight Testing

Who else do you know who can "get their eyes on this" and give you an objective appraisal? Too many entrepreneurs delude themselves in the early stages. They want so much to believe in their ideas that they listen only to what they want to hear and see only what they want to see. Venture capitalists do not want to be the first to validate an idea. It is not about hitting the bull's eye on the first attempt but it is about how quickly you can improve your aim and get another arrow on the way to the target. We recommend that you flight-test your Executive Summary with outside trusted individuals. Consider your banker, past business associate, leader at the non-profit trade organization, and business professors at the local universities.

Step 6. Focused Writing and Editing

Now the real work begins. It will be valuable to go through and read our book again, but this time begin studying it and applying it to the particulars of your venture. You will be need to be narrowing down your strategic options, alternatives, and begin working on the precise language and wording.

Step 7. Revising, More Flight Testing, Reworking

This step involves the details: proofreading, spelling errors, punctuation, and grammar. Following a more professional approach to business writing, discuss your opportunity in the third person. Instead of saying "we project" and "our projections," write "the Company projects," and "the Company's projections." Remember that your plan is a living document and that business planning never ends. Likewise, the preparation of a business plan must be seen as an iterative process, since both the assumptions and the projections those assumptions engender must be constantly refined. Therefore, the preparation of a business plan really never stops.

Designating Responsibilities

It is best that you do not work alone on your business plan, because working alone can get very frustrating and lead to many errors. This means that you will have to find someone who can help and figure out how to split up the work. A "stakeholder," with respect to your venture, is anyone or any group, within or outside your venture, who has a "stake" in your venture's future performance. Creditors, suppliers, employees, owners, investors, board members, are all stakeholders. From this group of potential stakeholders, consider who could help you with the business planning. This search can also help you find and recruit members for your venture team.

Some say that you should not involve outside consultants. But finding good advice, which is always difficult for an early-stage venture with limited resources, is more important than ever in today's uncertain times. As one successful entrepreneur pointed out, "If you have to learn just through trial and error, it's going to be very slow. If you can hire good advisers, the learning curve is shortened." Over the years, we have found that there are three broad types of professional advisory consultants.

1. **Strategists**. Strategists are what we call your general practitioners, providing business advice and knowledge about your business models and your directions, and a feel for the market environments. Strategists are the most important link in the information chain for new business ventures. They come in very early, and usually become more familiar with the venture over a longer period of time. But it is difficult to find one whose ego is not threatened by an occasional request to see a tactician or a field support specialist.

2. **Tacticians**. Tacticians are specialists—like engineers, lawyers, and CPAs—who focus on specific advisory services. Examples of their services are: a marketing consultant preparing a report about a new opportunity, an engineer issuing a report on how to get more throughput on a production line with existing machinery, a programmer crunching software code, and an accountant doing an end-of-month closing and preparing financial documents.

3. **Field Support**. Field support refers to all regular day-to-day services, including banking services, preparing and hosting a Web site, payroll and employee taxes services, and temporary hiring agencies.

Why Some Business Plans Fail

The cold reality is that no one is going to read the plan with the intensity you had when you prepared it. So knowing this, most entrepreneurs focus on just getting the plan done rather than on getting the *right* plan done. But what is the perfect plan? As Carl Jung pointed out in *Modern Man in Search of a Soul*, "The shoe that fits one person pinches another; there is no recipe for living that suits all cases." Obviously he did not have entrepreneurship in mind when he wrote it, but his observation is appropriate. We know that our advice is not the perfect fit for everybody, and not everybody is going to create the perfect business plan.

Simply remember this, that the probability of your success is directly related to the extent that your business plan is accurate and complete. So it is never a good idea to make your reader wade through typos, balance sheets that do not balance, upside-down slides, or "other troubling signs of inattention to detail."[21] Also stay away from getting into the spinning "teacup and saucer ride" we see at amusement parks. This is when investors continually have you revise your plan until it becomes spun too far from your true strategic vision. And do not assume that business planning software relieves you of having to think hard about how you intend to execute your idea and can sabotage your credibility.

Finally, as William A. Sahlman, professor of entrepreneurship at Harvard Business School, says, "All opportunities have promise; all have vulnerabilities. A good business plan doesn't whitewash the latter. Rather, it proves that the entrepreneurial team know the good, the bad, and the ugly that the venture faces ahead."[22]

Charting a Course

in New Business

Venturing Today

Discussions of Entrepreneurship

> There is nothing more difficult to handle, more perilous to conduct, or more uncertain in its outcome, than to take the lead in introducing a new order of things.
> —Niccolo Machiavelli, *The Prince,* 1532
>
> Entrepreneurship is neither a science nor an art. It is a practice.
> —Peter Drucker
>
> Entrepreneurship is the ability to create and build from a vision practically nothing: fundamentally it is a human, creative act.
> —Jeffry Timmons, professor of entrepreneurship

Entrepreneurship: A Historical Perspective

Few words are as abused in the lexicon of the business world, as ill defined in the management literature, and as open to multiple meanings as *entrepreneurship*. The concept of entrepreneurship has been in our modern society for thousands of years and in the history of economic study the word has been overused, and in some cases underused. Carl Voigt, dean of the Marshall School of Business at the University of Southern California, explains, "We sort of defined entrepreneurialism too narrowly as someone who wants to start their own business. But entrepreneurialism can also mean finding new business opportunities and expansion at existing companies."[1]

Starting with practically nothing, an entrepreneur is one who organizes a new venture, manages it, and assumes the associated risk. For this book the term *entrepreneur* is broadly defined to include business owners, innovators, and executives in need of capital to start a new project, introducing a new product, or expanding a promising line of business. We include technology transfer experts, technologists at leading universities, and consultants and advisors assisting in all aspects of venturing. An entrepreneur's principal objectives are profit and growth, and they will employ formal strategic management practices to achieve them.

Origins of Entrepreneurial Capitalism

To better understand entrepreneurship, it is useful to look back to the early development of capitalism. Capitalism depends on harnessing private motives

❖ **Case in Point: Sam Walton, America's Entrepreneur**

In 1945, with $5,000 of personal funds and $20,000 borrowed from his father-in-law, Sam Walton, perhaps the world's most successful businessman, became an entrepreneur and opened his first retail store. Later, as a franchisee with the Ben Franklin variety stores, Walton and his brother started buying up other variety stores. They began experimenting with "discounting" in certain departments in their stores. By 1960 they owned and operated some fifteen stores with total sales of $1.4 million.

In 1962, using a loan against his personal assets, he opened his first "free-standing" Wal-Mart discount store in Rogers, Arkansas. Wal-Mart has since then maintained a singular focus on providing the lowest prices to its customers. Eight years later, with thirty stores, Wal-Mart went public and raised $4.6 million, which was needed to fuel Sam's ambitious dreams. Some thirty years later a single share from that IPO would be worth 2,048 shares, with a total value of $116,736, or a return of 707,300 percent on the initial investment.

By 1979 the number of stores reached 276, and Wal-Mart reached $1.25 billion in sales. It became the nation's number-one retailer in 1990. In 1997 it was the largest employer in the United States, with 680,000 employees, and had sales of $105 billion. Wal-Mart was ranked #1 on the *Fortune 500* listing in 2002 and had its biggest single day sales in history on the day after Thanksgiving that year: $1.43 billion. By 2003, with nearly $245 billion in sales, Wal-Mart was the world's largest retailer, with nearly 4,700 stores, and it was growing at over 12 percent year over year. Sam Walton's story is about triumph over adversity and long, hard times. He got his retail start in 1940 as a salesman and management trainee at J.C. Penney. At the time of his death in 1992 he had a personal net worth of nearly $25 billion.

Sources: Wal-Mart company Web site; Amar V. Bhide, *The Origin and Evolution of New Businesses* (New York: Oxford University Press, 2000), p. 286; Robert D. Hisrich and Michael P. Peters, *Entrepreneurship*, 5th ed. (New York: McGraw-Hill, 2002), pp. 559–561; and *Sam Walton: Made in America* (New York: Bantam Books, 1993).

to produce the goods and services that the public wants as efficiently as possible. Historian Charles Van Doren leads us to the early roots of "primitive capitalism" in his book *A History of Knowledge: Past, Present, and Future*. He provides insight to the ancient Egyptians, economic life before the peasant, the introduction of the merchant, the king, the rise of the labor markets.

Defined today, *capitalism* is a political, social, and economic system. It is characterized by the private ownership of property—not only of land and buildings but of patents, know-how, and processes that are used by entrepreneurs to create profits for themselves. Capitalism sharply contrasts with other economic systems, like *feudalism* and *socialism*. In capitalism, entrepreneurs are responsible for such economic decisions as what to produce, how much to produce, and what method of production to adopt. Economist Lester Thurow writes, "Entrepreneurs . . . bring the new technologies and the new concepts into active commercial use. They are the change agents of capitalism."[2]

The French Connection

The concept of entrepreneur is borrowed from the French words *entreprendre*, "one who undertakes"—that is, a "manager." In fact, the word *entrepreneur* was shaped probably from *celui qui entreprend*, which is loosely translated as "those who get things done."[3] In the early eighteenth century, a group of thinkers called the *Physiocrats* surfaced in France around a school of new economic theory. They were the first proponents of *laissez-faire* and opposed all government intervention in industry, especially taxation. Their doctrine was that the economic affairs of society are best guided by the decisions of individuals.

One of the most famous among them was Richard Cantillon. In a paper he worked on between 1730 and 1734 and that was later published in 1775 as *Essai sur la Nature du Commerce en General*, he introduced the concept of entrepreneur. He developed these early theories of the entrepreneur after observing the merchants, farmers, and craftsmen of his time. Jean-Baptiste Say, a French businessman turned economist, followed Cantillon with his *Trait d'economie politique* in 1803. His work commented on the theory of markets and how the entrepreneur is involved in this transaction of goods for money.

Adam Smith's Invisible Hand and Pin Production

The economic system based on the capitalism concept was completed by the Scottish economist Adam Smith. Leveraging the work performed earlier by the Physiocrats, and in particular Francois Quesnay, Smith completed his famous book, *The Wealth of Nations,* in 1776 at the beginning of the Industrial Revolution in Britain. Some believe that his main contribution to economics is centered on free enterprise. Introducing the concepts of *liberal capitalism* and *entrepreneurial capitalism*, Smith is "known as an architect of our present system of society."[4]

Smith concentrated on the growing manufacturing and trade industries. In particular he studied the division of labor in the manufacturing of pins, which was beginning to incorporate new machines. His central argument in *The Wealth of Nations* is based on the concept of what he called the "invisible hand." He believed that human self-interest is the basic psychological driver behind economics, and that a natural order in the universe makes all individual, self-interested endeavors add up to the social good. He also studied the competitiveness of nations and multinational trade. His major theoretical achievement was to take the first steps toward a theory of the optimal efficient allocation of resources under conditions of free competition.

Joseph A. Schumpeter and His "Creative Destruction"

Joseph Alois Schumpeter, an Austrian-American economist, was one of the first to study entrepreneurs and the impact of entrepreneurial capitalism on society. As he wrote in *The Theory of Economic Development*, he believed that innovation and creativeness distinguished entrepreneurs from other business-people. He observed that innovation and entrepreneurship are closely inter-woven. He argued that the entrepreneur was at the very center of all business activity. He observed that entrepreneurs create "clusters of innovations" that are the causes of business cycles because their actions create disruptive dislo-cations and arrive in huge waves. In fact, Schumpeter believed that entrepre-neurs deserve the credit for the industrial revolution.

Schumpeter introduced the phrase "creative destruction," stating that the entrepreneur does not just invent things, but also exploits in novel ways what has already been invented. He identified five types of entrepreneurial activity: new product innovation or the introduction of a new service, new process innovation or new methods of production, market innovation or the opening of new markets, input or resources innovation, and organizational innovation, which is the complete restructuring of an entire industry or the breaking up of a monopoly.

Entrepreneurship in America

Entrepreneurship is deeply woven into the fabric of America's history, its economy, and its cultural beliefs. As Alexis de Tocqueville observed in his 1836 classic *Democracy in America*, "The Americans always display a free, original and inventive power of mind."[5] Milton Friedman, a Nobel Laureate in economics, wrote this in his timeless classic *Free to Choose*: "Ever since the first settlement of Europeans in the New World, America has been a magnet for people seeking adventure, fleeing from tyranny, or simply trying to make a better life for themselves and their children."[6] Fred Bollerer, from the Wash-ington, D.C.-based Morino Institute, said, "Entrepreneurship has been going on in this country since its inception. In fact, you can say the country really started because of its political entrepreneurs."[7]

According to research from Babson College and the Kauffman Center for Entrepreneurship, anywhere from 10 percent to 17 percent of adults in the United States take an active role in start-ups.[8] The *Global Entrepreneurship Monitor* reported that nearly one in ten working adults in the United States, or 18.3 million, were actively involved in the process of forming or leading early stage ventures.[9] As Federal Reserve chairman Alan Greenspan noted, "Competitive and open markets, the rule of law, fiscal discipline, and a culture of enterprise and entrepreneurship should continue to undergird rapid inno-vation and enhanced productivity that in turn should foster a sustained fur-ther rise in living standards."[10]

America's Silent Army Moves West

Entrepreneurs are as American as the Statue of Liberty and the "winning of the west." From its very beginning, America is a nation of opportunity seekers. As David Dary writes in *Entrepreneurs of the Old West*, early entrepreneurs were like Daniel Boone, who in 1798 at the age of sixty-five, settled along the Missouri River on about a thousand acres.[11] Boone and thousands of others were America's "Silent Army" that moved westward and laid the foundation to America's entrepreneurial capitalism. It was this silent army that "took such gambles with their lives and put their bodies through such physical torment," that moved even further west and opened up the Santa Fe Trail, a footpath that wandered through unsettled country for nearly 900 miles from Missouri to New Mexico.

This movement led to oxen-driven wagon trains and finally to the "iron horse," the steam locomotive trains. "The bigness of the West—the vast distances that had to be overcome—was a major obstacle for the silent army. Hurdling that obstacle required greater Eastern influence, especially of capitalism with its developing corporations. It was capitalism that built the railroads, greatly reducing the West's transportation problem." By the early 1860s the major railroad ventures commenced; none were as famous as the Central Pacific Railroad, led by the "Big Four"—Charles Crocker, Mark Hopkins, Collis P. Huntington, and Leland Stanford, the latter also the founder of the California university that bears his name.

America's Secret Economic Weapon

As Mark Heesen profiles in this book's Foreword, America's small, entrepreneurial firms have been the catalyst to our economy's growth in the past and will continue to be a key determinant of our future prosperity. According to Ernst and Young LLP, in the broadest sense of the term, there are over 40 million entrepreneurs conducting some form of business activity in the United States.[12] The U.S. Small Business Administration (SBA) estimates that there are about 25 million small businesses, defined as companies with fewer than 500 employees. According to the SBA records, there are about 180,000 companies that have between 100 and 500 employees, and about 5.7 million companies with fewer than 100 employees. The balance—the 12.8 million sole proprietorships and the 6.4 million limited partnerships or limited liability companies—have no employees.

In their landmark book *Venture Capital at the Crossroads,* William D. Bygrave and Jeffry A. Timmons refer to entrepreneurship as the American economy's secret weapon. According to the U.S. Department of Commerce, small businesses account for nearly 60 percent of the gross national product, produce some 75 percent of new jobs, and are a major source of new technologies and innovation. It has been estimated that 18 percent of the financial assets held by U.S. households, or $2.4 trillion, is invested in private ventures.[13] Sole proprietorships in the United States had about $969 billion in revenues in 1999.[14] Their combined economic power would rank them as the tenth largest economic power in the world—even larger than Canada, Mexico, or Russia.

Entrepreneurship Empowers All

Entrepreneurship is becoming more of a learned practice than business activity. Kim B. Clark, the dean of Harvard Business School, says, "The concepts of leadership that are going to be important in the future spring out of an understanding of entrepreneurship."[15] It is well researched that entrepreneurship empowers all, regardless of education, sex, color of skin, and nationality.[16] According to Amar Bhide, who studied the founders of successful ventures, about 80 percent had a college degree, 48 percent had a four-year degree, 15 percent had an MBA degree, 20 percent had some other advanced degree, and 11 percent were only high school graduates. As for their origins and backgrounds, 63 percent were from middle class, 26 percent described their backgrounds as working class, 5 percent were poor, and 6 percent came from affluent backgrounds.[17]

An important but neglected area in the study of entrepreneurship is the role of women in the building of high-growth ventures. Historically women have tended toward low-risk, slower-growth ventures. But things are changing as women in senior levels of marketing and management are being exposed to raising money and managing new business ventures.

Minority-owned businesses have grown explosively in the 1990s. Nearly 25,000 now have sales of more than $1 million. Information put together by U.S. Census Bureau's "Survey of Minority Owned Business Enterprises" found that Blacks own more than 800,000 ventures, and that there were some 3 million minority entrepreneurs by the end of the 1990s. Also, skilled immigrants are an increasingly important but largely unrecognized source of well-educated entrepreneurs. The Immigration Act of 1990 created significant new opportunities for foreign-born, highly educated professionals.

Defining the Types of Entrepreneurs

In this book we use a broader definition and scope of entrepreneurial activity, segmenting all entrepreneurial activity into seven types of entrepreneurs: small business and lifestyle, franchise, professional fast growth and serial, corporate, creative disrupters and innovators, extreme, and social and non-profit.

1. Small Business, Lifestyle, and Family Entrepreneurs

A small business entrepreneur is an individual who establishes and manages a business for the principal purpose of furthering personal goals. They comprise around 90 percent of all entrepreneurial activity in the United States. The business may overlap with family needs and desires. These ventures merely provide a reasonable lifestyle for the founding entrepreneurs. Their average net worth is less than $6 million, and they choose to stay small. These "lifestyle ventures" typically fall below 20 percent annual growth rates, their five-year revenue projections are below $10 million, and average net income does not exceed $2 million. Retailing is one of the few sectors where entrepreneurial activity is extensive. Each year, some 60,000 new retail businesses are started. The National Retail Federation in Washington, D.C., reports that 1.3 million retailers or over 95 percent of all retailers own and operate a single store.[18]

2. Franchise Entrepreneurs

Franchising started in the 1840s and became an American institution. One out of sixteen workers is employed at a franchise, and franchising accounts for nearly $1 trillion in retail spending.[19] Franchising is where a franchisor is offering a franchisee exclusive rights in return for their payment of royalties and conformance to standardized operating procedures. Franchising represents a great opportunity for entrepreneurs. An entrepreneur buying into a franchise increases the odds for survival to as much as 90 percent over starting up independently.[20]

There are three basic types: product franchising, like automotive dealerships; service franchising, like Century 21; and business format, like McDonald's. Since there are some 2,300 franchises to choose from, we suggest reading books like Ann Dugan's *Franchising: The Complete Guide to Evaluating, Buying and Growing Your Franchise Business*. Dugan will help you to find the right franchise and to negotiate the franchise lease; it also provides sample franchise agreements.

3. Professional Fast-Growth and Serial Entrepreneurs

Fast-growth ventures have been called "the backbone of the U.S. economy." Numbering less than 350,000, they create about two-thirds of all new job growth.[21] Professional entrepreneurs lead these ventures, which typically employ between 20 and 500 people, have sales growth of at least 20 percent each year for four straight years, and target five-year revenue projections between $10 and $50 million. Less than 10 percent of all start-ups make it to this level.[22] As can be expected, it is well documented that these high-growth ventures receive great investor interest. A small business entrepreneur will typically retain 100 percent ownership, since the primary motivation is financial independence and control. In contrast, serial entrepreneurs are comfortable with relinquishing control to "a more traditional chief executive." They also accept dilution because "taking significant outside investment" allows them to create a big venture very quickly. Basically, the serial entrepreneur creates a venture, builds it up to a certain point, and then walks away to start another.

4. Corporate Entrepreneurs and Intrapreneurs

A driving force for the corporate world is "innovate or die." As Drucker says, "Any organization that believes that management and entrepreneurship are different, let alone incompatible, will soon find itself out of business."[23] Entrepreneurship is beneficial for managing established businesses but not easily maintained. Large, mature conservative businesses need entrepreneurial leadership so they can perform the continuous renewal that has become a requirement for survival. For example, managers at 3M have set a long-term objective of achieving double-digit sales growth through innovation.

To survive, companies must "strive for a continuing change in the status quo." The National Science Foundation estimates that about $300 billion is spent annually on R&D in the United States, leading new opportunity analysis and roadways to entrepreneurial transformation. Microsoft spends almost $5 billion on R&D annually. In 2002 Microsoft began a five-year, $2 billion investment on the Xbox, a "stripped down personal computer in a VCR-sized electronics box" for home gamers.[24] Four veteran game developers led Microsoft's "Project Midway." They "were *intrapreneurs*, doing the same thing as entrepreneurs except inside a big company."[25]

The concept of corporate entrepreneurship has been around for at least twenty years. Broadly speaking, corporate entrepreneurship (also called intrapreneurship) involves the developing of new business ideas and the birthing of a new business activity within the context of large and established companies.

5. Creative Disrupters and Innovators

Shawn Fanning, the creator of Napster, appeared on the covers of *Time*, *Fortune*, and *BusinessWeek* before he could legally buy a beer. In 1994, John Doerr, a venture capitalist at Kleiner Perkins Caufield & Byers, met a twenty-three-year-old Marc Andreessen, who confidently declared that "his software would change the world." Their company, Netscape, went on to a record-shattering initial public offering in 1995. Like Edison in search of the electric light bulb, seeing only a better way to illuminate a room, these entrepreneurs are a rare breed, living on the *creative edge*. Most often, these brilliant "entrepreneurial-engineers" look to technology to solve problems in ways that "unlock value." They are visitors from the future, living among us here and now. They have an optimistic passion for an idea that borders on the embarrassing and a restless urge to make a difference in the world. They bring us innovations that will have a deep impact on how we live, work, and think in the decades ahead.

6. Extreme Entrepreneurs

Entrepreneurship is the last frontier where someone can explore individuality and pioneer a dream. In his work *Isolated State* (1850), German economist Johann Heinrich von Thunen described the entrepreneur as part "explorer and inventor."[26] Long before America's Silent Army, Christopher Columbus pitched his dream to Queen Isabella in Seville, Spain. His "discovery" of America in 1492 brought new prosperity to Spain, as it soon became a world economic superpower. John Sutter was even called a "soldier of fortune." It was near his lumber mill on the American River in California that gold was "discovered" in 1848, about 150 miles from Intel's headquarters in Santa Clara. Today's extreme entrepreneurs are Formula-1 race car drivers, North Atlantic fishermen, lumberjacks, and businessmen like Ted Turner and Richard Branson, the billionaire who started Virgin Records and Virgin Atlantic Airlines.[27] Branson says, "Being an adventurer and entrepreneur are similar. You are willing to go where most people won't dare."[28]

7. Social and Nonprofit Entrepreneurs

David Packard, co-founder of Hewlett-Packard, believed that giving to the local community was important. Social and nonprofit entrepreneurs who pursue endeavors for the benefit of society have existed since ancient times. In fact, the word *philanthropy* is derived from a Greek word that means "lover of mankind." Today it is believed that entrepreneurism and innovation can also help "spark positive social change." The Ewing Marion Kauffman Foundation is doing just that. Currently with over $1 billion in assets, its mission is to make a difference by encouraging entrepreneurship in all areas of American life. The Price Institute for Entrepreneurial Studies works to further the understanding of the entrepreneurial process. By generously providing grants to leading academic institutions, the Institute works to stimulate MBA programs and curricula development, encouraging and supporting students with entrepreneurial aspirations.

What Motivates Entrepreneurs?

Understanding common characteristics and what motivates entrepreneurs to start and sustain their venture is important to understanding the entrepreneurial life cycle. By definition, "entrepreneurs are optimistic and idealistic." They have great commitment, and a vision and passion that can be observed. According to Jack Stack, a judge for Ernst and Young's Entrepreneur of the Year (EOY) Award Program, "You can see it in their eyes. You can see it in their confidence. You can see it in the way they talk."[29] Although this topic of discussion is beyond the scope of this book and best left to the many experts in the field of human behavior, our research of the literature on the subject turned up common traits among famous entrepreneurs like Bill Gates, Steve Jobs, Michael Dell, Scott McNealy, Andrew Grove, and Larry Ellison. For example, entrepreneurs place an enormous value on creativity and are willing to take risks if they know they can influence the eventual outcome of the event. They are innovative, aggressive, self-confident, willing to work long hours, fiercely competitive, and intensely focused.

Intrinsic Motivation

But what motivates an entrepreneur to take all the risks and launch a new business venture? The most successful entrepreneurs are often not the most talented, but the ones with an "entrepreneurial obsession," who see an opportunity and pursue it with profound existence. They have conviction and believe in their ideas so much that "they will them into existence." It is not a question of *whether* they want to do it—they *have* to do it.

This drive is called *intrinsic motivation,*[30] defined as "the motivation to work on something because it is interesting, involving, exciting, satisfying, or personally challenging." This is the opposite of being *extrinsically motivated,* which means being motivated by expected evaluation, surveillance, competition with peers, dictates from superiors, or the promise of rewards. Entrepreneurs do what they love, and they love what they do.

For example, Robert Mondavi felt "reborn" after starting the winery that bears his name. "I was like a kid again, bursting with energy, ready to climb the mountain, conquer the world, go for the gold. Yes, at the unlikely age of fifty-two, the great adventure of my life had finally begun."[31] Michael Dell simply says, "Do you have any idea how much fun it is to run a billion-dollar company?"[32]

The Mythic Quest of the Entrepreneur

MIT professor Edward Roberts studied MIT graduates who had gone on to start technology-related businesses.[33] He discovered that the most successful ones did not seek "some intangible objective." They were not interested in devising brilliant ideas that only other brilliant people like themselves could recognize. In fact, they wanted to create something "significant and tangible" and did not want to go after it if it was not a challenge.

Schumpeter recognized this too. In his 1949 classic, *The Theory of Economic Development,* he proclaims, "The entrepreneur-innovator's motivation includes such aspects as the dream to found a private kingdom, the will to conquer and to succeed for the sake of success itself, and the joy of creating and getting things done."[34] Van Doren accurately profiled Columbus. He writes, "Brilliant as he may have been, and mad as well, Christopher Columbus was one of the most remarkable men who ever lived. He never turned aside from the opportunity of wealth, but wealth was not what he sought, what he was willing to give his life for. What he sought was eternal fame, for he knew, as perhaps no one else realized in his time, that the discovery of a New World would bring him that."[35]

Their Gift to the World

Wendell Dunn, professor of entrepreneurship at the University of Virginia's Darden Business School, believes that "entrepreneurs are in it to prove a point."[36] Steven Berglas, instructor at The Harold Price Center for Entrepreneurial Studies at UCLA, has devoted a career to understanding what makes serial entrepreneurs tick. He found they "leave as many intellectual and creative entities for others to derive developmental opportunities from as possible."[37]

After a ten-year period of teaching and studying entrepreneurship at Harvard Business School, Amar Bhide concluded that "it takes a really extraordinary individual to build a promising company—extraordinary in terms of someone who has an almost maniacal level of ambition. Not just an ambition to make a comfortable living, to make a few million dollars, but someone who wants to leave a significant mark on the world."[38] As technology guru George Gilder describes it, "Because an entrepreneur can never be sure of a return on his investment, starting up a business is like offering a gift to the world, in the hope, but never the certainty, that the gift will be reciprocated."[39]

It's About the Money Too

Entrepreneurs also want to be "rich." Out of the richest one percent of Americans, more than nine in ten are entrepreneurs who made their fortunes themselves.[40] In 1996 when Microsoft's stock soared by 88 percent, Bill Gates made nearly $11 billion on paper, or about $30 million per day. He was earning about $347 per second; *he could buy a Honda Accord every minute*. At the end of December 2000, Gates was worth about $55 billion, or about $200,000 for every living soul in the United States.[41]

On *Fortune*'s list of "Richest Under 40" for 2002, eight of the top ten were entrepreneurs. Number one was Michael Dell, worth $16.49 billion. Others were Pierre Omidyar of eBay worth $3.82 billion and Jeff Bezos of Amazon.com worth $1.66 billion. Entrepreneurs especially like cash for their hard work. Jeong H. Kim founded Yurie Systems, a high-tech communications equipment company, in 1992. In 1998 he sold it to Lucent Technologies for $1.1 billion. Kim, who came to the United States from Korea with his family at 14, was asked why. "I sold out to Lucent for two reasons. One, it was $1.1 billion, and two, it was in cash."[42]

Managing Entrepreneurial Risks

It is important to understand the construct of risk and uncertainty. Businesses have always faced risks. As we discussed in the Introduction, recent events around the world have provided dramatic evidence that, in today's business world, risk is now a reality. Entrepreneurship, risk, and uncertainty are long-time bedfellows, and they push the entrepreneur to the limit. Peter Bernstein, in *Against the Gods, the Remarkable Story of Risk,* describes that the modern concepts of risk dates back more than 800 years with the early principles of gambling. According to Bernstein, "The revolutionary idea that defines the boundary between modern times and the past is the mastery of risk." The period of global exploration and trade during the 1500s and 1600s transformed these principles into the creation of wealth and "the inevitable result was capitalism, the epitome of risk-taking." Bernstein writes, "You do not plan to ship goods across the ocean, or to assemble merchandise for sale, or to borrow money without first trying to determine what the future may hold in store."[43] In fact, when the Revolutionary War broke out, the Americans had to create their insurance industry from scratch and underwrite maritime business and life insurance policies for sea captains.

Uncertainty means that decision-makers do not have sufficient information about environmental factors, which increases the risk of failure. For this book we define risk as *the degree of certainty or uncertainty as to the realization of expected future financial returns in a business venture.*

Risks Specific to Entrepreneurial Capitalism

Risk-taking is essential to capitalism. Without risk the free enterprise system cannot function. Not all risks and challenges can be anticipated, but once identified, they can be managed by lead entrepreneurs, executives, and boards working together. We all have some kind of belief that entrepreneurship is risky, but the facts are startling. Estimates from the SBA's database suggest that of the 850,000 new businesses started each year, about 60 percent fail in the first six years and more than 70 percent fail in the first eight years. Risks that are specific to entrepreneurial capitalism are listed in Figure 1–1.

Unwinding this Knot of Uncertainty

Left unmanaged, these risks get tightly wound into a knot. When it is wound so tight, management skills, expert advice, and even hope are passed up as humans go into the survival mode. In fact, the human organism can tolerate

FIGURE 1-1. RISKS SPECIFIC TO ENTREPRENEURIAL CAPITALISM.

Economic Risk. How is the business world today? What is the window of opportunity for this venture? Includes geopolitical threats, economic cycles, interest rates, and governmental regulations.

People Risk. What about the venture team? How did they come together? Have they worked together before? Can they make it through the growth stage, or will there be too many cooks in the kitchen?

Market Risk. How are the dynamics of this industry sector? Is there going to be room for growth in this market? What about the risks of other competitors?

Technical Risk. Does the product work? What about some technology coming along in the future that will make this product/technology worthless like a buggy whip?

Strategic Risk. Is there a sustainable competitive advantage? Includes sharing the risk with strategic alliances and finding the right operations strategy with a viable business model.

Financial Risk. Can this venture or activity get funded now? What about later rounds of financing, when growth kicks in and it needs fed with cash?

Personal Risk. Can the lead entrepreneurs truly commit? There are many sacrifices, as other priorities in life, like family, friends, and vacations, that will have to come second.

anything except uncertainty, which causes so much stress that people are no longer capable of thinking in a cognitive, creative manner. They focus on survival.[44] What makes this "knot of uncertainty" so difficult to deal with is that all the entrepreneurial risks interact with each other.

For surviving the "deep, dark canyons of uncertainty" we again draw on Bernstein. He tells us that the essence of risk management lies in maximizing those areas where we have some control over the outcome while minimizing those areas where we have absolutely no control. Unwinding this knot, one risk at a time, starts with keeping your blood cool in the heat of the battle, or as military experts say, having a *sang froid*. You need this cool temperament and a clear head to separate the "controllables" from the "uncontrollables." Controllables are the elements that management can control like the cash burn rate, the activities of the venture itself, personnel, finance, and production. The uncontrollable forces are external forces over which your venture team has no direct control, although sometimes it can exert influence.

Becoming Risk Technicians

William J. McDonough, president of the Federal Reserve Bank of New York, says that taking calculated risks is part of any business venture. Each venture needs to have in place the systems and management processes necessary not only to identify the risks associated with the business activities, but also to effectively measure, monitor, and control them.[45] Identifying and being able to openly discuss the risks inherent in your venture is very key. It demonstrates your leadership and management skills. It increases the credibility of you and your venture with investors and strategic partners. It creates confidence that quickly clears open the channels of communication.

By reading this book and working hard to follow the strategies and concepts outlined herein, you will become expert risk technicians: experts at identifying risks, knowing how to manage around risks, and becoming comfortable in high-risk environments. Developing an effective strategy for dealing with risk and uncertainty sets apart the winners from those lost at sea. The strategy includes three key components. The business plan is the heading that provides guidance even in the roughest seas. Entrepreneurial knowledge is knowing where the rocks (or risks) are at sea. Entrepreneurial management is the skill of steering from the rocks.

Venturing into Stormy Seas

Historically, ventures that launched during economic downturns had difficulty in raising money and had to grow in a step-by-step approach. Tim Draper, a partner at Draper Fisher Jurvetson, believes that entrepreneurs launching today must find ways to build revenue and be more capital-efficient than in the past. Ventures that are watertight in stormy seas will last longer and become market leaders. Examples of great companies that started in economic downturns are Hewlett Packard, Sun Microsystems, Dell Computer,

Genentech, Palm Computing, Intuit, and even Starbucks. They did not go out and raise $50 million in venture capital. They became huge, successful companies because they watched money carefully.[46]

Even large corporations must batten down the hatches and watch each dollar more carefully. According to T. J. Rogers, founder of Cypress Semiconductors, "We've had two recessions in seventeen years. They were tough times, but I think I'm a better manager for it."[47] Don Valentine, founder of Sequoia Capital, has been around since 1972 and helped launch Apple Computer, LSI Logic, Oracle, and Cisco Systems in economic downturns. He says, "I think a retrospective from 2010 will show that 2001 was the beginning of (a new) golden era. Some of the great companies of all time have been started in prior recessions, and my forecast is they will be started (again) in this recession."[48]

Discussions of the High-Tech Revolution

Every generation needs a revolution.
—Thomas Jefferson
The further backward you look, the further forward you can see.
—Winston Churchill
Sometimes when I consider what tremendous consequences come from little things, I am tempted to think that there are no little things.
—Bruce Barton

The Long Waves of Modern Technology

As we take our first steps into the twenty-first century we can see that technology is central to the economic growth of nations, large companies, and individuals. Technological change plays a major role in industry structural change, as well as in creating new industries. Virtually all contemporary accounts of how technological change proceeds in capitalist economies are based on Schumpeter's work. Schumpeter relied on the works of Karl Marx, a German economist, to develop the concept of "creative destruction," and on the work of Nikolai D. Kondratieff, a Russian economist. In 1925 Kondratieff published *The Long Waves in Economic Life*, identifying "long waves" of economic growth, some lasting more than fifty years, from the end of the 1780s to the 1920s. These "Kondratieff Waves" were based on what Schumpeter called "clusters of technical innovations." There is much to be learned from understanding the dynamics of technological change. As Marx said, "History doesn't repeat itself, but it does rhyme." Before we discuss today's high-tech revolution, we first explore the five previous revolutions: industrial, steam, steel, electricity, and mass production.

The Industrial Revolution (1780s–1850s)

The term "industrial revolution" refers to the great change in the organization of work and production that began in England. This change was revolutionary, for it turned many things upside down and created a new class of wealthy and powerful persons. Recall that Adam Smith studied the "division of labor"

❖ Case in Point: IBM

Around 1890, during the height of the Industrial Revolution, the U.S. Census Bureau was in an information crisis. As a result, the Bureau sponsored a contest to find a more efficient means of tabulating census data. The winner was Herman Hollerith. His Punch Card Tabulating Machine used an electric current to sense holes in punched cards and keep a running total of data. Capitalizing on his success, Hollerith formed the Tabulating Machine Company in 1896. It was the world's first electric tabulating and accounting machine company.

In 1911, Charles F. Flint engineered the merger of Hollerith's Tabulating Machine Company with two other ventures. The New York-based company invited George Fairchild to become its first chairman of the board of directors. In 1914, Thomas J. Watson, Sr., joined the company as general manager. In 1924, the company was renamed International Business Machines Corporation, or IBM. In the 1940s IBM introduced the Selective Sequence Electronic Calculator system, which greatly increased the efficiency with which enormous quantities of data could be stored and processed, like payroll calculations, invoicing, and design calculations. Watson, Sr. died in 1956, and by 1957 IBM was completely reorganized, focusing on electronic computing; its revenues from the computer division topped $1 billion.

In 1964, IBM introduced the System/360, a broad line of compatible mainframe computers with peripherals for a wide range of uses. Total development costs including software were some $5 billion. By the late 1970s, they became the institutional mainframe computers. By the mid-1980s the 360 Series and its direct descendants had accounted for more than $100 billion in revenue for IBM. In the fall of 2002, with IBM topping $81 billion in annual revenues and 315,899 employees around the world, the U.S. Department of Energy awarded IBM a $290 million contract to build supercomputers capable of equaling the theoretical processing power of the human brain.

Sources: IBM Company Web site; Chris Freeman and Luc Soete, *The Economics of Industrial Innovations*, 3rd ed. (Cambridge: The MIT Press, 1997); Jon Palfreman and Doron Swade, *The Dream Machine: Exploring the Computer Age* (London: BBC Books, 1991); Martin Campbell-Kelly, *From Airline Reservations to Sonic the Hedgehog: A History of the Software Industry* (Cambridge, Mass.: The MIT Press, 2003); and Michelle Delio, "This Is Your Computer on Brains," Wired News Online, November 19, 2002. Delio writes that a human brain's probable processing power is around 100 teraflops, roughly 100 trillion calculations per second. IBM is contracted to build what will be the world's first 100-teraflops supercomputer.

in the pin factory and wondered why machines did what they did, and as a result thought about how to make them work better. Richard Arkwright's invention of the spinning frame in the 1780s replaced a "cottage industry" established by the wool and cotton companies. By 1850, cotton yarn and cloth accounted for 40 percent of all exports from Britain, and needless to say "Arkwright amassed a great fortune from his inventions."[1] These clusters of discoveries and innovations came one after the other, and each new discovery called for the next. But the most important invention of the 18th century was the factory, "the great machine which combined human and mechanical elements to produce undreamed-of amounts of goods, which in turn were absorbed by a market that was also viewed mechanically."[2]

The Steam Revolution (1740s–1890s)

Historian Charles Van Doren writes, "Steam power changed the city and the country, it revolutionized life and work."[3] The steam revolution was born in 1712, "when Thomas Newcomen erected a steam engine" to pump out water from English coal mines. The steam revolution wave crested some fifty years later. Leveraging James Watt's cluster of innovations that included the separate condenser, steam power began disrupting the handcrafting industry with machinery in the factory and mill operations. This age of steam-powered machinery produced two very significant offspring: steam locomotive trains and steam-powered dynamos. In 1830 the first "commercial" train was pulled in England, and soon after over a hundred railroad companies were started. Steam power created great wealth, and "some railroad magnates became richer than kings or emperors."[4] Later in the nineteenth century the steam engine was used to produce electricity, but the steam turbine, which is still in use today, displaced it in the next generation of electric power.

The Steel Revolution (1890s–1940s)

Modern business history in America started in the 1820s with a rail system that provided transportation between canals. The steel revolution brought clusters of innovations that affected every sector of industry and services, including this "railroadization" of America. Steel brought low-cost stronger rails, stronger, lighter steam engines, and huge bridges spanning wide rivers. Andrew Carnegie was dedicated to driving down the cost of steel. In 1875 he built his first plant based on the Bessemer process for the production of steel rails. The cost of steel was reduced as much as 90 percent from the early 1860s to the mid-1890s. By 1881 Carnegie was the "foremost iron and steel master in America." In 1901 he sold his business for more than $300 million to J.P. Morgan who incorporated it into an even larger venture, United States Steel. Steel led many other industrial innovations. The first high-rise building in Chicago was constructed of steel, the canning industry replaced the "tin" in tin-cans with steel, and electric power was "transported" through steel-wire power lines.

The Electricity Revolution (1830s–1950s)

The early 1830s introduced theories of electricity, and by the 1840s generators were commercially used in France. In 1877 Thomas Edison formed the Edison Electric Light Company with a group of investors that included William Vanderbilt and J.P. Morgan. By 1879 Edison developed the first successful electric incandescent lighting system, and by 1882 he started work on the Pearl Street Central Power Station in New York City. Between 1880 and 1890 a modern industrial infrastructure was in place, and soon the electricity revolution created a whole new set of industries and disrupted the production processes of every old industry. In 1890 the share of power for mechanical drive provided by steam was 81 percent, water was 13 percent, and electricity was a mere 5 percent. By 1930 electricity accounted for 78 percent, steam 16 percent, and water 1 percent of the power.[5] In the steam era a giant steam engine powered a central rotating shaft, and machine tools ran off pulleys in long linear factories. In the 1890s Westinghouse was making AC motors for industrial applications, which spawned the growth of machine tools. Because these small motors could be attached to each machine tool, very different, more productive configurations of machinery could be arranged on the factory floor. Quite interestingly, the "electrification of America" laid the roots of the next wave we discuss.

The Mass Production Revolution (1880s–1980s)

Perfecting the mechanisms of mass production meant decreasing the unit cost of products. In 1881 John D. Rockefeller, viewed by some as the "Entrepreneur of the Century," combined Standard Oil and nearly forty other allied companies to form the Standard Oil Trust Company. His goal was to achieve cost advantages that could only be realized by placing the companies' refining facilities under a single management. The cost per gallon dropped from 2.5 cents in 1879 to 0.4 cents in 1885. Standard Oil's successor is now Exxon Mobil, one of the largest corporations in the world. The first true mass production techniques were used by Henry Ford in 1914 at his Highland Park Plant in Detroit for the manufacturing of the Model T automobile. Ford modeled Highland Park after Armour's pig slaughtering system in Chicago, called the perfect "disassembly of a pig." Once perfected, 15 million Model T's rolled off Ford's assembly line—one every twenty-four seconds.

Introduction of Management Science

As we discussed earlier, for thousands of years entrepreneurial capitalism was, quite literally, *the* capitalism. That was the case until the early 1900s and the introduction of *Industrial Capitalism*. Giant firms such as U.S. Steel, Ford, DuPont, General Motors, General Electric, and Sears became characteristic institutions of the twentieth century. Managers had to learn how to handle huge forces of workers, miles of assembly lines, and deeply vertical integrated facilities like Ford's River Rouge plant, where iron ore and sand entered, and Model Ts made of steel and glass exited.

This transformation of American industry from small-scale manufacturing to large industrial corporations created new administrative needs and structural changes and innovations at all administrative levels. Simply the rethinking of the shop floors for electricity led to "organizational innovations" and displaced the old ways of running a business.

This transformation also led to the rethinking of capital inputs, like labor, resources, supplies, and inventory. And the creation of "best practices" led to the emergence of standardized information, accounting, and administration procedures using new office machinery and communication systems (typewriters, telephones, and telegraph) and linking branch offices, plants, and sales organizations with headquarters. The science of managing money and understanding return on investment was initiated by the DuPont family, who at that time in 1919 were the largest shareholders in General Motors. Simply by using the "DuPont Formula," finance for new investment, in procurement of materials, in establishing marketing networks, and in research, design, and development now became of equal or greater importance.

Diffusion of Fordism into the "Post-Industrial Era"

Paul David, an economic historian at Stanford University, noted that it took some forty years for industry to figure out how to reorganize itself and to take advantage of the "decentralizing power of electric motors."[6] Henry Ford was one of the first. He took the disruptive electric motor and incorporated it into an assembly line. Ford not only advanced electricity, he advanced an era of mass production never seen before. Historian David Lewis gives us an impression of Ford's grand scale. In 1925, Ford's workforce at the River Rouge plant approached nearly 60,000 employees. The facility occupied some seven million square feet, or more than 1,115 acres. It was known as the "greatest industrial domain in the world."[7]

This "Diffusion of Fordism" that followed captured the heart of industrialized America. Fordism meant economies of scale, low production cost, and fixed design. Production strategies were built on the notion that low cost required high volumes of standardized parts. The best examples surfaced during the massive buildup of military resources for World War II. Douglas Aircraft built some 30,000 aircraft, and the Kaiser shipyards in San Francisco were launching large ships daily. Following the war, on potato fields twenty miles from New York City, William Levitt pioneered the mass production of affordable housing. He built some 17,477 homes, putting up about twenty-four per day, each on a 750-square-foot concrete slab.

This radical change in the nation's system of production was not an easy one for the workforce and the management. In fact, some even countered Fordism. Alfred Sloan, the chief architect of the giant corporation that was later to be General Motors, triggered a shift from a "production focus" to a "market focus." Sloan established the first design group dedicated to automotive styling and developed a production system that pursued variety in body style and color.

Disciples of This Management Science Revolution

The industrial capitalists leading the corporate world laid down huge investments in production functions. They struggled on repositioning their companies to ensure future profitability and offset decline of their production infrastructure. They won, and business management had come to the forefront in America. Between 1880 and 1920 the number of professional managers climbed from 161,000 to more than one million. Harvard Business School opened its doors in 1908, and management journals were soon being published, such as *Administrative Management* in 1919 and *Management and Administration* in 1921. In 1923, Herbert Hoover convened the first International Management Congress in Prague and the American Management Association, publishers of this book, was founded.

Management science crested around the mid-1950s with work by Peter F. Drucker and William H. Whyte. Drucker's *Concept of the Corporation* in 1946 was a study of General Motors, and his *Practice of Management* in 1954 was a great attempt to organize and present the management science revolution as a discipline of knowledge.

Drucker saw that between 1950 and 1970 either big business or governments created three out of every four new domestic jobs. In other words, "the growth dynamics of the American economy lay in established institutions." William H. Whyte's influential study, *The Organizational Man,* was published in 1956. His thesis was that people have to work with others because "it is an age of organizations."

Andrea Gabor's book, *The Capitalist Philosophers: The Geniuses of Modern Business,* explores the other fathers of modern business management theory. The portraits in her book "provide a taxonomy of management's rich multidisciplinary heritage." She looks at individuals "who profoundly shaped the course of the twentieth century." They include Frederick Winslow Taylor, the "father of scientific management"; Robert S. McNamara, one of the original "Whiz Kids"; W. Edwards Deming, "a prophet of the quality movement and the learning organization"; and Herbert A. Simon, the "Leonardo da Vinci of the information age."

The Information Technology Tidal Wave

Throughout history, information had always been important. The problem was that information traveled at the speed of a human. In 490 B.C. a messenger ran the 41.3 kilometers to Athens from the plains of Marathon, Greece. He died after announcing the Greek victory over the Persians. For hundreds of years later, with the exception of the use of the carrier pigeons, information still traveled at the speed of man. In the 1700s the Rothchilds in Germany founded a money-trading empire. With branches in Germany, France, England, and Italy, the flow of business information and constant communication was essential to the growth of their business. Whenever important documents, news, or cash had to be transported, they had stables of horses and coaches and boats at the ready all over Europe.

Samuel Morse invented the electric telegraph service in 1837. He tapped out the first message that traveled faster than man on May 24, 1844, "What hath God wrought?" along thirty-seven miles of telegraph wires near Baltimore. New York to San Francisco service began in 1861, and by 1866 Western Union had more than 4,000 offices. John Steele Gordon tells us in *A Thread Across the Ocean* about a New York entrepreneur named Cyrus Field who came up with a plan to connect the New World to the Old World by laying cable on the ocean floor. After multiple attempts, the first cable was finally laid in place on August 16, 1858. Queen Victoria sent the first message to President James Buchanan. Sir Arthur C. Clarke proclaimed Field's accomplishment to be the "Victorian equivalent of the Apollo Project."

From Morse and Marconi to Satellites in Orbit

Information and communication technology (ICT) is the infrastructure and knowledge that is necessary to make information and communications readily available. There are four main categories of ICT:

1. Computers and peripheral equipment

2. Software

3. Communications equipment

4. Instruments.[8]

ICT literally began with the first telegraph service in 1837 when Guglielmo Marconi demonstrated wireless Trans-Atlantic radio signals in 1901.

The growth, integration, and sophistication of ICT today is rapidly changing our society and economy.[9] Our nation's capital stock of business equipment and software is twenty times higher than in 1950. In 1970 we had no fiber-optic cable in place, no cellular sites, no cellular towers, and no commercial satellites in orbit. By 2001, there were 39 million miles of fiber-optic cable in the ground, 128 million Americans owned cell phones, and there were 114,059 cellular sites, 104,000 cellular towers, and 700 satellites in orbit. According to *The Emerging Digital Economy*, a report published by the U.S. Department of Commerce, the share of the ICT sector grew from 4 percent of the U.S. Gross Domestic Product in 1977, to 6 percent in 1990, and to 8 percent in 1998.

In previous decades, companies used ICT and companies like IBM to automate and support specific business functions. Today, however, ICT is such an integral part of most businesses that it is hard to separate ICT from the company itself. Businesses use ICT networks even more extensively to conduct and re-engineer business activities and product processes, streamline procurement processes, reach and service new customers, and manage internal operations. Increasingly, a company's business strategy relies on information systems as an enabler and, in many cases, as a key source of competitive advantage for mature larger organizations.

ICT Fueled Productivity

The 1990s were an extraordinary period in U.S. economic history. For more than a decade we experienced sustained growth, low unemployment, and low inflation. Rising productivity growth, which signified higher living standards through new products, technologies, and management methods, surged unexpectedly in the second half of the 1990s. Martin N. Baily, senior fellow at Institute for International Economics, remarked, "The strong growth of the U.S. economy after 1995 is linked to a recovery of productivity growth."[10]

There is no doubt that the emergence of the information economy fueled this productivity growth. Baily found that information technology has affected productivity in two ways. First, computers and other ICT hardware have become better and cheaper, leading to increases in investment, employment, and output of the ICT sector. Second, advances in technology have also increased productivity in the more traditional sectors of the economy financial services, business services, and the retail and distribution industries.

Martin Feldstein, president and CEO of the National Bureau of Economic Research, believes that advances in information technology will lead to continued strong productivity growth.[11] Information and data has become the lifeblood of any supply chain system. The ability to access, process, and analyze vast amounts of information quickly and accurately is critical to a company's bottom line and long-term profitability. In other words, ICT slashes fixed costs in three areas: information, production, and distribution. As Michael Dell has said, "We substitute information for inventory and ship only when we have demand from real end consumers."[12] It adds up to higher productivity for Dell's business and a significant competitive advantage.

ICT Planted the Seeds of the New Economy

Long ago Henry Mintzberg said that information and control are essential components of organizations. He discovered that "management spends 80 percent of their time actively exchanging information."[13] In 2002, Tom Siebel, founder of Siebel Systems, said, "We are at a point where it's a stretch to understand how you could run a reasonable-size business today without information technology."[14]

Modern economies have evolved from the "invisible hand" and Fordism to the present, when the innovations of the "new economy" are powering changes in industry after industry. As U.S. Federal Reserve Chairman Alan Greenspan says, "A hundred years ago, physical brawn was critical to value-added determination. People who personally could lift rolled sheet steel and help haul it from one part of the plant to another performed an activity that was valuable in the marketplace. Today, several generations later, the structure of production has become, to a remarkable degree, idea-determined."[15]

The most principal characteristic of the new economy is that one's consumption of a good does not necessarily detract another's consumption. For example, when you are reading this book, no one else can be reading it at the same time. But if are reading it on the Internet, thousands can be reading it concurrently. Thomas Jefferson put it best, "He who receives an idea from me, receives instruction himself without lessening mine; as he who lights his taper at mine, receives light without darkening mine."

Drucker sees the future as a knowledge-driven society, where the basic economic resource is not materials, labor, or capital, but information and knowledge. As Greenspan said, "The revolution in information technology has altered the structure of the way the American economy works."[16] The collective market capitalization of five large ICT companies—Microsoft, Intel, Compaq, Dell, and Cisco—grew from less than $12 billion in 1987 to more than $588 billion in 1997, or more than 4,800 percent. In the next section, we look at how the information technology tidal wave that crashed on the world's economy in the 1990s came to be.

The Commoditization of Disruptive Information Technologies

It is important to understand the diffusion of disruptive innovations. This diffusion occurs when "innovators" buy and then, through an influence process, encourage others to buy. It always "starts with the first sale," and the innovation can "diffuse" through society very quickly. Consider how many years it took each innovation to reach 10 million users: Radio needed twenty years; television ten years, the Internet three years, Netscape twenty-eight months, and Hotmail seven months. In 2002 Hotmail had some 150 million users receiving 2 billion messages each day.

Some influential business thinkers have written about this "rate of adoption." Everett Rogers, who is best known for his classic *Diffusion of Innovations,* found that customers adopt an innovation at different times after it becomes available. This rate is illustrated in Figure 2-1. The curve exists because important innovations and new technologies typically diffuse through society often over many years rather than impact everybody at once.[17] Rogers found that there are five sets of customers:

1.   **Innovators.** The first 2½ to 5 percent of those who adopt the innovative product. They are willing to try innovative ideas along with the risk.

2.   **Early Adopters.** The next 13 to 15 percent of adopters. They are considered opinion leaders in their community and domain space. They adopt innovations early, but carefully.

3.   **Early Majority.** Perhaps the next 30 to 34 percent. They are deliberate in their decision making. They adopt innovations before the average person, but rarely are they known as leaders.

4.   **Late Majority.** Perhaps 34 percent or less. They are skeptical and adopt an innovation only after the early majority has proved it.

5.   **Laggards.** The remaining 16 to 20 percent. They are bound by tradi-

FIGURE 2-1. RATE OF ADOPTION.

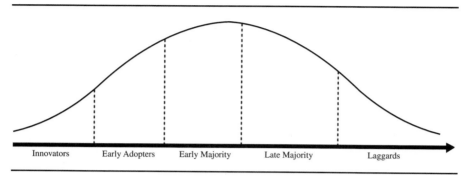

| Innovators | Early Adopters | Early Majority | Late Majority | Laggards |

tion, suspicious of changes, and adopt the innovation only after it becomes a commodity.

This diffusion process can be characterized as responding to both "technology-push" and "demand-pull" influences over time. Technology-push occurs when changes in scientific and engineering knowledge make new products or processes feasible or reduce their costs. Demand-pull occurs when the market for an innovation expands, causing the benefits realizable through innovation to exceed costs. Another great business thinker, Harvard Business School professor Clayton Christensen, released *The Innovator's Dilemma: When New Technologies Cause Great Firms to Fail* in 1997. Today it is a well-known book that explains how disruptive products or systems create entirely new markets or even industries. Here are some famous examples: Johann Gutenberg's printing press; the Watt-Boulton steam engine; Gottlieb Daimler's internal combustion engine; Edison's electric light bulb; Marconi's "ship-to-shore" wireless radio; the Wright brothers' first flight and their studies on aerodynamics; IBM's disk drive; Boeing's first trans-Atlantic jet, the 707; Sony's Betamax; and even the shipping containers found at thousands of ports today.

In *Crossing the Chasm: Marketing and Selling High-Tech Products to Mainstream Customers*, Geoffrey A. Moore describes how some innovations make the "leap" from early adopters and innovators into the mainstream consumer marketplace through incredible demand-pull. The pull is so strong that the innovation quickly becomes a "commodity." Commodity products are based on widely available standard components and typically have little differentiation. As Clayton Christensen explains, "A product becomes a commodity when product differentiation loses its meaning, when the features and functionality have exceeded what the market demands."[18] The introduction of HP's DeskJet in the early 1990s is a great example. It was "the death knell of the dot-matrix printer" industry.[19] The DeskJet was "commoditized" as its price went from just under $1,000 to $365 by 1994, and by 2003 we found one at Staples for $49.

We now circle back to Schumpeter and Kondratieff. Recall how clusters of innovations build up into a huge economic wave, or a revolution. The high technology revolution—or more accurately defined as the convergence of computer and telecommunication technology—began when Marconi formed his Wireless Telegraph Company in London in 1897. In 1908 Lee de Forest, an American electrical engineer, invented the audion (vacuum) tube in Palo Alto, California, and created the world of "electronics," leading up to television in the 1930s, and the military applications of electronics for detection and navigation. Between Marconi and Google, there were thousands of innovations grouped into hundreds of clusters. For this book, we condense the discussion of the high-tech wave into four layers. From the bottom up they are the computer, the Internet, the microprocessor, and the Web browser.

Commoditization of the Computer (1940s–1985)

Computers did not originate in Silicon Valley. Work on the first electronic computer, the ENIAC (Electronic Numerical Integrator and Calculator) began under the leadership of Drs. J. Presper Eckert and John Mauchly at the University of Pennsylvania in 1942. Designed to produce firing and bombing tables for the Army, it was 100 feet long, weighed 30 tons, and "contained no less than 18,000 vacuum tubes."[20] For years after the ENIAC, a computer was sort of a "shrine to which scientists and engineers made pilgrimage." Their use was strictly rationed and only those in white lab coats got anywhere near them.

In 1959 Kenneth Olsen and Harlan Anderson exploited their experiences at MIT's Lincoln Labs to start the Digital Equipment Corporation (DEC). They put the computer into the hands of the users who could interact with it directly via a keyboard, and see what was entered on a monitor. In 1965 their PDP-8 "minicomputer" cost around $80,000. Ten years later, Dr. H. Edward Roberts introduced a computer kit for $500. In 1981 IBM introduced the "personal computer" that sold for under $1,500, and *Time* magazine's "Man of the Year" award in 1982 went to the PC. The one-billionth PC was shipped in April 2002, and PC number two billion will ship sometime in 2007.

Commoditization of the Internet (1965–1999)

The Internet is a global network of computer networks that creates value by reducing the costs of transmitting information.[21] The seeds of the Internet were planted by the U.S. government when Russia's German rocket scientists, left over from World War II, were unleashed and launched Sputnik, the world's first satellite, on October 4, 1957. Its simple beeping back to Earth brought science to everyone's attention around the globe. In direct response, on January 7, 1958, President Eisenhower formed the Advanced Research Projects Agency (ARPA) to coordinate all U.S. technological research. One day in 1966, Robert Taylor at the Pentagon wondered why the three computers he was financing did not connect. He proposed the "ARPAnet" to provide interactive access between ARPA-funded computer resources around the country, and to save money that ARPA would otherwise have to spend on buying more supercomputers.

The first successful ARPAnet experiment was on September 2, 1969. Leonard Kleinrock conducted the first transmission of data across a 400-mile line from UCLA in Los Angeles to Stanford Research Institute (SRI) at Menlo Park, California.[22] In the years to follow, this ARPAnet grew into a parallel network for the research community, and an Internet "backbone network" for academic institutions was funded by the National Science Foundation (NSF) in 1986. In 1990 the NSF established a "commercial use policy" that cleared the way for applications beyond academic research and development. The networking of the research community was no longer confined to computer scientists.

By 1992 there were about 1 million homes in the United States connected to the Internet. In the fall of 1993 America Online (AOL) started providing "easy-to-use" access to home subscribers. Earthlink offered "all-you-can-eat" access in 1995, and NetZero was offering free access in 1999. Researchers at International Data Corporation (IDC) reported that there were about 550 million Internet users around the world in 2001 and predicted that more than 100 million new users will be added to the Internet each year through 2006, reaching just over 1 billion.

Commoditization of the Microprocessor (1971–1999)

The invention of the transistor is often called one of the greatest inventions of the twentieth century. John Bardeen, Walter Brattain, and William Shockley demonstrated their first transistor at AT&T's Bell Labs in New Jersey on December 23, 1947. They would later win the Nobel Prize in 1956. Their transistor was desperately needed. The nation's growing hunger for telephone services was eating AT&T alive. Their operating system relied on vacuum tubes; they realized that if demand continued to grow, they would have to hire half the nation as operators. The invention of the transistor reduced the size of computers considerably. But it was the invention of the microprocessor, a single piece of silicon etched with thousands of transistors, that launched the introduction of reliable, low-cost electronic computers into the economy.

In 1965, Intel co-founder Gordon Moore wrote in a paper that the speed and the power of computer chips had been doubling about every eighteen months. What "Moore's Law" means is that a computer twenty years from now will be able to calculate in thirty seconds what the average computer today would take an entire year to complete. In forty years, a computer would be able to calculate in thirty seconds what today's computer would take a million years to complete.

Employee number 12 arrived at Intel in 1971. His name was Marcian Edward "Ted" Hoff. His first job was to design a set of chips that would go into a calculator for Busacom, a Japanese company. But he wanted to put all the circuitry on a single integrated circuit and then program it.[23] Hoff's device was launched as Intel's first 8088 microprocessor chip in 1975. It proved to be "a *Magna Carta* moment in the world of technology." Intel's Pentium launched in 1993 had 3.1 million transistors, and designers can now routinely place 300 million on a chip. Intel's first chip with a billion transistors will arrive in 2007.

Likewise, the price of computing power has fallen by 99.9 percent in a single generation, and computers are delivering 66,000 times more power per dollar spent than the computers of 1975 did. Moore put it another way, "If the automotive industry paralleled those same advances in value and efficiency, the cars we drive today would cruise at a million miles per hour, cost about five dollars, and we'd be getting close to 250,000 miles to the gallon."[24] As a historical note, the public announcement of the transistor's invention in 1947 was buried deep in *The New York Times* in a weekly column called "The News of Radio." There, it was suggested that the device "might be used to develop better hearing aids for the deaf, but nothing more." In 1997 *Time* magazine named Andy Grove, co-founder of Intel, "Man of the Year."

Commoditization of the Web Browser (1993–early 2000s)

The Web is not a "physical" thing that exists in a certain "place." It is a "space" in which information exists.[25] J. Neil Weintraut called it "the Rosetta stone of the Internet for the masses."[26] In Robert Reid's *Architects of the Web*, Weintraut says, "The Internet was a massive library of some of the most advanced information and discussion forums in the world from leading research institutions, but locating and getting the information was obtrusively difficult. It was akin to walking down each aisle of a library, scanning each book just to figure out what is there, but doing all this in the dark!"

In 1989 Tim Berners-Lee sat down in the European Particle Physics Laboratory (CERN) in Geneva to invent the *World Wide Web*. When Berners-Lee started working on his Web project, there were about 800 different computer networks plugged into the Internet and about 160,000 computers filled with information. He invented a "Web client that allows a human to read information on the Web." It solved incompatibility among all the different servers, computing systems, and infrastructures.

In the winter of 1993, Marc Andreessen and Eric Bina posted the first version of Mosaic, a Web browser they developed for the National Center for Supercomputing Applications (NCSA) at the University of Illinois. They eventually made two key changes. They added graphics to what was otherwise boring text-based software, and more importantly, they translated the software from so-called UNIX computers to the Microsoft Windows operating system. Within a few weeks, tens of thousands of people had downloaded copies of it. By spring 1995 more than 6 million copies were in use on 85 percent of the computers surfing the net around the world.

Before Mosaic "you had to be a UNIX hacker" or a "computer nerd" to access the Internet. Andreessen's intent was "to make all the resources on the Internet available with one click." In December 1993 *The New York Times* described Mosaic as "an application program so different and so obviously useful that it can create a new industry from scratch."

But it took an Act of Congress to open "the floodgates to digital commerce." Up until 1991, free enterprise over the Internet was legally forbidden because the Internet was created for the military, research institutions, and academia. The "Boucher Bill" amendment to the NSF Act of 1950, introduced by Representative Rick Boucher, a congressman who represents Virginia's Ninth District, was signed into law by President George H. W. Bush on November 23, 1992. In the summer of 1995, an investment banker quit his job, headed west to Seattle, and launched a new venture. At the end of 2002, the sales for his venture, Amazon.com, reached $4 billion and he was leading a company worth nearly $9 billion. What happened was that "e-commerce exploded from $12.4 billion in 1997 to $425.7 billion by 2002, a 3,332 percent increase."[27]

Tim Berners-Lee's invention of the Web browser has forever changed the shape of modern life, altering the way people do business, entertain, and inform themselves. His invention is often compared to Gutenberg's printing press, Bell's telephone, and Marconi's radio. *Time* magazine hailed him as one of the 100 greatest minds of the twentieth century, saying, "He took a powerful communications system that only the elite could use and turned it into a mass medium." More than 375 million queries are made each day on the Internet. Google alone responds to more than 200 million search queries per day in 74 languages from 100 different countries. Tim Berners-Lee chose not to profit from his invention. In April 1993 CERN declared that they would not charge a royalty on the Web protocol and code created by Berners-Lee. *It was his gift to the world*.

Into the Eye of the Perfect Storm

The United States experienced an extraordinary surge in wealth in the 1990s that increased American's net worth by 75 percent.[28] John T. Wall, president of NASDAQ International, described the NASDAQ Bubble as a "total breakaway with no rationale."[29] It took sixty-eight weeks to go from 2000 to 3000; eight weeks to go from 3000 to 4000; and ten weeks to go from 4000 to 5000. NASDAQ peaked at 5048.62 on March 10, 2000, for 36 hours. Alice M. Rivlin, economic advisor to the Clinton Administration during the 1990s, said, "The world was treated to a vivid demonstration of how well free-market capitalism can work."[30]

But what goes up must come down. The NASDAQ crashed hard because the supply of the less experienced, less sophisticated, "marginal investors ready to buy overvalued stocks, had dried up."[31] And investors lost confidence in the securities markets in the wake of significant accounting scandals and bankruptcies.[32] Various numbers are given for the total amount of wealth lost in the United States. Henry Paulson, chairman and CEO of the Goldman Sachs Group, estimated that investors lost over $7 trillion since the market's peak in March 2000.[33] Tech leaders Microsoft, Intel, and even Cisco alone saw more than a trillion dollars in market capitalization wiped out. In 2002, almost 70 percent of the U.S. households had investments, in one way or another, in public equity markets.[34] The average loss per household in the United States was $63,500; Massachusetts lost the most at $138,100 per household, and California lost $112,500 per household.[35]

Some compare the fundamentals of the NASDAQ Tech Wreck to the great tulip mania of 1636–1637 in Amsterdam, when inflated prices of exotic tulip bulbs crashed on rumors of government intervention. We instead refer you to Ludwig von Mises, another Austrian economist, who stated that a cyclic downturn is a "cluster of errors." The cluster of errors we witnessed in the late 1990s was "something that we will never see again in our lifetimes."[36] It was, in fact, a "perfect storm."

A perfect storm is said to be one in which all the worst possible weather elements converge at the same time and place to create the mother of all atmospheric calamities—everything that can go wrong, does. Three elements converged in the late 1990s to create the Perfect Storm. There was "Internet anxiety" based on the commoditization of the Internet and fears that the "Y2K" problem would trigger a meltdown in the world's economy. The second element was the democratization of capital for entrepreneurs. Money was everywhere and investors were hot to invest. The third element was the triggering event that set off the Perfect Storm. It was the race to go public, following Netscape's initial public offering (IPO).

Commoditization of the Internet

The Internet was the greatest disruptive technology to hit the world since electricity. John Doerr from Kleiner Perkins described it as "the most powerful two-way global communication medium that we have witnessed, and probably will witness, in our lifetime."[37] America's business leaders were some of the first to see it as a revolution in the making, and their comments fueled the "Internet anxiety." Bill Gates called the popularity of the Internet the most important single development in the computer industry since the IBM PC was introduced in 1981. Like the PC, the Internet is a tidal wave. It will wash over the computer industry and many others, drowning those who don't learn to swim in its waters."[38] John Chambers, CEO of Cisco Systems, was quoted saying, "The Internet is not just a nice productivity tool. This is about survival."[39] Jack F. Welch, chairman of General Electric, was quoted in 1999 as saying that the Internet "was the single most important event in the U.S. economy since the Industrial Revolution."[40]

Thus technology was sold on fear. A lot of technology was sold. IT buyers were spending at roughly double the historic rate of IT investment: about 5 to 6 percent of a company's revenue, as compared to the historic rate of about 3 percent. In 2000 alone, ICT investment in the United States soared to $813 billion, or about $2,924 for every man, woman, and child.[41] According to Regis McKenna, ICT as a percentage of nominal business capital equipment spending peaked at 53 percent in December 2000, 48 percent above the forty-year trend line.[42] Official statistics from the U.S. Bureau of Economic Analysis (BEA) reported that total spending on business equipment and software accelerated to a growth rate of over 12 percent, accounting for more than one-fourth of total Gross Domestic Product (GDP) growth between 1995 and 2000.

The ICT spending boom was also fueled in part by concern over the "Year 2000" (Y2K) computer meltdown, the prospect that companies' "mission-critical" operations would be halted if computers misread 2000 as 1900. Economist Arthur B. Laffer reported that the U.S. Federal Reserve believed the Y2K problem was serious; they anticipated widespread computer failures and runs on banks.[43] The government estimated it was going to cost $6.8 billion to fix the Y2K bug in the legacy computer systems of federal agencies alone.[44] Estimates in 1998–1999 for fixing the bug in the corporate world ranged from $52 billion to as high as $600 billion. Chase Manhattan Bank was budgeting to spend $200 million to $250 million. And rather than making bare-minimum upgrades, or remedying the Y2K problems, many companies spent heavily on complete next-generation computer systems. In fact, too much was spent. Morgan Stanley estimated that companies overspent on technology by $130 billion in 1999 and 2000.[45]

Democratization of Capital

By its nature, and definition, venture capital thrives on capital gains, which in turn rely on the explosive growth of new business ventures. So like a huge tropical hurricane crossing warm water and growing even larger as more water gets sucked up into the eye of the storm, thus feeding the intensity of the storm, the democratization of entrepreneurs' access to capital fueled new business venturing, which in turn fueled the Perfect Storm's growth.

According to Mark Heesen, president of the National Venture Capital Association (NVCA), during the Perfect Storm $250 billion was being pumped into emerging growth ventures from venture capitalists, angel investors, and corporate investors.[46] Between 1994 and 2001, Internet-related investment activity alone totaled a staggering $175 billion. The majority, 48 percent or $84 billion, flowed into Internet-related ventures in 2000, compared to the early days of the Internet in 1994, when venture capitalists invested only $556 million in Internet-related deals.[47] This activity peaked in the fourth quarter of 1999, *when as much as $160 million was invested each day in about fourteen ventures,* for an average of about $11.6 million each. Or looked at another way, in 1995 the most venture capital raised by a venture in a single round of financing was roughly $85 million; in the eye of the Perfect Storm such a deal would not even have been close to the top of the day's press releases.

According to John Taylor, vice president of research at NVCA, the U.S. venture capital industry experienced one of its best years ever in 1999.[48] But there was a fine line to walk between being in and being out. The VCs basically could not afford to have their money sitting on the sidelines when the times were hot. According to Brad Jones, a partner at Redpoint Ventures' office in Los Angeles, "They have got to be in on the action when the action gets hot."[49] And during the Perfect Storm, "Everybody wanted to play in the venture business." Between 1995 and 2001 the number of VC firms grew 90 percent as 359 were added to the industry.[50] The average firm size grew 225 percent, from $103 million under management to $333 million, and the number of principals managing these firms grew 154 percent—from 3,498 to 8,891. So did their workload as the average amount managed per principal grew from $10 million to $28 million.

Taylor provided us these comments; "The industry grew very rapidly during that period. Venture funds were able to digest and put to use the amounts of money they were raising."[51] But did investors really put that money to good use? One consultant to entrepreneurs said in 1999, "You're fighting just to have investors remember who the hell you are when they write the check two weeks later."[52]

Race to Go Public

The old line with investment bankers on Wall Street is, "When the ducks quack, you feed them." Never was the quacking louder than during the race to go public in the late 1990s, and the ducks got fed as the IPO markets heated up. Since 1990, investment banks have raised nearly $24 trillion.[53] Bill Gates once said, "People are jumping into the market like it's a gold rush."[54] And gold investors found. Between 1996 and 2001, nearly $140 billion was returned on venture capital investments alone, 47 percent of which was returned in 2000.[55] NASDAQ IPOs raised an all-time high of $54 billion in 2000, which was 24 times as much as in 1990.[56] Between 1995 and 2001, 439 dot. coms went public, raising $34 billion.[57]

Netscape proved that dot.com ventures were good investments, and its skyrocketing IPO triggered Wall Street's five-year dot.com mania. Their sales campaign was simple. James L. Barksdale, CEO of Netscape, recalled that every businessperson he talked to was filled with greed or fear when it came to the Internet. They were asking, "How do I do it to them before they do it to me?"[58] Netscape made $75 million in sales the first year, $375 million the second, and just over $500 million in their third year. Netscape had grown in three years to be the same size that it took Microsoft eleven years to reach.

As Michael Lewis wrote in *The New Thing*, Netscape's IPO made 1980s' Wall Street seem like a low-stakes poker table. On August 9, 1995, the IPO shocked the world as the company's stock price opened well above its strong $28 offering price at $73, surged as high as $75, and closed at $58. (Three months later it was at $140.) Closing at a market value of $1.07 billion, it was one of the most successful IPOs in the history of the U.S. stock markets, and that's before it had made even one dollar in profits. The fifteen-month-old venture's IPO made the front page of *The Wall Street Journal*: "It took General Dynamics Corp. 43 years to become a corporation worth today's $2.7 billion. It took Netscape Communications Corp. about a minute."

Netscape's IPO was "the start of Year One in the Online era," and it "launched the Web in the mind of the public." In a little more than 2,000 days after, the world created some three billion Web pages on 20 million Web sites.[59] Doing business in "Netscape Time" became the inescapable process of rushing and working tremendously hard to get to IPO. The feeling inside Netscape before its IPO was nothing but "steady acceleration, with ever decreasing time periods between the initial product going to market and the company itself going to market."[60] Netscape Time was spreading. Said one CEO in 1999, "The idea of a competitor beating us to an IPO is very threatening."[61] This race to IPO was driven ever faster in part by the rising importance of stock options as a major form of compensation in the Silicon Valley. Twenty-four-year-old Andreessen, co-founder of Netscape, was worth some $80 million after his company's IPO.

The Good, the Bad, and the Ugly

During the Perfect Storm, more money was made available to invest, so people moved down the risk curve. Money was returned and more money was put back into riskier investments. Andrew McAfee, an assistant professor at Harvard Business School's technology and operations management unit, put it this way: "We will never see again a wave of enthusiasm and investment and speculation that rises and crashes the way the first Internet wave did."[62]

We can take away three broad lessons from the Perfect Storm: the good, the bad, and the ugly. First the good. As William Draper III, general partner at Draper Richards and managing director of Draper International, said, "It's been a fabulous period for the encouragement of entrepreneurship, and that is the route of success of the economic system in the United States."[63] The Perfect Storm actually helped usher in the real "new economy," where businesses, schools, and government agencies from around the world are steadily integrating Internet technologies into their normal business operations. And the dot.com crash did not kill anything except thousands of ill-conceived ventures and halted millions of business plans in the works. In 1999 Louis V. Gerstner, Jr., chairman at IBM, described the new Internet-only ventures that were going public at the time as "fireflies before the storm."

The bad was the loss of entrepreneurial discipline during the Perfect Storm. Venture capitalists threw caution to the wind and lowered the "validation bar" to getting funded. Bridget Karlin, serial entrepreneur and now venture capitalist, said, "We venture capitalists did a great disservice to entrepreneurs and entrepreneurship, funding ventures that were just in the idea stage."[64] Rob Glaser, who founded Progressive Networks in 1994, said, "In 1995 and 1996, if you said you were doing an Internet toaster, I'm sure you could find a venture capitalist to fund it."[65]

Everyone was racing to IPO "in Netscape Time," neglecting basic fundamentals to entrepreneurship. Sandy Robertson, who founded Robertson-Stephens investment bank, said this during the Perfect Storm: "With this huge injection of capital, companies are going public faster. And they don't have to perform quite as well. If you've got the cash, you can erase the mistakes."[66] And comments from Adam Reinebach, vice president of research at Venture Economics, support Robertson's. He said, "Back in late 1999 and early 2000, venture capitalists were really in a win-win situation when it came time to exit their investments. The IPO market was a virtual slam dunk, and there were plenty of companies with inflated stock values that were looking to grow through acquisition."[67]

This leads us to the ugly—the greed that surfaced and was leading the race to IPOs. William Hearst III, grandson of publishing magnate William Randolph Hearst and venture capitalist at Kleiner Perkins, told an audience of venture capitalists in 1999: "It's an Oklahoma land rush. It's not as much as how valuable the land is, but how much land you can grab."[68] Alan Patricoff, chairman of Apax Partners, a New York investment firm with $11 billion under management, helps us frame a closing to this chapter in the right direction by saying, "Real companies are built on earnings and cash flow. We gave away millions of dollars for crazy projects, and no one did the hard analysis of what companies could realistically earn. Rationality is coming back."

❖

THREE

Discussions of Risk Capital

Capital brings forth living offspring, or at the least, lays the golden eggs.
—Karl Marx

The essential point to grasp is that in dealing with capitalism we are dealing with an evolutionary process.
—Joseph A. Schumpeter

We are here to invest in companies that we believe can succeed, companies with both management teams and purposes that we can wholeheartedly embrace, companies that it will be fun to work with as we build and companies of which we will be justly proud when we succeed.
—**Mission statement for J.H. Whitney & Co. in 1946, one of the first formal venture capital firms in the United States.**[1]

Evolution of the Risk Capital Industry

Frank Knight, a professor of economics at Chicago in 1928, wrote in *Uncertainty and Profits*, "The only *risk* which leads to a profit is a unique uncertainty. Profits arise out of the inherent, absolute unpredictability of things."[2] Alfred R. Berkeley III, vice chairman of NASDAQ, said that "capital is like oil; it's stored energy. It's the fruits of someone else's labor ready to be put into play in businesses."[3] For nearly every entrepreneur, access to private equity capital, or risk capital, is a key ingredient to successful business growth. In the broadest understanding of the stratification of capital, risk capital is money for investment in innovative enterprises or research in which both the risk of loss and the potential for profit may be considerable.

In this book we use the terms *risk capital* and *private equity* to refer to the universe of that asset class—which includes angel investments, venture capital, leveraged buyout, and mezzanine financing—that make direct capital investments in high-growth potential ventures. The one element that binds this diverse group of investors is that they receive some type of equity or stock vehicle when they put money into a venture.

Conceived in France

Contrary to most media reports, the venture capital industry did not start in 1996, nor did it die in 2000. Many claim to be the "first venture capitalist," but the practice dates back as long as humans were exploring, inventing, pro-

❖ Case in Point: The Fairchildren and their Offspring

If venture capital is the engine that runs Silicon Valley, then Arthur Rock may be its James Watt—the guy who figured out how to harness steam. He once said, "I want to build great companies. That's how I get my kicks. I look for people who want the same thing." Rock's story starts in the spring of 1956, when William Shockley, who co-invented the transistor in 1947 while working at AT&T's Bell Laboratories, founded the Shockley Seminconductor Laboratory near Palo Alto. Despite his brilliance as a physicist, Shockley was a disaster as a business manager. Eventually, Shockley's core team could not stand it anymore. The renegade engineers—nicknamed the "Traitorous Eight"—decided to leave and form a new venture.

The eight were Julius Blank, Victor Grinich, Jean Hoerni, Eugene Kleiner, Jay Last, Gordon Moore, Robert Noyce, and Sheldon Roberts. They contacted the New York investment banking firm of Hayden, Stone & Company because Kleiner's father had an account there. They asked the bank to help them find a corporation interested in hiring the group to help establish a semiconductor operation, preferably on the San Francisco Peninsula. This attracted the attention of Rock, an analyst at the investment bank. Rock in turn introduced them to Sherman Fairchild, who at that time was IBM's largest shareholder. Fairchild was interested in redirecting his camera company toward the field of electronics and data processing. Together they created Fairchild Semiconductor in Palo Alto in 1957, the first venture to work solely with silicon.

Over the years, the departing "Fairchildren" helped to create the semiconductor industry. Between 1966 and 1969, no less than twenty-seven new chip ventures were formed by Fairchild émigrés. Two of the eight, Noyce and Moore, started Intel Corporation in 1968, and Rock also funded them with $2.5 million. Perkins and Kleiner founded Kleiner Perkins Caufield & Byers, one of the most influential and central venture capital firms in the world today. Together, the Fairchildren established the central philosophy of Silicon Valley—anyone with a good enough idea can get the capital, the workforce, and the markets to make it a reality.

Sources: Tom Wolfe, "The Tinkerings of Robert Noyce: How the Sun Rose on Silicon Valley," *Esquire*, December 1983, pp. 346–374; Robert Koepp, *Clusters of Creativity* (New York: John Wiley & Sons, 2003); Tom Quinlan, "The Start-up Culture," *Mercury News*, February 28, 2002; William D. Bygrave and Jeffry A. Timmons, *Venture Capital at the Crossroads* (Boston: Harvard Business School Press, 1992), p. 295; Daniel Gross, *Forbes Greatest Business Stories of All Time* (New York: John Wiley & Sons, 1996), pp. 247–265.

ducing, and selling. Although Britain already had developed a capital market late in the eighteenth century to fund the industrial revolution, it was the Parisian brothers Jacob and Isaac Pereire who leveraged the studies of the French economists discussed in Chapter 1, and who established *Credit Mobilier* as the first true entrepreneurial bank in 1852. Their work in France became "a philosophical system around the creative role of capital" and the prototype for the entire banking system in Europe, and it ushered in what we can call finance capitalism.[4]

Born in New York

The model for modern banking crossed the Atlantic after the turmoil of the Civil War. Its beachhead was established in New York by Jay Cooke and the *American Credit Mobilier*, which helped to finance the transcontinental railroad. Later, J.P. Morgan, who had been exposed to banking in London, established his bank in New York in 1865 as the "conduit for European investment capital in American industry." He is recognized as the founder of the "most successful entrepreneurial bank of the nineteenth century," and it still operates today. One of the first major deals in American history was in 1877 when Thomas Alva Edison formed the Edison Electric Light Company. In 1889, working with the investment bank Drexel, Morgan & Company, Edison established his electrical manufacturing firm, which today is known as General Electric.

Nurtured in Boston

The industry was still immature until the end of World War II. Three people stand out among those who put risk capital on a more permanent institutional base: John H. Whitney, a wealthy polo player and angel investor; Georges F. Doriot, a Harvard Business School professor of entrepreneurship; and Ralph E. Flanders, president of the Federal Reserve Bank of Boston. In 1946 Flanders helped Doriot form the American Research and Development Corporation (ARD) in Boston. It used a small pool of risk capital from individuals and institutions to make active investments in selected emerging businesses. Whitney was first to coin the phrase *venture capital*. On February 10, 1946, J.H. Whitney & Co. opened their doors with $10 million of Whitney's own money committed to invest in new business ventures.

Matured in Silicon Valley

Venture capital, which was born in New York and nurtured in Boston, did not really come of age until it moved to California. There it "joined forces with the brash young technologists who were using bits of silicon to create an information revolution as profound as the industrial revolution a century earlier" in Santa Clara County.

With only some 600,000 acres, about the size of Rhode Island, it is hard for some to believe that Santa Clara was seen as the seed farm to the world. But millions have visited Santa Clara, much like the nineteenth-century politicians, journalists, technologists, and revolutionaries, who made obligatory pilgrimages to Manchester, England, to pay homage to the steam revolution discussed in Chapter 2, and to meditate on the new economy that was then being created. Silicon Valley's investment banking community was firmly established in the late 1960s and early 1970s. It turned entrepreneurs' dreams into mountains of cash on the fertile soils first tilled by innovators like Bill Draper.

After he helped run the Marshall Plan in Europe for President Eisenhower, General William H. Draper founded Draper, Gaither & Anderson in 1958, together with Rowan Gaither (founder of the Rand Corporation in Santa Monica, CA) and Frederick L. Anderson (a retired Air Force general). After working three years at his father's firm, William Draper, General Draper's son, founded Draper & Johnson Investments with Pitch Johnson. The Drapers along with Arthur Rock are known as the few who "made Silicon Valley happen."

Educated in the SBIC Program

In 1958 Lyndon Johnson was seeking small-business support for his run as the Democratic presidential nomination, and he pushed the Small Business Investment Company Act of 1958 through the U.S. Senate. The SBIC program gave tax breaks to private investment companies that targeted small businesses and let them leverage their resources with low-interest loans from the U.S. Small Business Administration (SBA). During the late 1960s the program helped fuel the creation of today's formal venture capital industry by creating hundreds of venture capitalists overnight. These early firms were formed as limited partnerships, with the venture capital company acting as the general partner. The general partners received a management fee and a percentage of the profits earned on a deal. The limited partners, who supplied the funding, were institutional investors such as insurance companies, endowment funds, bank trust departments, pension funds, and wealthy individuals and families.

This pattern has pretty much been the same since 1978–1979, when pension funds began investing in venture capital funds after the Labor Department liberalized rules under the Employee Retirement Income Security Act (ERISA). One of the key milestones of the venture capital industry in the United States, the act changed not only the composition of investors in risk capital funds but also increased the total flow of funds into the venture capital industry. Before 1978 new commitments to VC funds had never exceeded $500 million (in 1993 dollars). In 1979, new commitments exceeded $1 billion for the first time and averaged over $4 billion in new commitments per year throughout the 1980s.

Perfected in the Reagan Era

Things changed with President Ronald Reagan's election in 1980, when the business environment shifted from President Carter's "Days of Malaise" as the Republicans produced political leaders committed to entrepreneurial capitalism. Their thrust took shape under "supply-side economics," which was first envisioned by economic adviser Dr. Arthur Laffer. His winning thesis was simply this: Lower the marginal tax rates. He believed that individuals should keep more of their hard-earned money, which would encourage them to make more.

On August 15, 1981, less than seven months after being sworn in, President Reagan signed the Kemp-Roth bill into law. It was the cornerstone of what would become the most successful economic policy for new business venturing in U.S. history. The bill's treatment of capital gains, a lowering of the top capital gains tax rate from 28 percent to 20 percent, made high risk investments even more attractive, causing a twofold increase in commitments to venture capital funds in 1981. Entrepreneurs then launched a boom that would last, except for a brief eight months following the Gulf War in 1991, until the end of the twentieth century. It was the longest period of economic expansion in the nation's history. Between 1983 and 2003, the Dow Jones Industrial average provided an annual return of 11 percent. For comparison, between 1965 and 1983 its annual return was 1 percent.

According to the U.S. Department of Labor Non-Farm Employment Data, the American economy generated over 27 million new jobs between 1980 and 1995. Over 24 million of these new jobs were created by small- and medium-size entrepreneurs operating high-growth ventures. As Dr. Laffer predicted, even Washington, D.C., prospered well, with the U.S. Treasury revenues increasing 28 percent to more than $1 trillion in 1990. At the closing of the last century, MIT economist Lester Thurow had this to say:

> In what will come to be seen as the third industrial revolution, new technological opportunities are creating fortunes faster than ever before. The United States has created more billionaires in the past fifteen years than in its previous history—even correcting for inflation and changes in average per capita gross domestic product."[6]

Understanding the Economic Impact of Venture Capital on the U.S. Economy

Entrepreneurship, combined with support from venture capital, is a major force driving economic growth in the United States. Thomas McConnell of New Enterprise Associates said, "Venture capital investment is a national phenomenon that helps set the U.S. economy apart from others in the world."[7] Venture capital financed groundbreaking research and untold improvements in infrastructure and technology. The average venture-backed company employs nearly 100 workers within five years and creates almost twice as many jobs as their nonventure-backed competitors. In his 2002 presentation before the U.S. Senate Committee on Small Business and Entrepreneurship, Mark Heesen stated it clearly. He said, "Investments by venture capitalists over the past thirty years have built companies that are responsible for nearly 11 percent of the U.S. gross domestic product, have created 12.5 million jobs, and have generated $1.1 trillion in revenue in the year 2000 alone."[8]

John Taylor from the NVCA provides more details.[9] A NVCA-supported study found that for every dollar invested in 1970–1999 there was $6.50 in U.S. revenue during 2000. And for every $13,775 of venture capital investment between 1970–1999, there was one job in the year 2000. In 2000, U.S.-venture-backed firms paid $58.8 billion in federal taxes, $7.8 billion in state and local taxes, had net income of $13.8 billion, exported $21.7 billion, and invested $157.3 billion in R&D.

There is no doubt that venture capital will continue to play an increasingly vital role during difficult economic times like we experienced after the Perfect Storm. It is one of the few sources of risk capital available to innovative businesses. In fact, as Heesen adds, "Some of today's most successful companies were founded in difficult economic environments."[10]

Construct of the Venture Capital Industry

In the course of one decade, the venture capital segment of risk capital went from a $3 billion industry to a $100 billion industry. Taylor describes venture capital as a unique alignment of interests between entrepreneurs, venture capitalists (VCs), and the VCs' investors. Depending on where you stand, venture capital can be cash investment, capital resources, leadership and contacts, economic development, commercializer of innovations, job creator, or research magnet. The NVCA defines venture capital as *money provided by professionals who invest alongside management in young, rapidly growing companies that have the potential to develop into significant economic contributors.*

Who are Venture Capitalists?

According to Steve Jurvetson, partner at Draper Fisher Jurvetson, "The venture capitalist works closely with portfolio companies to build the team, form partnerships, sign on key customers, gain awareness in the press, and secure follow-on rounds of financing."[11] Thomas Hellman at Stanford University's Graduate School of Business uses a sports analogy when looking at the entrepreneur/venture capitalist relationship. The entrepreneurs are the athletes and the venture capitalists are the coaches. The coaches choose which athletes get to play and the coaches train and motivate them and help create the plays and plans so that they all win.

Jim Clark, co-founder of Netscape, says the best VCs are like chess masters, always six moves ahead of the game. They finance new and rapidly growing ventures through the purchasing of equity securities. They add value to the venture through active participation, generally as a director, and assist in the development of new products or services. They have a long-term orientation and take higher risks with the expectations of higher rewards.

Such risk is inherent with the venture capital industry. In *Confessions of a Venture Capitalist*, Ruthann Quindlen writes, "Venture Capital is hard. It's stressful. It's lonely." It is a tough business because, like the saying goes, "You can count how many seeds are in the apple, but not how many apples are in the seed." Venture capitalists, as they count the dollars going out, assume that some deals will not work out. Vinod Khosla, a partner at Kleiner, Perkins who spotted winners like Juniper Networks (which returned some 5,000 times their capital invested), says this, "If things don't fail, it means we are not taking enough risk."[12]

As we first discussed in Chapter 2, the venture capital industry has grown to a size that could only be imagined in the recent past. Capital under management by venture capitalists increased from $226 billion in 2000 to $250 billion in 2001. Capital under management is defined as the cumulative total of committed funds less liquidated funds or those funds that have completed their life cycle. This $24 billion difference in capital under management, which represented an 11 percent increase, was due primarily because of the existing capital commitments from 1998 to 2001. This increase, however, was the lowest annual percentage increase since 1993 and the lowest dollar increase since 1997.

There are several types of venture capital firms. Most mainstream firms invest their capital through funds organized as limited partnerships in which the venture capital firm functions as the general partner. Thompson Financial Venture Economics and the NVCA classify venture capital firms into four main categories. The most common type is an *independent firm*. This category refers to independent private and public firms including institutionally and noninstitutionally funded firms and private family groups. This category manages about $204 billion, or 82 percent of the total capital under management in the United States.

The second category is *financial institutions*. This category refers to firms that are affiliates and/or subsidiaries of investment banks and non-investment banks financial entities. This includes commercial banks and insurance companies. This category manages about $31 billion, or 13 percent of the total. The third is *corporations*. This category includes venture capital subsidiaries and affiliates of industrial corporations. This category manages about $13 billion, or 5 percent of the total. The fourth category is all other firms, which may include government-affiliated investment programs that help start up venture either through state, local, or federal programs. This category manages about $2 billion, or less than 1 percent of the total.

At the end of 2001, there were 8,891 venture capitalists working at 761 firms, managing 1,627 funds. On the average, each firm had about 11 principals, who collectively managed two funds each worth $156 million, or a total of $333 million per firm, meaning each principal managed $28 million. Comparatively speaking, the number of firms managing large amounts of capital has increased over the last couple of years. In 2000, 106 venture capital firms managed over $500 million, with 56 of them managing over $1 billion. In 2001, 132 firms managed over $500 million, and 72 managed over $1 billion.

Finally, it is important to point out the difference between venture capitalists and angel investors. Venture capital firms are professional investors who dedicate 100 percent of their time to investing and building emerging growth companies. Most venture capitalists have a fiduciary responsibility to their investors. Most of the angel investment community in the United States is an informal network of investors who invest in companies for their own interests. And typically, angel investors invest less than $1 million in any particular company, whereas venture capitalists will usually invest more than $1 million per company.

Informal Angel Investors

Venture capitalists invest in more established ventures, but informal angel investors are the primary source of early stage risk capital for entrepreneurial ventures in the United States. Angels are private individuals that invest their own wealth in entrepreneurs who are not directly related to them through family or prior friendship, with the mindset that they will get higher returns as the ventures get "discovered" down the road by an attractive buyer. Active angels will make one to two deals per year, with investments ranging from $10,000 to $500,000, and the average being $175,000. They particularly focus on firms in the start-up stage. For example, the first angel investor in Starbucks Coffee was a doctor who was introduced to its founder, Howard Schultz, through their wives. The doctor's $100,000 investment grew to be worth more than $10 million.

Though not formally classified with the venture capital industry, angel investors are the largest pool of risk capital available to finance entrepreneurial activity in the United States, consisting of about $60 to $80 billion. Each year, as many as 250,000 active angel investors finance between 30,000 and 50,000 very early stage ventures with a total dollar investment between $7 billion and $20 billion. And according to one serial angel investor, as angel investors increasingly pool their funds and resources by connecting in networks, they are becoming more accessible to entrepreneurs.[13] Jeffrey Sohl at the University of New Hampshire's Center for Venture Research estimates that there may be as many as 170 formal and informal networks in the United States and Canada.[14] There are many different types of angels and this subject is well documented. Figure 3-1 provides a summary.

Corporate Venture Investors

Corporate venture capitalists will often co-invest along with traditional venture capitalists. They can add additional value by opening up access to corporate distribution channels, technology and know-how, and strategic partners. The typical distinction between corporate venturing and venture capitalists is that corporate venturing is usually performed through self-contained entities with corporate strategic objectives in mind, while VCs typically have investment return or financial objectives as their primary goal. The amount of venture capital invested by corporate investors grew from $267 million in 1995 to $17 billion in 2000, representing nearly 35 percent of the deal flow. Total capital under management by corporate investors has grown from $2 billion in 1991 to $13 billion in 2001 or about 5 percent of the total in the United States in 2002. Between 1995 and 2000, they invested $31 billion in 4,042 ventures. On the average, 18 percent of their investment dollars goes to early

Figure 3-1. Typology of angel investors.

Serial Angels. These are the super, high-flying formal angels that are most commonly associated with Silicon Valley. They may or may not work alone. Some have sold out of their ventures and work in established investment banking or venture capital firms.

Freelancing Angels. Sometimes angels can be found inside other businesses. Examples are Meg Whitman at eBay and Larry Ellison at Oracle. In addition to cash, they bring great credibility and connections.

Operational/Value-Adding Angels. These manager-investors are nearing the end of their careers and have earned their stripes working through the corporate ranks. They invest to keep themselves busy. They often start out as an advisor, board member, and/or consultant, and will even consider employment opportunities. Sometimes they are officers or board members inside established companies, looking to nurture and support emerging ventures.

Flock of Angels. A group of all types. But a formal angel investor participating in a legally structured angel group must be an "accredited investor." The Securities and Exchange Commission (SEC) states that that is someone whose net worth is greater than $1 million or who has an annual income of at least $200,000, or $300,000 for couples.

Enthusiast/Financial Angels. Also known as *Tourist* or *Checkbook Angels*, they are accredited by having great luck in the stock market, home values, or long and many years working within a large company. Typically investing purely for the financial return, they almost never invest on their own. Most like to hide in the background of formal angel groups. With no formal investing practice, nor entrepreneurial experience, they quite often spread money among many small investments in the range of $10,000–$25,000.

Socially Responsible Angels. This group includes great names like John Anderson of UCLA, The Price Institute, and The Kauffman Institute. They look for entrepreneurs with high moral values and ventures addressing major social issues, or they invest in educational and nonprofit organizations.

Neighborhood Angels. The largest group in the U.S., these unaccredited private investors are less experienced investors who like to tinker with entrepreneurial activities. Working solo, they are the doctors, lawyers, successful real estate developers, and other entrepreneurs. *Virgin angels* are included in this group. They are individuals with funds available and are looking to make their first investment but have yet to discover a suitable deal.

Celebrity Angels. These were entrepreneurs, or "bubble-babies," who were at the right place, at the right time, with the right idea, and made upwards to hundreds of millions of dollars. Fortunately, they are almost completely worked out of the investment community. They could have started a private equity firm, most likely disguised as an incubator. These angels do not add much strategic value and they dilute the capital structure.

Tire-Kicking Angels. Also known as *hobbyists angels*, they are the opposite of serial and formal angels. Sometimes they are accredited, but they almost never invest. They like hanging around the exciting world of entrepreneurship. It is something to tell their friends, or keep themselves busy, often having fun in a "men's-night-out" at gatherings of formal angel groups.

---

stage, 55 percent into expansion, 24 percent into later stage, and 3 percent into buyout/acquisition. In 2001 deal flow declined more than 71 percent as they invested just less than $5 billion. This represented 12 percent of the total investment activity in 2001.

How Does the Venture Capital Industry Work?

Marc Andreessen, co-founder of Netscape, vividly describes an insider's view to the venture capital industry's food chain:

> The best VCs can see ahead and are willing to think they can fix things, put the management team together, do all this stuff. Any huge success story like Netscape or Apple is like a sausage factory. Everybody likes to eat sausage; no one likes to see how it gets made. These things are all sausage factories inside.[15]

In their influential book, *Venture Capital at the Crossroads*, Bygrave and Timmons tell us that the lifeblood of the venture capital process consists of three essential components: entrepreneurial deals, money to invest in those deals, and a return on the money invested in them.

Depending on the investment focus and strategy of the venture capital firm, it will seek a liquidity event to exit the investment in the entrepreneur's venture within three to seven years of the initial investment. While the initial public offering (IPO) may be the most glamorous and heralded type of exit for the venture capitalists and founders of the venture, most successful exits of venture investments occur through a merger or acquisition (M&A). In the case of an M&A, the venture firm will receive stock or cash from the acquiring company, and the proceeds of the sale will be returned to its limited partners.

Just like the entrepreneurs they finance, venture capitalists have to go out and raise money too. They get the majority of their funds from outside the partners of the firms. Most VCs raise their funds from institutional investors, such as pension funds, insurance companies, endowments, foundations, and high net-worth individuals. These investors who invest in venture capital funds are referred to as limited partners. Venture capitalists, who manage the fund, are referred to as general partners. Each year, a venture firm will set out prospecting for investors with a target fund size. It will distribute a prospectus to potential investors and may take from several weeks to several months to raise the requisite capital. The commitments of capital are raised from the investors during the formation of the fund. In 2001 a total of $40 billion was committed to 299 venture capital funds. Private and public pension funds continued to dominate as limited partners, as 42 percent of the capital committed to venture capitalists came from them, 25 percent from financial and insurance organizations, 22 percent from endowments and foundations, and 9 percent from individuals and families; corporations committed the remaining 3 percent.

As an investment manager, the venture capital firm will typically charge a management fee to cover the costs of managing the committed capital. This fee ranges between 2 percent to 2.5 percent of the money they manage and will usually be paid quarterly for the life of the fund. This is most often negotiated with investors upon formation of the fund in the terms and conditions of the investment. "Carried interest" is the term used to denote the profit split of proceeds generated from a liquidity event between the VC firm and its limited partners. This carry is commonly paid to the VC firm only after investors have recovered their investment. See Figure 3-2 for how this comes together in the venture capital industry and where the venture capitalists provide their value in the food chain.

Not all venture capitalists invest in start-ups and early-stage ventures. Venture capital firms have different preferences and practices, including how much money they will provide, where in the entrepreneurial life cycle they prefer to invest, and the cost of capital or expected annual rate of return they are seeking. The sources of capital change dramatically for entrepreneurs at different stages of development and rates of growth. According to Dan Bas-

FIGURE 3-2. VENTURE CAPITAL INDUSTRY.

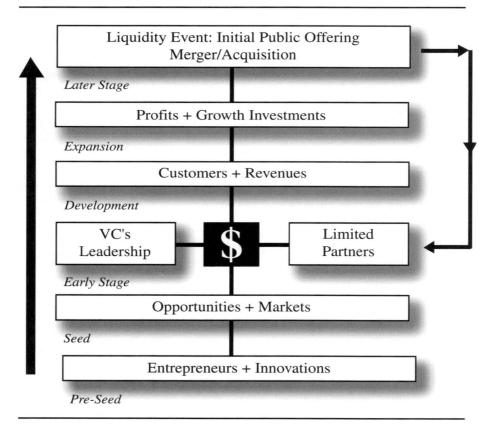

sett, a partner at InnoCal Partners based in Costa Mesa, California, "The number one piece of advice for entrepreneurs is to know where you are on the food chain. If you don't know, seek advice and make use of the very high quality people in your environment."[16] The five stages in the food chain of the venture capital industry are described in more detail in Figure 3-3.

Understanding the Types of Securities

There are two types of financial offerings available to entrepreneurs, equity and debt. In exchange for private equity investments, the venture issues equity securities. There are three basic types of securities.

❖   **Common shares** are most often issued to those who manage the corporation, bear the major risks of the venture, and yet stand to profit the most if it is successful.

❖   **Preferred shares** have liquidation and dividend preferences over common shares and may be converted into another class of shares, usually common shares.

❖   **Debentures** are long-term, unsecured debt securities.

Debt financing is a method involving an interest-bearing instrument, usually thought of as a loan, and it requires that some asset be used as collateral. Debt requires the venture to pay back the amount of the borrowed funds as well as a fee for the use of the money for the time it was loaned out, which is called interest.

All entrepreneurs interested in raising capital must decide which vehicle is most appropriate for their situation. An equity offering will give share ownership and some level of control to others. Also, with an equity offering, working capital and financial leverage of the venture improves, as interest costs and debt service in future years are avoided. On the other hand, debt financing has the distinct advantage that it does not dilute the existing shareholder value. While the main focus of this book is on private equity financings, the process and information required—like the business plan, marketing plan, and financials—are very similar to what is required for debt financings.

What Are Typical Returns on the Investments?

Entrepreneurs are the source of consistent high-performance returns on investments. Performance for the venture capital industry is traditionally measured by the internal rate of return (IRR). The IRR considers "cash-on-cash" returns from the sale of shares and disbursements from the liquidity events back to investors, such as dividends. It is calculated by taking inflows of cash as negative cash flows, and distributions of cash and stock to investors as positive cash flows. Venture capitalists have to have a good idea of the percentage returns they anticipate on their investments. Their limited partner investors—the "limiteds"—are IRR-driven, hence so are the VC's practices of

FIGURE 3-3. STAGE DEFINITIONS USED IN THE VENTURE CAPITAL INDUSTRY.

---

1. **Seed-Stage Financing.** The venture is in the gestation, or idea formation stage, as the product is not fully developed. A relatively small amount of capital is usually provided to an inventor or entrepreneur to prove a concept. This may involve product development and premarketing activities like market research, as well as building a venture team and completing a business plan.

2. **Early Stage Financing.** Early stage or start-up financing is used for completing product development and may include initial marketing efforts. Ventures eligible for this type of financing may be in the process of organizing, or they may already be in business for two years or less, but have not sold their product commercially. Investors want to see entrepreneurs that have conducted market studies, assembled the key players on their venture team, developed a business plan, and are ready to launch. Once launched, this opens the door to institutional investors, as the networking capabilities of the venture capitalists are used more here than in more advanced stages.

3. **Development and Expansion-Stage Financing.** Ventures here are usually more than three years old, demonstrating significant growth in revenues, and may or may not be showing a profit. Some of the uses of capital may include expansion of production capabilities, marketing, new product development, or developing new markets for the existing product line. The venture capitalists' role in this stage evolves from a supportive role to a more strategic role, often bringing in more institutional investors along with initial investors from previous rounds.

4. **Later-Stage and Bridge Financing.** Investors provide capital for ventures in this stage that have reached a fairly stable growth rate and have either stable streams of profitable earnings, or highly predictable streams of top line revenues. VCs will provide bridge financing when a venture plans to go public within a year or so. This can be structured so that it gets repaid from the proceeds of a public underwriting. It can also involve the restructuring of major stockholders/early investors who want to reduce or liquidate their positions, or if management has changed and the stockholdings of the former management, their relative and associates are being bought out.

5. **Acquisition and Leverage Buyout Financing.** Investors provide funds to finance the acquisition of another private venture or public company. This includes money for mezzanine financing using subordinated debt, bridge loans that are used to finance Leveraged Buyouts (LBOs), and recapitalizations. Financing for a Management Buyout (MBO) enables a group to acquire a product line or business, at any stage of development, from either a public company or a closely held private venture. An MBO usually involves the revitalization, or a "turnaround" of an operation, where an entrepreneurial management team acquires a significant equity interest in exchange for improving the venture's performance.

Based on definitions used by the National Venture Capital Association.

investing. Because VCs focus on delivering an average of 30 percent-plus back to their limiteds, they target for around 50 percent-plus on each investment. Private equity returns are derived from distributions back to investors and interim portfolio company valuations. Figure 3-4 illustrates a one-year, three-year, five-year, and twenty-year perspective of private equity returns.

Figure 3-4. Private equity returns.

Fund Type	1 Year	3 Year	5 Year	20 Year
Early Stage	− 28.6%	19.4%	44.1%	20.7%
Balanced	− 19.2%	19.4%	22.0%	14.7%
Later Stage	− 16.4%	4.6%	13.3%	16.1%
All Venture	− 22.3%	15.1%	26.8%	16.7%
All Buyouts	− 8.2%	− 4.3%	1.4%	12.4%
Mezzanine	− 1.6%	5.2%	7.7%	11.0%
All Private Equity	− 12.3%	1.0%	8.3%	14.5%

Source: Thomson Venture Economics/National Venture Capital Association 09/30/02.

The venture funds have lives on average of ten to twelve years. Their performance during the first three years of investment activity are volatile and difficult to measure. A typical VC investment might have one of five potential outcomes: "Bad," "Alive," "Okay," "Good," and "Great." The Bad, a complete "wipe-out," does not return anything; the Alive returns maybe 1 × the money invested; Okay returns 5×; Good returns 10×; and Great returns are 20× or higher. On the average, the gross returns on each $1,000 invested would be $4,400, and the net, less the Bad, would be $3,400. For longer periods of time, returns on venture capital investments outpace all others. For comparison, by the end of 2001, the five-year rolling averages were 38 percent for venture capital, 17 percent for NASDAQ, and 14 percent for the S&P 500.[17]

Understanding the Selection Process

Venture capitalists mitigate the risk of venture investing by developing a portfolio of companies in a single venture fund. They invest in a small percentage of the business plans that get placed and reviewed at their firms. When considering an investment, they carefully screen the technical and business merits of the deal before them. Jesse Reyes, vice president for Thompson Venture Economics, a New York-based venture capital research firm, says, "The key to this new environment, though, is that the venture investors can afford to be choosy about what deals they do, and they're exercising that right."[18] Therefore, the selection process profiled in Figure 3-5 can be quite comprehensive. We continue this discussion in Chapter 16.

Situation Analysis of the Venture Capital Industry

Returns have retreated from the record levels we saw during the Perfect Storm. As with the public markets, private equity returns also suffered a downfall in 2001 as measured by one-year returns. At the end of December 2001, each of the private equity sectors discussed above showed negative one-year returns ranging from a − 3.5 percent to − 33 percent. And for the first

FIGURE 3-5. HOW A VENTURE CAPITAL FIRM SCREENS ITS DEALS.

Placement of Completed Business Plan, through appropriate "warm" referrals.

Quickview and Routing, the plan is directed to the most appropriate reviewer based on partner's domain expertise.

Business Plan Review, one or more partners will review the plan and evaluate it based on a number of factors related to the firm's current area of focus. Based on the outcome of the review process, the entrepreneur will be contacted and informed of the next steps.

Informal Dialogue, whereby additional details are requested from the entrepreneur through email and phone calls. If there is significant interest, the entrepreneur and team will be invited to present before the firm's investment professionals.

Initial Pre-Screening Meeting, much like an interview process, provides opportunity for the interested partners to be introduced to the entrepreneur and team and see them in action with the presentation. They discuss the next steps in the funding process, and how the firm can assist the entrepreneur and team.

Informal Due Diligence, a step for pre-investment analysis, typically it can be conducted in about a week but sometimes takes as much as three weeks. The investment committee, which is made up of all the partners in the firm, reviews and discusses the due diligence that has been conducted up to that point.

Formal Presentation, if a decision is made to continue, they will ask the entrepreneur to formally present before senior partners. After the presentation, the investment committee would then make a decision whether or not to make an offer for investment.

Investment Decision, during the initial phase of either the informal and/or formal due diligence process, the investors will present and finalize details of a "Term Sheet." The Term Sheet will outline the general attributes of the relationship between the entrepreneur and the VC firm.

Formal Due Diligence, a full firm-wide effort is applied to the in-depth investment review process. Generally, one of the partners will take the lead in this extensive analysis. This process includes additional reference checks of the entrepreneur and team, dialogue with industry and customer references, and interviews with independent subject matter experts.

Closing Documents, a collaborative effort between the attorneys of the venture firm and the entrepreneur that will define the legal framework relationship between the venture and the investors.

Investment, provided that all reach an agreement, the VC then provides the funding and the two parties begin working together and creating sustainable value.

---

time since 1994, venture capital investment activity in 2001 actually declined from the previous year, dropping 62 percent from $106 billion in 2000 to $41 billion in 2001. This was the largest recorded percentage and dollar decline. On a more positive note, the 2001 total was the third highest year and was almost twenty times the amount that was invested in 1991 and almost twice the 1998 total. Viewed another way, if we removed the years 1999 and 2000, 2001 would be a record year with the most ever invested by the venture industry (see Figure 3-6).

The breakneck pace of entrepreneurial capitalism from 1998 to early 2001 was an aberration and is not worth using as a benchmark. Mark Heesen from the NVCA basically erases the data of year 2000 from everything he reads and sees, viewing it as an anomaly. Robert M. Metcalfe, the inventor of the Ethernet, the local-area-network technology in 1973 (LAN technology) and founder of 3Com, and now a partner at Polaris Ventures in Waltham, Massachusetts, simply says, "Just forget those years happened."[19]

In 2001, ventures in the expansion stage received 57 percent of this financing, early stage got 23 percent, later stage got 18 percent, and startup/seed stage ventures received only 2 percent. We found that as the total number of ventures receiving financing fell 40 percent from 6,366 in 2000 to 3,788, the number of first-round investments as a percentage of overall investments declined too from 27 percent in 2000 to 18 percent in 2001, as 1,172 ventures received financing for the first time from a venture capitalist. The total first-round activity in 2001 amounted to $7.4 billion, averaging $6.3 million per deal. For comparison, in 2000 venture capitalists invested a total of $29 billion into 3,333 first rounds, or an average investment of $8.7 million each. As a point of reference, looking over the years 1990–2001 venture capitalists invested $280 billion in 29,182 ventures. Further analysis shows that $132 billion, or 47 percent, went to ventures in their expansion round, $68 billion, or 24 percent, went to early stage ventures, $58 billion, or 20 percent, went to ventures in their later stage, and $23 billion, or just over 8 percent, went for ventures in the buyout stage. Specifically looking at first-round investments between 1990 and 2001, venture capitalists invested $93 billion in 13,867 ventures. This activity represents 33 percent of the total dollars invested and 48 percent of the total number of investment rounds for the period. Our analysis shows that the average amount invested in the first round increased dramatically from $2.7 million in 1990, to the peak of the decade at $8.7 million in 2000, and settled at $6.3 million at the closing of 2001.

Corpulent VCs, GPs, and LPs in Not So Heady Times

Unlike the ventures they support, venture capitalists learned that their industry just cannot scale. Venture capital under management increased tenfold between the late 1980s and 2001, from $25 billion to $250 billion, while the number of people making investment decisions at venture firms rose a little more than twofold, from 3,580 to 8,891. An increase in the fee income helped some venture firms expand operations, but the number of partners and staff did not increase nearly as quickly as did dollars under management. In fact, dollars under management per principal during the same period increased from $7 million to $28 million, which is four times the workload for the VCs. But as the limited partners saw it, much of the increased fee income went directly to the venture capitalists themselves.

Figure 3-6. Venture capital investments (1993–2003).

	1993	1994	1995	1996	1997	1998	1999	2000	2001	2002	2003 (1)
Total Amount (millions)	4,394	3,887	7,371	11,903	16,063	21,461	54,438	105,910	40,619	21,155	16,250
Startup/Seed	631	691	1,384	1,545	1,372	1,850	3,328	3,101	826	212	163
Early Stage	1,544	907	1,795	3,559	3,487	5,438	12,101	25,878	9,271	4,019	3,088
Expansion	1,684	1,351	3,070	5,094	8,173	10,840	30,278	60,992	23,025	13,328	10,238
Later Stage	535	937	1,122	1,706	3,031	3,333	8,731	15,938	7,497	3,596	2,763
Total # of Ventures (2)	905	955	1,568	2,098	2,583	3,456	4,480	6,366	3,798	3,028	2,290
# of 1st Rounds	349	417	901	1,151	1,315	1,809	2,448	3,333	1,172	756	595
# of Follow-on Rounds	611	608	773	1,156	1,473	1,892	2,481	3,723	2,801	2,393	1,786

(1) Estimates at time of publication.
(2) Number of ventures receiving financing can be less than the sum of the rounds because a given venture can receive initial and follow-on financing in the same year.

Sources: National Venture Capital Association 2002 Yearbook and PWC/VE/NVCA MoneyTree Survey.

Since the amount of capital raised by venture capitalists outpaced the amount of capital they put to use in investments in recent years, there is the issue of what some in the industry call "overhang," "dry powder," or simply uninvested capital. As much as 80 percent of the investments made by VCs since the Perfect Storm has been tied up supporting the portfolio ventures and not investing in new businesses. At the end of 2001, private equity industry experts first estimated that venture funds had more than $100 billion of dry powder, and buyout funds had more than $120 billion, for a total of $220 to $240 billion. By mid-year 2002, Jesse Reyes of Venture Economics concluded that about a total of $150 billion was available for all types of private equity investments.[20] In early 2003, John Taylor from the NVCA stated that some $80 to $85 billion in venture capital was still available for investment.[21] According to R. Glenn Hubbard, former chairman of the White House Council of Economic Advisors, this "capital overhang" will still take a while for the industry to actually digest.[22]

The Investors' Dilemma

This leads us into the discussion of what Vinod Khosla described as "the Investors' Dilemma."[23] The situation today is much like 1987, when the VC industry had negative returns. According to Khosla, there are good years, great years, and sometimes really bad years; we just got out of a couple of really bad years. He says we should still expect more losers than winners, and many will lose everything. But more will be won than lost and the value of winners in the future will exceed the cumulative market cap of the leaders today. He advises entrepreneurs that now is a great time to start a new venture. And as for his advice to venture capitalists, "This is a reckoning, but this is no time to retreat."

In fact, the venture capital industry is now returning to the discipline that made up their business prior to the Perfect Storm. Jos Henkens, a partner at Advanced Technology Ventures in Palo Alto, said that "2001 was a wake-up year. This was the year when people said, 'Hey maybe those rules set down by more experienced folks before 1996 weren't that crazy after all.'"[24] For example, we are witnessing the re-introduction of patience in investment decision making. As Thomas Jefferson wrote in a letter to George Washington in 1792, "Delay is preferable to error." And the timeline for success is back to normal: seven to ten years for a venture to complete the entrepreneurial life cycle to a liquidity event.

Innovation Did Not Go Out with the Perfect Storm

So all the necessary ingredients for entrepreneurial capitalism are still in place. With an unlimited ability to scale for global markets, we still have the culture that supports entrepreneurship, risk, restarts, and even failure. There is plenty of capital available and a perfected mechanism for putting it into play and exiting efficiently. The cost of building a venture is lower as talent and professional services are readily available. The number of competitors is significantly reduced and the established players in markets stop innovating and stop their R&D in economic downturns, leaving opportunities for new business ventures.

According to Leo Spiegel, a general partner at Mission Ventures in San Diego, the VCs' mindset must be based on investing through cycles in order to be successful. Tim Draper of Draper Fisher Jurvetson concurs, "We know that, and we know that historically, many of the best returns come from deals made while the rest of the industry is sleeping."[25] And it is highly unlikely that 2001 will mark the year that innovation and entrepreneurial capitalism ceased to exist. We close this chapter with a quote from Sunil Dhaliwal at Battery Ventures, a Wellesley, Massachusetts, venture capital firm with $1.8 billion under management. He says, "If you believe early stage funding can't be found, that's tantamount to saying there's no more innovation left to be funded."[26]

PART

Creating and

Engineering

Your Vision

New Business Venture Opportunity and Analysis

Chance favors the prepared mind.
—Louis Pasteur, father of microbiology

Profit is the payment you get when you take advantage of change.
—Joseph A. Schumpeter

I was seldom able to see an opportunity until it had ceased to be one.
—Mark Twain

Opportunity Recognition and Opportunity Formation

Ever since the day that Archimedes, the famous Greek mathematician, leapt from his bathtub and ran through the streets of ancient Syracuse triumphantly shouting *Eureka*, "I found it!," the history of science, technology, and business has been punctuated by exciting moments of true insight and discovery. It was during a visit to the baths that he was lost in thought, contemplating the problem of how to test the purity of the gold in King Hiero's crown without destroying it. He noticed the water overflowing from his bath and discovered his solution: Drop the crown into water and measure the amount of water displaced.

At the heart of even the most complex innovation there is usually a basic, and yet startling "entrepreneurial insight," a new way of looking at an old problem. James Watt's sight of snow on the Green of Glasgow in the spring of 1765 led to the invention of the condenser, and he went on to change the world. Peter Drucker says entrepreneurs are "kissed by the Muses" and have a "flash of genius."[1] Every business begins with just an idea, and opportunity recognition suggests that good ideas for new ventures are "waiting to be discovered by an astute observer."[2]

What Is the Strategic Inflection Point in Your Industry?

Whole industries can become vulnerable to "new rules," but entrepreneurs see such change as the norm and healthy. In fact, the entrepreneur always searches for change, responds to it, and exploits it as an exceptional opportu-

❖ Case in Point: Bill Gates, Paul Allen, and Microsoft

In 1973, after graduating from Lakeside High School in Seattle, Bill Gates went on to Harvard Business School. It was at Lakeside where Gates and his eighth-grade buddy, Paul Allen, discovered computing and developed an interest in writing software. In January 1975 Allen came to Harvard to share with Gates the latest issue of *Popular Electronics* magazine and shouted, "It's about to begin!" Featured on the cover was the Altair 8800. An Albuquerque-based company called MITS (Micro Instrumentation Telemetry Systems) had introduced a $500 computer kit called the Altair 8800 that was built around the Intel 8080 microprocessor. Edward Roberts, Altair's designer, said, "The idea that you could have your own computer and do whatever you wanted to with it, whenever you wanted to, was fantastic."

In his junior year, Gates then nineteen, left Harvard for Albuquerque to devote his energies to Micro-soft, a company he had begun in 1975 with Allen to sell software they were creating at that time. By the end of the year the start-up had three employees and $16,000 in revenues. By 1980 Microsoft had dropped the hyphen, moved to Seattle, and was a forty-person plus venture earning about $7.5 million. In the fall of 1981, IBM introduced its personal computer with Microsoft's 16-bit operating system, MS-DOS 1.0. In 1985, Microsoft's revenues were just over $140 million. The next year they went public at $21 per share. The Office Suite of software was introduced in 1989, and in 1995 Microsoft launched Windows 95. By 2002 the company had $28.4 billion in revenues and just over 50,500 employees in 78 countries and regions around the world. Leveraging the commoditization of the PC and Intel chips, Gates and Allen saw an opportunity in a time of disarray. In his book, *The Road Ahead,* Gates writes, "People often ask me to explain Microsoft's success, they want to know the secret. From the beginning, we set off down a road that was headed in the right direction

Sources: Microsoft company Web site; Howard Means, "The Man and His Money," *Upside*, June 2001; Stephen Segaller, *Nerds 2.0.1: A Brief History of the Internet* (New York: TV Books, 1999), p. 41; and Bill Gates, *The Road Ahead* (New York: Viking Books, 1995).

nity. Taking root in a disruption is the first condition that entrepreneurs need to meet to improve the probability of successfully creating a new growth business. In fact, research has shown that if they cannot or do not do this, their odds of success are much smaller.[3]

The disruptive technological changes we discussed in Chapter 3 are the principal drivers of competition in the world today. Technological change plays a major role in industry structural change, as well as in creating new opportunities. Many of today's great companies grew out of technological changes that they were able to exploit.

Andrew Grove, CEO of Intel from 1987 to 1997, was instrumental in making Intel one of the great success stories of entrepreneurial capitalism. In *Only the Paranoid Survive,* he defines "strategic inflection points" as major changes in the competitive environment that can threaten a company's livelihood if not addressed effectively.[10] He said that it is easy to miss the potential of new technologies and the impact of new competition that springs from these inflection points. Grove and co-founder Gordon Moore, in the wake of the disruptive processor chip, literally saved Intel with one question. Grove asked, "If we had to start all over, would we start with the DRAM chips?" Moore said "No," and they successfully transitioned Intel from DRAM chips to microprocessor chips.

Who Says It's Better Be a Domain Expert?

Physicist Niels Bohr once said that an expert is a man who has made all the mistakes that can be made in a very narrow field. In business, according to Michael Dell, "Opportunity is part instinct and part immersion in an industry, a subject, or an area of expertise."[5] The discussion and value of the domain expert in entrepreneurship is nothing new in the literature, considering that Karl Vesper had profiled Noyce and Moore, founders of Intel, back in 1979.[6]

In a popular *Harvard Business Review* article, "How Entrepreneurs Craft Strategies That Work," Amar Bhide looks at America's fastest growing private ventures. He found that "new ventures are usually started to solve problems the founders have grappled with personally." In fact, 71 percent were what we call domain experts, as they replicated or modified an idea they encountered in their area of expertise. Some 20 percent discovered the idea serendipitously. Of this group, 6 percent actually wanted the product or service as an individual consumer, and only 4 percent got an idea while they were reading industry publications. About 5 percent conceived their idea following a technological change, and only 4 percent "discovered" the idea through "systematic research." Bhide's advice: "However popular it may be in the corporate world, a comprehensive analytical approach to planning doesn't suit most start-ups."[7]

Brainstorming and Forced Analytics

As a corporate entrepreneur, what do you do to come up with great new ideas and winning innovations when competitive pressures, especially from start-ups, are nipping at your heels? For keeping your company "fresh, alert, and constantly innovating" we refer you to *The Business of Innovation* by Roger Bean and Russell Radford. It provides a powerful model and hands-on strategies for actively and systematically managing creativity throughout larger, established organizations. It also introduces a model for managing and nurturing innovation, and guidelines on measuring and evaluating innovations.

If you are stuck and need your creativity rebooted, or need some guidance leading group discussions, there are some techniques and books targeted for all entrepreneurs. Michael Michalko's *Cracking Creativity: The Secrets of Creative Genius* is a great workbook for reorganizing your thinking around idea-generating strategies. It will help you open up a fresh viewpoint that leads you to creating innovative solutions to everyday challenges. Other sources of ideas come from attending trade shows, listening to consumer feedback, formal competitive intelligence projects, R&D technology transfer projects, focused marketing intelligence reports, attending networking events, and hiring consultants to come speak to your company.

Creating Your Problem Statement

A problem is a situation that needs to be corrected. It can be experienced in a variety of ways but is looked on as a discomfort, or a pain of some sort. In the early days of the PC industry, computers were very expensive, having gone through many hands before reaching the consumer. The "street price" to the end-user for an IBM PC was around $3,000, but the components themselves were worth around $600. Michael Dell saw this as a problem and boiled it all down into one statement, "I started the business with a simple question, how can we make the process of buying a computer better?"[8]

An important early phase in analyzing your opportunity is creating your problem statement. This step is about carefully refining vague or general ideas, which can come from brainstorming, mind mapping, and the whiteboarding of all your discussions surrounding the problem. Then you need to clearly define your initial observations, drawing on domain expertise and research of existing literature, and generate a concise problem statement like Dell's. Consider these questions: How do you define the problem? Who decides there is a problem? Who owns the problem? What are the solutions? Who sees this problem too?

Industry Dynamics and Risk Analysis

Understanding the environment of the industry is most important when planting the seeds of a new business venture. The environment is defined as all elements outside the boundary of an organization including the industry, government, customers, suppliers, the financial community, and other business ventures. In the late 1970s, Harvard Business School's Michael Porter introduced his theories on business strategy formulation, and since then he has transformed the theory, practice, and teaching of business strategy throughout the world.[9] The ideas in this section build and extend on his discussions.

Your first step is defining your industry. Figure 4-1 lists the industry classifications that are based on the PricewaterhouseCoopers/Thomson Financial Venture Economics/National Venture Capital Association MoneyTree™ Survey.

The second step is to get a very basic fundamental overview of your industry by looking at key success factors, focusing in particular on the industry's average profitability. We use three very basic and simple characteristics to describe an industry: dynamic, technologically sophisticated, and hostile:

❖ **A dynamic industry** is emerging and growing with no leaders that dictate profits.

❖ **Technologically sophisticated industries** have a huge difference in profitability. The products range from highly sophisticated with great profits,

FIGURE 4-1. DEFINING YOUR SPACE.

Biotechnology. These ventures develop technology promoting drug development, disease treatment, and a deeper understanding of living organisms. Includes human, animal, and industrial biotechnology products and services. Also included in this sector are bio-sensors, biotechnology equipment, and pharmaceuticals.

Business Products and Services. These ventures offer a product or service targeted at another business such as advertising, consulting, and engineering services. Also included are distributors, importers, and wholesalers.

Computers and Peripherals. This sector includes manufacturers and distributors of PCs, mainframes, servers, PDAs, printers, storage devices, monitors, and memory cards. Also included are digital imaging and graphics services and equipment such as scanning hardware, graphics video cards, and plotters. Integrated turnkey systems and solutions are also included in this sector.

Consumer Products and Services. Ventures in this sector offer products or services targeted at consumers such as restaurants, dry cleaners, automotive service centers, clothing, toiletries, and home products.

Electronics and Instrumentation. Includes electronic parts that are components of larger products and specialized instrumentation, including scientific instruments, lasers, power supplies, electronic testing products, power supplies, and display panels. Also included are business and consumer electronic devices such as photocopiers, calculators, and alarm systems.

Financial Services. These ventures are providers of financial services to other businesses or individuals including banking, real estate, brokerage services, and financial planning.

Healthcare Services. This sector includes both in-patient and outpatient facilities as well as health insurers. Also included are hospitals, clinics, nursing facilities, managed care organizations, Physician Practice Management Companies, child care, and emergency care.

Industrial and Energy. Includes producers and suppliers of energy, chemicals, and materials, industrial automation companies, and oil and gas exploration companies. Also included are environmental, agricultural, transportation, manufacturing, construction, and utility-related products and services.

Information Technology Services. These ventures are providers of computer and Internet-related services to businesses and consumers including computer repair, software consulting, computer training, machine leasing/rental, disaster recovery, Web design, data input and processing, Internet security, e-commerce services, Web hosting, and systems engineering.

Media and Entertainment. These ventures are creators of products or providers of services designed to inform or entertain consumers including movies, music, consumer electronics such as TVs/stereos/games, sports facilities and events, and recreational products or services. Also includes online providers of consumer content like medical, news, education, and legal information.

Medical Devices and Equipment. These ventures manufacture and/or sell medical instruments and devices including medical diagnostic equipment (X-ray, CAT scan, MRI), medical therapeutic devices (drug delivery, surgical instruments, pacemakers, artificial organs), and other health-related products such as medical monitoring equipment, handicap aids, reading glasses, and contact lenses.

(continues)

FIGURE 4-1. CONTINUED.

Networking and Equipment. These ventures make and/or sell networking and communications equipment. Their products include switches, hubs, routers, gateways, ATM, network test, monitor and support equipment, and Internet communications and infrastructure-related equipment.

Retailing and Distribution. This sector includes venture-making consumer goods and services available for consumer purchase including discount stores, supercenters, drug stores, clothing and accessories retailers, computer stores, and bookstores. Also included in this sector are e-commerce companies, those selling their products or services via the Internet.

Semiconductors. These ventures design, develop, or manufacture semiconductor chips/microprocessors or related equipment including diodes and transistors. Also includes ventures that test or package integrated circuits.

Software. These ventures produce bundled and/or unbundled software applications for business or consumer use. These products include software created for systems, graphics, communications and networking, security, inventory, home use, educational, or recreational. Also included is software developed for vertical-specific industries such as banking, manufacturing, transportation, or healthcare.

Telecommunications. These ventures are focused on the transmission of voice and data, which includes long distance providers, local exchange carriers, and wireless communications services and components. Also included are satellite and microwave communications services and equipment.

Other. If the classification criteria in all of the other categories does not appropriately describe the product or service offered, the venture may be categorized in this sector.

Based on the PwC/VE/NVCA MoneyTree™ Survey.

to those that are commodities. There are widespread opportunities for growth and innovation for those who plan accordingly.

❧   **Hostile environments** provide little room for missteps. There are large, powerful, established firms who control the industry's profitability.

Other success factors include size and structure of the market, rate of year-over-year growth, profile of key customers, level of innovation, and pace of technological change.

The third step is examining the "product life cycle" of similar products in this industry. Porter states that the dynamics within an industry are often framed by the life cycle stages of its products and services. The industry or segments of an industry in the introductory and "emerging growth stages" can be expected to behave more aggressively in their pursuit of growth, sometimes at the expense of profitability. Industries with "mature" and declining products are predominantly characterized by the pursuit of profitability and the efficiencies required to obtain it.

According to Porter, emerging markets are newly formed or re-formed industries that have been created by technological changes, shifts in relative cost relationships, emergence of new customer needs, or other economic and sociological changes that elevate a new product or service to the level of a potentially viable business opportunity. He found the following to be true for emerging markets: The boundaries are not clearly established, buyers and needs are not well-defined, there is no base of experience about market behavior, the range of products are often limited, distribution systems will have to be developed, the scope and structure of the market are likely to change during the emerging stage, forecasting the direction of growth of the market may be difficult, and there is often a tendency to overestimate the speed and magnitude of market growth.

Industry Risk Analysis

The only certainty in the uncertain process of new business venturing and developing new products is that the unexpected lies ahead. The simple fact of bringing into existence products and services that currently do not exist implies that much of the information required by potential stakeholders—such as technology, price, quantity, tastes, supplier networks, distributor networks, and business models—are not reliably available.

So uncertainty means that decision-makers do not have sufficient information about environmental factors, which increases the risk of failure. Recall that for this book we define risk as the degree of certainty or uncertainty as to the realization of expected future financial returns in a business venture. But because it is important to have an understanding about the risk/reward scenario for each industry, we have identified certain industry risks in Figure 4-2 that capture the uncertainty of the industry and can help you measure the potential profitability of business activity.

For your industry analysis, start with the apex companies—the ones that are at the top of the food chain in your environment, preferably publicly traded. Your research should include their key success factors, how you can use them for business modeling, and financial analysis.

Working with Lead Users

According to Dawn Lepore, former CIO for Charles Schwab, everything—from defining your space to defining and analyzing your market, to creating the perfect product or new service—starts with a focus on the customer.[10] Segmenting the marketplace is one of the most important strategic moves that can be made by start-ups, high-tech companies, industrial companies, and firms that sell services to other businesses. However important, defining and segmenting a market is often overlooked by entrepreneurs.

For example, we found out from Marc Lautenbach, an IBM Business Partners vice president, that small- and medium-size businesses account for some $300 billion in IT spending around the world each year.[11] It would be

FIGURE 4-2. INDUSTRY RISK ANALYSIS.

Competitor Risk. As Michael Porter states, "The essence of strategy formulation is coping with competition." Entrepreneurs often neglect any strategic discussions about the competition, because all too often they tend to feel that their product is so new, so superior, that any competitors out there will not be significant. Many assume that competitors will be slow to react, or "fleet on their feet." But large established companies could come in after the market has been proven and buy up competitors, or even strategic partners/suppliers, and become a major direct competitor. And as one venture capitalist told us, start-ups even compete with other ventures outside their space for employees, resources, and financing. So underestimating the competition can be fatal to new business ventures and likewise, saying that there is no competition will most likely put an end to your financing potential.

Technology Transition Risk. We have learned that all business activity conducted in an industry faces the potential threats from disruptive technologies. As we discussed in Chapter 2, clusters of innovations can also spring up and create a technological change that as a whole, disrupt an industry. Such changes create strategic inflection points and opportunities for new entrepreneurs to entry or industry leaders to reposition and recreate themselves.

Substitute Risk. All industries are subject to the marketing attempts of companies in other industries to win customers over to their own products. Substitute products are often at the end of their life cycle in their respective market segments and reintroduced into another market, priced well below established products.

Customer Risk. It is important to examine the bargaining power, buying practices, and payment terms exercisable by buyers of the product. There is also substantial risk from buyers who are significant contributors to the revenues of a start-up, and it is important to consider the economic health of all buyers.

Resource Risk. Examines the bargaining power, selling practices, and selling terms exercisable by suppliers of inputs to the industry. It is important to look at whether the inputs are human resources, commodities, completed product platforms, or sourced overseas.

---

incorrect to boldly state in a business plan for a new computer that the total potential market is $300 billion. Obviously, the market opportunity needs to be further defined.

Philip Kotler, the marketing guru of our generation, helps in defining and segmenting markets. According to Kotler, the *market* is the set of all actual and potential buyers of a new product or new service. The *potential market* is the total set of buyers who have sufficient level of interest. The *available market* is the set of buyers who have interest, the cash, and access to buying the new product or new service. The *qualified available market* consists of buyers who have interest, the cash, access, and qualifications for the new offer. For example, they have the right computer operating system that is required for a new software application. He describes the *target market* as the part of the qualified available market, and the *penetrated market* is the set of buyers who have already bought the new product or new service.[12] See Figure 4-3 to better understand whether the market you are segmenting is attractive.

Identifying and Working with Lead Users

A common pitfall for a new business enterprise is the assumption that a large and interested market of potential customers is eagerly awaiting its arrival and offerings. Since venture capitalists do not want to be the first to validate a new business idea, start-ups that will be successful tomorrow are those that can get closest to their customers' needs today.

In fact, the single most important task in the new product development process is managing the "external integration" between the new product development team and the "sources of information about future consumption." Guy Kawasaki of Garage Technology Ventures simply calls this "Know Thy Customer," as in "Grill the Customer," and "The Art of Pressing Flesh." But external integration is more than being "close to customers," "market-oriented," or even "customer driven." There needs to be a very close connection and dialog with potential customers, and the new product developers must be capable of "translating subtle clues of latent customer needs into visions of future products and markets." In a sense, these "lead users" must become another "department in the organization" whose "concerns and interests need to be integrated."[13]

In his book *The Sources of Innovation*, Eric von Hippel, professor of business at the Sloan School of Management at MIT, describes lead users as those who are ahead of the majority of the marketplace. The "lead-user phenomenon" is that lead users are in a unique position to provide accurate, insightful data on needs related to future conditions of the industry, and they are also in a position to benefit significantly if they find a solution to their particular problem.

FIGURE 4-3. WHAT MAKES A MARKET SEGMENT ATTRACTIVE?

▲ The industry risks are identified and manageable.

▲ The customers have a distinct problem and a complete set of needs are identifiable.

▲ The customers will pay a premium to the venture that best solves their problem.

▲ The niche is not likely to attract other competitors.

▲ The niche has sufficient size, profit potential, and growth potential, what we call "headroom" for a venture to quickly scale up and grow.

▲ The resources and the skills required to succeed in this niche are readily available to the venture.

▲ The potential to gain certain economies of scale and industry-specific knowledge is possible.

▲ The early adopters are identifiable, and the venture has access to lead users.

According to von Hippel, because they often have had to struggle with the inadequacies of existing products, lead users are often able to articulate their emerging needs in new verbiage and concepts. And since they have such an urgent need to solve their immediate problem, they may have already created some sort of solution, parts of a solution, or can provide insights to a product platform that was not considered by the new product development team. In essence, von Hippel observed that "so much practical innovation comes from a small number of imaginative people who tinker with the latest technology."[14]

Working with lead users is very different from a sales call. The goal is to elicit an honest expression of needs, not to convince a user of what they need, or what they might be doing wrong. For example, Research In Motion (RIM) developed their successful BlackBerry in part by simply asking corporate users what they wanted from a remote e-mail system. It is possible to get valuable information through simple observations. The U.S. Honda automotive design team spent an afternoon in the parking lot at Disneyland observing how people loaded and unloaded the trunks of their cars. They ultimately came up with the design that lowered the opening down to the bumper, a first in automotive design.

There are only a few really important questions that you need to ask lead users: What is the real problem here or put another way, what if the product did not exist? What are the current attitudes and behaviors of the lead users toward the product? What product attributes and benefits do they want? What are their dissatisfactions, problems, and unfulfilled needs? How are they defining, in their own unique verbiage, what they see, need, and want?[15]

The research with lead users does not have to be expensive or complicated. Abbie Griffin and John Hauser state that as a practical guideline, conducting fewer than ten interviews or observations is probably inadequate, and fifty interviews are too many.[16] Lead users for new products and services can be found in existing customers, application laboratories in manufacturing partnerships, custom product groups run by industry and trade groups, and other nonprofit user groups.

Forging Your Unique Solution

In his book, *A Good Hard Kick in the Ass: Basic Training for Entrepreneurs*, Rob Adams argues that you never really know your customers as well as you think you do because, "All you have is a one-time snapshot." And besides having just a snapshot of the customers, the industry is constantly changing. As Vinod Khosla suggested to us, the entrepreneurs need to know what assumptions others in the industry are making, and what assumptions they are making that could be wrong. In essence, the business is trying to hit a moving target with an unproven product in an environment that is never the same. Quite often, because figuring all this out can be so difficult in high-tech markets, Khosla says that at Kleiner Perkins they see too many business plans that are distorted to reflect a "perfected marketing pitch" and not the underlying business opportunity capturing the interests of early adopters.

Being externally integrated with lead users is helpful in creating accurate customer profiles in the current market snapshot, since lead users have their pulse on the future of the industry. They have a sense of what is changing and how the industry is changing, and they are looking to profit from these changes. Analyzing your lead user insights begins by organizing the data collected, creating a "needs hierarchy," and understanding the importance of their needs. Helpful questions in this customer profiling are:

❖ Who are the existing/potential customers?

❖ How does the problem change from company to company?

❖ What are their characteristics?

❖ How do they decide to buy?

❖ What factors, other than customer characteristics and marketing efforts, will influence their buying?

❖ In what ways can they profit from the new product?

Conducting a SWOT Analysis

A SWOT analysis is an essential exercise for formulating new business strategies. It combines an internal analysis of strengths and weaknesses, with an external environment analysis of opportunities and threats. Objectively looking at the concept for the new business activity, the emphasis is on analysis, diagnosis, synthesis, and interpretation of the lead user information, combined with a careful industry analysis.

Sizing up your venture's strengths and weaknesses is like constructing a strategic balance sheet, where strengths represent your competitive assets, and weaknesses represent your competitive liabilities. The *strengths* are things that your venture is good at doing, or a characteristic that gives it an important capability over competitors in this space. Examples are marquee customers, proprietary technologies, proven domain experts on a venture team, and keen insight to lead users. *Weaknesses* are things that your venture lacks or does poorly, or conditions that put it at a disadvantage to others in the space. Examples are no clear strategic direction, falling behind in R&D/technology, lack of depth on a venture team, unable to self-finance, cost structures or revenue models that are out of industry/sector norms, weak distribution/ sales network, and below-average marketing skills.

The opportunities and threats not only affect the attractiveness of your venture's situation but more importantly point to the need of strategic action. You need to consider two simple questions: Are you headed in the right direction with the new product that could lead to other new opportunities? Or are you headed toward a disaster? *Opportunities* arise from moving on lead user insights, seeing a technological change before others, creating strategic partnerships with key suppliers and controllers of sales channels, hoarding cash, expanding overseas, and just plain luck. *Threats* to any new business venturing will most likely come from the industry risks we discussed earlier.

Strategic Mapping and Gap Analysis

Ralph Waldo Emerson has a famous line that is often quoted in business, "If a man can make a better mousetrap than his neighbor, though he builds his house in the woods the world will make a beaten path to his door." Making a play on Emerson is Garage Technology Ventures co-founder Bill Joos, who says, "It's not enough to come up with the idea on how to build a better mousetrap. You must really want to kill mice."[17] As we have stated earlier, you cannot just build it and expect that they will come. You need to look for a viable opening in your industry, learn what differentiates each offering, and create and market a better solution.

This leads us to a process called *strategic mapping*, a formal statistical technique with immense power to help you focus. You begin by strategically "mapping out the market" based on how all the product offerings are perceived by customers in the market. Once mapped out, you begin gap analysis, looking for "white-spaces" or gaps in the space, seeing where to attack, and where you will need to defend. The results of this thinking will prove to be quite handy when you are working on your slide presentation for investors, when communicating with your venture team, and in the later stages when you are working on your marketing strategies and sales tactics.

This exercise, especially when performed on a large whiteboard, is very important for entrepreneurs creating an innovative product or service, or for entrepreneurs who are new at new business venturing. Our experience shows that the step from the idea-in-the-head stage to the actual product stage—or as we say, from one-dimensional (1-D) to three-dimensional (3-D)—is quite often too great of a step. Strategic mapping helps by taking the 1-D idea in the head into a 2-D world on a whiteboard. Compressing all the work you have completed for this chapter—problem analysis, industry sector analysis, key competitor analysis, and internal SWOT analysis—you need to untangle just this one thought: How do you truly differ from your direct competitors?

It is important to consider an objective assessment of competitors' key strengths and limitations, product benefits and limitations, target-market strategy, product strategy, distribution strategy, price strategy, and promotion strategy. The net result of all this deep thinking should be presented in a very simple table, like the one shown in Figure 4-4.

Aspirin vs. Vitamins

When evaluating new product concepts, consider the advice we captured from Larry Page, co-founder of Google. He simply asks, do users really care? How does our solution help the experts who specialize in our space? Does it

FIGURE 4-4. COMPETITOR ANALYSIS.

Company	What do we do better than what they do?	What do they do better than what we do?
1.		
2.		
3.		
4.		
5.		

really solve a deep problem? And does our venture team surrounding the problem really understand?[18] Dan Bassett, of InnoCal Ventures, said that entrepreneurs have to ask themselves, "Is the product based on a need-to-have or a want-to-have?"[19]

Do not get confused between needs, wants, and demands. Again we turn to marketing guru Philip Kotler, who provides some basic understanding on how these three terms differ.[20] Kotler says that *needs* exist in the very context of doing business, or simply part of the condition for living. He calls *wants* "specific satisfiers of needs." In other words, a hungry person in the United States and a hungry person in a third-world country are both hungry, and they need to eat. But the person in the United States wants a Wendy's hamburger with French fries, while the other person may want rice and beans.

To Kotler, *demands* are "wants for specific products that are backed by an ability and willingness to buy them." What this means is that many people want a luxury car while only a few are able and willing to purchase one. So for a software application to be successful, there must be the following: a need, like a need for a computerized operating system to run a business process; there must be a want, like someone wanting Microsoft NT over Linux; and there must be a demand, such as people willing to pay for NT, especially when they can get Linux for free.

We all know that aspirin was created to alleviate pain, and vitamins are believed to prolong and support a healthy body. Similar to an aspirin being an immediate solution to a throbbing headache, does your solution immediately solve a significant and measurable source of pain? Imagine a hot summer day in July, and the problem is hot air. Are you selling an air conditioner or a fan that just pushes hot air around the room? Quite often we hear entrepreneurs claiming to have a proven aspirin painkiller, when in fact they are pushing vitamins. Around investors this becomes a real "stick-shaker," which is what commercial pilots say when an airliner stalls in midair, and the control stick is sending a warning signal to the pilot that the plane is falling from the sky. Know the difference; create a viable, real painkiller.

Recall our discussion in Chapter 2 about the diffusion of innovation. It occurs when "innovators" buy and then, through an influence process, encourage others to buy. It always "starts with the first sale," and the innovation can "diffuse" through society very quickly. Looking at the factors that affect rate of diffusion, here are a few questions that can help you "score" against the diffusion process.[21]

- ❖ What is the relative advantage of the new solution?
- ❖ How superior is the innovation to the other solutions it was designed to compete against?
- ❖ What about the compatibility? Does it fit with current end-user activity?

It is called a continuous innovation if little change is required, and a discontinuous innovation if much change is required by the end users. Also, incompatibility produces learning requirements, which will have to be overcome at the expense and time of the ventures launching against this strong headwind.

When looking at the complexity of the solution, will the end-users, sales people, or industry as a whole be frustrated or confused in understanding the concept of your solution? And what about "trialability," meaning how easily can your solution be sampled? For example, with a software venture, can your lead users download software from the Internet? Finally, look at "communicability." How likely is your product to sell on its own?

Creating Your Solution Statement

What is your unique business value proposition? According to Tim Koogle, employee number five at Yahoo, entrepreneurs need to be at the heart of their business and find out what customers consider to be truly valuable. He says, "Focus on what people can only do with your stuff."[22] And can you put your business purpose into a few words? As Drucker says, "There is only one valid definition of business purpose: to create a customer. What the customer buys and considers value is never just a product. It is always a utility, that is, what a product or service does for him."[23] For example, a shrink-wrapped box of Microsoft Office software is a product. But what you, the user, needs is a solution: How do I write a winning business plan on my computer? We can probably simplify things by calling products and services all one thing: a solution. The reason is simple, in that almost anything designed, developed, marketed, and used today has a tangible component and an intangible component.

Analyzing business opportunities must be viewed in a very discrete manner. You have identified a problem and you are now working on a solution. If it is a viable opportunity and worth pursuing, you need a problem statement and a solution statement. Without a doubt, creating your solution statement will be the most difficult analytical work you will have to do for your new business venture. This is what will separate the wanna-be entrepreneurs from the will-be's. As Henry Ford once said, "Thinking is the hardest work there is. That's why so few do it." Do not be afraid to aim high. Thomas J. Watson, Jr., past president of IBM, once said, "It is better to aim at perfection and miss than it is to aim at imperfection and hit it." But you must define the value precisely in terms of specific product or service, which meets specific customers' needs at a specific price.

Even with all these planning tools we have recommended in this chapter, we know that entrepreneurs will still get in trouble when screening new opportunities and creating new products. More often than not, entrepreneurs will become consumed developing and engineering their "patentable" technologies instead of creating end-user benefits. It becomes a new technical discovery in search of a market. And instead of conducting an organized search and analysis, sometimes they ask, "Who's got a new idea today?" The "me-too" efforts come from copying direct competitors' efforts without any analysis. The entrepreneurs who figure "let's run it up the flag pole and see who salutes it" produce many ideas, thinking that success comes in numbers. And finally, there are the entrepreneurs who have "got to do something fast" and end up rushing to market a less than premium product.

FIVE

Crafting a Winning Business Strategy and Sustainable Competitive Advantage

> If we could first know where we are, and whither we are tending, we could then better judge what to do, and how to do it.
>
> —**Abraham Lincoln**
>
> The great thing in this world is not so much where we stand, but in what direction we are moving.
>
> —**Justice Oliver Wendell Holmes**
>
> The important things are always simple. The simple things are always hard. The easy way is always mined.
>
> —*Murphy's Laws of Combat*

What Exactly Is Strategic Planning?

Your venture's goals and strategy define the purpose and competitive advantage that will set it apart from others. Your goals help define your intent, and strategy is the plan of action that describes activities for dealing with the environment and for reaching your venture's intended goals. When combined, goals and strategies define the scope of operations and the relationship with employees, customers, competitors, and other stakeholders. The term "strategy" is widely used in the business world today. It is one of those words that people define in one way and often use in another, without realizing the difference. It is derived from the ancient Greek word meaning "the art and science of the general deploying forces for battle."

Your strategy is a plan for interacting with the competitive environment to achieve your intended goals. Some think of goals and strategies as interchangeable. For purposes of this book, goals define where your venture wants to go, and strategy defines how your venture will get there. This formal process of setting goals and creating a strategy adds legitimacy, provides employee direction and motivation, helps form decision-making guidelines, and provides criteria for your performance. In essence, the process of strategy formulation sets the general directions in which your venture's position will grow

❖ Case in Point: Michael Dell and the Direct-from-Dell Business Model

In 1984, as a nineteen-year-old freshman, and going against one of the largest companies in the world, IBM, Michael Dell launched his company in his dorm room with $1,000. He had a vision that he could build computers made-to-order and sell them directly to consumers. His idea for a direct-sales business model came from observing the discontinuity in the way PCs were being sold at that time. He saw that 4,000 PC stores sprang up instantly across the United States. He saw problems with the cost structure of the supply chain to the consumer, where $600 worth of parts were being sold for $3,000. And there was no direct relationship with the customers or no ownership of the customers.

Touting a business model that sidestepped middleman markups for lower prices, Dell eliminated the middlemen of the computer industry supply chain—the value-added resellers and retailers—by offering its own brand of assembled to order from the same quality of components used by the established players. In 1985, the first year outside of the dorm room, Dell Computer made $33 million in sales, and in the first eight years it grew 80 percent or better. Following the worst years in computing industry ever, the mid-1980s, and in the week after the market crash of 1987, Michael Dell raised $20 million in a private placement, and a year later he went public. In 1992, Dell Computer was included in the *Fortune 500* roster of the world's largest companies, and by 1997 it shipped its 10-millionth computer system.

More than a "first-mover," Dell became a "first-prover." Ziff-Davis reported in 2000 that the "manufacturer-direct" business model became the largest single method of buying PCs, with 23 percent of the purchases, passing consumer electronics stores, which sold 19 percent of the PCs. By 2002, this dorm-room start-up had $35 billion in sales and 39,100 employees around the world.

Sources: Dell Computer company Web site; Michael Dell, *Direct from Dell: Strategies That Revolutionized an Industry* (New York: HarperBusiness, 1999); Richard Murphy, "Michael Dell," *Success*, January 1999, pp. 50–53; and Dan Briody and Eric Moskowitz, "Dell: the Antitechnology Company," *Red Herring*, October 1, 2001, pp. 96–98.

and develop—your goals and objectives represent the ends that you are seeking to attain.

Whereas the strategy is the means to these ends, strategic management is positioning and relating your venture to its environment in a way that will ensure its continued success and make it secure from surprises from competitors. This is competitive strategy, the search for a favorable competitive position in an industry, aiming to establish a profitable and sustainable position against the forces that determine industry competition.

Benefits of Strategic Planning for Entrepreneurs

Strategic planning is a logical, analytical process for choosing your venture's future positions *vis a vis* the environment. The most common defect of entrepreneurs is myopia, a lack of long-range perspective in thinking or planning.

In the sports world they say, "Luck is where preparation meets opportunity." Lance Armstrong, a bicyclist with five consecutive Tour de France wins to his name, prepares by "thinking the race through" before he ever starts down the road.[1] In the business world this preparation comes from strategic planning. As Michael Porter writes, "The essence of formulating competitive strategy is relating a company to its environment; the best strategy for a given firm is ultimately a unique construction reflecting its particular circumstances."[2]

So look at new business venturing as a chess game. To be successful you must be able to anticipate several moves ahead in advance. Thinking about your strategy is like thinking about the scenarios of plans, for example, what to do if/when competitors come into your space. Strategic planning is the process of thinking about and creating these scenarios, and the business plan is the document that communicates the fact that you have figured it out. According to Henry Mintzberg, the key to successful strategic decision making is not just looking out into the future, but having a capacity and willingness to learn from experience.

A new venture has to start somewhere, with a collective understanding of what it is supposed to be doing and where it should be going, and strategic planning aids in this learning. But entrepreneurs cannot wait until the competition is engaged before planning. The inevitable confusion that accompanies any battle and that renders the clearest plans difficult to execute is called the "fog of war," a term first coined by the nineteenth-century Prussian general Karl von Clausewitz (1780–1831).

Crafting Your Business Strategy

Strategic planning is the process through which you profitably match your internal resources with shifting market demands and based on an opportunity. In a must-read article for all entrepreneurs learning about strategic planning, "Crafting Strategy" in *Harvard Business Review*, Mintzberg states that a business strategy should be *crafted* because "craft evokes traditional skill, dedication, perfection through the mastery of detail." His point is that "strategies can *form* as well as be *formulated*."

There are two key components that need to be crafted together to logically spell out, as Drucker calls it, the business purpose. The first is a coherent encapsulation of your products and services, the markets and types of customers you serve, and the benefits they derive. The second component should identify the "key activities and how they will be carried out to realize the logic for competing." It is this the tight integration of the reasons for competing and for organizing lays the foundation for your venture's competitive advantage that becomes the basis of its superiority over rivals in serving a particular market or market segments.

Strategies are not set in stone. In fact, 84 percent of the CEOs leading fast-growth ventures said their business had changed target markets, even from the time when they launched.[3] Although the business may change, the questions that drive strategic planning remain fixed. Where are we now? Where do we want to be? How will we get there? Who must do what? And how are we doing?

Aligning Strategy, Metrics, and Rewards

A business has a purpose to market and sell a viable solution. And sales do not exist in a vacuum, they result from marketing and sales expenditures, R&D expenditures, and money committed to assets. Therefore, sales should be studied and analyzed in conjunction with other statistics that relate to their creation and impact on the bottom line. Jack Stack says that, "Numbers tell you where the problems are, and how worried you should be."[4] Bill Hewlett, co-founder of Hewlett-Packard, once stated, "You cannot manage what you cannot measure. And what gets measured gets done."[5]

Do you know what "critical numbers" really drive your business? Do you know what metrics are used in your industry? Do you know how you compare right now? How will you compare in the future? You need to know what critical numbers, or *value metrics*, are driving value for your venture. Value metrics help you monitor growth, costs, profitability, and return on investments; they help you define business plans and compare plans to actions.

As the value manager, you need to create an "executive dashboard" to your business that monitors all value metrics. These metrics are used to shape stakeholders' behavior in a way that ultimately allows the venture to achieve its goals. Expected performance criteria and performance measures of stakeholders must be aligned with the strategy and clearly defined because "people just don't get interested in a game if there's no scoreboard."[6]

Defining Your Core Competencies and Strategic Intent

In a June 1990 *Harvard Business Review* article, "The Core Competence of the Corporation," Prahalad and Hamel outline the concepts of core competencies that still hold true today.[7] A core competence is an intangible, not an asset that can be found on an accounting balance sheet, and not a patent. It is something your venture does especially well in comparison to direct competitors. Each core competence represents specialized expertise, know-how, or a bundle of skills and technologies that rivals do not have and cannot readily duplicate. As a set, they represent the sum of learning across your venture's activities that when combined, create unique organizational capability by providing a particular benefit and value to customers. They are extendable, they do not wear out; the more refined they get, the more valuable they become. And most importantly, they are the central subjects of your business strategy as they grow to become your distinct competitive advantage.

These roots of your competitive advantage lie in the viability and health of your core competencies. As Prahalad and Hamel suggest, think of your venture as a tree. The trunk and major limbs are core products; the smaller branches are business segments focusing on different market niches based on specific customer needs. The leaves, flowers, and fruit extending from each branch are your end products. The root system that provides nourishment, sustenance, and stability is your base of core competencies. As they say, "You can miss the strength of competitors by looking only at their end products, in the same way you miss the strength of a tree if you look only at its leaves." To that end, you cannot graft an orange branch on an apple tree, although both are fruit trees.

Let us consider Honda, whose core competence is in highly engineered small engines and power trains. It gives them a distinctive advantage in the car, motorcycle, lawn mower, and generator business. Their root system is based on Soichiro Honda's personal commitment and engineering skills that led him to create the world's finest team for designing small, high-perform-ance engines, first for motorized bicycles, then for motorcycles, and later for automobiles, including some of the most successful Formula-1 racecar engines ever built.

How do you identify your core competencies? First, is the competence a significant source of competitive differentiation and does the competence generate distinct value and benefits for your customers? Second, does the competence transcend a single business opportunity? For example, does it cover a range of businesses, market segments, and does it or will it provide access to a variety of product and market niches? Finally, is the competence hard for competitors to imitate and is it difficult for others to learn?

Blueprinting Your Strategic Architecture

Research has shown that successful entrepreneurs create visions of the future, which inspires others to get involved in the venture.[8] Howard Schultz, founder and CEO of Starbucks Coffee, says, "Vision is what they call it when others can't see what you see."[9] Entrepreneurs are those with a distinct vision or keen insight to an opportunity and drive it to its endpoint. Such a strategic focus is important because it fuels the persistence required to bring opportuni-ties to fruition once they are recognized as relevant. Also, employees "will go above and beyond the call of duty to help accomplish far-reaching goals."[10] Your strategic intent is based on your vision and focus. It is what you see your venture will be doing in the future, and what it should be doing today in order to get there. Think of what Jack Nicklaus, one of the most successful golfers of all time, said: "I never missed a putt in my mind." You need to be pursuing a certain long-term strategic objective that you have in your mind, and con-centrate strategic actions and resources on achieving that objective. And as Jeffrey Abrahams points out in *The Mission Statement Book*, "Companies are like people. They need a mission."[11] Abrahams cites Gene Roddenberry's mis-sion statement for the *Star Trek* TV series: "Space, the Final Frontier. These are the voyages of the Starship *Enterprise*. Its five-year mission: To explore strange new worlds, to seek out new life and new civilizations, to boldly go where no man has gone before."

Planting the Seeds of Your Sustainable Competitive Advantage

What is needed and quite often ignored by entrepreneurs is a business strategy. The business strategy defines a reason for competing and a reason for organizing. It is the tight integration of these two reasons that lays the foundation for your superiority over rivals serving a particular market.

Winning business strategies are grounded in a sustainable competitive advantage. A new business venture has a competitive advantage whenever it has an edge over rivals in attracting customers, attracting investors, and defending against competitive forces and industry risks. With a competitive advantage a new business venture has good prospects for above-average survivability, long-term profitability, and success in the industry. Without one, a venture risks being out-competed by strong rivals and locked into poor, to at best, average performance.

A competitive advantage is not only your venture's ability to perform in ways that other ventures can, but more importantly something unique that other ventures in your space do not have, and cannot get. Your competitive advantage comes from an internal analysis of your vision and core competencies. It is matched with your external analysis of the opportunity and industry risks. As an intangible, it only exists from focused efforts. A tangible has physical existence and substantial form. It is capable of being touched and seen. On the other hand, intangibles have no value of their own. They have no physical existence and depend on expected future benefits for most of their value.

We have found that entrepreneurs fall into one of two problem categories when it comes to their competitive advantage. Some believe they have a "first-mover" competitive advantage. This is based on the Civil War-era maxim, "Battles are won by who gets there first with the most." As we saw in our discussion of the Perfect Storm in Chapter 2, this first-mover advantage does not work. The second problem is when a venture team, in its business plan, lists five, seven, or even ten different items that represent the venture's "competitive advantage." In our research we found only six competitive advantages that have been successful for professional entrepreneurs leading early stage, high growth-potential ventures:

1. Branded-CEO
2. Code
3. Connections
4. Content
5. Commerce
6. Cash

When reviewing these advantages, consider what Pat Riley, one of the NBA's most successful basketball coaches, told us, "Excel at only one thing."[12]

Branded-CEO

In General Montgomery's World War II desert campaign in North Africa, the most important strategic decision was not one of Montgomery's field decisions, but rather Winston Churchill's selection of Montgomery.[13] All subsequent successes in the battlefield flowed from this fundamentally important decision. Branded-CEOs bring domain expertise, and professional and personal connections. They know that success comes from finding people smarter, better, more skillful than they are. Examples are: John Sculley with Apple, James Barksdale with Netscape, Meg Whitman with eBay, Eric Schmidt with Google, Ray Ozzie with Groove Networks, Charles Betty with Earthlink, Jeff Hawkins and Donna Dubinsky with Handspring, and Steve Wynn with his Belagio Resorts in Las Vegas. If a branded-CEO is not immediately available, a competitive advantage could be based on other human capital-related exclusives (see Figure 5-1 for examples).

Code

Entrepreneurs can become quite successful by first establishing some type of monopoly control over their intellectual property (IP) that prevents competitors from entering a market and then using this control to increase their economic return. Intellectual property is a set of intangible assets that includes patents, trademarks, copyrights, and trade secrets.

Dr. Paul Jacobs shared how Qualcomm became a leader in the wireless industry developing wireless voice and data solutions.[14] Qualcomm is best known as the company that pioneered Code Division Multiple Access (CDMA) technology, which is now used in wireless networks and mobile phones all over the world. By making very efficient use of radio frequency spectrum, CDMA allows wireless carriers to accommodate much more traffic on their networks than they can with other technologies. In other words, CDMA allows more people to share the airwaves at the same time without crosstalk, static,

FIGURE 5-1. BRANDED-CEO AND OTHER HUMAN CAPITAL-RELATED EXCLUSIVES.

Advisors	Employment contracts	Personality contracts
Board members	Executives and VPs	Security clearances
Buy-sell agreements	Management contracts	Shareholder
Certificated employees	Nationalities	agreements
Chairman	Noncompete	Trade group
Culture	covenants	memberships
Domain experts	Organizational skills for establishing offices, branches, divisions	Trained and assembled workforce

or interference. Although licenses on its 731 CDMA patents provided just 30 percent of the company's $2.7 billion in revenues in 2002, they made up 60 percent of its $942 million in pro forma operating income. See Figure 5-2 for other technology-related exclusives.

FIGURE 5-2. TECHNOLOGY-RELATED EXCLUSIVES.

Chemical formulations	Music compositions	Proprietary products
Computer software	Patent applications	Proprietary technology
Designs	Patents	Schematics and
Engineering drawings	Patterns	diagrams
Food flavorings and	Product designs	Technical and specialty
recipes	Product platforms	libraries
Know-how	Proprietary computer	Technical
Laboratory notebooks	software	documentation
Masks and masters	Proprietary processes	Technology
		Un-patented
		technology
		White papers

Connections

Michael Porter calls connections "advantaged relationships." Les Wexner, founder of Victoria's Secret, the chain of fashion stores for women's lingerie, called them a key element to his success. Wexner was well connected with Alfred A. Taubman, a real-estate developer who specialized in large urban shopping malls. Recall from Chapter 4 that Microsoft's first competitive advantage was not "code" in software programming, but their "connection" with IBM.

These connections as based on solid legal agreements and contracts that leverage business partnerships, special alliances, strategic partners, suppliers, buyers, buying groups, exclusive marketing relationships with market leaders, and exclusive access to sales channels. See Figure 5-3 for more examples. In

FIGURE 5-3. CONTRACT-RELATED EXCLUSIVES.

Agreements	Favorable leases	Proposals outstanding
Airport gates and slots	Franchise agreements	R&D partnerships
Broadcast licenses	Government contracts	Retail slotting/shelf
Contracts	Landing rights	space
Cooperative	Medical charts and	Rights of first refusal
agreements	records	Royalty agreements
Development rights	Mineral rights	Supplier contracts
Distribution rights	Natural resources	Technology sharing
Drilling rights	Oil rights	agreements
Environmental rights	Permits	Trade secrets
FCC licenses	Property use rights	Trademarks and trade
		names
		Use rights to air, water,
		or land

the battle for dominance in the VCR technology platform, the industry experts recognized that the Betamax system developed by Sony was of higher quality and technically superior to the VHS technology developed by Matsushita. But because of superior sales channel alliances with distributors and other sales companies—in particular with those outside of Japan—it became impossible for Sony to sustain its competitive battle. So connections can beat out code.

Content

Content relates to management, ownership, searching, storage, redistribution, re-purposing, or any combination of the exclusives listed in Figure 5-4. For example, MapQuest.com spun out of R.R. Donnelly & Sons and now serves up more than 10 million maps per day. And Hoovers.com, with information on more than 12 million public and private companies, provides rich data to the financial world. They have assembled and created proprietary content, which is the lifeblood of financial traders, researchers, and reporters around the world.

The use of the Internet for distributing all sorts of content—from text and photographs, to digital music and video, to clip-rights of sports broadcasting and video on-demand movies—is expected to grow once the digital rights management (DRM) systems become more robust. The Meta Group estimates that by 2004 $100 billion worth of content will be available over the Internet, which is about one-third of all electronic content available for distribution.

FIGURE 5-4. CONTENT-RELATED EXCLUSIVES.

Blueprints	Laboratory notebooks	Proprietary computer
Book libraries	Legal proceedings	software
Computerized	Literary works	Publications
databases	Manual databases	Royalty agreements
Consumer profiles	Manuscripts	Scientific studies and
Copyrights	Marketing/promotional	white papers
Credit information files	materials	Schematics and
Customer lists	Masks and masters	diagrams
Designs	Medical charts and	Spreadsheets
Directory information	records	Subscription lists
Email messages	Music compositions	Tables
Engineering drawings	News articles	Technical and specialty
Fashion designs	Patterns	libraries
Film libraries	Personnel information	Technical
Historical documents	Prescription drug files	documentation
Instant messages	Press releases	Technology
Inventory information	Procedural manuals	Trademarks and trade
	Product designs	names
		Training manuals
		Video files
		Word processing
		documents

CNN Technology expects to have available as much as 240 terabytes of data every year from its news footage.[15]

The amounts of content employees generate and store is on the rise. It will not be long before executives figure how to create revenues from their huge silos of unstructured corporate documents, which are quickly becoming a significant asset in most companies today. Wal-Mart now has the largest enterprise content management system (ECM) in the corporate world, with 200 terabytes. Proctor & Gamble and seven other manufacturers have started using Chicago-based Transora as a central clearinghouse, which collects 230 attributes per product sold in supermarkets and converts everything into XML, a Web-based software language.[16] Some are predicting that the ECM market will be worth about $10 billion by 2004.[17]

As we move toward terabyte storage becoming a commodity, we shall see uses of content that will go beyond the most creative imagination today. At the confluence of biology and information technology are experts called "bioinformaticians," who scour reams of data looking for the next secret combination of biomedical research and corporate capability. At the Lion Bioinformatics Research Institute (LBRI) in Cambridge, Massachusetts, bioinformaticians are scouring LBRI's proprietary database, which contains information from 480 public databases, looking for such clues as how to take years off the time needed to bring new drugs to market.

Commerce

This competitive advantage is based on marketing traction and momentum related to a disruptive technology or a cluster of innovations that are leading a technological change. "Platform leaders" like Intel, Microsoft, and Cisco are controllers of products or services that become "the foundation on which other companies build their products or offer their services."[18]

For example, in the early days of the PC, consumers were introduced to Hayes modems as they came installed on millions of computers shipped. Hayes was able to leverage this early competitive advantage of marketing momentum when it came to upgrading end-users to faster modems as they became available. A competitive advantage could also be having the right product at the right time, a complementary product to a disruptive product that is headed toward commoditization. For example, as the HP Inkjet and Laser printers were driven to commodities, the demand for high-quality printer cables increased, as did the price of the cables as they were repositioned and repackaged as critical accessories to high-quality printing. Other marketing-related exclusives are listed in Figure 5-5.

Cash

Cash flow is seen as the "Good Housekeeping Seal of Approval" by the investment community. Cash flow "on-its-way" is the next best thing. It could be coming from the winning of research grants from the government, universi-

FIGURE 5-5. MARKETING-RELATED EXCLUSIVES.

Acknowledgments	Government contracts	Retail shelf space
Advertising campaigns	Governmental	Royalty agreements
Awards	approvals	Sales force in field
Brand names	Logos	Sales in the pipeline
Broker contracts	Marketing	Supplier contracts
Claims	representatives	Trained and assembled
Co-branding	Open orders	workforce
Customer awareness	Package designs	Trademarks and trade
Customer contracts	Permits	names
Customer relationships	Production backlogs	Use rights to air, water,
Franchise agreements	Purchase orders	or land
	Regulatory approvals	Web site
	Reputation	Work in progress

ties, and strategic partners. Other examples of goodwill-related exclusives are listed in Figure 5-6. We also found that a little cash and the goodwill associated with the "bench-strength" from branded investors bring in more cash. In the Eye of the Perfect Storm, the start-ups that Vinod Khosla had launched were worth some $150 billion in the public markets. His "mere involvement" in any new such start-up instantly attracted tens of millions of dollars from other investors.

Business Modeling

References to "business models" are frequent whenever aspiring entrepreneurs pitch their business plans to potential investors. We feel that there has been a misguided approach of talking too much about business models, perhaps because the definition of business model is not clear. While the popular media and business literature use the term loosely and vaguely, we attempt to present a more precise definition. We prefer to lean more toward helping

FIGURE 5-6. GOODWILL-RELATED EXCLUSIVES.

Awards, judgments	Investors	Open orders
Cash on hand	Irrevocable letter of	Options, warrants,
Corporate partners	credit	grants, rights
already invested	Landing rights	Personal equity
Credit cards	Letter of intent	Purchase orders
Customer deposits	Lines of credit	Prizes and awards
Deposits/engineering	Litigation awards and	Retirement portfolios
advances	damages	Rights of first refusal
Endowments	Location value	Securities portfolios
Favorable financing	Mineral rights	Stock and bond
Home equity loans	Natural resources	instruments
Inventory	Noncompete	Terms of credit with
	covenants	suppliers

you create and develop your business strategy, competitive advantage, and unique business value proposition, that when assembled and functioning successfully together, become your business model.

A *business model* is a consistent, economically sound configuration of the elements comprising your venture's goals, strategies, processes, technologies and organizational structure, conceived to create and consistently add value for the customers you have identified and thus are able to successfully compete in a specifically segmented market. In other words, it is the entire system that allows your venture to capture and deliver value to targeted customers in a profitable business activity.

Elements of a Successful Business Model

Your business model may be the single most important element of your new venture, and getting any one of these following elements wrong can mean doom for your venture. You need to determine the following:

❖ How will your venture make money?

❖ Who is the target customer and how much money does that customer have to spend on your product?

❖ What is the fragmentation or concentration of competitors in the industry?

❖ Has any company been previously successful doing what you plan to do, and if not, why not?

❖ What are the pricing dynamics of the industry, the distribution channel and its economics, and the dependencies of your venture, such as other goods needed to make your solution useful or necessary?

Faced with the pressure of getting it all right the first time, some entrepreneurs choose to copy many elements of their strategy from other companies. As Bhide noted, "They creatively select and integrate ideas from several sources."[19] Based on our experience helping entrepreneurs create their business models, we have found that the most important concept is understanding that their business model is predicated on the assumption that greater value can be developed through the careful arrangement, implementation, and management of these unique elements discovered in other existing ventures. What we mean is to look for ideas not only within your industry sector, but also look at other industries, paying particular importance to fast-growing companies that are capitalizing on new trends and technological changes.

Communicating Your Business Model

Jose Ortega y Gasset, a Spanish philosopher, once said, "Metaphor is probably the most fertile power possessed by man." And using a simple business model as a metaphor to help in communicating your strategic intent is one of the most valuable skills an entrepreneur can learn. According to Regis McKenna, what makes a business model successful is that it has the capability to help the executives following in the steps of entrepreneurs to quickly grasp the strategic vision, and to think and plan ahead.[20]

As a case in point, consider the early days of the hardware industry. Retail hardware stores were few and far between. The depth and width of inventory on hand was limited; a typical store may have carried three kitchen sinks in its inventory. The knowledge and expertise was usually limited to the sole proprietor running the shop. In 1978, when Bernie Marcus and Arthur Blank were out raising money for their start-up, they called their concept "The Sears & Roebuck's of the home-improvement industry." Who today cannot see The Home Depot as the company that grew out of that concept they pitched?

Using a "Direct-from-Dell" business model, the airlines have slowly been cutting into the travel agency business by simply selling direct to their passengers. According to Scott Hayden, managing director for American Airlines Interactive Marketing, in 2002 American's site averaged 750,000 visitors that made some 15,000 to 20,000 reservations a day. About 67 percent of all the airline's tickets were sold through online or e-ticketing kiosks, totaling some $2 billion, and growing at about 90 percent year over year.[21]

Be Sure to Click Refresh

Your business model can only be successful if it was created by intensely focusing on a particular problem in a particular space, tinkering and tweaking through experimentation, and then sticking with what works. This "refreshing" of a business model is part of the evolutionary process of new business venturing today. Developing a modern business model is like a basketball game. You know what it takes to get down the court to the basket, and your job is to keep the ball moving forward by regrouping quickly and moving in response to events and circumstances. According to Leonard Riggio, the entrepreneur behind the Barnes & Noble bookstore chain, "Today's competitive advantage lasts about two hours."[22] But the concept of responding to fast-changing environments actually goes back to Charles Darwin, who stated in 1859, "It is not the smartest, nor strongest that survive, but the most responsive."

So transforming your business model to keep pace is par for the course. McKenna pointed out that Intel, with whom he was a marketing consultant, was in the memory business until 1985 and was actually licensing their processor technology to a Japanese firm that was going under. Recall from our discussions in Chapter 4 that they refreshed their business model to manufacturing microprocessors. Qualcomm changed their business from making cell phones to licensing their technology. In essence, once they saw how cutthroat the mobile phone marketplace was becoming they moved their competitive advantage from a commodity, selling phones to phone service providers, to code. These companies saw that they could move ahead with their next-generation technologies only if they cut away from their existing business model and competitive advantage and began profiting from their intellectual property.

Profiting from Your Intellectual Property

From the fifteenth century, when the first patent systems emerged in Venice, to 1790 when Thomas Jefferson served as the first patent examiner in the United States, intellectual property and the value in encouraging technological progress has been well-understood by governments through granting inventors sole rights to their creations for limited periods.

Intellectual property is a specific set of knowledge-based intangible assets that offers entrepreneurs superior means to create a sustainable competitive advantage and superior economic returns. Although this book is not intended to go into great detail on intellectual property, we have highlighted some key issues that should be understood before engaging the services of an attorney.

Patents

The U.S. Patent and Trademark Office (USPTO) received some 375,000 patent applications in 2001. In 2000 it granted 175,983 patents, which amounts to about 633 patents per million people. The three types of patents issued in the United States are utility, design, and plant. Only the original inventor may apply for patent protection. In the case of corporations, for instance, the patent, when issued, is always granted to an individual and then assigned to the corporation. While 11 percent of the 1.3 million patents issued by the USPTO from 1992 to 2001 went to independent inventors, less than 2 percent of these actually show a profit.[23]

Trade Secrets and Confidential Business Information

A trade secret is information that has been maintained in secrecy. It derives economic value from the fact that it is not generally known to the public or to anyone who can obtain economic value from its use or disclosure. Trade secrets can come in a variety of forms, including chemical formulas, patterns, compilations, programs, devices, methods, techniques, customer lists, product designs, employee lists, sales records, and manufacturing processes. Perhaps the most famous is the secret formula for Coca-Cola. It has been tightly guarded for more than 100 years in a security vault at a bank in Atlanta, Georgia.

Trademarks

The USPTO received about 296,000 applications for trademarks in 2000. A trademark is a word, name, phrase, symbol, or design, or configuration of these, that identifies and distinguishes the source of goods or services of one venture from those of another. When granted through the USPTO, trademark registration is good only in the United States. Ventures in the forty-nine countries that have signed on to the World Intellectual Property Organization's "Madrid Agreement" trademark protocol can register a mark with that organization and receive protection in all signatory countries.

Copyrights

In spite of the current quagmire of disputed rights involving content available on the Internet, including the downloading of music, copyright protection is available to artists and authors. It gives them the sole right to print, copy, sell, and distribute the work they produce. For example, books, musical and dramatic compositions, maps, paintings, sculptures, motion pictures, and sound recordings can all be copyrighted. Such copyrights are protected for a term of fifty years beyond the death of the author.

Licensing Your Intellectual Property

Intellectual property licensing is a $150 billion market. We define licensing as a special form of contract or an arrangement between two parties where one party has proprietary rights over some information, process, or technology protected by a patent, trademark, or copyright. This arrangement requires the licensee to pay a royalty or some other specified sum to the holder of the proprietary rights in return for the permission to use the rights.

IBM has topped *Technology Review*'s annual Patent Scorecard, which looks at the patenting activity of 150 top companies in eight key high-tech sectors. For nine years through 2001, IBM received 3,454 patents, almost ten per day.[24] IBM owns some 20,000 patents and gets $1.7 billion per year from the licensing of those patents to other vendors. Even individuals can get involved in licensing. From 1954 until his death in 1997, Jerome Lemelson had amassed some 550 patents and earned more than $1 billion on them. Ronald Katz is set on surpassing Lemelson, expecting to make around $2 billion on some forty-six patents.[25]

Managing and Protecting Your Intellectual Property

It is important to strategically manage your intellectual assets like any other vital asset. As Michael Porter writes, "Many firms have squandered technology-based competitive advantages through inappropriate licensing decisions."[26] And protecting your "crown jewels" from IP theft also requires a significant effort and focused strategy. We suggest that you consider performing an IP audit on a regular basis to maximize protection. In Chapter 16 we discuss how to handle your IP with potential investors and strategic partners.

Starting with the Right People and Organization

If you want one year of prosperity, grow grain. If you want ten years of prosperity, grow trees. If you want one hundred years of prosperity, grow people.

—**Chinese proverb**

When a crew and a captain understand each other to the core, it takes a gale, and more than a gale, to put their ship ashore.

—**Rudyard Kipling**

Surround yourself with the best people you can find, delegate authority, and don't interfere!

—**President Ronald Reagan**

What It Takes to Be the Lead Entrepreneur

It is not easy to be the boss if you have never been one, and the mistakes you make early on can come back to haunt you. In fact, the first-time entrepreneur faces perhaps no challenge greater than learning how to be the boss. But there is more. Does the opportunity fit with what you truly want to do? Are you really ready to quit your day job? Conducting an internal self-assessment is the hardest thing for entrepreneurs to do, but if you do not do it, you will really get into trouble.[1] And what makes you the right CEO to lead this venture now? Are you prepared to face an immediate tidal wave of responsibility?

It is normally assumed that the founder, or lead entrepreneur, serves at the outset as the chief executive officer (CEO). It is the CEO's job to build the venture team, and to provide the leadership, strategic vision, and motivation. Much like a project manager, the CEO first has to prepare a preliminary budget and schedule of activities (covered in Chapter 7), and then assign the routine details necessary to get the venture moving ahead. Then the tidal wave hits: motivating the venture team; meeting with legal and structuring the venture; acquiring adequate resources; dealing with obstacles, roadblocks, and challenges; making thousands of decisions and trade-offs among goals, cost, time, performance, and profitability; and finally, negotiating the risk and fear of failure.

❖ Case in Point: Edward Iacobucci at Citrix

In the fall of 1998, Edward Iacobucci, the founder of Citrix Systems, Inc.—a company based in Ft. Lauderdale, far from Silicon Valley—was awarded Ernst & Young's "Entrepreneur of the Year" in the Software and Information Services category. Before starting Citrix in 1989, Iacobucci was heading IBM's operating system development team in Boca Raton. IBM and Microsoft were in a joint venture to codevelop OS/2, an application that was subsequently replaced by the Windows operating system. It was during the development of OS/2 that Iacobucci saw a way to allow any platform of computers to work with each other. This "thin-client" system required very little in the way of hardware function. Basically, any computer, through a thin-client system, could run high-end applications off of a server.

After getting turned down at IBM to develop a thin-client project, Iacobucci packed his bags and brought along a team of developers from IBM. They put together a business plan and raised $16 million from brand-name Silicon Valley-based venture capitalist firms like Sevin Rosen, Kleiner Perkins, and Mayfield. Less than two years later Citrix had forty employees developing software. At the time of their 1995 IPO, they had eighty employees and almost $15 million in sales. By 1996 they reached a market capitalization of $1.1 billion, and by 2002, Citirx had 1,670 employees and $527 million in sales.

Iacobucci convinced a team of leading developers to leave IBM's Boca Raton's prestigious "Skunk Works." One of those developers, Andy Stergiades, said this about Iacobucci: "The way he thinks is very high and broad. He was kind of an entrepreneur even at IBM. An incredibly high caliber of people followed him without a lot of assurance. People wanted to make a real impact on the industry."

Sources: Citrix company Web site; and Ami Chen Mills, "It's A Thin Line," *Entrepreneur of the Year*, published by Ernst & Young LLP (Fall 1998), pp. 29–32.

Become a "Talent Magnet" for Team Building

It is well understood that creating a high-growth potential venture without a team is extremely difficult. While the "lone-wolf" entrepreneur may make a living in a "lifestyle" business, skilled teams are a requirement for growth; it is a "team-builder" who creates a venture where substantial value and harvest options are created. And leaders with high emotional intelligence and competence in social skills are therefore more effective in building the "social capital" that is needed to operate high growth-potential ventures. In other words, the people with talent will seize the right opportunity.

The ultimate mission for the CEO is to find great people, for two reasons: First, great people, like domain experts, are the only unique differentiator among ventures today. The business world is a huge, flat landscape where everything can appear commoditized except for human thought, spirit, and execution intelligence. The second reason is that people breed people, and like DNA, they breed in kind. In essence, "A-People" will hire "A-People," and "B-People" will hire "C-People." Avoid what we call the death spiral, when entrepreneurs make the mistake of recruiting and hiring B or C people in order to save money, and then do not trust their judgment and decision making. Instead, follow the advice of one successful entrepreneur who told us, "I was always be looking to hire someone better than I was." So choose your co-founders carefully; you will be married to them for a while, and divorce is painful and expensive.

Sense for Quickly Establishing Team Basics

It is important that entrepreneurs do not settle for average players on their team. If they cannot have or afford the best, they should not compromise and start the death spiral; it is better to have a smaller team. It is more important to focus on building a "solid people process" and having the right people in the right job.

Entrepreneurs must be more than just general managers. They must be able to spot the need for change and convince others of this change. And they need to get potential team members, including advisors and directors, to accept the idea of being on a venture team and to feel comfortable working with people from other functional areas and disciplines.

Establishing these "team basics," as Jon Katzenbach calls them, will "unleash real team capacity." According to Katzenbach, team basics come from an integrated balance of discipline and individualism. He has found that great potential is unleashed when a small number of people with complementary skills, who are committed to a common purpose, like the business strategy, and who have a business plan for which they hold themselves mutually accountable, are matched "with a burning desire for team performance."

Team Motivator, Team Leader

Success depends on the ability to think strategically and achieve results quickly. As Jack Stack says, "the challenge for entrepreneurs is to get people to follow their big idea, whether it's the investment community or the people inside the organization. When entrepreneurs are able to sell their ideas, they become leaders."[2] The goal of leadership is to quickly inspire and motivate a venture team with a common vision and purpose and then guide them in converting this shared vision into reality.

Richard Siegelman, general partner at Kleiner Perkins, probes to find out how people got together and what motivates them as a group. He asks, "Is there a shared vision and culture?" According to Siegelman, "Some people may have strong technical dreams, and others may be completely different—a warning signal."[3] John Hamm, a partner at Redpoint Ventures, believes that leaders who are able to scale their business quickly understand the importance of a focused, streamlined strategy. They learn to extract a handful of goals from a longer list and know how to focus their team accordingly.[4] Rebecca Smith, a judge with Ernst & Young's Entrepreneur of the Year Awards program, explains: "You have to be more than a strategist. You have to be dynamic, because once you develop a strategy, you have to lead people to your conclusion."[5]

An entrepreneur keeping everyone motivated in the right direction needs this "able-to-leap-tall-buildings-in-a-single-bound" characteristic that ignites and fuels a team in its early formation stages. What some call superhuman talents, we call leadership capital. Leadership capital is the collective management resources that are committed for executing an organized business activity. As Kim B. Clark, dean of the Harvard Business School states, "Part of what it means to be a leader is to identify the mountains people should climb—and this is no easy task because the mountains of true value are not well-climbed or thoroughly mapped. Climbing will inevitably entail innovating, using new tools, solving hard problems, and doing things differently.[6] It is like what General George Patton once said, "A leader is one who can adapt principles to circumstances."

Prepared to Be Alone at the Top

The corporate types need not apply for becoming entrepreneurs. First, entrepreneurs have their own unique way of looking at the world. It is this creative combination of insight and irrational behavior that makes entrepreneurs tick. Some entrepreneurs who previously worked at large corporations feel too comfortable with expensive furniture, office perks, large administrative staffs, and regular hours. And second, for CEOs leading a new business venture, there is "a pervading sense of loneliness" at the top, where the responsibility for everything that can and will happen resides. Entrepreneurs often lack colleagues with whom to share ideas and commiserate.

Few entrepreneurs expect that the emotional consequences will be other than positive. Entrepreneurs are genetically predisposed to be very optimistic. But there will be a lot of bad times, and then there may even be really bad times. In fact, as Bill Reichert, president of Garage Technology Ventures, advises entrepreneurs, "Plan for the worst, it's the most likely outcome."[7] Because, as Marc Andreessen, creator of Netscape, found out, "In the start-up world, you're either a genius or an idiot."[8] One study found that even successful entrepreneurs feel isolated and estranged. Said one, "I feel alone and lonely. I have difficulty enjoying the fruits of my labor."[9] As Fred Smith, founder of FedEx, once said, "The biggest risk that an entrepreneur has to face is internal. They have to decide that this is the thing that they want to do with their time and their life more than any other thing."[10]

Assembling the Winning Venture Team

It is very difficult to build high growth-potential ventures without a team that has a critical mass of skills and deep understanding and passion of the business space. This means understanding the customers, the existing relationships, and the current products. As Arthur Rock once said, "A great idea won't make it without great management."[11] He commits to and invests in people, not ideas. According to Rock, "If you can find good people, and if they're wrong about the product, they'll make a switch, so what good is it to understand the product that they're talking about in the first place?"

So the "people part" of your business venture should receive the utmost care and attention. After looking at highly successful ventures we found that 60 to 70 percent of the ventures involved two or more founders.[12] Multiple founders make possible a larger effort, drawing upon complementary skills, knowledge, and execution intelligence. This "collaboration under pressure" helped Jeff Hawkins, Donna Dubinsky, and Ed Colligan develop the Palm Pilot, and later at Handspring, to create the Visor.[13]

The founders, or partners, are the first raw strand of DNA assembled. When used in Securities and Exchange Commission (SEC) documents, the term "founder" means the person or persons employed or holding office in the venture the day it was incorporated. There are two other components of DNA that get assembled, usually within the first 100 days after the venture gets funded. The second strand is assembled by the investors; they bring in the early employees and the specialists. The third strand assembled is the board members. Although the literature indicates that what defines a venture team is not clear-cut, we say that, collectively, these three strands of DNA assembled are the venture team.

Structuring the Team

Planting the seeds for competitive advantage means creating a common body of knowledge and experience. Such organizational capability springs from three sources. *Financial capability* pertains to financial efficiencies—not just how to make a profit, but how to make wise investment decisions, and experience in providing a return to investors. *Marketing capability* pertains to building the right products, establishing a close relationship with customers, and having experience in effectively marketing products and services, preferably in this space. *Technological capability* pertains to technical innovation; R&D; being knowledgeable about new products, processes, and technologies; and having experience in successfully bringing a new product to market, preferably in this space.

There are some key positions that need to be filled. Marketing and sales positions, specializing in strategic sales and new business development, are the most important. The other key positions are in research and development and engineering, financial management, general management and business administration, personnel management, operations and servicing, and legal and corporate tax aspects.

Choosing an Organizational Structure

There are three generic choices: functional, geographical, and customer. For example, Dell, which has now settled on the third type of structure, a customer-centric organization, actually has about twelve different businesses focused on large customer segments based on end-users, needs, and uses. Dell's business groups are consumer business, small-business, K-through-12 educational, higher-educational, federal government, state and local government, medical, large-business, and global-business.

John Chambers of Cisco Systems realized early on that a "world-class engineer with five peers can out-produce 200 regular engineers." But what is the optimal size for a venture team? Some have determined that the size of the start-up at birth has considerable influence on its chance of survival. We found that ventures with one, two, or three members at birth have a much lower survival rate than a venture with five employees, and that a venture with five employees at birth has the same survival rate as those starting with ten, twenty, or more employees.

Venture Team Compensation and Incentives

In the early stages, when the intrinsic motivation we discussed in Chapter 1 is high, there are many intangible rewards for the venture team. They have the chance to change and experience personal growth, to exercise autonomy, and to be exposed to new business venturing. Larry Page, co-founder of Google, said he found that when you get a small group of people motivated in an innovative environment "work isn't just work—it becomes their enjoyment."[14]

Financial rewards are important too, as they can be offered to venture team members as a way of retaining and motivating them. Equity in the venture is first, and most important. Stock in the venture gives the member a direct financial stake in the overall performance of the venture. But there is no time-tested formula to cover how distributions should be planned with respect to the allocation of stock and timing, such as the vesting periods. Salary and bonuses are money paid directly as paychecks, or indirectly to consultants by agreement. Commissions are given based on percentage of sales made and usually reserved only for the marketing and sales executives. And profit sharing is cash distributed to eligible employees based on the venture's profit.

Key Success Factors

Simply by definition, a new business venture is short on human resources. A common pitfall is not being prepared for how dynamic the process of team building is and for the changes that will most likely occur over time. It is important that initial talks and agreements have understandings and mechanisms to "facilitate and help structure graceful divorces" as the venture grows.[15]

Remember that no venture team is ever perfect; do not expect to find a "venture team in a box." But there is a growing body of research in the venture capital community that suggests that most of the reasons for new business failure may be traced to specific flaws in the venture team. So investors will expect that you have worked with consultants and advisors to perform an objective analysis, and that you have some kind of plan to fill in the flaws and weak spots.

There is no doubt that the combination of the right team of people and opportunity can be a most powerful venture. Bill Coleman is a co-founder of BEA Systems, which claims the distinction of being the fastest software company to reach $1 billion in revenue. His advice for finding the best team members is key: "I wanted all of them to have the following four experiences: To be the best at what they do; to have been a successful executive in a large, high-growth company; to have been an executive in a start-up; and, most importantly, to have survived at least one failure."[16]

Venture Team Management

A business organization is composed of people and groups of people. It is goal-directed, meaning that it exists for a purpose, it has structured activities, and it is chartered or incorporated with the intention of profitably operating a business activity. It has an identifiable boundary, distinct from the environment, and a place in the ecosystem of capitalism. Richard Schulze, the founder of the consumer electronics retail chain Best Buy, built his company from kitchen-table to a retail empire with almost 1,900 stores, 94,000 employees, and $20 billion in sales.

In discussing what makes up an entrepreneurial operating environment, Schulze said that it has to instill the vision and values of the entrepreneurial leader. It builds on talent, becoming a "talent powerhouse." The leaders are on the lookout for barriers to remove and look outside the organization for new ideas and creative viewpoints. And everyone must learn how to measure and adjust to cover gaps because the customers' demands are always changing.[17]

Defining Corporate Culture

An organization's culture is the underlying set of key values, beliefs, understandings, and norms that are shared by its employees. These underlying values may pertain to ethical behavior, commitment to employees, efficiency, or customer service, and they provide the glue to hold organization members together. Most importantly, an organization's culture is unwritten but can be observed in its stories, slogans, ceremonies, dress, and office layout.

If organizational structure is the "hardware," then culture is the "software," much as patterns of thinking, feeling, and acting are behaviors that arise from a person's mental programming, or "software of the mind."[18] Tom Siebel, founder of Siebel Systems, said the number-one reason for his company's success is the corporate culture.[19] According to Siebel, the primary job of a chief executive is "to first articulate and communicate the corporate culture."

How Should Venture Teams Function?

The venture team must learn to work together, learn how to divide up the work, and learn how to divide up the responsibilities. It must determine how decisions will be made and how to handle disagreements and conflicts. Drucker talks about how venture teams should work like sports teams.[20] For example, tennis doubles team players work with and support each other. The team scores a point or wins a match only when partners are dedicated and work in synch with each other.

Charles Deneka, chief technology officer at Corning's R&D lab, describes their culture as a jazz ensemble, as opposed to a symphony.[21] The R&D lab's employees operate like a soccer team as opposed to a traditional football team. It is a collection of talent, all with roles to play, all able to keep performing in a game that is constantly changing.

Be Prepared to Learn and to Change

It takes some time for the team to fully come together because it takes constant learning and "recalibration." To learn more about what it takes to be a great organizational leader, we listened to the CEO of the world's largest organization, Richard Danzig, the chief naval officer (CNO) of the U.S. Navy.[22] During the late 1990s, CNO Danzig was in charge of some 200 separate organizational networks, over 100 ships deployed around the world, a $90 billion budget, and 900,000 employees. He said that the CEO has to project a theory that is deeper than the once popular mission statement. This "theory of the organization" leads the culture and expectations. The CEO also provides what he calls "the central nervous system" that draws the whole organization around to support the theory of the organization.

Among some of the sports leaders we talked to, John Elway, former quarterback of the Denver Broncos, is one who stands out. As the CEO on the football field between 1987 and 1999, he led his team to five Super Bowl games and two Super Bowl championships. In the 1999 game he was given the Most Valuable Player award. According to Elway, leaders must have the vision and capability of seeing through endless walls and roadblocks. Facing times of uncertainty, they must spot the possibility and motivate the team to success. Elway cited a championship game against Cleveland in 1989 when Denver moved the ball 98 yards in fifteen plays to win the game, still today referred to as "The Drive." Finally, there is the persistence that is required to keep going. According to Elway, "Nothing in the world takes the place of persistence; not talent, not education; nothing."[23]

How to Lead During the Tough Times

During the easy times, everybody can make things happen. But tough times, especially economic downturns, require a different approach to managing. In fact, the ability to re-assemble the team and manage the interpersonal conflicts that arise during tough times is seen as very key to potential investors. But what can you do to maintain morale when tough times strike?

❖   First, be honest with yourself. Do not end up believing in your own marketing and PR campaigns. Do not lose your intellectual honesty.

❖   Second, refocus on your true competitive strategy. Do not overreact to current industry conditions and chase trends. Start by investing in a strength instead of shoring up weaknesses, and do not work on anything where you might be just average. It is important to emerge from tough times without compromising the potential future growth.

❖   Third, revisit your value metrics and look hard at what you truly need to measure and analyze. Consider what may happen during growth periods, when inexperienced venture teams may be hiring "B" bodies (called "under-hiring") instead of going after quality "A" team members. Once the growth curve (topline sales) flattens in tough times, these "B" bodies become dead weight and the organization will lose its lift. In such down times entrepreneurs often stay in denial, then not cut deep enough or quick enough. Tentative or partial cuts will only slow the bleeding, not stop it. Do not be afraid to "prune the tree deeper than imagined." If you need to reduce headcount, make your cuts based on performance, rather than on arbitrary factors like seniority, nepotism, or friendship. Focus on keeping the people who can help you drive value.

❖   Fourth, you need to create and communicate a positive agenda for your remaining workforce that creates a sense of purpose, and strategic direction for keeping the venture moving forward. It is important to clearly communicate that the decision to retain each of them was based on an objective examination of their contributions to the venture. Make it clear that they are still with you because your management team wants them there.

❖   Fifth, a reduction in headcount is an excellent time to revise or implement an effectively targeted incentive program. In the middle of tough times, such an effort by the venture team makes it clear to the remaining employees that your venture is looking ahead through lean times and will not be passive in its pursuit of success. In tough times, great teams pull together. Like Elway's "drive," this action reassures the remaining employees that management not only has a strategy to address the tough times, but more importantly is committed to sharing the upside benefits of achieving that strategy with its people. It is financially sound too, because by relying on incentive programs instead of salary increases, you can motivate targeted behaviors that drive value while simultaneously holding down fixed salary costs.

Legal Issues in New Business Venturing

To manage the relationship with any lawyer we feel it is important to know what they do, how they can help you, and how they think. This section is merely intended to help guide you and to prepare you for your discussions with any legal specialist.

The basic legal steps before doing business are handling issues with your prior employers, choosing a company name, filing all the documents with the secretary of the chosen state and paying all the required fees, working on the capital structuring of the equity, and drafting employee agreements and legal documents for incentive stock options.

We know that you will need legal help in the following areas: incorporation, copyrights, trademarks, patents, contracts and agreements, personal needs of the venture team, real estate and leasing agreements, employee stock ownership plans, franchising and licensing, formal litigation, delinquent accounts, liability protection, merger and acquisitions, employee benefit plans, tax planning and review, and government and regulatory reporting. There are many books that can help you communicate with your legal specialists. The *Small Business Formation Handbook,* by Robert Cooke, covers all types of business formations, including S corporations, C corporations, limited liability companies, partnerships, and sole proprietorships. Included in the book are sample legal forms and relevant IRS forms.

New Employees and Issues with Intellectual Property

More than ever, potential investors are looking for ventures that are run and operated by professional entrepreneurs and domain experts who are specialists in their respective fields. Likewise, it is assumed that most will have existing or prior relationships immediately before joining the new business venture. It is important that during this formation process that all such potential members of the venture team, and employees that are to be hired directly following the launch, do not misappropriate the intellectual property we discussed in Chapter 5.

If you plan to leave a company and intend to compete with that company through your new business venture, be very careful with the solicitation of fellow employees, business accounts, and even professional service providers. Check with your legal representatives because IP laws are different for each state and are changing each year. Bottom line, be very careful in hiring employees from competitors, how you hand out and expect employees to sign non-compete agreements, how you will handle non-solicitation clauses, and how you will manage intellectual property issues in your new venture.

Corporate Structuring

One of the key issues you must resolve at the outset of your new venture concerns the legal structure of your venture. There are three basic legal forms of business: sole proprietorships, partnerships and LLCs, and C corporations. The right legal structure for your business can save you money, help you get more money, and save you from future headaches. The wrong one can take years to unwind, especially if the corporate documents are not in order.

Since this book's main thrust is helping you raise money for your venture, your decision on entity selection should be driven by the financing strategy of your business. The corporation, because of its advantages over the two other forms with respect to personal liability, is the form of business we recommend for raising capital. The modern corporation has been around for the last 160 years, and its capital-raising advantage is ensured by corporate law. It allows people to invest their money in a corporation, and to become owners without imposing unlimited liability or management responsibility on themselves.

Capital Structuring

Ann Winblad, a venture partner from Hummer-Winblad, simply states, "If you're serious about pursuing professional capital in your company you ought to learn how you should orchestrate the stock structuring of your company on day one." Because, she adds, "More often than not that the capital structure is a train wreck that makes it uninvestable by venture capitalists."[24]

Equity capital, which we discuss here, is the money invested in fixed or hard assets, such as building, equipment, land, machinery, and fixtures. The excess cash, or working capital, which we discuss in Chapter 7, is money used to pay ongoing expenses, such as your payroll, supplies, marketing costs, and rent. In exchange for equity capital, every corporation issues equity securities, of which there are three basic types. Common shares are most often issued to those who manage the corporation, bear the major risks of the venture, and yet stand to profit the most if it is successful. Preferred shares have liquidation and dividend preferences over common and may be converted into another class of shares, usually common shares. Debentures are long-term, unsecured debt securities. It is not uncommon for debentures to be convertible into one of the other securities.

Securities Laws and Private Financing Issues

Be advised that it is illegal to offer for sale, or even solicit investors for, any type of security without registering your offer with federal and state agencies that control such offerings, or filing your offer under a federal or state exemption from such registration. The most serious consequence of violation of the securities laws is potential civil liability that may be incurred by anyone deemed to have violated such laws or to have aided and abetted violations.

Like many areas of the law, securities regulations are a complex, ever-changing territory fraught with many pitfalls for the entrepreneur in the race to get funded. And the consequences of violation not only affect the individuals, but also the officers, and they also can preclude present and future business financings. A good securities attorney will be able to steer you clear of the land mines and misconceptions. For example, these statutes apply to issuers of all "securities," not just the issuance of stocks we defined above. All securities include common and preferred stock, notes, bonds, debentures, voting-trust certificates, certificates of deposit, warrants, and options subscription rights. In fact, the definition is broad enough to encompass just about any financing transaction you may plan to do through your venture.

Building Your External Team

Recall that the founders are the first of three strands of DNA assembled, the second being the early employees and specialists, and the third being the board of director members. Effective directors play a key role in ensuring an early stage venture's future growth and value. Such a corporate governance system offers clear lines of reporting and responsibility, prevents or resolves conflicts of interest, captures and organizes expertise, and also provides oversight and accountability to the equity owners, as well as setting standards by which corporate management practices and conduct are carried out.[25]

A common pitfall with entrepreneurs assembling a venture team is that they do not seek out the advice of competent advisors, most likely because effective networking is a challenge for most entrepreneurs, for whom time is a valuable resource. We highly recommend the use of creating a formal external advisory board. Such a board of experts can begin working with you on an informal basis very early on. They can immediately help fill in the gaps in your venture team and even help you recruit new executives and employees. They bring you immediate execution intelligence, domain expertise, and connections, all without the legal entanglements and formalities of a regular board. You gain control of advice and counsel from outsiders without being legally bound by their decisions. It is easier to "remove" someone from an advisory board. It is also less expensive (we suggest providing advisory board members with honoraria of $1,000 to $2,000 per month, or around $5,000 a quarter). And your external advisory board is a great way to screen and test-drive a number of people in action, to see how they can help you before you consider selecting one or two as regular directors.[26]

Developing Your Board of Directors

Why are there boards of directors? A high-quality board of directors provides a new business venture with instant credibility and opens doors that would otherwise forever remain closed. Great directors have access to people who can make things happen. Today, the corporate board is no longer just a legal formality. It is a competitive necessity. As William J. McDonough, president of the Federal Reserve Bank of New York, states, "The board of directors is meant to oversee the development of the overall strategy of the organization and the decisions made by senior management in pursuit of those objectives."[27] Jay Lorsch, a subject matter expert at Harvard Business School, says that the board's duties are to monitor what is going on in the venture and the business space, correct and/or adjust business strategies as needed, and "to get rid of the CEO at the right time."[28]

Experienced boards can also help lead entrepreneurs through uncertain times. Michael Dell discovered this: "If a company is having problems, the role of its board becomes greater. Many board members may have seen recessions and downturns more closely than the people who are operating companies today. Because most managers have probably not been through something like this, the board can provide perspective."[29] And marquee board members can lead the venture to funding. Eugen Chan, CEO of U.S. Genomics, recruited Dr. Craig Venter, president of the first company to map an entire human genome, and by the end of 2002 U.S. Genomics received $25 million in funding.[30]

It is challenging to find directors who are sufficiently independent but still knowledgeable about and engaged in the business of the company on whose board they will sit. Susan F. Shultz, the author of *The Board Book: Making Your Corporate Board a Strategic Force in Your Company's Success,* writes that ventures should strategically recruit board members and that such a strategy requires a plan and a dedicated commitment. A great resource, her book details "nine steps to strategic recruiting" of board members and provides some tips for interviewing board prospects.

Working with Professional Service Providers

Recall what we said earlier in this section, that you select your board members from your advisory board, and that you select your advisory board from your professional service providers. Your universe of available consultants includes the following: legal counsel, accounting/CPAs, banking, insurance, business plan developers, financial intermediaries, marketing consultants, business strategists, technical specialists, scientific advisors, patent counsel, angel investors, new product consultants, real estate brokers, business brokers, public relations, executive recruiters, nonprofit trade groups, academicians, professors, and other scholars.

An advantage of working with service professionals, besides the fact that outsourcing saves cash, is that each professional brings a different perspective based on a particular needed discipline by your venture as it grows. As we said in the book's Introduction, there are three types of consultants: strategists, tacticians, and field support. We found that the most successful ventures begin cultivating relationships with consultants before they open their doors, usually starting with respected legal and accounting firms. The impact can be great when the venture begins moving forward. For example, a business plan whose financial statements were reviewed by a reputable accounting firm adds instant credibility to the deal.

It pays to start with an excellent legal firm that knows its way around the specific legal needs for new business venturing, such as incorporating, legal structuring, private equity, venture capital, taxes, legal issues in hiring employees, stock options for employees, contract law, securities, M&A, transactions, and real estate. Richard Riordan, of Los Angeles-based Riordan and

McKinzie, confirms the importance: "The start-up CEO needs to use a lawyer that will structure the deal today to take care of the events of tomorrow. That is why the lawyer needs to know venture capital well and also have a good sense of business."[31] Other legal needs include intellectual property issues, employee agreements, strategic partner agreements, and litigation.

Choosing a commercial banker is one of the most important decisions you will have to make for your venture. But what are the key factors in selecting a bank? Richard Shuttleworth, senior vice president at Silicon Valley Bank, told us that he provides his emerging growth ventures "coaching, consulting, and connecting."[32] All in all, it is important to manage these consultants, especially because their ideas are often in competition with the ideas of other consultants, and they can become "organized around competition rather than collaboration."[33]

Gathering and Allocating Critical Capital Resources

Skill comes by the constant repetition of familiar feats rather than by a few overbold attempts at feats for which the performer is yet poorly prepared.
—**Wilbur Wright** [1]

Never buy new what can be bought second-hand. Never buy what you can lease. Never lease what you can rent. Never rent what you can borrow. Never borrow what you can salvage.
—**Ian C. MacMillan, professor of entrepreneurship at Wharton's Snider Entrepreneurial Center**

We were always focused on our profit and loss statement. But cash flow was not a regularly discussed topic. It was as if we were driving along, watching only the speedometer, when in fact we were running out of gas.
—**Michael Dell**[2]

Assessing Your Critical Capital Resources

Leadership, as we discussed in Chapter 6, requires marshalling resources co-operatively toward a goal while simultaneously preserving and encouraging a strategic vision. To successfully execute a business plan, in order to translate the business concept into a reality, entrepreneurs have to surround themselves with the right mix of resources, which includes people, capital, and partners. But they first need to assess the resources that the venture will require, and they are often required to do more with less. In fact, many successful entrepreneurs pursued their new business opportunities relentlessly, without becoming deterred by the limited resources that they initially controlled. Simply put, by definition, entrepreneurs are attempting to achieve goals that will require considerably more resources than they currently control. One of the key skills of entrepreneurial success lies in distinguishing between those resources that are absolutely critical and those that would be nice to have but are not so critical. The other skills are knowing how to get the resources, and knowing how to manage or allocate them.

❖ Case in Point: Sir Edmund Hillary and the Hillary Step on Mt. Everest

At 28,900 feet, just 135 feet below the summit of Mt. Everest where the South Summit takes a slight dip, is a forty-foot treacherous ice and rock face that can only be scaled one person at a time. It is the last obstacle all climbers who desire in making it to the true summit must climb. It is called the Hillary Step.

It was named after Edmund Hillary, a thirty-three-year-old beekeeper from New Zealand, who first successfully climbed Mt. Everest with Tenzing Norgay on May 29, 1953. Many times Hillary doubted that the pair would reach the top—deep ravines and crevasses, avalanches, and extreme rock walls stood in the way of their success. In *View from the Summit*, Hillary recalls in vivid detail the account of that fateful morning in late May. "Ahead of me loomed the great rock step which we had observed from far below and which we knew might prove to be a major problem. I gazed up at the forty feet of rock with some concern." A slip at this point would most certainly result in a fatality. There was no other way to the top but up, one footstep at a time.

Looking back on that day, Hillary commented, "I didn't know whether we were going to be successful or not. I knew we were going to give it everything we had." With this fortitude, scraping at the ice and snow with his ax, Hillary chimneyed between the rock pillar and an adjacent ridge of ice to surmount this daunting obstacle, which was later to be known as the Hillary Step. "I pulled myself out of the crack onto the top of the rock face. I had made it! For the first time on the whole expedition I had a feeling of confidence that we were going to get to the top."

Following the first attempt to climb Everest in 1921 by the British, there had been at least ten major expeditions before Hillary's. Since Hillary and Norgay, more than 1,200 men and women from sixty-three nations have reached the summit; a total of 175 climbers have died trying, with as many as 120 bodies interred on the mountain. Today, it takes more than six months to move the required 30,000 pounds of gear up to 17,500 feet. More than 5,000 items are needed just to get a pair of climbers to the top. It is all about getting all the resources in the right place at the right time. According to Todd Burleson, director of Seattle-based outfitter Alpine Ascents and organizer of more than eleven Everest climbs, "We take the bare minimum to make this work. But if you get up there and find you've forgotten, say, even a fuel cartridge, you've just killed the expedition." Everest veteran Ed Viesturs said, "You don't assault Everest. You sneak up on it, and then get the hell outta there."

Sources: Sir Edmund Hillary, *View from the Summit* (New York: Pocket Books/Simon & Schuster 1999), p. 14; Dianna Delling, "Excess Baggage," *Outside*, May 7, 2003, p. 35; David Roberts, "50 Years on Everest," *National Geographic Adventure*, April 2003, pp. 56–57; Brad Wetzler, "Everest's Destiny," *Outside*, May 7, 2003, pp. 29–30; Ray Lilley, "Remembering the Biggest Climb of them All," *The Associated Press*, June 2, 2002; and James Brooke, "This Year, Everybody's Doing Everest," *New York Times Online*, May 27, 2003.

Resources are scarce because people want more than they currently have or more than what other humans can produce. Henry Ford found that humans on an automotive assembly line have limits to their outputs. And the world itself has a limited supply of resources. Such resources that immediately come to mind are the natural resources that have not been modified by man— land, water, oil, metals, minerals, and wildlife. The central theme of new business venturing is one of understanding this scarcity because many start-ups fail due to circumstances relating to resources.

Because resources are scarce, entrepreneurs must make clear choices as to which resources they must obtain, and in what time period they are needed. There are five basic types of capital resources that are absolutely *critical* to the entrepreneurial process. They are human capital, opportunity capital, economic capital, financial capital, and entrepreneurial capital (see Figure 7-1).

Product Development Issues

New product development is the set of activities that begins with the perception and analysis of a market opportunity, and ends in the production, sale, and delivery of a new product. Risk and uncertainty accompany new product development, and there are many challenges to "integrating the fuzzy front-end of new product development." The best way to manage the front-end process is to use a systematic approach to integrating your business strategy and technology strategy.

Such a formal process requires a sequence of steps that transforms a set of inputs into a desired set of outputs. A technology strategy defines the venture's approach to the development and use of technology. It specifies the venture's "technological goals and the principal technological means for achieving both those technological goals and the business goals of the organization."[3] The significance of a technology strategy is that it explicitly links the management of a venture's technology activities to its larger business strategy. From the technology strategy perspective, technology must be planned and managed so that it is consistent with, and supportive of, the overall business objectives of the venture. A technology strategy aids in quality assurance, coordination of the venture team as informing them on what to do and when, establishing milestones that anchor the schedule of the overall development, management for comparing the plan to action, and helping to identify opportunities for overall improvement.

Establishing Product Specifications

This book provides you with an oversimplified conclusion of the product development process for a new business venture. You need to efficiently flesh out the minimum set of features to ensure that the targeted customer will buy

FIGURE 7-1. CRITICAL CAPITAL RESOURCES FOR ENTREPRENEURS.

Human Capital. Includes physical labor, one of the most important resources. Can be classified in a number of ways: direct or indirect labor, recurring/nonrecurring, designated/nondesignated, exempt/nonexempt, wage/salary, blue collar/management, union/nonunion, executive management, and other employees. It also includes the board of directors, professional service providers, and consultants on the advisory board.

Opportunity Capital. This is the lead time before others see a problem. It is insight to the opportunity and particular know-how to solving a problem. Also called intangibles and goodwill, it is the first of two business assets that includes patents, trade secrets, trademarks, confidentiality agreements, exclusive customer relationships, technological know-how, knowledge capital, and relationship capital, which is especially important for strategic partnerships and outsourcing. It could also include exclusive access to sources of financial capital, primary marketing research and business models, special leasing/rental agreements to a winning location, and can even include "social capital" or "social assets," which are special friendships, access to lead users, and unique obligations, that provide access to or framework for the opportunity.

Economic Capital. The second of two business assets is called tangibles. There are two types of tangibles: fixed assets like land, physical building, manufacturing plant, office space, and machinery, all called "property, plant, and equipment" (PP&E) in accounting terms. The second type is called current assets, which includes inventory, materials, direct materials, and subcontract materials, like components, parts, and assemblies produced by a supplier or vendor in accordance with designs and specifications.

Financial Capital. This includes cash in the checking account, and cash equivalents like publicly traded stocks, U.S. bonds, sometimes accounts receivables from marquee customers, and personally secured loans made to the venture. Clearly, these financial resources are the most frequently needed.

Entrepreneurial Capital. This includes the collective domain expertise, the execution intelligence, the time and commitment, and combined intrinsic motivation of a venture team. It is assembled to assume the risk and begin a new business enterprise in a specific space to accomplish a specific thing. It is the entrepreneur, who quite often includes other entrepreneurs, that creates and drives value out of unique, and sometimes exclusive combinations, of the four other resources above. In other words, without entrepreneurs, the resources would not be gathered and allocated toward a common goal—without this last resource, the venture never takes place.

---

the new product, the minimum resources required to accomplish this, and the fastest, most efficient method to getting it done.

We now present a methodology for helping you to establish product specifications. First, it must be assumed that lead-user input and customer needs, discussed in Chapter 4, are already established. Generally, these customer needs are expressed in the "language of the customer." And in order to provide specific guidance about how to engineer, develop, and market a new product, your team needs to establish a set of specifications that will indicate in precise, measurable detail what the product has to do in order to be commercially successful for your venture.

Taking this step not only ensures that the product is focused on true customer needs, but it can help you identify latent or hidden needs as well as explicit needs, provide a database for justifying the product specifications, create an archival record of your development process, ensure that no critical customer need is missed or forgotten, and develop a common understanding of customer needs among the venture team. New product specifications also help determine the following: annual production volume, sales for total lifetime, sales price, number of unique parts, development time, development team size, development cost, and production investment.

Start with a Limited Objective Experiment

It is important to stay very focused, looking at the venture's first new product development process as a one-time-only "project" with very fixed time, firm objectives, and using limited resources. Too often entrepreneurs complicate the process with "too many moving parts" in a complex product. As Alan Patricoff states, "Instead of just blasting out, this is walking carefully and figuring out things in a more measured environment."[4] George Abe, venture partner at Palomar Ventures based in Southern California, says that by going the "experiment route" entrepreneurs can start small and look at uncovering and understanding the vital economic drivers of the opportunity.[5] Venturing in these early days becomes a continuous work-in-progress through experimentation and through a series of small successes and noncatastrophic failures.

All the entrepreneurs and so-called experts in the early days of aviation tried to accomplish too much, too quickly. It was on a cold morning on December 17, 1903, at Kitty Hawk, North Carolina, that the fragile aircraft of Wilbur and Orville Wright proved, in a span of sixty seconds, that powered, heavier-than-air flight was possible.[6] They did not start out by engineering a Boeing 747 with hundreds of thousands of working parts. They practiced with a glider, researching and learning as they went, how to do a most difficult thing, flying. They broke a huge accomplishment into its parts and proceeded with only one task at a time. They started with one original idea, what they called "wing-warping," a method for redirecting airflow to provide lift and directional control. They had no books to read, nor engineering schools to attend. In fact, they had to create their own formulas, and in a few weeks at the end of 1901, "they rewrote and vastly extended the entire store of man's aerodynamic knowledge."[7] Today, a fully loaded Boeing 747 takes off weighing some 750,000 pounds; before the Wright brothers's flight, man could not successfully fly a single pound.

Allocating Your Critical Capital Resources

Many entrepreneurs tend to underestimate both the costs and time that it takes to launch and later manage an early stage business. For the first-time entrepreneurs, especially, there are major challenges, such as having to think in advance and how to plan for expenses. This section about budgeting will help you to accurately estimate the cash required for starting up your venture so that you will avoid the pitfall of underestimating both the money and time it takes to start your venture.

First, circle back to the discussion in Chapter 6 about founders' contributions. Such contributions vary in nature, extent, and time. In exchange for this equity capital contributed, the founders are issued securities of equal value from the corporation. It is easiest to discuss and value cash, as long as U.S. dollars are used. Other contributions might also have value, but it is up to the founders to agree on how to assign that value. These include: tangible property, intellectual property, business plan preparation, commitment and risk, business knowledge and domain expertise, responsibilities for day-to-day managing, and specific contacts like bringing connections to other executives, marquee customers, technology partners, and potential investors.

Keeping in mind that your first product is like a one-time project, you must do the following tasks. First, record this equity capital, then determine the minimum amount of working capital required to gather and control the specific labor, direct materials, subcontractors, facilities, and equipment. Next you need to determine what engineering resources are needed to get the product developed and start some revenue coming in. There are specific critical capital resources for launching your venture and getting your first product developed or service launched. Figure 7-2 lists the most common start-up costs you may need to consider.

Importance of Setting Milestones

Launching a new product is essentially an experiment. The "hypothesis" is the business purpose, and the assumptions can only be validated or negated by real-world experience. Going back to classical Chicago School of Economics, it was F.A. Hayek who pointed out that "entrepreneurs are rewarded by markets when they are right and show superior judgment, but punished when they are wrong."[8] Today, Dr. Paul Jacobs of Qualcomm simply states, "It's OK to make mistakes, just don't make a career of it."[9]

Entrepreneurial success comes from this continual process of rearranging resources continuously in search of greater value. Moving ahead through challenges and roadblocks increases the learning, which, when focused on what went right and what went wrong, uncovers the risks and uncertainties. Collectively, this learning improves the chances of successes. The secret to "maintaining collective momentum" means launching new ideas, rebalancing the team, and re-evaluating individual elements of the approach.

Milestones are the formal breaks that allow the team to evaluate performance along the way. Also known as stage-gates, or check-points, milestones enable you to learn from the results of the experiment to date, and make adjustments in modeling, strategy, and objectives as necessary to pro-

FIGURE 7-2. START-UP SPECIFIC COSTS.

Project/Product/Technology Specific. Includes development and ramp-up costs, inventory and supplies, direct labor and consultants' fees, subcontracting and outsourcing, machinery, tools, printing of technical or special product-related literature, and measurement and testing instruments. It is important to also understand the payment terms and timing and forecast accordingly.

Overhead Specific. Includes plant equipment and installation costs, improvements in office location or business space, deposits for utility companies, special fees for licenses, special real estate and other consulting fees, and logistical, storing, shipping, and packaging needs for the product.

Organization Specific. Includes business plan development costs, business and legal fees, banking fees like check printing and opening a checking account, incorporation expenses, and tax registrations or deposits.

Market Specific. Includes marketing studies, special promotional and advertising needs like advertisements in phone books and upcoming print publications announcing the new product or launching of the venture, product-specific marketing information or sales-related data, and special packaging needs.

Entrepreneurial Specific. In addition to the contribution of cash, this includes completion of specific venture and product-related tasks. The assignment and timing of these tasks is based on the availability and existing agreements or understanding among the founders and venture team. Also included are expenses for raising money. Entrepreneurs should budget as much as 15% of the money they are seeking for additional expenses.

---

ceed. As Ross Cockrell, general partner at Austin, Texas-based Austin Ventures with over $2.4 billion in committed capital, says, "It is important to maintain and support your credibility with investors today." According to Cockrell, "Milestones make sure you're doing what you said you would do."[10] See Figure 7-3 to determine which milestone you have passed in your product development process.

Preparing Your Cash Budget Table

Entrepreneurs who fail with their first venture almost always put the blame on lack of capital, saying they were undercapitalized. But all too often we hear about entrepreneurs who create wildly optimistic sales projections, to cover their fear of failing, and then go out and spend their money on noncritical capital resources like fancy offices, computer systems, new cars, global-travel, slick brochures, and launch parties.

Every entrepreneur planning a new venture faces the same dilemma. What are the critical capital resources? How much cash is needed? When is it needed? How will the funds be used? How soon will the venture reach profitability? To answer these questions, it is important to first gather all the pieces of the puzzle that are known. These pieces are related to one of three basic groups: cash coming in, cash going out, and sources of financing. Cash

FIGURE 7-3. PRODUCT DEVELOPMENT MILESTONES.

Eureka: Idea Formation and Evaluation Stage. At the heart of even the most complex innovation there is usually a basic, and yet startling "entrepreneurial insight," a new way of looking at an old problem. As this point, the idea and opportunity has been analyzed, as we discussed in Chapter 4. Maybe the conceptual and engineering design work has been completed and even a working prototype developed.

Alpha: Concept Testing Stage. An in-house process that can run parallel to engineering activities. The developers can also interview, and work in real-time with lead-users, early-innovators, and other fellow "bench-testers" like friends and family, investors, or their experts. Objectives are to learn more about expectations, and how end-users will most likely be using the product. It is important to get the early bugs fleshed out, create the service and support/technical guides, get new ideas, verbiage on how to explain, discuss, and hopefully insight to selling more.

Beta: Product Use Testing Stage. Takes place on the premises of intended end-users, or where they will be using the product and preferable under actual usage circumstances. Objectives include finalizing the complex set of customer needs and specifications. May concentrate only on whether the product performs as expected or on whether the performance meets the direct needs of the end-user or as perceived by that user group. It is then determined to take the product to full production or return back to bench-testing and even concept evaluation. If proceed, need to determine how to convert lead-user contacts into the first customers.

Gamma: Market Testing Stage. Where the product is put through its paces and thoroughly evaluated by the end-users. More than field-testing, it is working with the pre-production units, or the first units produced from the production line that is not yet operating at full capacity, but making limited quantities of the product, or low-rate initial production (LRIP). At this stage, the key objectives are to check on the effectiveness of the marketing and sales strategy. If there is a solid fit with business strategy the product is fully launched. If needed, the manuals are printed, the sales and service representatives are trained, and the channel is stocked.

Delta: Post-Launch Testing Stage. Usually occurs some time after the product launch. A small number of products are repurchased from customers. Objectives are to carefully evaluate wear and tear of the production product under actual usage circumstances. Usage and other performance problems are identified for product improvement aid in determining how to scale, modify, and evaluate the production process. If conducted formally, new product teams can discover ideas for upgrades, new products, product extensions, and even entirely new uses for the same product.

---

inflows pertain to payments from customers, and terms for how these customers will pay. Cash outflows pertain to the critical capital resources needed, precisely when they are needed, from whom, and the terms for how the venture will pay these suppliers. Financing sources pertain to probable sources, when the money comes in, and repayment obligations.

It is impossible to know exactly all the details, but it is possible to come up with realistic financial estimates based on information, domain expertise, execution intelligence, and sound financial management practices. Financial management has three parts: short-term planning, long-term planning, and financing and capital structuring. We discuss short-term planning in this chapter and leave the other two topics for Chapter 12.

At the heart of short-term financial planning is the preparation of your cash budget table. The cash budget table provides much more detailed information concerning your venture's future cash flows than do the more common financial statements that you may have seen before. A cash budget table is a forecast of cash funds your venture anticipates receiving and disbursing throughout a specific period of time, and it also projects the anticipated cash position at specific times during the period being projected.

Budgeting is the perfect exercise before venturing into uncharted waters and perhaps the most important activity of your business planning process. Venture capitalists expect entrepreneurs to be able to budget and forecast their operations at least weekly for the next twelve to eighteen months and monthly for the following three to five years. Unfortunately, the practice of preparing a cash budget table is not "taught" anywhere nor found in any popular business literature.

Budgeting deals with information based on data derived from cost estimating and "conjectures of future activities." The budgeting process forces all members on the venture team to apply comprehensive critical thinking skills and begin considering how to allocate resources for the future. Unfortunately, too many entrepreneurs spend most of their time dealing with daily emergencies, thinking that putting out the daily fires is entrepreneurial management instead of budgeting.

The budgeting process not only provides a means of allocating resources to those activities that will drive value in the venture, but also can help uncover potential bottlenecks before they occur. The budgeting process is a very important formal management practice that coordinates the activities of the entire venture team. The budget itself provides a clear means of communicating management's plans throughout the entire organization and ensures that everyone in the venture is pulling in the same direction. And since the cash budget clearly defines goals and objectives that can serve as benchmarks for evaluating subsequent performance metrics, the budgeting process can also help in preparing a financing strategy such as the activities, worksheets, and schedules. These items prepared for the cash budget table can be used to create the pro forma financials required for presentations before investors.

Distinguishing Cash Flow vs. Net Income

It is important to understand the differences between "cash flow" and "net income" or "profit." Many in the business world do not understand these differences because executives and managers of existing businesses are not used to having to watch or worry about cash flow, and they definitely do not oper-

ate their businesses on a cash-in, cash-out, and cash-only basis. For an entrepreneur, when times are good, cash flow is the oil that keeps a venture
running smoothly. Even when a venture shows a negative profit but maintains
a positive cash flow, life goes on. But cash is like oxygen at the summit of
Everest, run out of cash and trouble brews really fast.

Cash is needed to purchase inventories, pay employees, and purchase
all the supplies needed to start up the venture. The profit and loss statement
indicates profitability of firms, but accounting profits generally do not give a
true picture of the firm's cash flow. Besides, you cannot spend net income.
This difference becomes more clear when the firm is beginning to experience
rapid growth, has tons of orders coming in, and there is no money in the
checking account to meet the payroll at the end of the week.

Nolan Bushnell, founder of Atari game systems and a pioneer in the
electronic gaming industry, comments about entrepreneurship and cash flow:
"I used to say the difference between an entrepreneur and an employee is
how you feel about payday. If you love them, you're an employee. If you hate
them, you're an employer. And the number of times that it was Wednesday
and payday was Friday and there was not enough money in the bank to make
the payroll . . . it happened over and over and over again."[11]

Understanding the Cash Flow Cycle

The cash conversion cycle, or cash flow cycle, is the length of time between
the disbursement for the purchase of materials and labor, and the receipt of
cash for the sale of goods and services. The shorter the cash flow cycle, the
more liquid the venture is said to be. Preparing the cash budget table helps
entrepreneurs better understand their cash flow cycle time, which is essentially the length of time cash, including the cash from investors, is "tied-up"
in working capital before that money is finally released back into the venture
and used to create more value. In essence the shorter the cycle the faster the
venture can "re-deploy" its cash and become more valuable.

The longer the cash flow cycle, the more critical cash-flow management
becomes. This issue of timing becomes most apparent when the terms for
incoming supplies on a "COD-basis," or cash-on-delivery, and when the targeted marquee customers pay in ninety days. So obviously, the longer the
cash cycle the greater the need for cash.

There are three key variables to the cash flow cycle:

1. **The inventory-conversion period.** This is the average time between the
receipt of raw materials or finished goods and the sale of those goods.

2. **The receivables-conversion period.** This is the average length of time
between the sale of goods, materials, or business services, and the receipt of
cash for those goods.

3. **The accounts-payables period.** This pertains to the length of time between the purchase of materials or labor and the payment for them.

Bootstrapping Yourself up the Hillary Step

Traction to move the venture forward comes from capturing one specific slice of a market. This *focus-first approach* needs to lead to other follow-on markets. But committing to a focus is difficult because of the unknowns. Nothing gets an entrepreneur more focused than uncertainty and fear. And at no other time in the entrepreneurial life cycle is there more uncertainty and fear than in Stage 3, Commitment of Resources, when the entrepreneur and venture has to commit to one direction. The only way to get to the top is by climbing. It is now time to "concentrate your powers" and focus your "organizational intelligence"—which is your venture's capacity to mobilize all of its brain-power—and to commit to the mission at hand. Commitment means it is now time to "bet the company" and "go for the summit."

Innovative products and technology are good things but not enough to build a sustainable business. However, in the aftermath of the Perfect Storm, entrepreneurs need to flush out of their systems the beliefs that technology alone will drive a business to the top. One leading venture capitalist succinctly told us, "If you build it, no one's going to come." There was too much enthusiasm for entrepreneurship, now new business venturing gets down to going for the summit and surviving. Today's entrepreneurs need to figure out the pathway to successfully launching the venture, and then bootstrap themselves to the summit and plant a first prover flag. Or as Michael Dell says, "The ultimate test of an idea is whether the customers actually buy."[12]

German philosopher Friedrich Nietzsche once said, "That which does not kill me, makes me stronger." Sir Edmund Hillary proved that Mt. Everest can be climbed, just like the Wright brothers' sixty-second flight proved that man can fly, and Edison's first light bulb burning for forty hours straight proved that electricity can safely light a home. Psychologically, making it up the Hillary Step is vitally important. It gives you the assurance that you can fight and be successful, that you can believe in yourself as an entrepreneur, and that your team is a winner. The Nepalese saying goes, "The summit of Everest can deliver you from the prison of ambition."

Richard Shuttleworth of Silicon Valley Bank told us that it is very important for entrepreneurs to break through this "transition stage" from entrepreneurial risk to a more traditional business risk.[13] More often than not, new business ventures fail because the business and revenue models were not clearly defined and tested in the real-world environment. We heard of venture capitalists who lost their confidence and ability to quickly pick out winners based on concepts. Only exposure in the bitter cold at the summit is a true test of a workable model.

In addition to validating your product, you need to validate your price point to help you determine how much money your product can generate. And only after a race to the summit can you determine whether you need to change the technology, the core components of the product, or your pricing structure in order to get traction in the market. After the climb, down at base camp, you will need to determine the headroom for this market, meaning how many customers there will be, how many will continue to rely on your new products or additional services, and how many will remain as a part of your customer base over the long term. It is also important to uncover pitfalls about industry risks and competitor threats. Only a focused, limited experiment can reveal hidden problems and force the venture to solve them. Taking care of them early on increases the chances of success, and likewise increases the value to potential investors.

Successful entrepreneurs know that new business venturing cannot be taught, even at the best business schools, and it cannot be learned from working at the biggest and best-run organizations in the business world. It can only come from experiencing and surviving a climb to the top of the world at Mt. Everest.

Bootstrapping: Unlocking the Door to Self-Financing

Serial entrepreneurs understand that all resources are scarce to a start-up, and that cash must be as cherished as the oxygen that is required to reach the summit of Mt. Everest. Weight on a climb to the summit is like overhead to a start-up. David Breashears, the first American to scale Everest twice, says that climbers cut their toothbrushes in half to save weight. Tom Siebel founded Siebel Systems in 1993 with $50,000 in East Palo Alto, California. Ten years later his company had nearly $2 billion in revenues, with 8,000 employees working out of some 136 offices in twenty-four countries. Said Siebel, "We didn't spend much money. We had the crummiest space in Silicon Valley. All of our furniture was the crummiest furniture that we could buy at auction."[14]

Start-up financing is very dependent on paid-in equity capital by the founders, their credit histories, and heavily collateralized banking financing. This "bootstrapping" is self-financing by employing highly creative ways of gathering and allocating critical capital resources without raising equity from outside investors, or borrowing money from traditional banking sources. Bootstrapping requires a different mindset and approach, because the principles and practices imported from the corporate world will not serve well. Entrepreneurs need to become a "cash management fanatic."

One report on successful bootstrappers found that 73 percent tapped into their personal savings, 27 percent used credit cards, 14 percent had repayable loans from friends or family, 7 percent had a loan against personal property, 5 percent had a bank loan, 2 percent found equity investors in friends or family, and 14 percent found other sources of cash. Almost two-thirds, 63 percent, started their business in their homes; 49 percent did not start paying themselves until a year later; and 33 percent waited more than a year to pay themselves.[15]

Additional research on bootstrappers found that 87 percent of the CEOs leading high-growth ventures had on the average 43 percent of all their personal assets at risk in their start-ups.[16] About 28 percent of them raised their seed money from co-founders, 24 percent from friends and family, and about 7 percent raised seed money from strategic partners and customers. Two-thirds of them launched using $50,000 or less, and 22 percent needed more than $100,000.[17] It takes, on the average, twenty-eight months for successful ventures to grow from the seed stage to sales ranging between $1 million to $50 million.[18] Another recent study found that ventures with seed capital of $100,000 or more grew, on average, some 2,074 percent over five years, employed about 150 people, and had nearly $21 million in annual sales.[19]

Strategies for Covering Gaps in Financing Needs

There are two bootstrapping strategies you can employ.

Focus on Cash

Get operational quickly and generate cash creatively. What you do at this early stage is not struck in stone for the life of the venture. Be sure to start with premium-priced products and services in niches. Be advised that start-ups will not survive pricing wars with established competitors. Focus on cash flow and remember that each stage of new growth will require additional cash.

Cultivate Business Relationships

Strategic partnerships, business partnerships, and outsourcing partnerships, formed before you need them, are critical to the successful execution of your business plan. Surround yourself with the right mix of people, capital, and business partners. Such "relationship capital" is an increasingly important resource for entrepreneurs. Your venture's success depends less and less on the resources within your "corporate walls" and more and more on the strategic alliances your venture is able to establish within your sector. Strategic partnering, corporate partnering, and strategic alliances all refer to "the establishment of long-term collaborative agreements" between smaller entrepreneurial ventures and larger corporations.

We found that two-thirds of the fastest-growing ventures in the United States participate in multiple strategic alliances. Service companies typically have five to six alliances, and product companies have four alliances.[20] About 70 percent of all these firms are in a joint marketing or promotional alliance, 58 percent are in a joint selling or distribution alliance, 32 percent license technology, 29 percent have R&D contracts, 26 percent have e-business partnerships, 24 percent conduct design collaborations, 23 percent have product development arrangements, 15 percent are going global together, 13 percent are outsourcing partners, and 5 percent are involved in some other alliance. Be sure to look to your board of advisors and directors for guidance on finding strategic alliances that can fill out your critical capital resources.

PART

Launching and

Getting Traction

Creating Your Market Entry Strategy

> Building a castle is difficult. Defending and maintaining it is harder still.
> —**Asian proverb**

> Competition is not really company versus company, but supply chain versus supply chain.
> —**Warren Hausman, business professor at Stanford University** [1]

> The biggest mistake an entrepreneur can make is to invent a distribution channel and a new product category at the same time.
> —**Dave Brown, former CEO of Quantum Corporation**

The Value Chain Concept

There are five objectives for this chapter. They are to help you:

1. Understand the value chain concept.
2. Understand the value chains that interlink in your industry sector.
3. Figure out a way to untangle yours.
4. Decide on a market entry strategy.
5. Create barriers of entry to prevent others from following you.

Some influential business thinkers, most notably Michael Porter at Harvard Business School, have introduced the concepts of value chains that we discuss here. When a company enters and competes in any industry it performs a number of discrete but interconnected value-creating activities. Examples are engineering and designing, producing and marketing, warehousing and shipping, and servicing and supporting. These activities are connected with the activities of suppliers, internally with marketing channels, and ultimately to the end-users. Linked together, they must include a markup, which is also called a profit margin, over the cost of performing these value-creating activities. The value chain is the sum of all these business activities—even if all the activities add up to producing just a pencil. For fun, we suggest that readers take a look at Milton Friedman's thoughts on the "infinitesimal

❖ Case in Point: Steve Case and America Online

Steven Case created America Online from scratch, building it into the world's largest online service by making the power of the Internet available to the average consumer. He describes his source of pain. "In 1982, I bought my first computer and wanted to hook it up and be part of this online world, and I went to great lengths to make it happen. It took many months, and hundreds of dollars to get the modem to work with the software to work with the cable to work with the computer to actually connect to this world. So it was very frustrating." In 1985, at a time when General Electric launched Genie online services, and IBM and Sears together launched Prodigy online services, Case launched Q-Link, an online service based in Virginia. In the early 1990s he watched the development of modems and believed that faster modems would become commoditized in the near future, which would mean more potential customers for his online service.

In 1991 he changed the name of his business to America Online (AOL), and he took the company public in 1992. By fall 1994 they had one million users plugging into the Internet through AOL. Between 1992 and 1999 AOL added 13 million more subscribers. That is more new subscribers than *The New York Times* and *The Washington Post* together have added in the past fifty years. In 2003, America Online, now the Internet division of AOL Time Warner, is the world's largest Internet access provider (with more than 35 million subscribers using its AOL online service). Nearly 400 million e-mails are sent and received daily through the AOL network, over 13 billion Web pages are served up daily, and more than 2 billion instant messages are sent daily.

Sources: AOL company Web site; Stephen Segaller, *Nerds 2.0.1: A Brief History of the Internet* (New York: TV Books, 1999), p. 268; Thaddeus Wawro, *Radicals & Visionaries: Entrepreneurs Who Revolutionized the 20th Century* (Irvine, Calif.: Entrepreneur Press, 2000); and Ruthann Quindlen, *Confessions of a Venture Capitalist: Inside the High-Stakes World of Start-Up Financing* (New York: Warner Books, 2000), pp. 61–65.

amount of services that each of the thousands contributed toward producing the pencil."[2]

Porter separated all these services into two groups of business activities: primary and support.

Primary Business Activities

Purchasing includes activities, costs, and assets related to buying the inputs and supplies, and inbound logistics like receiving, storing, and distributing. Operations include activities, costs, and assets associated with converting inputs into final product form, such as production, assembly, packaging, equipment maintenance, and quality assurance. Outbound logistics include activities, costs, and assets dealing with physically distributing the product to buyers like warehousing, order processing, order picking, packing, shipping, and delivery vehicle operations. Marketing and sales are related to sales force efforts, advertising and promotion, market research and planning, and dealer/distributor support. Service is associated with providing assistance to buyers, such as installation, spare parts delivery, maintenance and repair, technical assistance, buyer inquiries, and handling complaints.

Support Activities

Research, technology, and systems development includes all activities, costs, and assets related to product R&D, process R&D, equipment design, data-basing, and computerized support systems. Human resource management includes all activities, costs, and assets associated with the recruitment, hiring, training, development, and compensation of all types of personnel and development of knowledge-based skills. And general administration relates to general management, accounting and finance, legal and regulatory affairs, safety and security, management information systems, and all other overhead functions.

Untangling the Value Web in Your Industry

For your start-up to survive, you must find a defensible market not dominated by any major players. In the years prior to and during the Perfect Storm, many entrepreneurs ignored Gause's *Principle of Competitive Exclusion*, named after Professor G.F. Gause of Moscow University. Today known as the "father of mathematical biology," Gause simply deduced in 1934, after observing proto-zoans fight it out in the same bottle, that "No two species can coexist that make their living the same way."[3] This fact is clear: An entrepreneurial strategy aimed at exploiting an innovation must achieve leadership within a given environment. Otherwise, the venture will simply create an opportunity for the competition.

Business today is tremendously interwoven and complex. Understanding this complexity is the first major challenge for any entrepreneur. Like a taxonomist classifying organisms in an ordered system that indicates natural relationships in a biological ecosystem, an entrepreneur needs to have a deep understanding of the ecosystem and how the venture will survive in it. The ecosystem refers to the large, loosely connected web of all stakeholders, including competitors, their partners, suppliers, customers, investors, and even regulators particular to each industry. Some ecosystems are hundreds of years old, have complicated cultures, regulations, and systems, and have hundreds of billions of dollars invested in them by some very large protozoans. How can anyone expect a small start-up to change the science of biology?

For example, business concepts not integrated into a value web are merely science projects that have little chance to survive in the open air. Sky Dayton is founder of Earthlink and a co-founder of eCompanies, an incubator that was based in Santa Monica, California. When eCompanies failed to launch any winners after some $20 million was thrown at a dozen "half-baked ideas," Dayton noted that what he learned is that "just because you have a great idea, that doesn't mean the world's ready for it."[4] As Ray Ozzie, founder of Groove Networks and creator of Lotus Notes, says, "There has to be an ecosystem. This is something I learned from the Notes experience—the value of this ecosystem."

We now return back to Porter, who developed tools to help companies analyze their respective ecosystems, and to learn how to create more value. He created value chain analysis as a means to organize and understand the customer-value-creating activities and processes within a company. It is a tool that helps a company focus on and analyze its internal business activities that affect (1) a company's costs, and (2) the activities that add value to the end-users through its end product or service. To help you arrive at a sound diagnosis of your venture's true competitive capabilities, we now turn to the task of "untangling the value web" in your space.

First, identify the leaders in the industry, or maybe the niches you want to enter, and collect as much information as you can on their business models and value chains. Then determine which activities in their value chains are exclusive to these businesses. For example, identify which are internal and core competencies, and which are outsourced or at least have the potential to be outsourced. Also identify as many stakeholders as possible, including the key customers, suppliers, competitors, strategic partners, and investors. Finally, disaggregate their value chains, activity by activity, into strategically relevant activities and business processes. Only then it is possible to better understand the cost structures, and to see where the major cost elements are, because each activity in the value chain incurs costs and ties up assets. Then look for problems where you can provide an immediate solution.

Only to those with skilled, keen eyes will these "value gaps" become apparent. These gaps are weakened links of ownership in an established value chain. For example, during periods of high growth, such gaps will be overlooked by the big players. And other macroenvironmental pressures can create value gaps. They include: keeping up with information and communication technologies, increasing dependence on strategic partnering and outsourcing, race for global expansion, and the increasing pace of introducing new business concepts, products, and services.

Following any one of these disruptions comes a new set of wants. The end customers want instant fulfillment, more perfect information, and increasing choices of new and improved products. Competitors fighting for survival want better integration of customer fulfillment, information integration, and facilitation of globalization. Suppliers want consolidation, improved information visibility, and management of strategic alliances. The marketing channels want more perfect information, lower prices, and personal service. Finally, even the government has wants, including enforcement of anti-trust laws, rulings on digital rights, and information usages.

Clayton Christensen says that new business organisms have the best chance for survival when "minimizing the need for customers to reorder their lives." He also states that "if an innovation helps customers do things they are already trying to do more simply and conveniently, it has a probability of success."[5] But as a rule, entrepreneurs who exploit competitor weaknesses stand a better chance of succeeding than those who challenge competitor strengths head-on, especially if the weaknesses represent important vulnerabilities and the rivals are caught by surprise with no ready defense.

Finally, whatever disruptions lie ahead, one thing remains certain: Companies are pushing information up the value chain, and out to the edges. According to one group of consultants, "The business world is hurtling toward the day when customer purchases at the end of the value chain will be acknowledged at the start of the chain within hours or minutes. The purchase of an espresso by a tourist in Italy, for example, will trigger a sequence of signals that will ultimately be seen on the PC of a coffee farmer in Columbia."[6]

Market Entry Strategies

Daniel Spulber's book *The Market Makers: How Leading Companies Create and Win Markets* helped us understand the importance of this subject. To quote him:

> Entry strategies take advantage of the company's ability to create and manage markets. This opens up a wide range of strategic alternatives and allows the company to develop its market relationships and profit from its unique knowledge.

Success comes from insight about the markets, insight about the opportunity, and an ability to execute. Market entry is a strategic challenge and cannot solved with brute corporate force.

The value web, composed of many integrated value chains, represents a significant industry-wide commitment to a large number of players in the particular markets and the customer connections they serve. Normally, it takes many years for an industry to build an established value web; it is not easily changed, because building one involves great sums of capital investments. Woven in among all these players is an extensive set of long-term relationships, a commitment to an established set of policies, industry norms, standards, regulations, and other particular practices.

Facing these facts, some questions pose an immediate concern. What is your proposed entry strategy? What is the best way to move a new product into a market? How can you get immediate traction? Will you have problems with your technology, if it is too disruptive, to overcome the cultural/organizational dynamics of the industry norms? Are you facing any particular seasonalities unique to your industry? What about "must-attend" trade shows, and when are they? Do you have to make alliances for suppliers or marketing channels? Are there any governmental hurdles, barriers, or approvals to go through? What about special regulations, like third-party spec'ing and testing?

Choosing one of the following market entry strategies depends on the ecosystem that you are going into, the positioning that you seek, and the product portfolio of the existing organisms in the space. Once you select a market entry strategy, it begins to drive everything else. This includes your business strategy, your business model, how you recruit and build your venture team, the resources you will need, your marketing and sales strategy; it even drives how much money you will need and your leads on potential investors. Good luck!

Trailblazers and Creative Disrupters

In his book *Winning In High-Tech Markets: The Role of General Management*, Joseph Malone presents the case for the pioneering trailblazer:

> If the firm that pioneers a market is capable of continuing to pioneer new generations of technology, it is almost impossible to catch. It develops a learning-curve advantage, which is constantly reinforced as long as the pioneer continues to press ahead with ever-newer technology.

The trailblazers and pioneers should go after nonconsumers, where the alternative is nothing at all. HP provides us a great example, as they, according to David Packard, "single-handedly created the revolution in color printing" when they introduced the Deskjet 500C in 1991.

Christensen once stated that "Sony was history's most successful disrupter."[7] In an average year Sony introduces 1,000 new or updated products, or an average of four every working day. Typically, about 200 of these products are aimed at creating entirely new markets.[8] Between 1950 and 1980 Sony introduced twelve disruptive technologies that created exciting new markets and ultimately dethroned industry leaders, everything from the first transistor radios to televisions to VCRs and the Walkman.

Fast Followers

Despite the supposed existence of "first-mover" advantages, first-to-market innovators and trailblazers do not always win. In Schumpeter's view, life is easy for the fast followers because all they need to do is to follow in the footsteps of the pioneering entrepreneurs who have led the way and established a dominant design or product platform, and whose earlier activities have resolved all the major uncertainties. Such fast followers can also leapfrog the pioneers.

There is perhaps no better fast follower than Microsoft. In 1985 Microsoft's Excel followed Lotus's 1982 release of 1-2-3, which in turn followed VisiCalc's 1979 release. Richard Belluzzo, a former Microsoft president who oversaw MSN and the XBox games division, commented on their online strategy as they pursued AOL: "It's typical Microsoft. It takes them a while to find their groove, but once they do, all they have to do is execute."[9] And in the early days of the PC industry, IBM's penetration of the corporate market was so successful that the company could not satisfy demand for approximately eighteen months. This created an opportunity for many start-ups to develop IBM-compatible machines, or "clones" that followed IBM's footsteps.

Innovators and Enablers

Much like how the stirrup changed riding horses, weaponry, and warfare, and even the entire feudal system, history has shown us that one simple idea, or a cluster of innovations, often enabled the emergence of entirely new industries. In more modern times, electrification (the enabler) and the rise of supermarkets (the innovators) in the late 1930s led a boom in refrigerator sales and introduced food marketing. And like the stirrup, the Internet enabled Amazon.com to trigger a fundamental change in the balance of power between buyers and sellers. Think of the first time you went online and actually purchased a book from Amazon, and then thought, "Why can't every bookseller conduct business like this?" Well, the innovator looks at Amazon.com and thinks, "Why can't all business be conducted this way?"

At Ducati they did just that. In early 2000, the sixty-year-old Italian motorcycle company sold about three years' worth of their $26,000 limited edition 996R street bikes in less than one month online, one day selling 350 units.[10] But these innovators and enablers of a "miniature revolution" do not have to be leading a technology-based product or service. As Dave Thomas, founder of Columbus, Ohio-based Wendy's, once said, "We did not invent the salad bar or the stuffed baked potato, but we were the first ones to put them into a national chain of quick-service restaurants."[11]

Evolutionary Components

In Chapter 2 we discussed how Carnegie's fortune was amassed during America's period of "railroadization," when his steel replaced wooden bridges and trestles, and when existing rails were replaced with his stronger and cheaper rails. Evolutionary components are incremental innovations, the replacement spikes and ties of any industry that is experiencing a technological change or a period of accelerated growth. According to Les Vadasz from Intel Capital, "The infrastructure that will be defined as the Internet is going to be developed over the next ten or fifteen years, and it's going to change. It's going to require a new generation of communications and computing infrastructure and applications that will run on it."[12]

Early stage ventures can "supply the suppliers" or enter through a gap they see in a particular ecosystem. Typically, there are small gaps between the evolutionary waves and the market leaders, either because of poor insight, weak defensive measures, or just poor management. Also the market leaders can "miss a shift" during a lap in the race, and competitors will blow right by them. For example, IBM lost 64 percent of its market share in the disk-drive business between 2000 and 2002 to Hitachi of Japan, because in 1999 IBM experienced internal delays in relocating its manufacturing operations overseas.[13]

Substitutes and Alternative Solutions

"Paper or plastic?" is seldom heard at the grocery market anymore, but plastic bags were a substitute that overturned the paper grocery bag industry. Porter also provides an example of how high-fructose corn syrup replaced sugar for soda drink-makers. Substitute products and services offer a viable alternative to what is already being offered in the space and "perform the same function as the product of the industry."[14] Once a symbol of software's counterculture, Linux technology has become a mainstream technology and is now a serious substitute for UNIX technology-based servers. Said one corporate user, "Linux unshackles us from a proprietary world."[15]

The market is ripe for substitutes when a huge macroenvironmental change surfaces, such as when there is a change in the economics of the industry, or a technological change. Like a fast follower, substitutes are viable once the market has been broken open, and once customers are trained and comfortable at buying in the segment. But unlike fast followers, substitutes make a play on pricing. Opportunities for substitutes come from price-reduction demands, increases in the cost of supplies or capital, and increased regulatory pressures.

Creating Your Value Map

Today's venture capitalists look to market traction, or "referenceability," as the single most important element before investing in a new business venture. Brooke Seawell, general partner of Palo Alto-based Technology Crossover Partners, which invests primarily in expansion and late-stage start-ups, says, "The most important thing is, can I go to four or five referenceable customers who can tell me why they like this company over competitors."[16]

In the old days, an entrepreneur could sit at the closing table in a venture capitalist's office and point to a slide showing the cumulative number of years behind the sales force that will be coming from the corporate world to work for the new venture. This left the investor to guess what might happen on day one after the investment. Well no longer, as investors are not too comfortable with guessing today. The historical track record of the sales team alone is not enough to get a venture to the launching pad and get it fueled, especially in an environment of constrained capital expenditures across all sectors of buyers.

Today, in these uncertain times, it is imperative that you identify the marquee customers. Validation means you have placed betas and working hack models with customers who believe in what you intend to build out. You must have them lined up and ready to tell your potential investors, your strategic partners, and your competitors that your product is a "must-have." Remember, the VCs do not want to be the first ones sold, they want to see traction.

The "Catch-22" is the fact that marquee customers want to see traction too. Recall from Chapter 5 where the domain expertise and what Porter calls "advantaged relationships" come into play. Any customer worth having today got burned yesterday. Expect a comprehensive due diligence process, even from customers. They will be assessing your financial health, even to the extent of going over your financials with their accounting/finance experts. They will be asking tough questions about how much cash you have in the bank, how well funded you are, and who your investors/backers are. For technology-related products, they'll want to know how much you are investing in R&D, whether you have a famous, well-known "mad scientist," and who else is on your R&D team and what are their credentials. They will be conducting reference checks, checking up on current customers, and reviewing your client list. Is it growing? And who are considered your major accounts? Finally, they will be looking over your business partners. Who are they? Are they solid financially? And how much and what of the total solution will be outsourced by your venture?

Mapping Your Traction in an Emerging Market

Creating a strategy in an emerging marketplace can be quite tricky. In his book, *Competitive Strategy: Techniques for Analyzing Industries and Competitors,* Porter points out some challenges. There is technological uncertainty as to which platforms will be leading and which will die. There is strategic uncertainty. Which approach to the market is best? Who will be the market leaders? And in which direction will they be taking the market? There is a very steep learning curve and there are high costs related to production. But once the product begins to move through the adoption curve, there are also steep cost reductions. There is great potential for spin-offs and product extensions as the fast followers and evolutionary products enter later. In the absence of any market infrastructure, the "first-time" buyers must be informed, introduced, and convinced with expensive marketing and sales efforts. Most likely the early products will suffer from image and credibility problems, and from poor quality. There is tremendous pressure to quickly develop new versions of the product in response to customers' interests and suggestions. Although there are low barriers to entry, and the market might be unregulated, there is difficulty in finding the right suppliers and inputs. For example, in the early days of the semiconductor industry, the pioneers had to literally invent the processes and work hand-in-hand with their suppliers, sharing daily discoveries and feedback on quality controls.

Outside the venture, the external environment that every organization must interact with must be clearly understood. Your value map is the schematic diagram for your business that helps you demonstrate a graphical representation of your complete business model and like a chessboard, helps you strategically manage the challenges listed above. It clearly demonstrates where, how, and with whom you create value, and how you intend to survive in an established ecosystem. There are three general types of value. The first is delivered through tangible value, the goods, services, and money. The second is intangible value derived from branding, customer loyalty, customer ownership, and connections. The third is knowledge derived from strategic information about the markets, competition, technologies, processes, and ownership of customer behaviors and customer knowledge.

In order for the product to deliver value to the end-user, it must be sold or utilized in some way in the ecosystem. Most often it is combined with other products, solutions, services, or processes. In other words, it must be integrated and "utilized in conjunction with the services of other assets." There are five sets of these "complementary assets."

The first set is called *buyer complementaries*. This set is not only the physical product that the customer "buys," but it includes a number of other factors. For example, for the PC to be successful, it needed to be available, have operating and application software, and have peripherals available, such as printers and keyboards.

The second set is called *supplier complementaries*. This set includes the other parts of the value chain that the innovators must organize, partner with or otherwise access, and in some cases assemble, in an acceptable and profitable order to ensure that the product is produced and delivered to the customer as promised.

The third and fourth sets are technology-centric. *Complementary technologies* come from the combined potential of two or more technologies. For example, the processor chip needed a motherboard and stable operating software for it all to work together. *Complementary innovations* are innovations that will occur down the road. The success of AOL depended on a system of complementary innovations that were outside the venture's control, such as phone modems and e-mail, to help move the business along. Sometimes the complementary innovations may or may not be in the industry. In fact, they may be introduced by the innovators and enablers we described earlier. The key point is that "the impact of invention A will often depend upon invention B, and invention B may not yet exist."

Finally, the fifth set of complementary assets are called *specific assets*. For example, the suppliers to the semiconductor companies had to invent specific assets so that the industry as a whole could scale to meet the fast-growing demand. There can also be specialized assets on the buyer side. For example, Webvan, the home-delivery service for groceries, crashed hard because its business model required the building of a billion-dollar-plus national infrastructure before it could create any positive cash flow.

A value map is a snapshot of right now, which identifies the major flows of product, information, revenues, inputs, and outputs. It details the major benefits, roles, and relationships among your venture's stakeholders: customers, alliances, and suppliers. Figure 8-1 is an example of a value map. It provides a high-level view of AOL and the value it brings to particular markets. The resources that the venture consumes, or requires as inputs, are shown on the left. The outputs the venture generates—products and services—are

FIGURE 8-1. VALUE MAP.

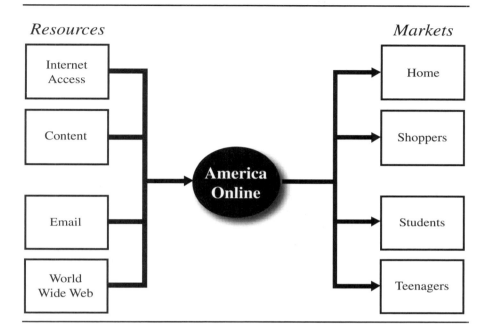

shown on the right. Create a work-in-progress value map on the largest white-board in your office, so that you and your venture team can look at it every-day. In a presentation, your value map on a PowerPoint slide helps your investors immediately understand your business model, and helps them see how familiar you are with your chosen market. It quickly leads them through a visual display of your current assumptions.

Establishing Your Barriers to Entry

As you prepare your value map, consider how you can create an antibiotic against harmful organisms. Antibiotics have long existed in the biological world before Alexander Fleming's work on penicillin in 1928. They are chemicals produced by one microorganism in order to prevent another organism from competing against it. These "barriers to entry" enable an organism to create space for itself in an overcrowded ecosystem. Basically, watch out for *value gaps* in your value maps and have plans for strengthening weak links in your value chain. As they say at Oracle, "Lock in customers, lock out competitors." Barriers to entry can lengthen your venture's lead time and provide important advantages, including helping your venture strengthen its brand name, broaden its solution set/product line, and achieve cost advantages through the learning curve. A venture should consider using any or all the barriers discussed in Figure 8-2.

FIGURE 8-2. BARRIERS TO ENTRY.

Technical Barriers	Strategic Barriers
Includes: intellectual property, patents, trade secrets, lead times with technological developments, "man hours" in code crunching, a "mad scientist" on board, unique design features and/or functions, compatibility with proven products, access to developers' tools and research and development through strategic partners, and scalability of production line.	**Includes:** domain experts on team, experienced executives, long-term contracts with distribution channels, history and credibility of team/founders in marketplace, traction with marquee customers, investors in the deal, branding, service marks, co-branding with strategic partners, employment contracts, first to get research grants and awards, and special connections to lead user groups.

Put on Your Tire Chains Here

The best barrier to entry is sales traction in the market. We now provide some ideas and suggestions for finding traction in different market environments, based on the work of some influential thought leaders, especially Porter and Kotler.

Finding Traction in an Emerging Market

Remember, you have to persuade marquee customers that they need you; you become a "must-have." It involves educating the marketplace, maybe going against the biggest competitors and some established norms in the industry. Are you prepared to be in the education business, as well as your original business? Examples are holding seminars, conferences, and meetings in order to educate the industry about the benefits of your solution. Can you be supplying the supplier rather than a direct participant?

Finding Traction in a Growing Market

Growth and profits will come easily to anyone who drops a line in the water. You will need to satisfy the customers quickly or someone else will. Also, a growing market attracts new entrants, which will force "reactionary pricing" by the established players. You know, this could be your only chance to make it big really quickly. Are you structured for this growth, do you have a growth strategy?

Finding Traction in a Mature Market

Growth can be achieved but it will be difficult. The market is proven, the rules are written, and the norms are established. You will find that the "pie" is not finite. You will have to come in through a niche and be prepared to defend it. Consider how fragmented is the industry? Who are the leaders? Do you really have the best product for this ecosystem? Have you considered being an innovator and enabler in another industry? Or can you identify subsegments of your industry that might be growing faster than the other segments? Can you identify micro-niches where being small can provide an advantage? Would it be possible to enter a market with a product you have now, then introduce innovative upgrades? How about seeing opportunities visible to you but not visible to leaders in your industry? Finally, are you prepared to lead the industry change, as there might be fast followers in your wake?

Finding Traction in a Declining Market

How can you position your venture as viable and growing in a declining industry? Consider that some competitors will be dropping out of the market, which might be enough to leave you some headroom for growth, or at least some breathing room to quickly plant some roots, and then later move into other markets. Can you get started here and then diversify into other industry sectors? Or you could be known as the "last-to-leave" in the industry, meaning you could buy up other inventory, their customer accounts, know-how, even partner with industry leaders to takeover their accounts.

Creating Your Marketing and Sales Strategies

The entrepreneur all too frequently tends to forget that marketing is key to the success of most businesses.
—Arthur Lipper III

Success is on the side not of the heavy battalions, but of the best shots.
—Voltaire, French philosopher

One person with a belief is equal to a force of ninety-nine who only have interest.
—John Stuart Mill

Setting Your Marketing and Sales Objectives

The first objective of any business venture is to figure out how to gain paying customers. A great product without customers is not a business, though it may be a little more than a science project. Marketing involves increasing customer awareness, delivering a well-thought-out message about your product or service, and identifying customer prospects. Sales involves various efforts to convince those potential customers to buy your product. According to Steve Wynn, who sold his Mirage Resorts in Las Vegas to MGM for $4.4 billion in 2000, "Marketing is about getting through the clutter, telling your story; why you have a better product than the others."[1] And Edward Iacobucci, whom we discussed in Chapter 6, put it in a matter-of-fact manner, "Nothing happens until you sell something."[2]

Just like an effective strategic plan helps you focus on your competitive positioning relative to your chosen "battleground," your marketing strategy helps you understand your effectiveness of your marketing and customer relationship management efforts. After all, as we discussed in Chapter 8, your venture does not compete in a vacuum, you need customers to survive. There are five basic steps to preparing your marketing strategy:

1. Choose a market entry strategy for each niche you intend to serve.
2. Set objectives for each target market.
3. Design a sales program for each one.

❖ Case in Point: Finis Conner, a Sales Force of One

In 1961 Finis Conner headed for California with $100 in his pocket. After a studying at San Jose State University, he worked at the Memorex Corporation, where he met his future business partner, Alan Shugart. Together they founded Shugart Associates in 1973, where they produced and sold 8-inch disk drives. The company was sold to Xerox Corporation in 1977. In 1979, Finis Conner approached Shugart to create and market 5.25-inch disk drives. Together they founded Seagate Technology, and by the end of 1979 had announced the ST-506 drive. This drive is known as the father of all PC disk drives.

In 1985 Conner "went in search of a product to sell." That product was the 3.5-inch disk drive. In 1986, he left Seagate, founded Conner Peripherals Inc., and built the first high-volume 3.5-inch disk drives. Without Conner's pioneering development of compact hard disks, the current crop of light, rugged, powerful notebook computers would still be a dream. By 1987, Conner Peripherals had sales of $113 million; the company had sales of $256 million in 1988, $705 million in 1989, and $1.4 billion in its fourth year of sales. By Conner's sixth year of full operations, the company had attained an astounding sales level of $2.2 billion, with $1.4 billion, or 61 percent, of those sales coming from overseas. In 1996, Seagate Technology and Conner Peripherals merged under Seagate Technology Inc., which became the single-largest company in the storage industry. Industry insiders said this of Finis: "Conner's reputation as a salesman and entrepreneur was set." Conner said this of himself: "What did it take to make these kind of sales? First, 95 percent sales ability, and second, lots of hard work—as in twelve days a week of hard work with 400,000 air miles per year."

Sources: Jimmie T. Boyett, *The Guru Guide to Entrepreneurship: A Concise Guide to the Best Ideas from the World's Top Entrepreneurs* (New York: John Wiley & Sons, 2001); and Jerry Borrell, "Selling the Valley," *Upside*, October 2001, pp. 122–144.

4. Implement and manage the marketing strategy.

5. Set metrics; measure, control, and adjust as you go.

Growth in your venture can only come from your marketing team's efforts. Marketing and marketing strategy wins 90 to 95 percent of the time over any other activities. And investors know this. They will go with an "A" marketing team and strategy with a "B" product and technology strategy over an "A" product and technology strategy with a "B" marketing team and strategy.

Three Types of Marketing Objectives

It is very important to pick your fight carefully, which means finding the right niche, driving the opportunity to reality, converting lead users, working on expanding the niche, and then working on controlling and protecting the niche. As William F. Miller, professor at Stanford's Graduate School of Business, points out, "You control your fate by controlling your market. Once an entrepreneur focuses on gaining control of his or her market, all other desired outcomes follow."[3]

The marketing and sales functions are central to your business success; without them everything else becomes irrelevant. Your marketing strategy is based on the results of your market research, feedback from your beta users, and a good "rule-of-thumb" insight from the domain experts on your team. Establishing marketing objectives help you prepare and focus for action. As Louis Pasteur once said, "Where observation is concerned, chance favors only the prepared mind."

An objective is something that you prepare in advance. It indicates something that you want to accomplish. An objective should indicate a desired level of performance. It should be understood how each objective will be measured, and who will be responsible for meeting it. Setting good marketing objectives will be one of your venture team's prime responsibilities. The task is very demanding, because it requires close coordination among all of your team's members, who must work in close synchronization to ensure that all objectives correspond to your business strategy and mission.

Every sales opportunity that you are tracking should drive some kind of incremental value to the overall value of your venture. In addition to measuring the basic objectives, like an estimated closing date, probability of closing, and the revenue, each sale should correspond to one of the three broad marketing objectives highlighted in Figure 9-1.

Characteristics of Good Marketing Objectives

Well-stated marketing and sales objectives possess several important characteristics. When evaluating your objectives consider the following questions: Who is responsible for approving the objectives? Is each objective relevant to overall results? Is each objective consistent with the other marketing objectives and with non-marketing objectives as well? Does each objective provide a clear guide to accomplishment? Has the objective been quantified and a time frame specified? Is the objective realistic, and is there a reasonable chance of meeting it? Is responsibility for each objective assigned to someone inside the venture? Are joint responsibilities indicated? When is the objective scheduled to be reviewed and, if need be, updated or dropped?

Marketing Through Crusaders

There are many great marketing, sales, advertising, and branding books and courses out there. They all say the same thing, that you need to create a marketing strategy that goes out looking for the customer. Unfortunately, all this literature and great in-class discussion accomplishes little for the emerging venture. Because the strategy, the execution, and the venture's potential upside should be keyed on only one element: the founder. Put more suc-

FIGURE 9-1. TYPES OF MARKETING OBJECTIVES.

Technical Objectives. These sales are especially important for high-tech ventures lower on the food chain. Could be making a sale to someone to help work out the kinks in your pre-production "hack model," your production line, and/or delivery of product. In exchange, these customers could be getting the product priced at a discount for having them assist in the development and providing feedback.

Strategic Objectives. More important for ventures a little higher up on the food chain. This could be going out and getting the "low-hanging fruit." Could be used to get traction in one niche, knowing that you can use this as leverage to gain access to more financially viable customers. Could also go after early adopters in special user groups to increase industry awareness and help provide "referenceability" when soliciting marquee customers down the road. Could be sales activities that will lead to high-quality customers and streams of strong recurring revenues. Could be defensive too, to prevent others from having direct access to the best customers. A simple example is like giving away razors to sell razor blades later on.

Financial Objectives. The one most associated with sales objectives; cash flow and making money. A word of note: If you are getting into full production of a product or service, made it through the Hillary Step and survived, and targeting the right customer with the right product, then there is no reason why you should not be charging a full premium on your product. As William Cockrum, entrepreneurial finance professor at Anderson School of Management at UCLA, states, "New companies, afraid of losing a sale, often underprice their products." And still, a start-up's best source of raising capital is from internally generated funds from sales. As Tom Siebel says, "Sales is often an overlooked opportunity." Finally, for a venture suffering from any one of the common maladies, listen to Mark Cuban, co-founder of Broadcast.com and now owner of the Dallas Mavericks professional basketball team. He told us, "Sales cures all."

---

cinctly, Steve Wozniak, co-founder of Apple Computer, discovered that he didn't have to understand a market of several million, since nobody had a computer. All he had to understand was himself.

Second only to raising the money for the venture, the founder's job is building momentum on the top line revenues. Like we learned from Finis Conner, the job entails working 24/7 day-to-day, traveling tens of thousands of miles each year, figuring out new ideas, being exposed to new experiences, and then discussing them with the venture team, the board of directors, and the venture's advisors. In the early-stage days, building top line revenues becomes a nonstop adventure for the CEO; no other marketing plan should be considered. In essence, sales begin with a sales force of one. It is up to the CEO to get on the road and to flush out discrepancies in the business and revenue models. No amount of marketing planning experts back at the desk can possibly conceive what the CEO will discover on the road talking to prospects, at trade shows, reading trade literature waiting on planes, and dealing with the industry on a daily basis. It is the CEO who needs to go out in the field, press flesh, and be *the one person* responsible for driving like hell to get the numbers up. This task cannot be assigned, cannot be outsourced, and cannot be buried deep in elaborate marketing plans.

Do Not Outsource Your Sales

Many individuals who start businesses without prior experience or training in sales do not know the basics in sales techniques and have fundamental misconceptions about the mindset required for getting orders. Having a CEO who is effective in face-to-face selling is critical for an emerging venture's survivability. Gone are the days of Super Bowl commercials, elaborate Las Vegas "launch parties" with *The Who* rock group, and trade show rollouts with stretch limousines for the media. Entrepreneurs leading new ventures now have to rely on their CEO leading an internal sales force. They have to secure orders by calling on prospects and customers themselves. It is nothing new, and as we learned with Finis Conner, it is a common practice with the most successful entrepreneurs.

In his book, *The Origin and Evolution of New Businesses*, Amar Bhide, a professor at Harvard Business School, reports that only 12 percent of the most successful entrepreneurs used sales intermediaries. The other 88 percent of ventures sold directly, and all but a handful were principally responsible for making the sale. In other words, the founders themselves were experts in the hand-to-hand combat of selling. Bhide found that 82 percent of the founders were the main salesperson, and 10 percent were heavily involved. [4] Conclusion: Unlike large corporations that usually rely on specialized sales forces, new business ventures cannot outsource others to do the selling that is required in early stage ventures.

As for the entrepreneurial engineer, or the founder who has trouble with the hand-to-hand combat of selling, it will be tough to recruit the first marketing executives to lead the sales at emerging ventures. Vinod Khosla recalls when he was a twenty-six-year-old co-founder of Sun Microsystems spending more than one year and placing hundreds of calls trying to recruit an experienced marketing executive. He discovered that nobody wanted to leave established companies to join someplace where they wouldn't even see any salary for six months.

In the very early turbulent days of early stage ventures, conflicts of interests will appear, most apparent when trying to figure out the pricing and market entry strategies. Pricing for the new venture and the new product becomes more of an art than science. This draws a line of conflict with the sales force, as sales force compensation packages are often driven by commissions. So naturally the sales force team will want the product to be priced high, which goes against two of the marketing objectives we discuss above. We recommend that initially the sales executives, if other than the CEO, should be rewarded for meeting objectives, such as delivering a proven product on time, and recruiting referenceable or marquee customers. Then as sales begin to ramp up, the overall compensation strategy can eventually evolve to a more traditional commission-based model.

Some influential business thinkers, most notably Amar Bhide, suggest other reasons why outsourcing sales is not an option for entrepreneurs. Maybe the process of making a sale requires making on-the-spot strategic choices, which the venture team cannot easily entrust and outsource to nonfounders. Besides, being in the trenches exposes the venture team to excellent feedback and intelligence from the front lines. Some other reasons include that hired-help employees may not have the same "zeal and passion," and that the outsourced field agents cannot provide marquee customers with the *psychic benefits* of dealing with a founder. It might be impossible to attract a really competent sales agent until the venture has established a track record in the marketplace. Good salespeople often tend to seek out "hot" items to push that can quickly generate high commissions. Few nonfounders have an interest in the arduous task of selling and educating customers about new, innovative products and services. Finally, with the average cost of a sales call of around $350 in 2003, it is very expensive to operate with outside sales agents.[5]

Marketing Starts with a Crusader

In his book *Marketing High Technology: An Insider's View*, William H. Davidow presents the case for marketing through crusaders. Davidow is a general partner with Mohr Davidow Ventures in Menlo Park, California. Before forming this venture capital firm, he was senior vice president of sales and marketing for Intel Corporation and helped lead the renowned Intel 8080 and 8086 processors to their rightful success. According to Davidow:

> "The most important ingredients of great high-tech marketing aren't taught in business schools. Most marketing people don't even like to handle them. They require personal commitment to the product's success that is consistent with the company's philosophy, a dogged pursuit of customers, and an untiring commitment to service. Those are the soul of the product."[6]

We believe that an "evangelist" is one who simply preaches and conducts lots of missionary work. Today, new business ventures do not have the luxury of time and resources of evangelism. A crusader is one who undertakes military expeditions, focuses on one front at a time, and fights for a very specific task. Davidow adds that "crusaders" are not managers. Business schools have programs to help people become "product managers" and "product champions," but with a new product, there is nothing to manage and there is no such thing as a champion without a hard-fought battle. The crusaders are like Jerry Sanders, founder, chairman, and CEO of Advance Micro Devices, "who can lead in the tough times, who can fight the odds and win." The crusaders, as Davidow stresses, "were willing to lay their lives on the line," something that is surely not taught in business schools!

Choosing Your Sales Tactics

There are three distinct buying situations: the straight rebuy, the modified rebuy, and the new task. The straight rebuy is buying from an approved vendor, product list, or a well-stocked retail store. The modified rebuy is where the buyer is interested in modifying the product; this usually involves others in the buying process. The new task is what all entrepreneurs must go through at least once. Their difficult task involves getting a customer interested to buy the product for the first time.

Since it is the least-discussed buying situation in literature and academic circles, and the most important for new business venturing, from this point on we shall direct our discussion to the entrepreneurs choosing their sales tactics for facilitating a new-task buying situation. There are only a few basic tactical choices: promotion, advertising, public relations, printed materials, and personal selling. To repeat from above, outsourcing the sales force, like working with sales representatives, part-time sales folks, or working with unqualified sales agents at the front lines of battle, is out. And expensive advertising is out. Dave Power, a partner at Charles River Ventures, a venture capital firm in Waltham, Massachusetts, says, "Start-ups have no business spending money on ads. If you can't measure it, don't do it."[7]

Guy Kawasaki suggests "everyday evangelism" as a sales tactic for entrepreneurs, but we found that it takes too much time and leaves them poorly focused. "Low-hanging fruit" is another tactic that many unwillingly resort to when faced with a revenue crisis. This is a tactic of quickly going around to capture the sales within easy reach of the venture, and then making the mistake of thinking the next round of sales will be just as easy. "Piggy-back marketing" through business partnering programs can be a very successful tactic, especially for high-tech firms. One-third of IBM's revenue is generated through such partner relationships. It is a good tactic that leads to funding too. Tony Sun from Venrock says, "We are looking for capital-efficient companies, which generally means enterprises that sell through partners, rather than those who need to build huge direct sales forces in order to be successful."[8]

Introducing the Catalysis Sales Approach

There are five stages in the new task buying process: awareness, interest, evaluation, trial, and adoption. There is much work involved in leading a customer through this process, so much more than one can imagine; it is especially complicated if combined with launching a new venture. One of the greatest errors in new business venturing is not knowing this difficult work that lies ahead. Many entrepreneurs proceed by looking at a hundred different opportunities and ideas for their product, with the belief that their success will come in numbers. But only the most experienced entrepreneurs know there is just no way to go after all of them. As David Packard of Hewlett-Packard stated, "Many companies die from indigestion of opportunities rather than starvation."

So the most important strategic decision facing any new venture is choosing only a handful of the right customers. The right customers can be found in lead users, which we first discussed in Chapter 4. Recall that lead users face needs that will be general in a marketplace, but face them months or years before the majority of that marketplace encounters them. In fact, they can serve as a quasi-forecasting service, providing critical data for your marketing research. And lead users are positioned to benefit significantly by obtaining a solution to their particular problems and needs. Most importantly, lead users know other lead users, and they are most likely in a position to help you identify and contact other lead users either directly, or indirectly, based on your early work with the first group of lead users. They will communicate their experience (good and bad) with your products and venture to others. Recall from our discussions about the diffusion of innovations in Chapter 2 that late adopters look to the lead users for opinion leadership, which will encourage or discourage them from adopting your products and services.

The sales tactic we recommend is what we call the catalyst sales approach. This approach involves a crusader, like the CEO who is committed to the venture and has a personal stake in the outcome of the new product, someone who works as a catalyst to stimulate the early sales. Chemically speaking, a catalyst-crusader is one who modifies and increases the rate of a reaction with lead users, especially without being involved or consumed in the consequences. The sales task is to catalyze, or to initiate and produce a fundamental change in the lead users, and then get out of the way. When Tom Siebel started his company in 1993, he focused on companies and prospects that fully understood the need for his software from the get-go. His sales tactics were profoundly simple, "We were looking for people who understood the need and wanted to use it. A core part of our strategy was not to evangelize—we wanted customers where the demand was very salient."[9]

The Critical Elements to Catalyze Sales

Remember, as you head out as a *customer problem solver*, not a sales agent, your goal is to get yourself up the Hillary Step, stimulate key sales, and get back down in one piece. So how do you find, as Siebel calls it, strikingly notable demand? First, recall from Chapter 4, it is imperative that you have in place an external integration between the new product development team and the lead users and early adopters. From this integration, your goal is to find and contact what Geoffrey Moore calls the right "technology enthusiast" or "visionary." In his book, *The Secrets of Word-of-Mouth: How to Trigger Exponential Sales Through Runaway Word of Mouth*, George Silverman goes one step further. Based on the Ayn Rand novel, he calls it *The Law of the Fountainhead Influencer*, boldly proclaiming, "Give me the right person to start and I'll change the world."

Dan Bricklin is a person who changed the world. In 1979, as a Harvard Business School student and former programmer at DEC, he and his friend and collaborator, Bob Frankston, created VisiCalc. It was the first spreadsheet software application for IBM PCs. It was a practical solution for anyone with a personal computer to do financial modeling and simulation previously available to only corporations with mainframe computers. Bricklin recalls those early days, "I remember showing it to one accountant around here and he started shaking and said, 'That's what I do all week, I could do it in an hour.' They would take their credit cards and shove them in your face. I meet these people now they come up to me and say, 'I gotta tell you, you changed my life. You made accounting fun.'"[10] What really catalyzed the sales in the early days was when the accountants shared their financial work with others in the office and with their clients. It was basically a sales demonstration of the unique capabilities of VisiCalc.

The catalysis sales approach is combining the right visionary with the right product, at the right time. The product can even still be in the prototype stage. Gamma testing, which we discussed in Chapter 7, lets you know early on what kind of reception your new product is likely to receive. The upside is that you may also find companies that want to buy. For example, Polycom, a manufacturer of speakers for conferencing tables, had an order for 600 Soundstations as a result of their gamma testing at Intel, prior to having perfected their design. As a fast follower to Amdahl selling 250 scaled-down mainframe computers that cost $3 million to $9 million in 1985, IBM began test-marketing their AS/400 minicomputer in 1987.[11] By the minicomputer's introduction date, IBM had potential buyers field-testing about 1,700 units. Some 25,000 of the AS/400s were sold within the first year, making it the most successful new product launch in IBM's history. By 1992 more than 200,000 were placed in service around the world. And by 1999, IBM's AS/400 became the world's most popular multi-user, commercial business computer, with more than 700,000 systems installed in over 150 countries.

Chemical Experimentation

Measurable success from the catalysis sales approach is more than just "word of mouth," where the chatter from early adopters about a new product drives new customers to try it. Success is about shortening the customer decision cycle time for new task buying. As Silverman points out, such "decision acceleration" will turn into your "secret weapon." We leverage some more of Silverman's points. The sales process should be independent, not needing additional nurturing from the sales crusader's time. For example, like we describe with VisiCalc, the sales process should be deeply integrated in the product itself. Each presentation of VisiCalc by an accountant, and each use of the Soundstation at Intel, was a sales presentation in itself. This is what ignites the catalysis sales—it originates from a single source, or from a relatively small number of sources, and it "grows exponentially," or "sometimes explosively."

Marketing and sales tactics comes from a process of chemical experimentation that includes a careful mix of people, product, pricing, sales, placement, market timing, sector awareness, and creating the right buzz. Sales channel relationships are complex, vary greatly from industry to industry, and this book is not intended to go into great detail on this topic. But it is important to understand the basic channel options and how to manage the channel partners in your value chain. We suggest Kenneth Rolnicki's *Managing Channels of Distribution: The Marketing Executive's Complete Guide*. He covers very well channel design, channel selection criteria, and channel management and communication, including managing channel conflict.

Building Your Revenue Model

Put simply, no business can exist without top line revenues from sales, no matter how well the other functions are handled. Your business plan must detail how you plan to price and sell your product, and how much money you plan to make. The basics should cover three broad aspects: your selling tactics, your revenue model, and your sales cycle. There are seven steps that can help you build your first revenue model.

1. **Set your pricing objective.** Pricing is the only element in your marketing strategy that produces top line revenues. It is also one of the most flexible elements. Unlike product platform features and channel commitments to business partners, prices can be changed and modified quickly as you grow. At the same time, pricing is perhaps the number-one problem for entrepreneurs, who have great difficulty in predicting demand, how to set and modify prices, and understanding what actually affects prices. Faced with these challenges, many entrepreneurs set their pricing objectives based on how they make personal purchasing decisions rather than on entrepreneurial experience; they decide to enter a market by starting a pricing battle, which is usually the first step to failure, not success. When competing on price, especially when competing against larger, established firms with substantially greater resources and better access to stakeholders in the ecosystem, the best outcome a start-up can expect is a tie, and a tie is equal to losing. It is more important to establish a clear price objective that is connected with one of the three main marketing objectives we discussed earlier: technical, strategic, or financial.

2. **Determine demand.** The reliability of any cash forecast and profitability depends on the anticipated forecast of sales. In fact, the cash forecast can never reach a higher degree of reliability than the sales forecast on which it is based. We all know that forecasting demand for a new product—or what we call forecasting in a "whiteout," where the snow is blowing so hard that one cannot see the road ahead—is close to impossible. But investors expect to see some components of marketing research and reasoning behind the numbers. Start with your domain experts and advisors, looking for insight from that will catalyze sales and build momentum. We also suggest looking to models and examples in other industries.

3. **Estimate costs.** Unlike trying to forecast demand, estimating costs

can be done with greater accuracy as long as all the cost components are well understood. Both demand and costs should be based on the work we discussed in Chapter 7 and on the results from your limited objective experimentation.

4. **Review competition.** This is based on your work from Chapter 4. After analyzing competitors' costs, prices, and potential new offers, consider a response to each competitive pressure and how it will affect top line sales and profitability of the proposed venture.

5. **Establish a pricing method.** This includes pricing options and strategies. In essence, this is where the sales team creates the venture's first brochure, or sales sheet. It is important to consider up-front deposits, nonrecurring engineering (NRE) fees, licensing and maintenance fees, follow-on revenues, and any potential changes for terms of sale.

6. **Select the first price.** Remember the first rule with marketing a new product, especially during bootstrapping days: Charge what you can get. Be prepared to change the prices; in effect, test the elasticity of pricing. Realize that this will take time, especially when you are introducing a new product or service and are not sure what you can charge.

7. **Rework accordingly.** Likewise, look at the influence of other factors on your prices that are outside your venture, such as feedback from customers (no one is buying and they tell you why) and competitor responses. You will need to adapt the prices to each situation. This means providing new service plans, offering discounts with upgrades or referrals, and considering new terms of sale, which can include financing or extending payments.

Mapping Your Selling Process

We have found it to be very helpful for entrepreneurs to categorize and map each person they meet in their selling process into one of these seven roles. *Initiators* are typically the lead users who request something new. *Users* help define product requirements in addition to sometimes initiating the request. *Influencers*, related to the decision-making process, provide information for evaluating the alternatives, substitutes, and competing products. *Deciders* drill down on exact specifications and/or on suppliers. *Approvers* authorize the proposed actions of deciders or buyers. *Buyers* play a major role in selecting suppliers and negotiating, and they have the formal authority to select and arrange the purchase terms. *Gatekeepers* are basically anyone else who is in the way to others above.

Detail Your Revenue Event

Quite simply, we define the term "revenue event" as "when the check clears." Getting to a revenue event can take a long time, and usually longer than most entrepreneurs care to admit. The most successful entrepreneurs know that figuring out the sales cycle for new products is a nerve-wracking and arduous learning experience they only care to go through once. There are five steps for every revenue event: call, contact, close, contract, and cash. Time and time again we have seen an entrepreneur drop the ball in a presentation before a group of potential investors, when one of them asks, "Walk me through one sales cycle—from first talks with calling on a prospect, to when you actually get paid." Be prepared!

Where Are You Now in the Sales Titration Process?

Being prepared also means knowing who is on your key prospects list. But where are you at in the sales cycle with each of these key prospects? And can you describe your best salesperson, and his/her experience and connection within this niche? Do not make the mistake of relying on some pie charts representing large generic markets based on some big-name market research reports. Instead, go back and review what we discussed in Chapter 4 about defining and segmenting viable markets. Next, clearly understand your Sales Titration Process, as shown in Figure 9-2. Having a diagram like this clearly demonstrates the following: You have domain expertise, you know how to call on customers and on whose door to knock to make a deal, and you know to whom to talk for closing deals and getting paid. In essence, you have figured out how to focus your team's efforts on nothing else but sales and moving your venture forward.

Marketing and Sales Controls

Finally, it is important to establish measurements that focus on key controllable variables that reflect performance results in your marketing and sales efforts. Philip Kotler provides us with a list of the most common performance metrics. They are average sales calls per week per salesperson, average dollar sales per contact per salesperson, average cost per sales call and/or per sales transaction, number of new accounts established per salesperson, number of lost accounts per salesperson, number of customer contacts per salesperson, and total selling costs. But these metrics are most relevant to larger, more established ventures.

For early stage ventures we recommend revenues per employee as a benchmark of efficiency. First, it demonstrates how your venture stands up to competitors and leaders in your space. Some of the highest benchmarks are in the high-tech world, as shown by these examples of revenues per employee for 2002: Palm, $1,189,000; Dell Computer, $874,000; Cisco, $594,000; Siebel Systems, $561,000; Apple, $558,000; Microsoft, $531,000; and IBM, $268,000.[12]

Second, and most importantly, this benchmark controls "employment creep," or when head count grows faster than sales. Conversely, a steady rise in sales per employee is a sign of improving efficiency. But too great of an increase suggests that you may have an understaffed venture, and that you'll need to keep an eye out for employee burnout. A static number signals ineffi-

FIGURE 9-2. SALES TITRATION PROCESS.

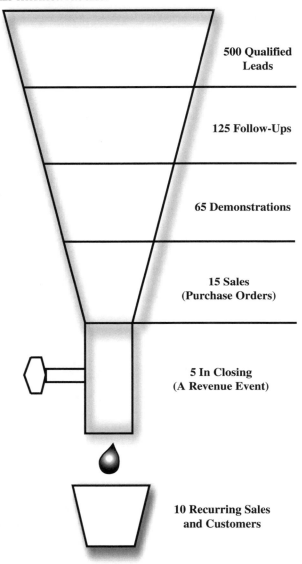

500 Qualified
Leads

125 Follow-Ups

65 Demonstrations

15 Sales
(Purchase Orders)

5 In Closing
(A Revenue Event)

10 Recurring Sales
and Customers

ciencies that might otherwise go unnoticed. For example, "bureaucracy build-up" occurs through paperwork and meetings. Such inefficient systems can stall your venture pretty quickly.

The benchmark can also be used to compare and measure the productivity of one salesperson, or one sales team, against another. As a result, inefficient performers can get trimmed, and critical capital resources can get reallocated and marshaled into activities where they will count the most. As John Dillon, CEO of Salesforce.com, says, "It's like organizational Darwinism. It forces you to make a selection."[13]

TEN

Managing the Rapidly Growing Venture

We are what we repeatedly do. Excellence, then, is not an act, but a habit.
—**Aristotle**

You can go into a corner slow and come out fast. Or you can go into a corner fast and come out dead.
—**Sterling Moss, Formula-1 racing legend**

First year, 1985, $6 million; second year, $34 million; third year, $70 million; fourth year, $159 million; fifth year, $258 million . . . year sixteen, $25 billion.
—**From various Dell Computer annual reports**

Creating Your Growth Strategy

Growth is the very essence of entrepreneurship. Growth is the only vehicle that will deliver returns to your investors. And as we discussed in Chapter 1, uncertainty and risk are a vicious cycle in high growth-potential ventures. Uncertainty and risk increase because the number of elements in the venture increases, the differences among those elements increase, and the interdependencies among those elements also increase. Thus, high growth leads to managerial complexity, which requires entrepreneurs to establish business practices and organizational management systems to get a hand not only on the increasing organizational complexity, but also on the increasing macroenvironmental complexity and risk.

The beginning, launch, and transition to growth depend on the industry, the assets, and marketing team required, and on the time to acquire the industry-specifics know-how. As Bhide points out, Dell used his college dormitory room and less than $5,000 to launch Dell Computer in less than a year. Sam Walton was first a franchisee of the Ben Franklin variety store chain, and he spent years developing the know-how of operating a retail store, therein discovering many opportunities in discounting before launching Wal-Mart. However rapid growth occurs, once it does, entrepreneurs face unusual challenges. Like the weightlessness of space, it is unknown until you are there. But you can and should prepare to grow, to change, and to handle such challenges.

❖ Case in Point: Cisco Systems

In the early 1980s Stanford University had some 5,000 computers of various types. There was no campus-wide network, the systems were like islands. Bridges were needed to connect them together. Cisco Systems was founded in 1983 in Len Bosack's and his wife Sandy Lerner's living room. Their solution was to create the bridge that networked the networks. For more than five years, they struggled and bootstrapped their venture by running up bills on their credit cards. In 1987, Cisco had $350,000 in monthly sales but was facing a serious shortage of cash. They needed capital to support their growth and found an interested party at Sequoia Capital.

Cisco's founders and Sequoia agreed, according to partner Donald Valentine, that besides providing financing for Cisco "Sequoia would find and recruit management, and we would help create a management process. None of which existed in the company when we arrived." Valentine hired an experienced manager, John Morgridge, to run Cisco in 1989. Morgridge immediately installed a professional management team and formal management processes. With these assets and resources coming together he established a revenue goal of $100 million, more than a twenty-fold increase from their revenues of some $5 million in 1989.

By 1991 they reached $183 million and along the way paved the road for an IPO in 1990. Between 1995 and 2000, Cisco's revenue grew an average of 53 percent annually, an unheard-of rate for a multibillion-dollar company. Cisco had reached a $100 billion market capitalization value in 1998. In March 2000, Cisco became the most valuable company in America, with $531 billion in market capitalization, briefly eclipsing Microsoft as the world's most valuable company. In 2002, with 36,000 employees and nearly $19 billion in sales, Cisco's networking solutions were the foundation of the Internet and most corporate, education, and government networks around the world.

SOURCES: Cisco Systems company Web site; Scott Thurm, "After the Boom, Cisco Is Learning to Go Slow," *Wall Street Journal Online*, May 7, 2003; Stephen Segaller, *Nerds 2.0.1: A Brief History of the Internet* (New York: TV Books, 1999), p. 242; John K. Waters, *John Chambers and the Cisco Way* (New York: John Wiley & Sons, 2002), pp. 71–88; Robert Slater, *The Eye of the Storm: How John Chambers Steered Cisco Through the Technology Collapse* (New York: HarperBusiness, 2003); and Amar V. Bhide, *The Origin and Evolution of New Businesses* (New York: Oxford University Press, 2000), p. 163.

How Fast Is Really Fast?

One thing for certain, successful high growth-potential ventures do not stay small very long. When they do launch they can be as exciting as a rocket racing to the sky. Siebel Systems tops the list of the fastest-growing technology companies in the United States. In 1999 they recorded a five-year revenue growth rate of 782,978 percent! Founded in 1993 with $50,000, they had $391 million in revenues in 1998, and by 2003 had nearly $2 billion in revenues, with 8,000 employees working out of 136 offices in twenty-four countries.

Each year since 1982, *Inc.* magazine has recognized 500 of America's fastest-growing private ventures. The 500 ventures on the 2002 list had $12.3 billion in sales and employed just over 80,000.[1] The averages per each company were: five-year growth, 1,521 percent; sales, $25 million; age, 8 years old; number of employees, 160. The average revenues per employee were $154,375. From the top ten we prepared the following averages: five-year growth nearly 9,000 percent; sales, $56 million; age, 7 years old; employees, 240. And the revenues per employee were a phenomenal $2,321,408. In fact, these top-ten ventures accounted for just over $500 million in revenues. Five years prior, each one had about ten employees and $695,000 in top line sales. This means they had about $70,000 per employee in the early stage. So on the average, sales per employee grew some 3,216 percent during the five years prior. And employee growth meant that, on the average, each venture had to be hiring a new employee per week for five years straight!

Defining Growth Expansion Strategies

With respect to growing, Bhide tells us that there are two basic types of business ventures. One is the "precocial" venture, which, like a horse, is relatively mature and can walk the day of its birth. These ventures are capable of moving on their own when launched. The "altricial" venture is born helpless, naked, and blind. These ventures take years to build the assets and proceed sometimes through management of "trial and error" rather than through the execution of a growth strategy. A growth strategy is about investing in a broad base of assets, developing professional management know-how and mechanisms to coordinate these assets, and having a formal plan in place to overcome growth constraints.

Instead of relying on opportunistic adaptation to exploit niche opportunities by chance, successful entrepreneurs have to formulate and implement ambitious long-term strategies. According to the *2002 Inc. 500* winners, 71 percent said that they actively and systematically search out new markets for existing products or services, 45 percent actively and systematically search out new products or services, 38 percent concentrate on selling "more of the same" to existing customers, and 12 percent seek growth through an acquisition or merger (see Figure 10-1). The growth-through-acquisition strategy,

FIGURE 10-1. SUCCESSFUL GROWTH STRATEGIES.

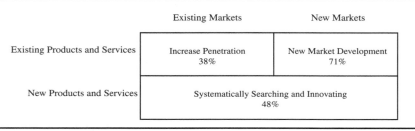

Source: *Inc. 500 Special Issue, October 2002.*

like Cisco's "cookie-cutter" approach, involves numerous risks, including difficulties in integrating the operations, technologies and products of the acquired companies; increasing capital expenditures to upgrade and maintain combined businesses; increasing debt to finance any acquisition; diverting management's attention from normal daily operations; managing larger operations and facilities and employees in separate geographic locations; and hiring and retaining key employees. Global expansion, which is creating and developing opportunities through multinational business activities, is perhaps the most difficult expansion strategy and beyond the scope of this book.

Getting Your Framework for Growth in Place Today

Growth is a strategic issue; it is willed, not wished. For example, 59 percent of the *2002 Inc. 500* CEOs said their industry had been growing slowly or not at all in the past five years. Coming from a unique group of CEOs, where the average five-year growth rate was 1,521 percent, prompts this question: "How did they do it?" We also looked at data from the *Inc. 500* class of 1985, whose average annual percentage of growth from 1984 to 1994 was 23 percent, or 3.8 times the rate of growth for the U.S. GDP of the same period.[2] Our conclusion is that they strategically planned for growth to occur. Recall BEA Systems, which claims the distinction of being the fastest software company to reach $1 billion in revenue. According to co-founder Bill Coleman, "It's not magic. It is all about an addressable opportunity, great people, focus, and execution."[3]

Douglass North, a Nobel Laureate in economics, said, "Organizations evolve in a way that is no more predictable than the evolution of science and technology." Even with this in mind, we can find some lessons to share from the launch and transition of Netscape. Netscape generated $80 million in sales in its first full year, and in three years reached $500 million. For comparison, Microsoft took almost fourteen years to reach comparable revenues. The five key lessons from Netscape's meteoric growth are:

1. Create a compelling vision of your complete product.
2. Hire and acquire managerial experience in addition to technical expertise.
3. Always consider how you can gather and allocate your critical capital resources for building a big venture while organizing like a small one.
4. Manage through continuous decentralization, which means breaking the organizational structure into smaller, flexible, and creative groups.
5. Continuously build external relationships to compensate for limited resources controlled internally.

Now is the time to map out a growth plan for the upside. Take time to go off-site with your venture team to discuss. Prepare a growth strategy. The key to successful growth is establishing clear goals and objectives that are matched with organizational skills, but at the same time, always being prepared to adapt to changes and opportunities in the markets and overall business environments.

Transitioning: Entrepreneurial Management to Professional Management

When an organization is born, the emphasis is on creating a product and surviving in the ecosystem. Certain features characterize an entrepreneurial management style and structure. The founders devote their full energies to the technical activities of producing the first product and later marketing it. The work hours are long, and work procedures are typically informal. At this stage there is little need for formal procedures, systems, and structures because the venture is small enough that activity can be monitored through the daily, personal interaction of the entrepreneur, the venture team, consultants, and hired employees. More importantly, because the venture is young and inexperienced, it has not yet learned the patterns and routines that are required for rapid growth. Since there is little specialization or formalization, coordination, command, and control are from the top. This centralized decision making is where one or a very few number of individuals are responsible for making all the major decisions, and generally, one person can comprehend all the information required for decision making.

In the mid-1950s, in response to Remington Rand and UNIVAC's leadership of the early days of the computing age, Thomas J. Watson, who was then IBM's patriarch, was forced to make a decision on restructuring the company. Thomas J. Watson, Jr., recalls the situation his father faced, "If we had organization charts, there would have been a fascinating number of lines—perhaps thirty—running into T. J. Watson."[4] In late 1956, after months of planning, they called the top one hundred or so people in the company to a three-day meeting in Williamsburg, Virginia. They came away from that meeting decentralized.

Who has the key to the Coke machine in your venture? We tell entrepreneurs that Michael Dell had two Eureka moments, the first was creating the "direct-from-Dell" business model. The second was learning about delegating business responsibilities. In the early days of Dell Computer, while working on a complicated business issue, he was interrupted by an employee complaining that he lost a quarter in the Coke machine. Dell wanted to know why the guy was complaining to him. The employee responded, "Because you've got the key to the Coke machine!"[5]

Professional Management Structure

According to Bhide, "To assume that all firms are equally endowed with enterprising management seriously misrepresents the realities of growing businesses."[6] Co-founders Pierre Omidyar and Jeff Skoll of eBay realized they needed help when they started seeing a 70 percent compound monthly growth rate. In his book, *The Perfect Store: Inside eBay*, Adam Cohen captured Omidyar's comments, "We were entrepreneurs and that was good up to a certain stage. But we didn't have the experience to take the company to the next level."[7]

Professional management structure creates an environment where people set goals, and put into place formal activities that make things happen on time, over and over again. It is where issues of accountability and responsibility for delivering results become very key. Three key features characterize professional management. First, there is the delegation of decision-making responsibility. Like we saw with Dell and the Coke machine, the entrepreneur and the venture team cannot make all of the decisions required to manage a fast-growing firm. The team must begin by delegating responsibility to middle managers, and later to front-line employees. Like we saw with IBM, how the venture team and board members determine how this gets done will eventually determine the venture's organizational restructuring.

The second feature is the introduction and use of formal controls and systems to manage the venture. These systems include mechanisms for setting goals and objectives, performance metrics, and methods for monitoring performance against clearly established measures. The third key feature is repeatability. To accomplish this, many hired managers develop policies and standard procedures that are used to guide and manage the actions of the employees that will be hired later on.

Making the Transition to Professional Management

We have found that the most distinctive factor in the transition is the change in the decision-making process, moving from *intuitive decision making* to *organizational decision making*. In her *Inc.* article, "Founding CEOs vs. Second CEOs," Carole Matthews writes that typically the founding CEO has "fingers in every part of the business—a desire for total control," while the Second CEO has a "desire to establish a management team" and a "track record of building a company from initial funding stages." The formalization and transition to professional management style and structure involves the installation of rules, procedures, and formal control systems. The top management has to delegate responsibilities, and communication becomes more formal and less frequent. During this period, goals are shifted from survival to maintaining internal stability and creating growth expansion strategies.

Like we saw with eBay, after a certain point the founders cannot do everything and will have to start hiring professionals. One person can be stretched to lead an emerging growth venture that has revenues of $10 to $25 million per year, and up to fifty employees. After that point, the venture will need to find the right executives or the business will die. There are five formal steps that are required for a successful transition to professional management.

❖   **The first step is simply recognizing the need for change.** This is often extremely difficult because it is a by-product of success, which means that the venture may be growing and the growth rate may be accelerating into escape velocity, but with little or no chance of survival. What happens is that success reinforces beliefs and behavior that may be appropriate for the start-up stage of the venture but that may not fit the needs of a fully scalable, larger, more complex venture.

❖   **The second step is formally developing the human resources.** This means hiring "A" people to hire more "A" people and not starting the death spiral we discussed in Chapter 6.

❖   **The third step is delegating responsibilities.** Entrepreneurs should not wait until someone comes pounding on their door for the key to the Coke machine, nor wait until competitors threaten to smother the flames that are powering rapid growth.

❖   **The fourth step is developing formal controls and a control system that shifts to performance rather than behavior.**

❖   **The fifth step is stepping aside once the ball is put into play.** This re-quires a fundamental change in the attitudes and behaviors of the founders and the venture team. Michael Roberts, executive director of entrepreneurial studies at Harvard Business School, knows why the transition to professional management is often so difficult. It requires far more than changes in organizational systems and structures. He says, "It requires a fundamental change in the attitudes and behaviors of the entrepreneur."[9] Merely creating organizational structures and systems accomplishes little if the entrepreneur is unwilling to step aside, truly delegate, and finally hand over the key to the Coke machine.

Building Organizational Change Capabilities

It takes little time to destroy a high growth-potential venture. One turn-around expert says, "Ninety-five percent of the failures are due to internal problems. I can't tell you how many companies I've been to that have the fast-growing-company plaque on the wall and are about to go under. They don't have the systems and the people in place. Accounting is lagging. Purchasing is not done in the most efficient manner. Inventory gets out of control. All of a sudden, all these mistakes compound, and the least little burp kills them."[10] Michael Dell discovered this, "As success followed on success, it was hard to imagine that growth would at some point become our greatest vulnerability. We didn't understand that with every new growth opportunity came a commensurate level of risk—a lesson we learned the hard way."[11]

Entrepreneurs make one of three approaches to the launching pad. The first we classify as *unconscious incompetence*. These entrepreneurs do not know what they do not know. Because they lack the skills and resources, they proceed on guesses and "friendly advice." Most often they self-detonate on the launch pad.

The second approach is *conscious incompetence*. These entrepreneurs know that they do not have the best-engineered rockets, but have great confidence in their guidance system. Once poor choices in early-stage decision making begin to come to light, they are confident that they can make in-flight adjustments.

The third approach is one of *conscious competence*—having an internally prepared culture. These entrepreneurs know the risks and uncertainty of rocket launches. They know that everything comes down to people. They know that the only way to be successful, particularly in a rapidly growing and rapidly changing market, is to hire the "A" people and point them in the right direction.

Flexible Organizational Structure

Transitioning the operational model on a fast-growth venture is like changing the tires on a racecar going 100 miles per hour. Kathleen M. Eisenhardt, professor of strategy at Stanford University, advises entrepreneurs that they should stay flexible. She says speed comes to those organizations that are formed as loosely as possible without coming apart.

One year after Hewlett-Packard was formed in 1947 it had 111 employees and sales of $679,000. Over the next ten years revenues grew to 1,778 employees and $30 million in sales. By the time co-founder David Packard retired from HP in 1993, it had 96,200 employees and $20.3 billion in sales. In his book *The HP Way: How Bill Hewlett and I Built Our Company*, Packard made some interesting points related to fast-growth organizations. First, in rapidly growing ventures organizational changes occur quite frequently. Second, organizational structure, once created, should be flexible and responsive to the developing needs of the organization and changes in the marketplace. And third, HP's organizational structure was based on "creating an environment that fostered individual motivation, initiative, and creativity, and that gave a wide latitude of freedom in working toward common goals and objectives."[12]

Build from Day One for CEO Succession

Very rarely does the original founder who had the Eureka moment make it all the way through to the point of maturity. According to Scott Gordon, a managing director for Spencer Stuart, an executive search firm that places CEOs who displace founders, "Many of the qualities that you need to be an entrepreneur—passion, charisma, self-confidence—can make it hard to subordinate yourself to the CEO of your own company. Many companies have been destroyed because the founder pays lip service to being just a member of the team but never gives up the reins."[13]

Omidyar at eBay had planned for his succession: "It was in our heads from the start to try and bring in a world-class CEO to grow this thing as big as it could possibly get."[14] Meg Whitman, who joined eBay in 1998 after leaving Hasbro Toys, is arguably the best CEO ever recruited to an early stage venture. During her tenure at eBay revenues grew from $47 million in 1998 to $749 million in 2001, and the number of employees grew from fifty to over 3,000. When the online community only had some 300,000 users, she brought in disciplined management. She worked as a seasoned general manager whose mission was to ensure that an emerging venture with promising technology could "master all the classic challenges of strategy, marketing, and finance that are necessary to succeed at a higher level."[15]

By 2001 eBay was number one on Deloitte & Touche's Fast 500. In the five years prior, they had grown 115,874 percent, from $372,000 in sales in 1996 to $431 million. Founders who made millions from exiting their ventures in a transition have told us it was a matter of weighing self-worth against net worth. Omidyar would probably agree. Recall from Chapter 1 that he was on *Fortune*'s list of "Richest Under 40" for 2002, with a net worth of $3.82 billion.

Hitting the Growth Wall

According to Michael Porter, "The desire to grow has perhaps the most perverse effect on strategy."[16] Factors that drive initial successes are seldom enough to sustain a venture as it begins to accelerate through the growth stage. The external demands and opportunities change constantly, the venture's value chain and internal capabilities must adapt, and the venture's growth and evolution will ultimately necessitate a shift to professional management. Simply put by Jack Stack in his book *The Great Game of Business*, "The more successful you are, the bigger the challenges you have to deal with."

When faced all at once, these challenges will suddenly appear as an impenetrable wall. Thus "hitting the growth wall" is a phase in a venture's life cycle where operations reach out-of-control proportions: Cash runs out, top line revenues flatten out, and key employees leave for more stable jobs. The only way to avoid the growth wall is by being prepared to lead and manage growth with effective strategies grounded in sound management skills and controls.

What Is the Source of the Stall?

Why is growth so hard? Why do so many ventures fail to escape their initial entrepreneurial stage? Reasons include inadequate growth capital, exceeding the entrepreneur's personal span of control, the lack of developing bureaucratic practices, and the loss of entrepreneurial spirit. Ventures also develop poor management practices that can stall successful long-term growth. Some of the popular ones are profiled in Figure 10-2.

FIGURE 10-2. What management practices stall emerging growth ventures?

▲ **Treadmill Mentality.** A poor management practice where the venture team is working harder than ever. Because they are not moving forward, they then believe that they to have work even harder.

▲ **Management by Insanity.** The venture team is doing things the same as they have always been done, but expecting different results.

▲ **Rear-View Mirror Management.** The team knows where it has been but has no firm idea where it is going.

▲ **Management by ESP.** A practice when the CEO says the business plan "is in my head" and the team is expected to be "mind-readers."

▲ **Midas-Touch Management.** The CEO and/or executive egos are in the way. With so much politics, the venture team is focused on keeping internal superiority. They lose touch with customers, competition, and what is actually going on in the environment.

Sometimes ventures just need a clean restart. Alan Patricoff learned this lesson from the Perfect Storm, "You don't have to build a $100 million company in a year. Some companies aren't meant to be built that fast. They get ahead of themselves."[17] And many ventures just do not have the right DNA to support growth. According to Amar Bhide, "My analysis suggests that most new businesses aren't just large businesses in miniature and that their trajectories do not point to noteworthy size and longevity."[18]

Breaking Through the Growth Wall

Only exceptional entrepreneurs have the capacity and the will to make changes that enable them to break through the growth wall. The passage from a fledgling venture to a large corporation requires entrepreneurs to develop new skills and to perform new roles. The basics include: creating a growth task force, planning and staffing for growth, working on maintaining a growth culture, learning from all mistakes, and using the advisory board and board of directors for insight and advice.

Innovation is the driver that breaks through the wall. Frederick Smith, founder of FedEx, believes that "the first step in trying to perpetuate innovation in an organization is to develop a common set of goals or a common philosophy so that everybody understands what you are trying to do. That way there should be a lot of mental concentration focused on just a few things."[19] For example, in its first year of release in 1996, Starbucks sold $52 million, or 7 percent of its total annual sales, of their Frappuccino drinks. *BusinessWeek* named it one of the best products of the year. Howard Schultz, founder and CEO of Starbucks, remarked, "If we had been a typical leaden corporation, Frappuccino would never have emerged as it did. Its story epitomizes the enterprising spirit we still have at Starbucks, an innovative edge that keeps our customers coming back and our competitors grousing."

Influential business thinkers like Katherine Catlin and Jana Matthews agree with the above. In their book *Building the Awesome Organization*, they discuss key characteristics that leaders must have in order to drive innovation throughout their organization, making extraordinary ventures out of ordinary ones. What they found is that leaders spend time thinking because they believe in the process. They are visionary and they listen to their customers understand how to manage ideas. They are people-centered and maintain a culture of change. They maximize team synergy, balance, and focus. They hold themselves and others accountable for extremely high standards of performance. They do not take no for an answer. And finally, they love what they do and have fun doing it.

Forge Tomorrow's Leaders Today

According to David Packard, "I have always felt that the most successful companies have a practice of promoting from within."[20] At Dell Computer they say that they "hire ahead of the game." As Michael Dell says, "It's not enough to hire to fill a job. It's not even enough to hire on the basis of one's talents. You have to hire based upon a candidate's potential to grow and develop."[21] But how do you focus and "unlock the organization's human asset potential" and grow your own leadership?

We found that it is important to develop a strong bench that works together very early on. For example, Tom Siebel created what he calls the "Founders' Circle," which includes some seventy key employees who are not necessarily founders. This designation is the highest honor at Siebel Systems. These carefully selected individuals "can drop everything and get the job done." By meeting on a regular basis to discuss corporate values and vision, they give Siebel Systems the benefit of an experienced management team that has been around for a while and knows how to get things done.

Managing in High-Growth Environments

When a venture reaches Stage Five on the entrepreneurial life cycle, Full Launch and Growth, the venture team needs to be sensitive to certain high-growth management issues. Usually, rapid growth is seen as a positive sign of success. However, uncharted rapid growth can quickly change the status of an emerging growth venture from profitable to bankruptcy. Uncharted growth causes the venture to stray from its goals and objectives and to take on too many ideas and opportunities. It can quickly dilute leadership effectiveness and result in weak management, poor planning, and poorly allocated resources. Quite often, delegation is avoided and control is maintained by only the founders, creating bottlenecks in management decision making. It also leads to communication barriers between individuals and all other stakeholders. New product programs are put on hold, and quality control is not maintained in the current products. Uncharted growth can also lead to stressed, overworked, and burned-out employees, with little attention given to training and employee recruitment.

How Will You Become a Recruiting Machine?

Recall from Chapter 3 that the average venture-backed company employs nearly 100 workers within five years. The U.S. Department of Labor reports that the national average of employee turnover is 21 percent. Added together, the cost of staffing a fast-growing venture can become quite toxic unless well planned. Recall that the top-ten winners on the *2002 Inc. 500* were hiring about one new employee per week for five years straight. Staffing.org, a non-profit organization focused on staffing metrics and measurements, found in 2002 that the cost per hire for firms with less than 100 employees was $7,122.[22] This means that these fastest-growing *Inc. 500* ventures spent on the average $1.8 million on just recruitment costs through their growth stage.

To get started recruiting, first embrace a "talent mindset" and craft a "winning employee value proposition." One of the CEO's chief tasks is recruiting new talent, picking the right people for particular positions, grooming young stars, developing global managers, dealing with underperformers, and reviewing the entire talent pool. We have found that your first five to ten hires will come through your insider contacts: your board members and your professional service providers. Also keep your eyes and ears open for potential candidates among your vendors, buyers, and even competitors. Finally, you must really believe in what you are doing. As Michael Dell says, "If you've got an idea that is really powerful, you've just got to ignore the people who tell you it won't work, and hire people who embrace your vision."[23]

Sharing the Rewards with Those Who Produce

Frederick Herzberg, who studied employee motivation, contends that key motivators are recognition, achievement, the work itself, responsibility, advancement, and the chance to learn something new and exciting. But the key question is how to reward people financially.

One of the simplest practices we have come across for ventures with less than a dozen or so employees is to set aside a percentage of gross sales to be paid out to employees. Because this means that each worker's piece of the reward-pie would shrink with every new hire down the road, this becomes a built-in incentive for current employees to help each other become more productive. Siebel Systems focuses on maintaining high levels of satisfaction among customers. Tom Siebel found that "all our compensation is tied to those customer satisfaction scores. It's the best way to go, because it ensures that we have a customer-based environment."[24]

Previous research has demonstrated that equity compensation is the most important incentive for venture growth and profitability.[25] As Tim Draper from Draper Fisher Jurvetson says, "With the equity-based model, everyone pulls their own weight." Stock options provide employees the right to purchase a given number of shares of company stock at the "strike price" between the vesting date and the expiration date of the options. T. J. Rogers, president and CEO of Cypress Semiconductors, says that "broad employee stock ownership is the genius behind Silicon Valley's economic miracle." He adds that "stock options promote long-term thinking, astonishing innovation, progress, and broad wealth creation."[26] Bill Gates shared his wealth through stock options like no one else before. At the end of 1998, he had created more than 20,000 millionaires at Microsoft, from code-crunchers to secretaries.

Managing in Economic Downturns

We found a common approach to holding your own in economic downturns. First, focus on doing one thing well. If you do one thing better than your competitors, in a downturn your customers will dump everyone else first. Keep innovating, especially with R&D investments and new product projects, as innovation makes extraordinary ventures out of ordinary ones. Watch your wallet, especially with inventory or accounts receivables, and be more conscious of what you are buying. In slow times make protecting cash flow everyone's responsibility. Seek out and develop advantaged relationships with companies or organizations like the U.S. government, where spending is based on long-term planning and will continue during economic slowdowns. Finally, have reasonable expectations. Be slower to expand and have backup strategies. The bottom line is that you will have to be well prepared to scramble and work multiple alternatives to quickly pursue opportunities as they arise when the economy rebounds.

Creating and Managing the Networked Enterprise

The notion of community has been at the heart of the Internet since its inception.
—**Arthur Armstrong and John Hagel**

It's all about using your community to support your brand in 360 degrees, multiple channels; everywhere you intercept the user, the stakeholders, and the constituents.
—**Denise Benou Stires, executive vice president, global marketing, The NASDAQ Stock Market, Inc.[1]**

Treat people you do business with as if they were a part of your family.
—**Konoske Matsushita, founder of Matsushita Electronics Company (makers of Panasonic, Techniques, and Quasar brands)**

Construct of Today's Networked Enterprise

In a *Journal of Marketing* article entitled "Marketing in the Network Economy," Ravi Achrol and Philip Kotler introduced the concepts of a networked organization.[2] They define a networked enterprise as an interdependent coalition of task- or skill-specialized business entities (independent ventures or autonomous organizational units) that operates without hierarchical control but is embedded by dense lateral connections. It has shared objectives or purposes that interact and build relationships with each other in an online environment across time and space. They are created to reduce hierarchy and open ventures to their ecosystems. They are organized around customer needs and new market opportunities. They maximize the productivity by creating partnerships among independent skill-specialized firms and often seek horizontal synergies across industries to meet new partners and access resources.

As a result, an online "community" of people becomes unified around a common purpose, place, or interest. This community can make decisions, nurture inspiration, solve problems, and learn and innovate faster. The more participation that occurs in the network to identify and respond to customer needs, the greater the value that is created for the members as a whole. The fact is that you worked so hard to bootstrap up the Hillary Step, get market

❖ Case in Point: eBay and Its Digital Biosphere

Created in September 1995 by Pierre Omidyar, eBay is "The World's Online Marketplace" for the sale of goods and services by a diverse community of individuals and businesses. Eight years later the eBay "biosphere" includes some 62 million registered members from around the world. It is the most popular shopping destination on the Internet. On any given day, there are more than 12 million items listed on eBay across 18,000 categories. In 2002, eBay community members conducted $14.9 billion in gross merchandise sales. The San Jose, California company, which employs more than 4,000, has long enjoyed one of the Internet's most profitable and efficient businesses, with revenues in 2002 passing $1.2 billion and sales growing at 62 percent year over year.

Through discussion and chat boards, community members meet and get to know each other, discuss topics of mutual interest, and provide one another with helpful information on trading on eBay. These discussion boards are public forums that encourage open communication between members. Such community involvement and development became clear to Omidyar in eBay's earliest days, when he was working on the feedback forums and discovered that sellers and buyers used it for praise as well as airing out complaints.

"As it turned out," he said, "I learned that it became more about creating standards for a way a community operated." Meg Whitman, eBay's CEO, agreed: "You can put up a new feature, and within twenty minutes you will have a very good sense of what the adoption rate is going to be. And within an hour, we'll have 4,000 responses." As Adam Cohen writes in *The Perfect Store: Inside eBay,* "The implications of the eBay model are revolutionary."

Sources: eBay company Web site; Mark W. Vigoroso, "What Makes a Great E-Biz CEO?," *E-Commerce Times Online,* February 26, 2002; Kara Swisher, "eBay Founder Puts Profits to Use to Help 'Rediscover Community'," *Wall Street Journal Online,* October 29, 2001; Martin J. Garvey, "The Brawn Behind eBay's Always-On Auctions," *Information Week,* December 10, 2001, pp. 84–86; Penelope Patsuris, "The eBay Economy," *Forbes Online,* April 16, 2003; and Stephen S. Cohen, J. Bradford De Long, and John Zysman, "The Next Industrial Revolution?" *The Milken Institute Review* (first quarter 2000), p. 10.

traction, and get on the road to growth, so it is important to focus on keeping your customers.

Creating Your "Womb-to-Tomb Strategy"

Marketing expert Regis McKenna tells us that traditional marketing is disappearing into the information and communication technology (ICT) world: computers, software and communication networks. In *Total Access: Giving Customers What They Want in an Anytime, Anywhere World,* he frames a discussion of what marketing is quickly becoming by stating that ICT will do most of the marketing activities, such as data gathering, decision making, customer response and care, and much more. We advise that you should have woven throughout your venture, from front-office to back-office, a digital "womb-to-tomb" strategy for community management and community ownership. This closed-loop integration will give you the management tools to get your finger on the pulse of your venture for the entire cash-to-cash cycle. You need to be monitoring from when you first invest in a new product or service, to when you get your first inquiries from customers. This continues through when each salesperson engages a customer in the sale titration process, to finally when you deposit the customer's check in your bank account.

There are three levels of relationships each venture must maintain. The first is *customer specific,* of which eBay is an excellent example. The second is *enterprise specific,* which is structured around the roles that are found inside your organization. For example, Hewlett-Packard has one of the world's richest intranets, featuring more than 100 news groups and many "knowledge bank" databases, which makes possible the global collaboration between their engineers.

The third level is *strategic partner specific,* which focuses on vendors and other stakeholders outside the organization. One of the best examples is Dell Computer. As a value advisor providing information and services, and in helping customers make the best decisions about computing technology, Dell gets real-time daily input from thousands of customers. This input regarding their products, service, and views on new product ideas gives Dell a sustainable competitive advantage in tailoring its product offerings. Also, this strong womb-to-womb connection from Dell's customers to suppliers like Microsoft and Intel creates a formidable barrier to entry.

Creating a Collaborative Advantage

Created within each of these three relationships should be a system of constant interface to a value-added environment for information exchange. Rosabeth Moss Kanter, a business leadership series professor at Harvard Business School, describes this interface as a "collaborative advantage."[3] A collaborative advantage helps ventures gain strength to compete through real-time integration and relationships, providing information to all stakeholders in complex value chains. For example, software companies, for whom ties with independent developers, venture partners, and customers are a critical asset, actually dedicate senior executives and large departments solely to the management of alliances and partnerships. Recall that one-third of IBM's revenue is generated through such collaborative partner relationships.

Kanter notes that such collaboration throughout today's "extended enterprise" requires interpersonal as well as organizational sensitivity. Skills in listening, self-awareness, and ability to read others, along with a "dose of humility," are vital. Success comes from sharing information with partners, networking among all the stakeholders at multiple organizational levels, and keeping everybody's interest in mind when crafting new business strategies. Michael Harris is a senior vice president, products and strategy at FileNet Corporation based in Costa Mesa, California. He believes that true "collaborative commerce" is based on an established strategy that combines content management and process management, and which integrates technologies to automate and streamline business processes among all four relationships: internal staff, external partners, suppliers, and customers.[4]

Benefits of a Networked Enterprise

It is important that your networked components of business become an extension of your business model and business practices rather than just some adjunct service to a complex revenue event or a small element of your value chain. The most important benefit is getting your loyal customers to perform tasks of rebuying and modified rebuying. Recurring revenues substantially increase profit margins only to those ventures that are ready to accommodate such business activities. Too many entrepreneurs get stuck chasing too many markets pursuing new customers. And with each new market come new uncontrollable variables, learning curves, and deployment of critical capital resources. The objective is to become more and more efficient in delivering the complete solution for the right customers when they need it. Tom Siebel helps to support our thinking when he writes that "loyal customers have always been important to an organization's long-term success. . . . A 5 percent increase in customer retention can increase an organization's profitability by 25 to 100 percent."[5] Indeed, these are pretty healthy numbers, which a start-up—or any business organization for that matter—needs to hear.

There is an interesting study conducted by the Kauffman Center for Entrepreneurial Leadership that provides more support for recurring revenues.[6] They analyzed 1,100 entrepreneurial businesses across nine different industries in seventeen countries. All were recipients of Ernst & Young's prestigious Entrepreneur of the Year (EOY) awards program. The study, which provides insight for achieving and sustaining higher than normal growth and profitability, concluded that entrepreneurs who focused on profitability obtained as much as 67 percent of their sales by selling existing products to existing customers.

Other Benefits

We now have to accept that the value of a venture is no longer multiples of the top line revenue, but the combined value of the venture's customers. In fact, we found that the best customer care of the industry becomes the standard by which all others are measured. Besides recurring revenues, there are other ways a networked organization can increase a venture's bottom line.

Improved Customer Service

Being networked means you are able to offer outstanding service to all your customers, allowing them to easily interact with your venture $24 \times 7 \times 365$. Using Web-based self-service applications, customers can receive personalized products and services each time they visit. When all of your systems are integrated, your organization will always be equipped with accurate, timely information necessary to quickly respond to customer needs and queries. This includes product demonstration, simulations, automated order acceptance, new product training, and e-learning.

Increased Customer Satisfaction

By offering improved customer service, you increase customer satisfaction. You will know who your customers are, what they want, and how to respond to and even anticipate their needs. And, with a completely integrated venture, you will deliver your products and services faster and cheaper than ever before. By offering improved customer service, you increase customer satisfaction. You will know who your customers are, what they want, and how to respond to and even anticipate their needs. As a completely integrated venture, you will deliver your products and services faster and cheaper than ever before. And satisfied customers will share their satisfaction to other potential customers, thus facilitating the catalysis sales approach we discuss in Chapter 9.

Lower Operating Costs

As a networked enterprise not only are you more efficient, but you realize unprecedented savings as well. Taking full advantage of ICT (i.e., facilitating self-service for your customers, employees, and business partners over the Internet) you will significantly cut costs in every area of your business, including procurement costs, selling costs, reduction in inventories, financial management, human resources, and data processing.

Better Quality Products and Services

Being networked means that you not only lower operating costs, but actually improve the quality of your products and services. With improved customer intelligence you know what your lead users and best customers want. You have access to suppliers around the world that bid for your business, which allows you to pick and choose based on quality, price, and date of delivery. And because your value chain is completely integrated (customers to suppliers and suppliers to customers), your quality of service also improves. You deliver exactly what is needed, when it is needed. You can work online with your suppliers to facilitate supplier-managed inventory, providing products and services faster and cheaper than ever before and even help manage recalls.

Greater Business Efficiency

Your entire networked enterprise becomes more efficient. Your systems are integrated, processes streamlined, and everyone is sharing the same accurate, timely information. You can realize greater business efficiency when you integrate all of your systems to create one comprehensive, connected value chain.

You can shorten buying times or accelerate the revenue events, have suppliers deliver parts and inventory on a just-in-time basis. And you can streamline your administrative processes using self-service applications, which is helpful in managing your outsourcing business partners.

Better Business Intelligence

When your supply chain, operations, and customer-facing systems are integrated, it gives you a new, extended enterprise supported by suites of integrated, Internet-enabled applications. With this digital "executive dashboard" you can employ the information generated by these systems in real time, which will help you run your operations and more effectively capture and retain customers. You are now able to deliver insight throughout the organization, supply logistical information in real time to all stakeholders, discover opportunities quickly, better understand business risks, and better align operations with corporate objectives.

Increased Market Coverage

With your Web site on the Internet, you instantly have a global audience. No matter where your headquarters is located, your venture is now accessible to the entire world. Your Web site will enable you to sell more effectively to large marquee companies, to make limited explorations into other markets, and to support global business initiatives.

Fewer Administrative Errors

As part of a networked enterprise, your employees, customers, and suppliers can all perform transactions themselves using Web-based self-service applications. No more data entry clerks. No more lost paperwork. Transactions are now processed quicker, cheaper, and much more accurately. This self-service eliminates intermediaries and delays, significantly reduces administrative errors, accelerates billing and accounting procedures, lowers stakeholder communication costs, and helps deliver critical documents to professional service providers, such as your law firm.

Increased Competitiveness

You will be able to operate in a global economy, giving your customers what they want when they want it. Staying ahead of the curve means you are providing personalized products and services at the lowest possible price. You are accessible $24 \times 7 \times 365$. You have a 360-degree view of your venture and a comprehensive view of your customers and your space. You have suppliers bidding for your business. You will have the business intelligence to make accurate, timely decisions and the ability to monitor its impact across the enterprise. Your employees are focused on relationship building, improving service, and benefiting the venture. You are more competitive than ever before by improving the relationships with suppliers and partners, promoting the image of your venture and can even speed joint product development programs.

Managing Customer-Specific Relationships

Customer relationship management (CRM) combines a strategic business approach with technology. Managing customer relationships begins with a strategic awareness based on customer-focused themes. They are: matching the right problem with the right solution, developing and test marketing the solution, producing and providing it in a timely manner, implementing a full-scale marketing and sales effort, getting customer lock-on, and maintaining customer ownership. As we have discussed above, managing customer relationships through a networked enterprise helps you respond quicker to customer inquiries, increase efficiency through automation, gain a deeper knowledge of your customers, improve customer loyalty, and increase revenues through marketing or cross-selling opportunities.

It all starts with one simple premise: "How can you make it easier for your customer to do more business with you?" Maintaining the lifetime value of customers means creating a long-term servicing franchise. Customer satisfaction leads to customer retention, which leads to recurring revenues. For example, Charles Schwab, the world's largest discount brokerage service founded nearly thirty years ago, has over 8 million customers and maintains an 88 percent retention rate. So if Charles Schwab did nothing else, if they got no new customers, they would still have a profitable business, thirty years from now, servicing the 7 million customers they currently have locked-on.

Getting Customer "Lock-On"

On the average, U.S. corporations lose half their customers in five years, half their employees in four years, and half their investors in less than one year. But getting customers as part of an "installed base" means you have to have a group of customers who want your products as their dominant, or sole, choice on an on-going basis. They should have a good and sufficient reason—you solved a major problem for them before and they are sticking with you. Likewise, this lock-on becomes a significant barrier to entry for competitors.

As Philip Kotler and many other marketing experts point out, the economics of customer lock-on and ownership are quite simple: It lowers the cost of customer acquisition, and the marginal cost of transaction, the longer and stronger the customer relationship becomes. For example, the cost of marketing, advertising, and customer support for loyal customers is as much as 25 to 30 percent less in overhead than for first-time customers. Loyal customers are better than your sales force at converting prospects into clients, because they are trusted to be objective and because prospects identify with them. Loyal customers provide excellent feedback. They are the first ones to spot a negative trend in your products, sales, or service and they are an excellent source of advice on how to run and how to improve your venture.

Customer Relationship Management

CRM is about managing the customer's activity cycle, from customer acquisition and retention, to sales and servicing. Siebel is known as a leader in CRM applications. Just look at how their Web site describes their business: "The Company designs, develops, markets, and supports Siebel eBusiness Applications, a leading Web-based application software product family designed to meet the sales, marketing, and customer service information system requirements of even the largest multinational organizations."

Peter Weedfald, vice president of strategic marketing and new media for Samsung Electronics America, Inc., oversees 4,000 dealers and channel partners in North America. He says that "CRM stands for customers really matter." Weedfald also provides us with some CRM secrets: First, remember that every contact point is valuable, and this includes phone calls, service people, follow-up mailings, Web site, products and packaging, partners, and e-mail marketing. Second, realize that marketing and sales are deeply integrated. A salesperson's goal is to close the sales cycle and get to a revenue event. Likewise with marketing, an ad or press release can work on closing too. Third, experience your own CRM by calling your toll-free numbers, buying your own products, receiving your own newsletters, and getting on your mailing lists. Fourth, use CRM as a form of research, collecting intelligence from competitors' CRM programs. And the fifth secret is to know that CRM is choice not chance. Your customers will have access to more information than ever on products and services to help them make decisions that will lead them to your venture, so do not leave it up to chance.[7]

Facilitating Rebuying

When a sale is complete, a customer is left with not just a tangible product but also with feelings like elation, surprise, delight, satisfaction, frustration, confusion, disappointment, anger, resentment, and so on. It is important to know how your customers feel. It is also important to keep working them toward one thing: *satisfaction to the point of referrals, renewals, and recurring revenues*. As mentioned above, very early in the buying process Dell Computer becomes a value advisor, going beyond selling products and solutions. Dell helps customers understand and stay ahead of the fast-changing technology curve, which facilitates the decision-making process. Dell begins the first contact points delivering expert advice "with no strings attached." This does much to demonstrate that Dell can be trustworthy not only with the advice regarding the current product, but as a point of reference for facilitating future technology purchases at Dell. In addition to providing advice on upgrades and new purchases, through their extended enterprise Dell monitors and tracks customer satisfaction, tames service problems, handles complaints and suggestions, surveys customers, and conducts online focus groups and new product surveys, always trolling for new product ideas.

New Product Development

Michael Dell found that managing customer relationships is a two-way street. He found that it is as important to listen to customers as it is to advise and counsel them. According to Dell, "If we had consulted our customers first about what *they* needed we could have saved ourselves a lot of time and aggravation. Involve your customers early in the developmental process. They are your most valuable focus group. Listen early and listen well."[8]

If you listen, you'll get early insight to what customers are interested in and, better yet, where they are going in terms of needs and solutions. Hence this integrating of information, customer intelligence, and collaboration with lead users that we first discussed in Chapter 4 becomes even more important for extending the venture's value into the future. Keeping your finger on the pulse of your best customers will become a requirement, as customer priorities will change so rapidly. So if you are not out there directing them, as Dell does, helping them discover what they need in the future, you are going to lose them to competitors through the gaps in your value chain.

This customer knowledge will help your venture predict what sorts of services and support offerings customers are likely to want or need, and to develop more effective strategies for meeting those needs before they are even articulated. Being networked can even prevent new product projects from getting launched. For example, Arrow Electronics, based in Melville, New York, has a suite of digital tools connected to a real-time database that customers can search for information about electronic components. The database tracks product life cycles, parts availability, multiple sources of information, breadth of customer usage, lead times, and component cross-referencing. As a result, the company's online network helps engineers avoid the problem of designing parts that become obsolete before the company gets to production.[9]

Managing Strategic Network Specific

In his book, *Direct from Dell*, Michael Dell advises companies to "keep your friends close, and your suppliers closer." But we know that in the old economy there were natural limits to the power a corporation could have. It was restricted to how many businesses, customers, or suppliers it could draw into its sphere of influence, because there were natural limits on how many could utilize the service at one time and how many could have access to the company's assets in the value chain, as was true of store fronts, drive-through windows, or manufacturing lines.

There were always tremendous costs and risks when a new business venture created its own distribution channels, logistical network, manufacturing plant, and R&D function for every key market. Strategic alliances are important hedges against uncertainty. For example, Siebel Systems creates software products and coordinates a huge team of more than 750 consulting companies, technology providers, implementers, suppliers, and vendors in its value web. When taking their product to the global marketplace they reduced their risk by creating strategic networks. Tom Siebel once said, "We only have 8,000 people on our payroll, but more than 30,000 people work for us. The models for business success today are hermetically sealed firms but dynamically evolving networks of cooperating players."[10]

In a *Thunderbird International Business Review* article, Hans Hinterhuber and Andreas Hirsch state that a strategic network is not "coordinated coordination" between Web-blogs, message boards, and online chat groups—but can only exist between formally structured for-profit, legal, business enterprises that promote long-term strategic cooperation.[11] Motives for and objectives to entering into such networks are quite clear. As mentioned above, the number-one reason is risk reduction. Such networks spread the risk of large projects between two or more companies and can facilitate faster entry into the marketplace, thus speeding return of cash flow on investment. These networks also create economies of scale, rationalization, and synergy. They reduce capital expenditures, reduce inventory in the value chain, and are particularly helpful to ventures transferring production and support activities to lower-cost locations around the world or supporting launches into new marketplaces around the world. Members of these networks can share technology, know-how, and information about marketplaces, like access to channels and changing customer preferences, which helps manage demand volatility. Finally, these networks as a whole can block competitors' moves and potential new entrants. The following are examples that help illustrate the benefits of strategic networks.

❖ **Michelin North America, Inc.** Based in Greenville, South Carolina, Michelin empowers their tire dealers and national fleet account customers with online information and services. They can use the site to look for inventory, order tires, check on orders, create and submit claims, check the status of an account, and obtain technical data. And Intel's CEO Craig Barrett pushes his company toward a 100 percent electronic corporation, where suppliers can access their account information online to see internal demand forecasts, engineering changes, and orders and invoices. Its factory systems automatically communicate demand, inventory, and receipt information to suppliers, without an Intel buyer's involvement. When Intel is developing new products, they work closely with suppliers, particularly those that build manufacturing equipment or provide direct materials such as silicon.

❖ **NASDAQ International.** They established a proprietary network exclusively for NASDAQ-listed companies. It is continually updated and contains comprehensive market information to help companies manage relationships with analysts, market makers, and institutions. It also provides access to up-to-the-minute market commentary. Its community members can use NASDAQ online to see how their stock is trading, follow their competitors, and track the market's activity at any given moment. NASDAQ online also provides key information on institutional ownership, research coverage, performance ratios, and more.

❖ **The Cisco Collaboration Center of Excellence (CCOE).** This network coordinates, delivers, and drives solutions across the company to enable virtual, Internet-based capabilities that increase productivity across geographical, cultural, and technical boundaries while reducing expenses. With only 30,000 employees, the network manages some 584,000 extranet relationships. The primary emphasis is on bundling new technologies that allow stakeholders to communicate and network into a "collaboration space." The intent is to leverage the skills and knowledge of people who work across a variety of social, geographic, industry, and cultural boundaries.

❖ **Ingram Micro.** Guy Abramo, chief strategy and information officer at Ingram Micro, based in Santa Ana, California, has been instrumental in transforming the $30 billion company from a technology distributor to a global Internet business and supply-chain management services firm.[12] His network accesses more than 1,800 vendors, including Microsoft, HP, Compaq, and Cisco. When combined, these vendors stock some 280,000 products; each day Ingram Micro ships more than 90,000 orders, and every year it processes over 60 million electronic transactions globally. Ingram Micro's strategic networks are segmented by customer needs and special interests. Their value-added resellers (VARs) segment contains retail stores like Best Buy and CompUSA. Their Partnership America network targets government and education, their VentureTech Network targets small and medium business ventures, and their National Service Network targets service professionals in 800 markets.

Developing and Managing Your Network

The development and management of an enterprise's IT infrastructure has long been a challenge for businesses of all sizes. IT systems and network management are critical functions because poorly performing and nonfunctioning systems can be very costly. IT management encompasses a wide range of critical-function tasks including the buying of applications and systems; the monitoring of network components, operating systems, and application performance; and the troubleshooting of the network, applications, and system outages.

Our discussion here is to help you begin mapping out your IT infrastructure and organization—for it should be scalable for rapid growth over the next twenty-four to forty-eight months. Then, as your venture does grow, it can better reap the benefits in terms of efficiencies, profit margins, and higher valuation. Although we started out discussing technology, our best advice is to put your customers first. Kevin Turner is the chief information officer (CIO) of Wal-Mart, a retail chain with annual sales of $245 billion, 4,700 stores, 30,000 suppliers, and nearly 1.4 million employees around the world. Wal-Mart has the largest database outside of the U.S. government. They can update their database of what is being purchased in every one of their locations every ninety minutes. But Turner responds, "We're merchants first, technologists second. Technology at this point is simply a means to an end. What is really strategic is the use of the information and how we exploit and maximize it."[13]

What Will It Take to Keep Your Customers?

Today, "staying in business means staying in touch." With increasingly sophisticated and easy-to-use analytical tools, early stage ventures have an array of options for obtaining customer information that can support data-driven business decisions. These technologies and internal processes must be in place for integrating customer relationship management, for maintaining a customer-centric focus throughout the venture, and for monitoring activity from the 360-degree view of the business relationships you are cultivating. Leonard Kleinrock, early pioneer of the Internet and chairman of Nomadix, based in Westlake Village, California, translates what all this means: "Just figure out how to stay ahead of your core users. You will keep your customers through continuous community creation."[14]

Basics of Creating Your First Network

Becoming a "customer-centric" organization is easier said than done. Although the scalable technologies are readily available, you first must lay out explicit objectives that are linked to your business model, to your strategy, and of course to your limited resources. Then you must develop an implementation plan, and be prepared to actively monitor and measure the performance—all in real time, adjusting as you grow. Because once in the fog of war, it will be very difficult to sit down and try to implement the technologies, let alone think strategically about these issues. Besides, it will be too difficult for most ventures to circle back, and to collect, manage, maintain, and analyze all the information, on top of soliciting for new business from the customers.

For three years running, Kenosha, Wisconsin-based Snap-On Tools, Inc., with $2.2 billion in revenues, has placed first among manufacturers in the *InformationWeek 500* survey, which ranks U.S. companies according to their levels of technological, procedural, and organizational innovation. They placed ahead of Cisco Systems (#37), Intel (#53), and General Electric (#68). How did an old-world-economy automotive tool maker far away from Silicon Valley succeed in implementing a network strategy, when so many of the most aggressive and sophisticated companies have had such a hard time? The answer lies with Snap-On's decision to take a practical, ground-up approach. They first identified what they wanted to get out of their network and devised a development strategy that drew on the company's resources. Alan

Bilan, Snap-On's CIO, said, "You don't start with an implementation; you start with a strategy, and from strategy comes structure and then tactics."[15]

Bilan first established a special thirty-member team, which began by listing all the different stakeholders, including customers, dealers, distributors, employees, investors, suppliers, and others, that might be interested in using their network. Then they identified all the things these stakeholders might like to do on the network. The result was a list of hundreds of items and activities, which were condensed down into a five-step strategy. Bilan envisions a day when an automobile technician will be able to sit down at a computer and access all the repair information for a particular make and model of car. This information would include the history and description of any problems, updates and advisories from the maker, and advice on the best tools to use. And of course, the technician will be able to order those special tools for overnight delivery or contact the local sales representative.

Blueprinting the Architecture for Your Network

The scope of our book is not intended to go into great detail on this topic. But to sum up what we discussed so far, the networked enterprise initiative must be led from the customer-focus, with appropriate support from the venture team and appropriate resources allocated. The technology, however, must be developed from the bottom-up. Together, these two paths must align with identifiable business objectives, solid business ownership, clear metrics for success, and methods for measuring progress on a regular basis.

Basically, for functionalities, community users expect a format, a place, a formal process, and a destination to organize the information that is behind not only the buying decision process, but also supporting the products and the community of users. The community needs to provide processes and solutions for sharing knowledge and information by giving them comparatives. Other functions could include: email newsletters and product updates, message boards, online advice, forwarding of sales leads, dealer directories, online technical guides, peer-to-peer infrastructure, white papers, and case studies. There are five basic technology enterprise-wide platforms to consider: warehousing management systems, supply chain optimization, call center technologies, sales force automation, and knowledge management systems. For more details on the tactics, see *Corporate Portals* by Heidi Collins, which is an excellent guidebook for creating your first network solution.

The challenges to maintaining a networked enterprise are numerous, so we highlight only the ones that are key. Upgrading the network and maintaining high-quality community members means weeding out the dead wood and aggressively recruiting new stars. It is important that the community continuously provides true value, not just the creation of digital mass. The community needs to be segmented properly and differentiated. For example, what problems can this network solve in the marketplace? Finally, you need to consider maintenance issues like online privacy and self-policing.

PART IV

Reaching Escape

Velocity

TWELVE

Financing the Emerging Growth Venture

Success breeds its own brand of capital problems.
—**John L. Nesheim, in** *High-Tech Start-Up*

When you can measure what you are speaking about, and express it in numbers, you know something about it.
—**Lord William Thomson Kelvin, British physicist who developed the Kelvin scale**

Once we sign the check, we are the team. We consider it our responsibility that our companies never run out of money. We help them hire the right people, and we help them identify the risks and put those risks behind them. If anything, we have been accused of being too involved.
—**Thomas Perkins, founder of Kleiner Perkins Caufield & Byers**[1]

Why a Financing Strategy?

In Chapter 7 we discussed the importance of finding out what works in your business model and then creating an operating plan with a detailed cash budget. In this chapter we help you determine the capital you will need for financing the growth strategy you outlined in Chapter 10. But, exactly, how much money do you need? When do you need it? How do you value your venture and structure a "good" deal? Who are the best investors for your deal? And what are your financing alternatives? A concise financing strategy threads these important elements together.

If you are looking for outside funding, you are not alone. We found that 49 percent of the CEOs leading the *Inc. 500* companies, who raised later-stage financings, got it from venture capitalists or other private-equity investors.[2] But entrepreneurs leading an emerging growth venture face a myriad of challenges: an ever-increasing pressure for recruiting and retaining skilled workers, the need to defend against new entrants, and shortened product life cycles that demand higher investments in R&D to continually pioneer and introduce new products. As a result, today's average venture-backed company needs to raise some $16 million of venture capital during its first five years, and complete five or six financing rounds to get from start-up to a liquidity event.[3] This is a 129 percent increase from the amount raised by the average

❖ **Case in Point: Kleiner Perkins Caufield & Byers**

At the top of Sand Hill Road in Palo Alto sits the home of America's most famous venture capital firm with the most celebrated venture capitalists, including John Doerr and Vinod Khosla. Founded in 1972, Kleiner Perkins Caufield & Byers became successful by funding and building over 350 ventures that were disrupters in their days. Kleiner Perkins has supported hundreds of entrepreneurs leading ventures that include household names like Amazon. com, America Online, Compaq Computers, Genentech, Google.com, Juniper Networks, Lotus, Netscape, and Sun Microsystems. In 1995, Pradeep Sindhu, an engineer at the Xerox Palo Alto Research Center in San Jose, created an improved algorithm that could be used to build a better router than Cisco was selling at the time. Khosla gave him a check for $275,000 to build out some hack models, and Juniper Networks was on its way. It is considered one of the best investments anyone has made to date in Silicon Valley. Khosla's decision to invest a total of $3 million in Sindhu returned some $2 billion.

Kleiner Perkins was formed with the goal of providing operating advice and resources to entrepreneurs in addition to capital investment. Over the years, the firm's partners have been instrumental in helping to create some of the most innovative and rapidly growing businesses of the 20th century, with assets measured in tens of billions of dollars. From fund to fund, the billions Kleiner Perkins invested have returned over $550 billion, creating some 130 companies that generate over $75 billion in revenues and employ some 250,000 people. In 1996, Jeff Bezos, the founder of Amazon.com, closed an $8 million round with Kleiner Perkins being the sole investor. Said Bezos at that time, "Kleiner and Doerr are the gravitational center of a huge piece of the Internet world. It's the equivalent of prime real estate."

Sources: Kleiner Perkins Web site; Carleen Hawn, "The Man With the Golden Touch," *Forbes*, February 19, 2001; Anthony B. Perkins and Michael C. Perkins, *The Internet Bubble* (New York: HarperBusiness, 1999), pp. 67–103; Jerry Borrell, "Big Iron and Its Lessor Relatives," *Upside*, October 2001; and Melanie Warner, "Inside the Silicon Valley Money Machine," *Fortune*, October 26, 1998.

five-year-old venture capital-backed company in 1985. And the median number of months between financing rounds is about fifteen months.[4]

The fund-raising process can ruin a venture's prospects if it is not prepared for the harsh realities inherent in the process itself. It cannot be done casually nor can it be delegated to another party. The process can drain the entire venture team's time and energy. In fact, about 25 percent of the CEO's time and 20 percent of the time of those reporting directly to the CEO will need to be dedicated to raising capital during the first four years.[5] Not knowing this critical fact, many of the venture teams and entrepreneurs we have worked with over the years first show us their business plan, and then ask us to help them with their financing strategy.

It could not be more backwards. You need to have a financing *strategy* before you do the business plan, but you don't actually start to seek financing until you have your business plan complete. In fact, your business plan communicates not only your vision and business strategy but should also complete and support your financing strategy. You need to be prepared and take the necessary steps to ensure that you get the capital you need to fund your growth strategy, when you need it, and most importantly on terms that do not sacrifice your future upside. There are five steps to getting your financing strategy and financial plan together, as shown in Figure 12-1.

Is Your Financing Strategy Realistic?

First, do you truly know how much is needed to finance the long-term growth of your venture? Knowing the answer to this before you meet with investors is key. As Michael Hirsland, a general partner with Boston-based Polaris Ventures, says, "We are more interested in the total capital needed for the life of the company."[6] And is it realistic? For example, the typical average sought by entrepreneurs from angel investors is about $750,000, with a range from $50,000 to $5 million. Also, consider the fact that Cisco Systems got launched with $1.8 million and Yahoo was launched with some $1 million. How much can you capture from your retained earnings? eBay was self-funded from day one; it did not need outside funding but needed the credibility of being venture-backed. When the $5 million check arrived from Palo Alto-based Benchmark Capital, co-founder Pierre Omidyar proved this by depositing it in the bank, "where it remained untouched."

Second, although bad things will happen to your business overnight, be advised that good things take time. Desh Deshpande, chairman and founder of Sycamore Networks, advises entrepreneurs to set a deadline—decide to

FIGURE 12-1. STEPS TO PREPARING YOUR FINANCIAL PLAN.

Step 1. Complete your projected financials. They will be used to analyze and model the effects of integrating the operating plan you first created in Chapter 7 and your sales forecasts and revenue model from Chapter 9.

Step 2. Determine the funds needed to support a 5- to 7-year growth strategy we discussed in Chapter 10. This includes funds for capital investments in property, plant, and equipment (PP&E), and working capital investments for inventory, human capital needs, and marketing and sales expenses.

Step 3. Forecast funds available to you over the next five years. This involves the funds that your venture will generate internally as well as those that must be obtained from external sources like venture capitalists, strategic partners, founders, and board members.

Step 4. Establish a system of controls for governing the allocation and use of funds within your venture, making sure that the basic financial plan is carried out properly. This often includes the hiring of a Chief Financial Officer (CFO) to develop procedures and practices.

Step 5. Establish the field tactics and timeline. Utilizing your advisors' connections, develop a list of potential investors, prioritize that list, and begin knocking on doors. Bring your advisors into the feedback loop and discuss potential investors' objections. Revise the financing plan, while expanding the networks and contacts as needed.

---

spend six months raising money and *make sure to go all out*: "If there are no investors that you pick up along the way then you should probably reconsider the venture and maybe even try to come up with something new."[7]

Finally, understand that the path to getting financed is neither clear nor predictable. The financing strategy should be driven by corporate and personal goals, by financial needs, and ultimately by the available alternatives. However, it is the entrepreneur's relative bargaining power with investors and skills in managing and orchestrating the venture drill process that actually govern the final outcome. So be prepared to negotiate with a financing strategy and complete financials. As James Stancill writes in a classic *Harvard Business Review* article, "It's impossible to know exactly how much a new business will need during its first five years, but it is possible to come up with realistic estimates."[8]

Putting Together Your Financials

Professor William Sahlman writes, "Entrepreneurs are value creators, investing today in hopes of generating cash flows tomorrow."[9] So the main purpose of the financial section of a business plan is to formulate a credible, comprehensive set of projections reflecting a venture's anticipated financial performance. Therefore, if your projections are carefully prepared and convincingly supported, they become one of the most critical yardsticks by which your venture's attractiveness is measured by potential investors. Since the value of your venture ultimately depends on what the business will accomplish in the future, reasonable estimates of future cash flows will help in arriving at a value. So when a venture team produces convincing financials it will likewise command a higher value than one that does not!

But what exactly are financial statements? According to the American Institute of Certified Public Accountants (AICPA), the term *financial statements* refers to a package of financial data, including accompanying notes, derived from accounting records. They are intended to communicate an entity's resources or obligation at a point in time, or the changes therein for a period of time, in accordance with a comprehensive basis of accounting. Four traditional financial statements, along with the assumptions and notes, together comprise the financial statements of a business entity. They are *Income Statement, Balance Sheet, Statement of Cash Flows*, and *Statement of Stockholder's Equity*. Although there are no true ground rules for levels of preparation in the venture capital industry, accountants prepare financials to one of the three levels. The first, "audited financials," are prepared for publicly traded companies and prepared by independent auditors. For the second, "reviewed financials," the accountant expresses limited assurance; the accountant might or might not have been aware of all significant matters. The third, "compiled statements," are management's representation presented in the form of financial statements; the accountant has not undertaken any efforts to express assurance on the statements.

Pro forma financials are simply projected financials. The exercise for completing your pro forma financials should not be about demonstrating Excel spreadsheet skills. Your pro formas should accurately support the storyline you are creating in your business plan. Practice on building financials from the ground up, using the market potential and feedback from lead users and key customers, to describe your upside. Many times financials are done through a "CFO" mindset, using an artificial linear model to make projections. These tend to result in the infamous "hockey stick," where the revenues are flat for a period of time, then launch in a perfectly straight line at a 45-degree angle. In reality the start-up process is very lumpy, not linear. It is not that the CFO or CPA doing the numbers is wrong; what's wrong are the thought process and assumptions underlying the numbers.

Below we discuss the financials that investors need to see in a business plan, and we have provided additional guidance in Appendix E, "How to Prepare Your Financials." Be careful with your financials and keep them limited to supporting only your storyline. As Johann Wolfgang von Goethe once said, "The first sign we don't know what we are doing is an obsession with numbers."

Pro Forma Income Statement

We repeat what John Nesheim wrote in his book, *High-Tech Start-Up*: "Remember that cash flow and ROI (return on investment) are the measure of success for the venture capitalist." Your pro forma income statement is based on your cash budget table (Chapter 7), integrated with your sales forecast (Chapter 9) and your growth strategy (Chapter 10). For most VCs, you will need five-year projections and a very detailed (sometimes week-by-week) cash budget table for the first year. Be advised that getting your "gross margin" nailed down is *most important*. It demonstrates and presents the true value of your product to the customer. The investors do not just expect to see some huge top line sales numbers, but they do want to see how you determined the revenue model and how you discuss the soundness of your assumptions behind the gross margins.

We want to briefly discuss the "break-even" analysis, which is a financial exercise to determine some point in the future when your volume of sales neither makes a profit nor incurs a loss. It is that point in time when the next unit to be sold will contribute to profitability. This analysis originated in the academic world, mostly based on the research in consumer products, such as Procter & Gamble selling bars of soap from established production lines, through established sales channels, to an identifiable base of consumers. In other words, the break-even analysis works great on linear assumptions where the financial models are sound and the research supporting the sales forecasts is solid. We repeat, for all early stage ventures, that the cash flow will move in lumps, and quite often the financial modeling will be adjusted on the go. Sorry, but your financials cannot be formed and compressed into one nice, neat algebraic formula at this time.

Pro Forma Balance Sheet

Although a pro forma balance sheet should be included, it will not be a primary concern for venture capitalists unless you have high inventory needs, large current liabilities like accounts receivables, or unless you anticipate capitalizing a large amount of R&D. More of a formality, it shows retained earnings, how the venture is being financed along the way, and what types of assets are being purchased. If you have any debt you will need to address the principal terms of the debt, type of debt securities, interest rates, repayment installments and prepayment terms, convertibility of the debt, subordination, affirmative and negative covenants, defaults or material breaches, and security or collateral used in the notes. Finally, if you are expecting to purchase other companies along the way as a part of your growth strategy, the balance sheet should reflect the consolidation of the ventures and the goodwill.

Statement of Stockholders' Equity

Commonly referred to as the "Cap Table," or "Capitalization Table," it is a list of equity owners that includes each owner's name and usually the number of shares held by each as of the valuation date. It details your capital structuring and demonstrates how you intend to fund your growth through selling equity. Investors need to know the details of your intended distribution of ownership, cost per share, and types of securities issued: preferred stock, common shares, warrants, and option pool projections for sharing with new employees. Family members and other relationships among the equity owners should be identified in the endnotes.

Capital Requirements

Also called "Use of Proceeds," this can be a simple one-page document that clearly articulates your financing plan. It demonstrates the effect of investors' money on the venture. The most common examples are presented in Figure 12-2. As for restarts, it is perceived in the VC community that entrepreneurs who have been baptized by the fire of failure tend to have better understanding and appreciation for new business venturing, especially when it comes to financial management. If you have made some mistakes, fess-up to your foibles and carefully explain what you learned. However, the best insurance plan is to avoid financial trouble, or at least have a strategy in place to help minimize the painful consequences. For restarts, you just need to have a good understanding on where the venture is, how it got there, and some plan of corrective measures.

Assumptions and Notes

Finally, know that investors expect to see financials that are supported by thoroughly documented assumptions and detailed notes. Because there are many decisions that management makes with respect to operating an early

Figure 12-2. Use of proceeds.

Early Stage Financing	**Engineering the Runway.** Relatively small amounts to conduct research, prove concepts, and finance feasibility studies. Also to complete product development, initial marketing, and organize the venture team. **Constructing the Runway.** Focusing on getting to the "proof-of-concept" with the product, working capital for test marketing. Includes expenses for patent and intellectual property protection.
Development or Expansion Financing	**Accelerating to Full Throttle.** There is proven market acceptance, here is heavy investment in marketing and sales. Includes working capital for initial capital equipment required for putting the plan to action. And includes creating partnerships with major contracts or customers, and seeding the executive management team. **Building Production Facilities.** Investments for scaling to meet the future needs with the major of the market. The big orders are not only coming in, but they are getting even bigger! Cultivating strategic partnerships around the world, and leading/nurturing the ecosystem. **Getting Key Branded Executives.** Completing the venture team and completing the transition from entrepreneurial management practices to professional management practices. Here, shifting the fulcrum from development to execution.
Acquisitions and Buyout Financing	**Buying Up Capacity.** For buying up competitors, facilitating quick expansion, scooping up executive management teams at weakened competitors. Also used for buying up partners for national expansion plans, and/or establishing beachheads in global markets.
Restarts and Subsequent Rounds	**Extending the Runway.** Sometimes even moving the runway, or creating a temporary runway on a new location utilizing a new business model, new products/new technology platform. Sometimes to salvage operations in order to sell out. More often, for resetting and recharging the executives' option pool too, when the venture is in a down round and exposed to "cram downs" in valuations.

stage venture, your assumptions and notes not only give potential investors the data they need to evaluate your deal, but more importantly they speak volumes about how you arrived at your assumptions. They can be listed separately on a page as endnotes to the financials or included as footnotes to the financial statements and budgets.

How to Value Your Deal Like an Investor

One of the entrepreneur's most difficult challenges is assessing and determining a value for the emerging growth venture. Simply put, value is determined by the interaction of three major ingredients: cash, risk, and time. Valuation depends mainly on understanding the venture, its industry, and the general economic environment, combined with a very prudent job of forecasting. Investors know that careful thought and hard work leads to foresight. The financial world has developed many methods that can be used for valuing an ongoing firm or a publicly traded company. Since no single method is universally accepted to all purposes, valuing a private venture can be complex and often confusing due to the different types of values that can be considered. Likewise, there are certain difficulties with attempting to value a new business venture. It has no track record of earnings and will not pay dividends for a long time, if ever, so common methods like P/E ratios or dividend yields are therefore useless. And many early stage ventures have no tangible assets, like property, plant, and equipment, so they have no "book value." So most of the value lies on the capability of the venture team and future professional management team on putting the plan to action, hence, demonstrating the potential future streams of income.

In our research we discovered that there are a multitude of methods, ideas, and concepts developed by schools, organizations, and individuals used to measure future streams of income. Harvard Business School Professor William Sahlman created the "Venture Capital Method." The "First Chicago Method" was developed at First Chicago Corporation's venture capital group. There is even a "Rule-of-Thumb Method" developed by Frank Singer, an angel investor.[10] Finally, there is the discounted cash flow method. Shannon Pratt, in *Valuing a Business: The Analysis and Appraisal of Closely Held Companies,* provides us with a comprehensive definition of value, using the discounted cash flow method. He states:

> In the simplest sense, the theory surrounding the value of an interest in a business depends on the future benefits that will accrue to the owner of it. The value of the business interest, then, depends upon an estimate of the future benefits and the required rate of return at which those future benefits are discounted back to the valuation date.[11]

There are two approaches to making investment decisions by means of discounted cash flows. One is the net present value method (NPV), and the other is the internal rate of return (IRR) method.

Discussing Net Present Value

NPV is an intuitive and powerful financial concept all entrepreneurs should understand. The NPV approach to investment appraisal was introduced by American economist Irving Fisher in *The Nature of Capital and Income* (1906). In essence, NPV is simply a recognition of the fact that value of a dollar today is worth more than a dollar tomorrow. NPV calculations help you evaluate the value today (*present value*) of some future cash flows or expenses related to your venture.

The NPV is calculated by adding the initial investment (which is considered as a *negative* cash flow) to the present value of the anticipated future cash flows. A comparison of the NPVs of alternative investment possibilities indicates which of them is most desirable. An NPV of zero signifies that the investment's cash flows are exactly sufficient to repay the invested capital and to provide the required rate of return on that capital. If an investment has a positive NPV, then its cash flows are generating an excess return. In essence, the greater the NPV, the greater the increase in the financial value of the investors' assets.

Obviously, in a perfect world, venture capitalists would never consider a deal with a negative NPV. However, there are reasons large, profitable corporations may choose to pursue an entrepreneurial endeavor like a new product project even if the financial analysis reveals a negative NPV.[12] The reasons are:

- ❖ To finance the development of core competencies or new product platforms
- ❖ To create complementary products to more profitable products in the company's product line, like creating a new razor to sell more blades
- ❖ To develop innovative products for lead users
- ❖ To implement environmental policies and other projects based on ethical grounds
- ❖ To make a competitive response, either to signal a new lead into a space or to increase barriers to entry
- ❖ To develop goodwill with customers and ecosystem
- ❖ To bet that the cost of capital will decrease in the future as the project progresses

In using the NPV method, it is necessary to choose some rate of return for discounting cash flows to present value.[13] The interest rate used in these calculations, also called the discount factor or hurdle rate, is what the finance world calls the "opportunity cost of capital." This rate converts all of the expected future return on investment to an indicated present value. It is the financial return forgone by investing in this deal rather than making other investments. In other words, the discount rate is the reward that investors demand for accepting delayed return on their investments.

There are entire books and courses on calculating NPV and dealing with uncertainty and the impact of risk in cash inflow and outflow estimates. In fact, some financial analysts will add special premium factors to the discount rate to offset uncertainty about the outcomes. However, such factors are invariably arbitrary and are used to offset the uncertainties inherent in the forecasting of cash flows. Instead of using such arbitrary adjustments, we advise venture teams to focus on creating very realistic forecasts of cash flows and uses. These forecasts should be supplemented with careful sensitivity analysis, in order to understand and communicate the full impact of the range of possible outcomes.

Brief Evaluation of the NPV Method

As we first stated in Chapter 7, cash flow is more accurate than net income as a measure of economic value because it avoids distortions due to accounting presentation or comparability issues. The NPV method links value to expected performance, and thus eliminates reliance on historical performance. It also reflects risk and time value of money.

But you will find that the NPV method involves numerous uncertainties and forces you to make certain assumptions. The first and most significant is the projection of future cash flows, both in amounts and timing, since they are based on pure conjecture by the entrepreneur, the venture team, and its stakeholders. Others include the determination of the appropriate periods of projection and the discount rate or risk premium. As a result, the specific numbers used in the financial analysis may create the illusion that they are the actual or correct numbers. More often than not, the assumptions for the projections may be obscured by weak and unsubstantiated business logic.

Overall, we feel it is always better to be approximately right than to be exactly wrong. Diligent professional investors know that the NPV method is widely agreed upon to be the superior method for evaluation and ranking of investment proposals.[14] One advantage of the NPV method is that it is very popular. It is part of a common language among all financial managers because it completely exposes all business logic behind the economics of the deal and financial modeling. The time required performing NPV analysis is very minimal, as it can be accomplished with Microsoft's Excel and HP-12C calculators using your pro formas. Using NPV, the details are in the budgeting, assumptions, and financial modeling, not in creating comprehensive audited financial statements. So the future income can be expressed year by year with any desired detail in pro forma income statements. This exercise becomes the final and most important check on a business plan's overall consistency and attractiveness to potential investors.

We have found that it can be a serious mistake to approach the valuation task in hopes of arriving at a single number, or even providing a narrow range. All one can realistically expect is a range of values with boundaries driven by the different methods and underlying assumptions for each. So keep it simple. As Michael Curry, CFO for Kleiner Perkins, says, "The valuation process is not numbers-crunching. It's really based on experience. If you can't do the math in your head, it's probably not a venture deal."[15] We hope that this analytical exercise in valuation will help entrepreneurs create a mindset of "cooperative value building" instead of "individual value surrendering," or the feeling that investors are "claiming" more than their share. We know that the NPV method can be a simple exercise to help determine how much value the venture is actually expected to create in the future.

Discussing the Internal Rate of Return

Recall from our discussions in Chapter 3 that performance for the venture capital industry is traditionally measured by the internal rate of return (IRR). The IRR considers "cash-on-cash" returns from the sale of shares and disbursements from the liquidity events back to investors like dividends. It is calculated by taking inflows of cash as negative cash flows, and distributions of cash and stock to investors as positive cash flows.[16]

Now, before we discuss the IRR in more detail, it is important to understand the concept called the "time value of money." This means that investors would rather receive a dollar today than wait a year from now. If they had that dollar now, they could invest it, earn interest, and end up with more than one dollar. Hence, those investments that promise favorable returns earlier in time are preferable to those that promise returns later in time. In essence, IRR is defined as the interest yield promised by an investment. For instance, the IRR answers this question for an investor, "How much interest would I have to receive on my money today in order to equal the return on investment I will get from investing in this deal?" Technically speaking, the IRR is the rate of return at which the discounted future cash flows equal the initial investment. It is the discount rate at which NPV is zero.

From a venture capitalist's viewpoint, the IRR relative to the present value discount rate indicates the net result of the investment. For example, if the IRR is greater than their desired rate of return, the investment is financially attractive. Since the IRR exceeds the costs of the funds used to finance the growth, a surplus remains after considering the cost of the capital, and this surplus is passed on to the venture capitalist's investors, the limited partners. If the IRR is equal to their desired rate of return, the investor is indifferent toward the investment. If the IRR is less than their desired rate of return, the investment is not financially attractive. Once the IRR for your deal has been computed using your pro formas and a financial calculator, go back to Chapter 3 and check with the historical returns for venture capitalists presented in Figure 3–4. If your IRR is equal or greater to their requirements, then your deal could be acceptable to a venture capitalist.

Venture capitalists and their limited-partner investors also tend to think and discuss valuations in terms of "capital gains multiples." For example, a venture capitalist might say something like, "We expect to see a 10× in our investment within four to six years." With this in mind, we have included a conversion table for IRRs and multiples over time (Figure 12-3). So what makes a deal attractive to venture capitalists? What is the "sweet spot" for each type of investors? Remember, since there is more risk involved in financing a venture earlier in its development, more return is expected from early stage financing than later stage ventures. For a comparison, see Figure 12-4, which shows what investors prefer in their deals according to each development stage of the venture.

Figure 12-3. Capital gains and multiples conversion table.

Multiple	Exit Year with Internal Rate of Return (IRR)			
	3	5	7	10
3×	44%	25%	17%	12%
4×	59%	32%	22%	15%
5×	71%	38%	26%	17%
7×	91%	48%	32%	21%
10×	115%	58%	39%	26%

Figure 12-4. What makes a deal attractive to venture capitalists?

For Start-Ups:	58% IRR, 10 times the investment in 5 years
For Ventures Under 1 Year Old:	48% IRR, 7 times the investment in 5 years
For Ventures 1–5 Years Old:	38% IRR, 5 times the investment in 5 years
For Ventures over 5 Years Old:	25% IRR, 3 times the investment in 5 years

Discussing Capital Structuring

There are many choices available to an emerging growth venture that needs expansion capital, but basically the choices are limited to two flavors: debt and equity. Defining your "optimal capital structure," which those in the financial world use to describe the proper balance between the two, is a challenge, as is finding those sources of capital at affordable rates. What is considered affordable varies, depending on whether you are pursuing debt or equity. Figure 12–5 lists some important factors that affect capital structuring.

Affordability in the "debt" context refers to the terms, the interest rates, the amortization, and the penalties for non-payment. In the context of "eq-

Figure 12-5. Factors that affect capital structuring of a new business venture.

▲ Availability of sources of funds to the venture and founders, i.e., bootstrapping vs. internal sources like revenues, debt vs. equity, local vs. foreign

▲ Marketing and sales traction, market acceptance, marquee customers

▲ Degree of entrepreneurial risk in deal

▲ Degree of industry risk in deal

▲ General appetite of investors and lenders in the marketplace

▲ Liquidity needs and timing of exits for investors

▲ Financial markets composition and depth locally

▲ Prevailing general terms of the current investments like term sheets, etc.

▲ Negotiation skills of entrepreneur and completed business plan; deal making is ultimately a combination of art and science and it comes down to the human components

▲ Handling "hairs-on-the-deal" and "deal-killers," which we explore and discuss in Chapter 14

uity," affordability refers to valuation, dilution of the shares or control held by the current founders, and any special terms or preferences such as mandatory dividends or redemption rights. As we discussed in Chapters 3 and 6, your first available option is to issue securities. Recall that there are essentially three types: common shares, preferred shares, and debentures. Each has certain characteristics, variable features, and attendant costs.

To continue our discussion with the equity route, understand that professional investors focus on the IRR to them and their investors, not the amounts of equity they own in each deal. In fact, the equity percentage is a function of the IRR and the risk in actually putting the entrepreneur's business plan to action. Our research has shown that, as a rule of thumb, the investment community defines a successful entrepreneurial venture as one that returns at least 40 percent IRR to investors over a holding period of four to five years.[17] Figure 12-6 outlines the percentage of ownership required to provide investors a 40 percent return on a $1 million investment. So if your projections support a valuation of $15 million in five years and you needed $1 million to get there, then investors would need 36 percent ownership.

Keep this example in mind when analyzing the capital structure of your deal. One of the best hits over the fence in the modern era of private equity investing was Netscape for Kleiner Perkins. Jim Clark, founder of Silicon Graphics and partner at Kleiner Perkins, was a very tough, professional, experienced negotiator. In 1994 they placed a $20 million valuation on Netscape, investing $5 million for 25 percent in equity. Kleiner Perkins in turn made some $400 million, or 80× their money in the deal.

As we discussed in Chapter 10, the message is clear, strategically "spreading the wealth" through equity to employees who produce is critical to the simultaneous pursuit of growth and profitability. Winning big requires a great team, so be prepared with a stock option pool to offer, attract, and retain great people. Siebel Systems, the fastest-growing company ever, issued more options as a percentage of diluted shares outstanding by 2001 than many of the other technology companies.[18]

However, be advised that there are no tried and proven formulas for setting aside stock for key players on your team. But Figure 12-7 shows the

FIGURE 12-6. CAPITAL STRUCTURING.

Percentage of Ownership Required to Provide Investors a 40% Rate of Return on a $1 Million Investment

Exit Year for the Investors	Future Value of the Venture (Millions)			
	$10	**$15**	**$20**	**$25**
3	27%	18%	14%	11%
5	54%	36%	27%	22%
7	*	70%	53%	42%
10	*	*	*	*

* = An investment would not be made.

FIGURE 12-7. STOCK OWNERSHIP OF EXCEPTIONAL VENTURES.

	Private Ventures	Public Ventures	Average
Entrepreneurs/Founders, Venture Team, and Family	73%	26%	65%
Outside Investors	10%	54%	18%
Top Executives	4%	5%	4%
Board Members	11%	12%	11%
All Other Employees	2%	3%	2%
	100%	100%	100%

*In 2001, Ernst & Young LLP, the Entrepreneur of the Year Institute, and the Kauffman Center for Entrepreneurial Leadership published the International Survey of Entrepreneurs. This unprecedented research involved over 1,000 Entrepreneur of the Year finalists in seventeen countries. About 78% of the firms had less than 250 employees. The majority, 35%, had annual sales between $5–25 million. Their annual growth rates ranged from 20% to 260%, and about 80% of the ventures had net profits between 15–30%.

interesting results of stock ownership of key stakeholders. For attracting a branded CEO, expect to offer 8 to 10 percent in stock; for attracting marketing and technical executives, expect to offer 2 to 3 percent each; for attracting salespeople, be prepared to offer 1 to 1.5 percent, plus commissions; and set aside 20 to 30 percent in an option pool for future employees. Be sure to get advice from the legal experts, who can help you set up the initial capital structure correctly. Otherwise, the venture could be "plagued with problems throughout its life."

As with most start-ups, the entrepreneur and members on the venture team have probably made considerable sacrifices, called "opportunity costs," such as not having worked full time in the workforce and perhaps having been without earning an income from the start-up for a while. Entrepreneurs commonly refer to such endeavors, and sacrifices, as "sweat equity." But when discussing capital structuring in the financial world, this sweat equity is considered "sunk costs" and bears no immediate entitlement to equity in the venture. So while information about the venture's past and the founders' great efforts in getting the venture launched help tremendously in demonstrating commitment and assessing future performance, investors are only interested in the equity capital that has been invested into the venture to date.

Process Leads to Success

Often valuation and the process of putting a deal together is an "arm wrestling contest" between the entrepreneur and the investors. It becomes a struggle what investors are willing to pay and what the entrepreneur is willing to "give up." But there is a little-known insider secret we would like to share. In valuating a venture, investors actually look more into the process of the negotiations with entrepreneurs than at the cold-hard numbers. The way entrepreneurs handle the initial stages of valuation demonstrates their maturity. It also demonstrates their ability to understand the environment and the job of putting together a venture using risk capital. So the process itself is almost as if not more important than the end results.

This means that you shouldn't get stuck in the "valuation trap." Why struggle with this? Focus more on working with your investors, growing your venture, and moving forward. Arguing over a split between 23 percent and 25 percent of equity versus owning 100 percent of nothing is not worth it. As Pyrrhus said, "One more such victory, and we are lost." A higher valuation may mean you have done well in the negotiations but it may become a Pyrrhic victory, meaning you have won the battle, not the war, and at what cost? You could end up with ill feelings instead of mutual respect and support. Think about developing relationships with your investors, not winning.

Finding the Right Venture Capitalist for Your Deal

Before we help guide you to the right VC for your deal, here is a quick situation analysis of their investment activity. The amount of money that venture capitalists have invested has declined every quarter since the start of 2000. To summarize what we discussed in Chapter 3, in 2001 venture capital investment activity decreased 62 percent—to $41 billion from $106 billion in 2000—as the venture capitalists concentrated more on building up their previous investments than dealing with new investments. This $41 billion was invested in 3,798 ventures through 4,679 rounds. In 2001, the number of first-round financings as a percentage dropped from 27 percent in 2000 to 18 percent. A total of 1,172 ventures received first-round funding in 2001 compared to 3,333 ventures in 2000 and 2,448 ventures in 1999. The amount of first-round financings dropped harshly from $29 billion in 2000 to $7.3 billion in 2001. The average first-round investment was $6.3 million, and the average valuation of the investee at the time of the first-round investment was $27 million.

For a broader perspective we examined more than ten years of datum. Between 1995 and 2001, venture capitalists invested $258 billion in 24,349 ventures through 30,458 rounds. A total of $74 billion went to first-round investments, representing 29 percent of the dollar amounts. There were a total of 12,156 first rounds representing 50 percent of the deal flow. The average first-round investment was $5.6 million, and the average valuation of the investee at the time of the first-round investment was $24 million. For a more granular analysis of first-round investments, sector by sector, see Figure 12-8. In this chapter, to simplify our sector-by-sector analysis of first-round investment activity, the seventeen sectors we identified and discussed in Chapter 4 have been pared down to nine sectors.[19]

FIGURE 12-8. ANALYSIS OF FIRST-ROUND VENTURE CAPITAL INVESTMENTS (1995–2001).

Sector	Total $ Invested (Billions)	Total # of Deals	Total # of Ventures	Total First Round (Billions)	Total # of First Round Deals	Average First Round (Millions)	Average Valuation (Millions)
Communications	$63.6	4,761	3,659	$16.0	1,841	$6.95	$32.4
Retailing & Media	$63.6	7,261	5,673	$18.4	3,081	$5.12	$23.7
Computer Software	$47.6	6,733	5,426	$11.4	2,502	$4.10	$18.2
Computer Hardware	$25.5	3,120	2,509	$7.9	1,287	$5.00	$21.4
Biotechnology	$15.8	1,866	1,503	$3.3	574	$5.73	$20.9
Healthcare Related	$14.1	2,602	2,062	$3.6	789	$4.59	$19.5
Semiconductors & Electronics	$10.4	1,272	1,073	$2.9	496	$5.35	$21.3
Business & Financial	$8.8	1,228	1,056	$5.1	698	$7.33	$24.8
Industrial & Energy	$8.4	1,615	1,388	$5.2	888	$6.30	$40.5

Source: National Venture Capital Association 2002 Yearbook.

What Makes a Great Venture Capitalist?

Now that you know and understand the specifics of your business—you know your numbers cold, you have the financials prepared, you understand how much you need, and grasp the fundamentals of valuation—it is about finding and evaluating the right investors for your specific deal. But navigating through the universe of investors can be confusing, even for the most experienced entrepreneurs. As a start, examine Figure 12-9, which provides a comprehensive summary of our discussions with respect to financing an emerging growth venture.

Today, uncertainty dominates the venture capital industry. Unsure of their ability to guess at what will be the next big thing, venture capitalists are choosing to work together. According to Greg Galanos, managing director at Palo Alto-based Mobius Venture Capital (formerly known as Softbank Venture Capital), "The big change between the bubble and now is everyone was in 'hog-the-puck' mode before."[20] Investing in early-stage new business ventures is a very risky business, and the risk is commonly mitigated among other venture capital firms by sharing information and due diligence at the beginning, and sharing the combined efforts in relationship building. In these syndicated or conjoined deals, the role of the lead investor first agrees to the term sheet and then helps put together the syndicate, helps set the value, and starts the due diligence process. But it will most likely be up to the entrepreneur to manage all the different interests and informational needs.

Venture capital is an "eyeball-to-eyeball" business, meaning they personally get involved in venture building. Venture capitalists help entrepreneurs and their venture teams build great companies. They see themselves more as builders than financiers. Brad Jones, a partner at Redpoint Ventures, once told entrepreneurs, "The great value VCs bring is experience and helping avoid making mistakes. They can help you step back and take a look at your markets and your strategies. Based on experience of working with perhaps hundreds of entrepreneurs like yourself, they have a sense of what direction to turn in tough times."[21]

Besides providing cash, venture capitalists add value in a variety of ways. See Figure 12-10 for some examples of roles they can play. After they make an investment, VCs will spend about 50 to 70 percent of their time supporting their portfolio companies. The most intense involvement is with early stage ventures. As Bill Stensrud, a partner at San Diego-based Enterprise Capital, said, "A good venture partner will not only provide money. They are a good test of the quality of your business opportunity and, when you get funded, your investors should be great partners in helping you succeed."[22]

Segmenting the VCs: Objective Research

During the 1990s, the number of venture firms in the United States more than doubled to somewhere around 1,200, and settled around 1,000 at the start of

(*text continues on page 206*)

FIGURE 12-9. FINANCING THE EMERGING GROWTH VENTURE.

	Informal Angels	Formal Angels	Venture Capital		
			Early	Growth	Later
Stage	Preseed to Seed	Start-Up <1 Year			
Number of Contacts	3 Million Individuals	200,000 Individuals	8,000–10,000 Professionals		
	250,000–400,000	100–170 Groups	750–1,100 Firms		
Business Risk	Active				
	Highest				Lowest
Return (IRR)	58%	48%	48%	38%	25%
Multiple	10×	7×	7×	5×	3×
Equity Share	20–30%	30–35%	20–50%	20–30%	15–20%
Average Round	$145,000	$600,000	$6.3M	$11.9M	
Range of Investment	$5,000–$500,000	$50,000–$3M	$125,000–$10M	$5M–$60M	
Deals per Year	30,000–50,000+	1,500–2,500	580	1,400	390
Amount Available	$60–$80 Billion		$70–$85 Billion		

Figure 12-10. Roles venture capitalists play in venture building.

Strategic

▲ Serve as a sounding board in crafting and flight testing ideas and strategies.

▲ Business consultant with unique industry experience.

▲ Developing negotiation agreements, and executing strategic partnerships.

▲ Developing and executing an acquisition strategy.

▲ Developing financial plans and assisting in follow-on rounds of funding.

▲ Developing a global business strategy.

▲ Negotiating licensing or royalty agreements.

Social and Supportive

▲ Company-building experience.

▲ Can help manage the transition from entrepreneurial to professional management structures.

▲ Been in the trenches, written payroll checks—they know the ropes of entrepreneurship.

▲ Been around in hard times, now providing sound advice and encouragement.

▲ Have a complete repertoire of mistakes and stories to share.

▲ Knowledgeable of industry trends and exposed to insider knowledge seeing deals and plans.

▲ Vital business coach, mentor and personal friend, confidant.

▲ Support for, during, and after initial public offerings or other liquidity events.

Network Effect

▲ Credibility to venture team.

▲ Helping recruit key management and board members.

▲ Providing access to industry experts and knowledgeable advisors.

▲ Providing access to the right professional service providers, in particular legal and accounting firms.

▲ Instrumental in opening doors to key marquee customers that otherwise might not take a new venture seriously.

▲ Instrumental in opening doors to key suppliers.

▲ Introducing the venture team to other private equity investors.

▲ Providing access to the investment bankers for preparing a viable exit.

▲ Providing access to executives overseas for strategic alliances, investments, and resources.

▲ Making key contacts with banks and leasing companies.

▲ Providing a close-knit relationship with other ventures in the portfolio.

the new century. There are many kinds of venture capitalists who invest in different types of opportunities. Some venture capitalists prefer to provide only seed capital; others prefer investing in mature companies looking for expansion capital; others might invest only in specific industries and locales. It will take a concentrated effort to objectively research the industry and screen out potential investors. In one study of entrepreneurs who received venture capital, they spent on the average forty hours gathering and evaluating information about their potential investors, with 29 percent spending more than one hundred hours.[23]

We suggest that you start your search at the National Venture Capital Association (NVCA). Founded in 1973 to foster a broader understanding of the importance of venture capital to the vitality of the U.S. economy, it is the trade association that represents the venture capital industry. Its membership consists of professional venture capital firms and organizations that manage pools of risk equity capital designated to be invested in young, emerging companies. In 2003, the NVCA had some 450 member firms, representing the majority of the $250 billion of venture capital that was invested in U.S.-based companies in the decade of the 1990s.

Another source to search is the *MoneyTree™ Survey*, a quarterly study of venture capital investment activity in the United States. A collaboration between PricewaterhouseCoopers, Venture Economics, and the NVCA, it is the definitive source of information on emerging companies that receive financing and on the venture capital firms that provide it. The study has become a staple of the venture capital industry, entrepreneurs, government policymakers, and the business press worldwide.

Based on your searches through these and other resources, and considering your financing strategy, narrow the universe of investors to a workable shortlist of twelve to fifteen firms with the following questions:

❖   When in the entrepreneurial life cycle do they prefer to invest?

❖   What business sectors/niches do they prefer?

❖   How much do they typically invest per deal?

❖   Do they have any industry experts in their firm?

❖   In which ventures in your space have they already invested?

❖   How are their investments typically structured?

❖   Do they prefer to lead deals? With whom have they completed conjoined deals?

❖   What is their geographic focus?

❖   Who are the key partners?

❖   What are their backgrounds (schools, degrees, companies, etc.)?

❖   Who are their limited partners? And how are their interrelationships?

❖ What is their average size of investment?

❖ What is their record with IPOs and other exits?

❖ What do they consider their best investments?

❖ What is their network effect potential?

❖ How much "dry powder" do they have available to invest?

Segmenting the VCs: Subjective Research

According to Brian Bedol, founder of *ESPN Classics*, it is important to "choose your investors well. They need to be supporting you during rough times as well as sharing in the good to great times."[24] In other words, subjective due diligence is a two-way street, and unless you are talking with the top tier of venture capitalists, you should be equally interested and concerned about the qualifications of your potential investors. Especially if you are dealing with angels, you will need to ask for references and resumes that detail their professional and educational backgrounds. Venture capitalists are surprised that most entrepreneurs do not take this step. So besides performing a general search on Google, ask for the names of your investors' bankers, accountants, and attorneys, and then have *your* banker, accountant, and attorney check their professional reputations. You also need to consider which investors might hurt your venture, and which ones, once invested and involved, might steer your venture the wrong way.

Before you accept an investment, ask your investors for a list of their portfolio companies available for you to research, and also find out about any of their investments that have failed. It is important to understand these relationships between investors and the entrepreneurs in the portfolio companies. Ask the entrepreneurs who have received funding these questions:

❖ What pre-investment support did they provide?

❖ How would you describe the chemistry between your venture and the VC firm?

❖ Were they reasonable to work with?

❖ Were they difficult to deal with, and if so, how?

❖ What is it like working with them now?

❖ How have they been most helpful?

❖ What is the best thing they have done for you to date?

❖ How active are they in your business? How often do you talk to or see them?

❖ How did your investors behave during the rough times?

❖ Have you gone out for other rounds? If so, how have they helped?

❖ What did you learn in the negotiations?

❖ How long did it take to get your financing from the VC firm?

❖ Who are the investors' representatives on your board of directors?

❖ What's the one piece of advice you could give us?

❖ How are their relationships with their limited partners?

❖ Are they involved in any litigation with stockholders? With their limited partners?

❖ If you could sell out today and start all over again, would you do it with the same VC firm? Why or why not?

Personalize the Connection

Finally, while performing this research on the firms and managing partners with whom you may soon be negotiating a deal, consider how you can personalize the connection. Work through your contacts in the industry, through your networks and advisors, and through your consultants and board members. Find out from them which venture capital firms on your list are good candidates for you to approach and how they can help you place your plan. Great chemistry begins at the first point of communication. Consider how you can work your first contact point with a potential investor to help create a positive relationship, rapport, and optimistic negotiating environment at the closing table.

Alternative Sources of Financing

We realize that not all companies are venture-fundable. As we first discussed in Chapter 3, venture capital is a unique form of financing and needs these three elements in a deal: It must have rapid growth, get really big sooner rather than later, and remain profitable for a long time. Our book is not intended to explore and discuss other sources in great detail. But we do intend to give a broad view of this topic and refer you to additional resources.

Dealing with Corporate Venture Capitalists

Corporate strategic investing differs from conventional venture investing that we have discussed so far.[25] Unlike venture capitalists, corporate investors can eventually be a part of the liquidity event, as they could buy you out. Generally, a corporation's goals are strategic: to enhance their innovation, gain early exposure to new markets, and invest in new technologies. In the eye of the Perfect Storm, over 350 corporations were involved in corporate venturing. By the end of 2002, only about 150 were "somewhat alive." Early stage ventures are not always of interest to corporate investors. But Cisco built an empire by investing in high-tech start-ups and acquiring them. Cisco completed seventy-one acquisitions from 1993 to 2001, and twenty-five in 2000 alone.

R&D limited partnerships are possible source of funds for high-tech entrepreneurs, where corporate partners invest in the technology development and share the upside by splitting royalties. But Richard Siegelman, general partner at Kleiner Perkins, provides this sage advice: "Get pure financial players first. Then the outside strategic investor will know it can't twist your arm. Also, the strategic investor's agenda may make it hard for VCs to come in later. Use a VC, then raise money from a strategic investor at a higher valuation."[26]

Small Business Investment Companies

Small Business Investment Companies (SBICs), which we first discussed in Chapter 3, operate like a hybrid among a group of angels, a venture capital firm, and a bank. These privately owned and funded investment companies are licensed and regulated by the SBA. They use their own capital, along with funds borrowed from the SBA, to provide equity investments and long-term loans to small businesses. Their "bread 'n butter" is working with early stage ventures, and working closely with informal and formal angel investors at a very local level. From 1960 through 2001 the SBICs have made about 125,757 investments, for a total of $33 billion. Since 1992 when the first steps were taken to rejuvenate the SBIC program, total capital under management has grown from $3 billion to $17 billion, in 407 funds. In 2000 the SBA provided $5.6 billion in financing through some 400 SBICs. The average was around $1.2 million in financing; the majority of their investments—56 percent—went to ventures that were three years old or less. Some notable companies that got SBIC help in their early years include Federal Express, Apple Computer, Teledyne, Cray Computer, America Online, Staples, and Outback Steakhouses.

Federal Funding for Technology Transfer

According to one entrepreneur, who in 2002 received $2 million from the Advanced Technology Program (ATP) of the National Institute of Standards and Technology (NIST), "In the dot-com heyday, people turned their nose up at government funding. It's much more accepted now."[27] And the recent increase in worldwide terrorist activity has pressed the need for the United States to quickly develop high-tech countermeasures. For this reason President George W. Bush appointed E. Floyd Kvamme, a partner from Kleiner Perkins, as a co-chair of the President's Council of Advisors on Science and Technology (PCAST). In 2002, PCAST prepared reports on advising the new Department of Homeland Security (DHS) how the government will meet the needs of technology transfer through Cooperative Research and Development Agreements and intellectual property licenses. PCAST's proposal stresses the need for a streamlined technology transfer system to help bring to surface quickly new technologies that could be used in the DHS. The opportunity for an entrepreneur is that such a new development encourages participation by innovative companies that otherwise avoid government funding and contracts.

Private Placements

If you intend to raise a relatively small amount of money from a relatively small number of sophisticated investors, you might be able to use one of the exemptions from federal and state securities law. These exemptions allow you to do what is called a private placement. The Small Business Investment Incentive Act of 1980 increased the opportunities in private placements. More than $60 billion was raised in 2002 in the United States through private placements.[28] A private placement is selling stock directly to a few private investors instead of the public at large. It can be faster than going to the venture capital community and less expensive than an initial public offering.

There are primarily three sections of operative rules under Regulation D of the Securities Exchange Act of 1993: Sections 504, 505, and 506. They deal primarily with the amount of capital you can raise, the time period in which you may raise the capital, whom you can approach, and how you can approach potential investors. You can raise money through an investment banker who specializes in private placements or consider going alone. Investment bankers can charge anywhere from 3 to 25 percent of the total amount raised. For more information, we refer you to a workbook that explains the basics of raising capital through private placements and that can help you through the process.[29]

Asset-Based Financing and Debt Capital

Asset-based lending is financing that is secured with assets that have an easily determined value. Ventures can leverage a variety of assets as collateral, including accounts receivable, inventory, property plant and equipment, and securities. The financing can take the form of anything from loans to revolving lines of credit to equipment leases. A study by the New York City-based Commercial Finance Association found that companies had $343 billion in outstanding asset-based financing in 2000.[30]

Start-up financing is very dependent on paid-in equity capital by the founders, their credit histories, and heavily collaterized banking financing. In fact, 62 percent of the *Inc. 500* CEOs who raised additional financing borrowed money from a bank.[31] One report found that about 91 to 98 percent of the small businesses in the United States have had access to credit for financing their businesses.[32] The economic slowdown can actually benefit entrepreneurs, since we now have the lowest cost of capital in forty-five years. This, and the "democratization of credit" in recent years, means that more people have access to credit through home equity loans and credit markets. They can convert their personal assets into cash and into paid-in equity to launch new business ventures. Also there are the SBA's main lending program and loan guarantees. The maximum loan guarantee is $750,000 and the average loan amount is $178,000. Funds can be used for working capital and typically have seven-year terms.

Somewhere in between debt and equity financing is "debt capital." This is also known as trade credit, project financing, cash flow financing, purchase order financing, trade capital, trade financing, supplier credit, and factoring. It is reflected on the balance sheet statement as "accounts payable," as it is in essence a loan for 30 to 120 days. Venture bridge financing, bridge loans, and mezzanine financing are all short-term financing. They are usually loans backed by equity and used by a start-up to pay for operating expenses during negotiations for a second-stage round of venture capital investment. Understand that all forms of asset-based financing require careful planning. As Warren Buffett said, "Leveraging a company is like driving your car with a sharp stick pointed at your heart through the steering wheel. As long as the road is smooth it works fine. But hit one bump in the road and you may be dead."[33]

THIRTEEN

Creating Your Exit Strategy and Exit Goals

The end is where we start from.
—T.S. Eliot, poet

Success generally depends upon knowing how long it takes to succeed.
—Montesquieu, eighteenth-century French philosopher

What George Bernard Shaw said about love affairs is also apt for business:
Any fool can start one, it takes a genius to end one successfully.
—William D. Bygrave, professor of entrepreneurship

Harvesting from Your Venture's Value

This chapter supports our belief that having a harvest goal in mind and creating an exit strategy to achieve it are what separate successful entrepreneurs from the rest. Clearly, the main objective of professional entrepreneurs is to create economic value. It is unfortunate that little attention in the entrepreneurial world has been given to exiting a business venture, or what has come to be called *harvesting the business*. In their book, *Venture Capital at the Crossroads*, William Bygrave and Jeffry Timmons help introduce this topic: "Just like farmers, venture capitalists seed, tend, and feed portfolio companies in the hopes of reaping a bountiful harvest."[1] The professional entrepreneurs and investors know that harvesting an entrepreneurial venture is the approach taken by the owners and investors to realize terminal after-tax cash flows on their investment. It defines how they will extract some or all of the economic value from their investment.

But just because a venture team can build a successful business doesn't mean they can become rich from it. Investors who provide equity financing to high-risk ventures need to know how and when they are likely to realize a return on their investments before they commit any funds. They invest not for eternity but on average for three to seven years, after which they expect to make a profit that reflects the scale of the risk they have taken on in making their investment. An exit should be seen as a critical milestone that focuses on the transferring of ownership. It is at this stage in the entrepreneurial life

❖
Case in Point: Intel Capital

Les Vadasz, an entrepreneur at heart, left Fairchild Semiconductor in 1968 to help run a high-tech startup called Intel Corporation. He was hired as employee number four. In 1991 he started up a corporate venturing program that became Intel Capital. At first, Intel began investing and nurturing a few private ventures, whose products and services helped fill in the gap in their own product line, capabilities, and capacity. But their plans soon grew beyond that goal. They did fifty deals in their first year. By 2002 they were investing anywhere between $1 million and $10 million per deal.

Intel does not typically lead the deal. Instead it co-invests with other venture firms and takes an active role in assessing the technology potential of start-ups. By fall 2002, Intel Capital had made some 475 to 500 investments, and their portfolio was valued at $1.7 billion. In 2002, Intel Capital was ranked as the top investor in information-technology start-ups, and as the second-largest investor in start-ups overall. They have a global perspective: nearly 45 percent of its investments were in thirty-one countries outside the United States.

Kirby Dyess, vice president and director of operations for Intel Capital, managed the successful integration of Intel's mergers and acquisitions. At one time there were more than 300 people working at Intel who did nothing but facilitate acquisitions and help integrate the new ventures into Intel. In 1999, Intel completed fourteen acquisitions for about $6 billion, and in 2000 they completed fifteen. About 80 percent of the ventures Intel acquired were introduced to them through financial intermediaries and investment bankers. Although most of the details behind Intel's venture group and acquisition activities are not publicly known, some of their largest publicly known acquisitions included Level One Communications for $2.2 billion in 1999, and Xircom for $748 million in 2001.

Sources: Intel company Web site; and Charles R. Fellers, "Inside Intel Capital," *Venture Capital Journal Online*, April 1, 2002.

cycle that the capital gains (or losses) occur, or, in other words, that there is a harvest (or exit) from the investment.

Why Is an Exit Strategy Important?

Your exit strategy is important because it helps you define success in business. When entrepreneurs have not thought through an exit strategy, it may be an indicator that they are not focused on the eventual transition of the venture. There is a saying among venture capitalists, "It's easy to get into an investment, but how do we get out?" And investors do not want an exit strategy to be difficult or bloody. In essence, having a harvest goal and a strategy to achieve it is indeed what separates successful entrepreneurs from the rest of the pack.

Investors will shy away from ventures that do not have an exit strategy because it may be an indicator that the entrepreneur is more interested in building and running a lifestyle business rather than in building a potential high-growth venture. So like the North Star guiding Columbus across the Atlantic to America, your definition of success should be used as your strategic heading. It launches you off in the right direction, helps keep you on track, but also illuminates the way when you feel uncertain or feel you are off track. Trust us, every stage of the entrepreneurial life cycle becomes clearer and easier to take if you know precisely what you plan to do with the business in the end.

Investors know that millions of people start new businesses every year. They know that the right exit strategy protects wealth, attracts valuable employees, and ensures a smooth transition. The wrong one could mean financial ruin. One study of successful high-tech entrepreneurs found that 60 percent wrote an exit strategy or gave thought to exiting prior to their harvest.[2] Dick Kramlich, general partner at New Enterprise Associates, says his firm actually maps out the exit date with entrepreneurs at the time of every investment. William Link, co-founder of Newport Beach-based Versant Ventures, believes that the exit strategy is one of the most important aspects of starting a business venture. According to Link, "It gives you, the entrepreneur, a focus for your efforts and allows you to set up your entrepreneurial endeavor with the end in mind. It also allows you to clearly communicate your goals and expectations to your venture team and investors."[3]

Shaping Your Exit Strategy

Shaping a harvest strategy is an enormously complicated and difficult task. Crafting an exit strategy can never begin too early. Stephen Covey writes in *The Seven Habits of Highly Effective People* that one of the keys to being effective in life is "beginning with the end in mind." Although Covey is speaking of one's personal life, the statement also rings true with respect to the entrepreneurial life cycle.

We share with you some important advice on helping you shape your exit strategy. First, you need to determine the personal goals of the lead entrepreneur and the venture team. For each, what defines success for this venture activity? Second, research and understand what options are available, and try to plan and fit the options to the venture, and likewise the venture to the options. Consider the conditions that will trigger an exit, and the conditions that will preclude an exit. Remember that success comes to those who are prepared and can quickly be positioned to spot and respond to triggering events when they occur.

Next, with a strong, clear vision that will get you through the tough, challenging seas that lie ahead, go build and grow the venture. Make it happen. And be patient, because it will take at least five years and as long as seven to ten years. Periodically conduct a formal, realistic valuation of the venture that includes a refreshed list of potential buyers, investors, strategic partners, and even professional service providers. This will not only help you keep your eyes and ears on what is going on in your space, but also provide checkpoints for your exit goals.

It is also important to seek outside professional advice when crafting your exit strategy. It will be difficult to find an objective advisor who can help you not only craft an exit strategy but also keep tabs on your valuation. For example, professional service providers—such as investment bankers or brokers, who deal on a commission-only, success-fee-only basis—will be looking for the quick deal and may not be able to assist early stage ventures with their exit strategy.

Recall from our discussion above that an exit is the transferring of ownership. Figure 13-1 identifies the ten principal exit strategies that are available to entrepreneurs.

Discussing Initial Public Offerings

Looking at the 9,796 start-ups that were venture-backed between 1992 and 2001, there were 1,331, or about 14 percent, failed outright; 1,902, or 20

FIGURE 13-1. TYPES OF EXIT STRATEGIES.

1. **Increasing the Free Cash Flows and Milking Them.** With small businesses it is retained earnings; with venture-backed deals it is paying dividends; with corporate entrepreneurship, it is increasing shareholders' earnings.

2. **Private Sale for Cash, Debt, and/or Equity to the Management Team.** Most often through a leveraged management buyout (LBO) or management buyout (MBO).

3. **Private Sale for Cash, Debt, and/or Equity to the Employees.** Usually in the form of an employee stock option plan (ESOP). More often, ESOP plans are used as a way to buy out a retiring owner.

4. **Family-Specific Transaction.** Transferring to heirs, family members, which is more of a personal exit strategy.

5. **Partial Sales or Liquidation of Assets.** Parts of the venture, like its tangible and intangible assets, are sold separately in a piecemeal fashion.

6. **Enforced Liquidation, Bankruptcy, and Reorganization.** In all cases the management and ownership will be out of the control of the original venture team and investors.

7. **Strategic Sale.** To a supplier, customer, or competitor as a part of vertical or horizontal integration.

8. **Selling to a Financial Buyer.** To a venture capital firm or private equity group either to be restructured and rolled into or merged with one of their portfolio companies, and sometimes to be run as a stand alone.

9. **Global Integration, Merger, or Acquisition.** Companies from overseas could buy the venture to get a beachhead into the U.S. as a part of vertical integration or horizontal integration.

10. **Initial Public Offering (IPO).** Long considered the benchmark for venture-backed deals. The IPO Journey is a long and arduous process.

percent, were acquired or merged; and 5,706, or 60 percent, are still privately held. Of the latter, some may not be good enough to sell, some are too young, and some are classified as "walking dead," which means there have not been any returns to the investors and none are really expected any time soon. The balance, 857, or 9 percent, went to initial public offerings (IPOs).

There were 1,919 IPOs recorded for the years 1997 to 2002, of which 756, or 40 percent, were venture-backed. But the economic downturn following the Perfect Storm has affected the number of IPOs. According to Alfred R. Berkeley III, vice chairman of NASDAQ, the "system is broken" as venture capitalists cannot push out any more new companies into the public markets until the system gets fixed. We saw the total number of venture-backed IPOs drop 86 percent—from 257 in 1999 to 37 in 2001. And just between 2000 and 2002, the average offering size fell 18 percent, from $93 million to $76 million. Using the definitions from Chapter 4, Figure 13-2 presents a sector-by-sector analysis for venture-backed IPOs.

The IPO Journey

An IPO should not be viewed as an end to the business, but as an important milestone in the entrepreneurial life cycle. Getting to an IPO is often described as the "IPO Journey." In 2001, the IPO Journey, or the amount of time from initial equity funding to IPO, was longer than it had been in years. The average age of a venture at time of IPO was around fifty-four months, compared to thirty-four months in 1998, and forty-eight months in 1994.

FIGURE 13-2. ANALYSIS OF VENTURE-BACKED IPOS (1991–2001).

Sector	Total $ Raised (Millions)	Total Number of Deals	Average Offering Size (Millions)
Biotechnology	$8,358.8	221	$37.8
Business Products & Services	$1,302.0	33	$39.4
Computers & Peripherals	$3,801.1	103	$36.9
Consumer Products & Services	$3,308.1	82	$40.3
Electronics & Instrumentation	$1,866.1	62	$30.1
Financial Services	$3,499.9	60	$58.3
Healthcare Services	$2,766.4	57	$48.5
Industrial & Energy	$7,730.3	148	$52.2
IT Services	$5,483.6	85	$64.5
Media & Entertainment	$5,052.0	85	$59.4
Medical Devices & Equipment	$6,259.4	199	$31.5
Networking & Equipment	$8,817.1	118	$74.7
Retailing & Distribution	$9,302.6	133	$69.9
Semiconductors	$2,821.1	66	$42.7
Software	$14,060.8	321	$43.8
Telecommunications	$10,638.8	145	$73.4
Other		No Deals	

Source: NVCA Yearbook 2002.

How long does the IPO Journey usually take? We examined in detail, industry by industry, the ages of 1,825 ventures that went public in the years 1997 to 2001.[4] The average was 79 months, or six-and-a-half years. The range goes from 55 months for telecommunications ventures to 94 months for healthcare ventures. The others were: industrial/energy, 92 months; semiconductors and electronics, 90 months; retailing and media, 87 months; computer software, 82 months; computer hardware and services, 78 months; business/financial, 70 months; and biotechnology, 66 months.

To some, eighty months may seem like a long time, but the importance of advance planning for the IPO Journey cannot be stressed enough. In fact, we found that some simple day-to-day management decisions and corporate transactions made years in advance of an IPO can create significant legal problems and the need for "corporate cleanup" and housekeeping later on. Randy Lunn, general partner at Palomar Ventures based in Southern California, has been involved in more than forty IPOs over the past twenty years. He has invested over $300 million in early stage ventures. He expects each one to be "IPO worthy," because it will still be attractive for someone to buy if the IPO gets pulled. Plus, as he says, "It sort of leaves a hook out for strategic partners to quickly snap 'em up." Most importantly, it directs the venture team on how to build and successfully guide the growing venture. Quite simply, and to paraphrase Covey, always begin a venture with the IPO Journey in mind.

Advantages of IPOs

In addition to providing a "liquidity event" for the venture team and the investors, IPOs offer many financial advantages. According to a report published by Babson College, 85 percent of the CEOs who led an IPO wanted to raise capital for growth, 65 percent wanted to increase their working capital, 40 percent wanted to facilitate the acquiring of another company, 35 percent wanted to establish a market value for the company, and 35 percent wanted to enhance the company's ability to raise more capital.[5] There are nonfinancial advantages too. Most importantly, an IPO is the benchmark for the credibility and viability of a young business venture with prospects, customers, and suppliers. It is also a great opportunity to create equity incentives for existing employees and for help in recruiting executives.

Disadvantage of IPOs

The chance of a high-tech venture to become a successful company that goes public is about one in six million. First of all, it is too difficult to time the markets. According to Jay Ritter, a professor at the University of Florida who studies the behavior of IPO markets, "The IPO market is never in equilibrium; it's always too hot or too cold."[6]

Second of all, a large amount of management effort, time, and expense is required to comply with SEC regulations and reporting requirements. For example, consider the Sarbanes-Oxley Act of 2002, which was signed into law as a direct response to the deterioration of public confidence in financial governance of prominent public companies. It has tightened boards of directors' audit committee responsibilities, imposed new CEO and CFO certification requirements, and raised the "standard of care" obligations on management dramatically. In other words, getting the S-1 registration documents through the approval process is taking much longer today than before and during the Perfect Storm.

Third of all, during the IPO process, the venture undergoes a tremendous amount of stress testing. According to one CEO, "There are so many parallel processes going on simultaneously. It takes a strong and well-organized team to get the job done."[7] In a survey of *Inc.* magazine's top 100 firms, the CEOs who had participated in IPOs reported that they spent 33 hours per week for four months on the offering.[8] Also, the cost of raising $5 million averages some $700,000 and involves 900 total hours of the principals' time to complete an IPO. Those pursuing an IPO will need to do so with a steady pace, not a wild scramble. Basically, it becomes a marathon, not a sprint, although you will need to sprint from time to time to meet deadlines.

Discussing Mergers and Acquisitions

The M&A market has changed considerably since the Perfect Storm. Around 1995, the new economy prompted a reallocation of capital previously unseen in the corporate world and drove M&A activity to record levels from 1995 on to 2000. In 2003, considered the worst economic downturn in a decade, M&A activity had not ground to a halt, however. For many ventures that are unable to arrange for an IPO, or for whom conventional bank financing during these uncertain times becomes a stretch, M&A deals still remain one of the few viable options for raising capital. They also allow venture capitalists and others to cash out their investments.

There are three basic types of mergers:

❖ **A horizontal merger** involves two ventures operating and competing in the same kind of business activity.

❖ **A vertical merger** occurs between ventures in different stages of production, operation, or the value chain.

❖ **A conglomerate merger** involves ventures engaged in unrelated types of business activities.

Drucker once commented that the drive for mergers and acquisitions comes less from sound reasoning and more from the fact that doing deals is a much more exciting way to spend one's day than doing actual work. Actually, we found that acquisitions occur for sound reasons. In a comprehensive survey conducted by Deloitte Consulting, 91 percent of the executives surveyed acquired another venture to grow their business, 60 percent were after econo-mies of scale, 50 percent were interested in expanding their product portfolio, 52 percent were facing pressures to consolidate, 37 percent were pressured by globalization, 35 percent were diversifying, and 37 percent thought it was an opportunistic deal.[9] Cisco Systems' approach was, "We don't do R&D, we do A&D: acquire and develop." During their hyper-growth days in the mid-1990s they were in hot pursuit of serial entrepreneurs; 45 percent of the ventures they acquired had entrepreneurs who had been acquired before, and some in fact had already sold their previous ventures to Cisco.[10]

Situation Analysis: Sector by Sector

In 2001 there were some 7,500 acquisitions in the United States, totaling $819 billion, or about half the world's M&A volume. M&As continue to be the preferred exit strategy for venture capitalists. During the period of 1996 to 2002, 57 percent of the venture-backed exit strategies were through M&As. Mark Heesen, president of NVCA, concluded that "the M&A market continues to be an extremely important exit strategy for venture capitalists, especially in years when the IPO market experiences high levels of volatility."[11]

In 2001 a record number of 322 venture-backed companies were ac-quired, but at much lower valuations than in recent years. In 2000, M&A activity accounted for $67 billion, through 190 known deals, or an average $355 million per deal. In 2001, of all the known deals, we saw a sharp de-crease in the activity—a decline of 77 percent to $15 billion. There were 146 deals, or an average $105 million per deal. For a point of reference, looking at venture-backed M&A deals between 1991 to 2001, we researched and found 1,693 deals worth $156 billion, or an average $92 million per deal.[12] Using the definitions from Chapter 4, Figure 13-3 presents a sector-by-sector analysis for venture-backed M&As.

Overview of the M&A Deal Process

The M&A deal process is second only to preparing for an IPO as the most stress testing a venture team will encounter. Like the preparation and plan-ning involved before an IPO, the M&A process will last most of one year. We briefly outline what to expect in selling a venture.

❖ **Months 1 to 2:** The preparation for the transaction; discussing the seller's decision and preparation, which involves the mental aspects, person-nel planning, tax and estate planning, business review and method of sale; assembling the team with investment bankers, accountants, and lawyers; de-termining the confidentiality treatment and limitation on use of disclosed in-formation.

❖ **Months 3 to 4:** Contact of potential buyers, maintaining confidenti-ality through the process; receiving and analyzing all indications of interest; assembly of data room.

FIGURE 13-3. ANALYSIS OF VENTURE-BACKED M&A DEALS (1991–2001).

Sector	Total $ Deals (Millions)	Total Number of Deals	Average Deal Size (Millions)
Biotechnology	$3,512.5	97	$36.2
Business Products & Services	$3,820.9	46	$83.1
Computers & Peripherals	$5,780.5	108	$53.5
Consumer Products & Services	$1,861.0	53	$35.1
Electronics & Instrumentation	$4,968.2	48	$103.5
Financial Services	$3,880.7	49	$79.2
Healthcare Services	$1,625.2	58	$28.0
Industrial & Energy	$7,021.0	124	$56.6
IT Services	$4,412.3	84	$52.5
Media & Entertainment	$16,635.5	110	$151.2
Medical Devices & Equipment	$3,671.7	94	$39.0
Networking & Equipment	$40,749.1	109	$373.8
Retailing & Distribution	$6,353.2	124	$51.2
Semiconductors	$8,461.7	50	$169.2
Software	$29,331.6	411	$71.4
Telecommunications	$14,374.6	125	$114.9
Other	Only 3–5 deals for this period.		

Source: NVCA Yearbook 2002.

❖ **Months 5 to 6:** Start of the management presentations; conducting extensive buyer due diligence; evaluating proposals.

❖ **Months 7 to 8:** The beginning of the end. Negotiating and executing the chosen Letter of Intent (LOI). Facilitating requests for information and buyer's due diligence. Negotiating and finalizing terms of purchase agreement, stock versus asset deal, tax planning, use of earn-outs, and termination or hiring of key employees.

❖ **Months 8 to 12:** The closing. Continuing involvement of seller includes honoring covenants not to compete, no shop clauses, and determining consulting vs. employment agreements. Reaching the closing means discussing employee issues, change of control agreements, and indemnities for directors and officers. Other issues include managing the communications in public M&A transactions, such as media and government-relations strategies, road shows, Web sites, and analysts calling U.S. Regulation FD.

Dealing with Investment Bankers

The role of investment bankers is to assist you in the M&A process outlined above. They help determine valuation, prepare and assist with the "selling memorandum," and identify potential candidates. Their assignment is usually undertaken on an exclusive basis, meaning that each party—the seller and the buyer—bears their own costs associated with their investment bankers. Typically, the seller pays the banker a retainer and a "value-added" success fee upon the completion of the deal. It is well understood that investment bankers will do more than earn the money back you may pay them. To avoid million-dollar mistakes, it is important to find a firm that knows its way around a deal like yours, and one that has deep experience in deal making rather than in specialized niche sales.

Obviously, venture-backed firms have the assistance of their board members and of an extended network when it comes to choosing an investment banker. A great start would be making contact with the best research analysts at investment banking firms that understand your particular industry space, sector, customers, and technology. Find out who has done deals similar to your venture, compare their success records, and finally ask around. While an investment banker can be brought in at any point in the M&A process, having one as a permanent part of your advisory team enhances the value of your business and, of course, guarantees you ready access to one.

Briefing on Getting Acquired

In *Solving the Merger Mystery*, Deloitte Consulting suggests that you should plan and structure for integration early on and focus on speed only when the opportunity to be acquired comes along. This is true because all things being equal, the faster you can get acquired, the better. Being prepared increases not only the probability of your deal going through, but also the probability of success. This is enhanced even more if the integration is well planned and orchestrated, and if it begins very early in the transaction, namely as early as the introduction phase between buyer and seller. In other words, performing internal due diligence *prior* to selling a business venture enables management to identify and address weak spots and hidden opportunities that affect its value.

Deloitte Consulting further suggests that you should be prepared to address retention issues early on. The key to M&A integration success is to view retention across three dimensions: the employees, the customers, and the suppliers. Also, having a high-level transition team comprised of well-respected executives allows your venture to rapidly mobilize the integration effort. But remember there is still a business to run, as they will face the challenges of delivering on day-to-day operating commitments. Finally, keep your M&A strategy updated and discuss it with your board and venture team members regularly.

Getting on the Radar of Potential Buyers

First, consider that from the viewpoint of potential buyers, there are five strategic alternatives to acquiring a venture. They could "build internally," form a joint venture, form a strategic alliance, enter into a licensing arrangement, or form a business partnership. Knowing that they are faced with these strategic alternatives, you should ideally be in one of these relationships today in order to facilitate getting acquired tomorrow.

Second, if you don't have any such strategic relationships today, go create some. Consider all the players on your value map. Get to know CEOs, CFOs, and CTOs in your ecosystem. Get known in your ecosystem—get analysts writing about what you are doing. Analysts at private boutique investment banks are always looking for something new to write about. The bankers they support are always looking for something to talk about, and likewise, the bankers could be helping clients look for a deal.

Third, be a first prover, and buyers will come knocking. Cisco Systems is one of the most acquisitive companies ever. They completed seventy-one acquisitions from 1993 to 2001, and twenty-five in 2000 for $12 billion, paying between $500,000 and $2 million per employee. Most importantly, 75 percent of their acquisitions were start-ups with no products shipped![13]

Managing the Deal Process and Beyond

As the saying in the M&A business goes, "Finding the right partner is the easy part. The hard part is making the marriage work." But we know that getting to the altar is no easy part either. It is your job to keep the momentum in the deal, as the longer the deal process drags on, the more likely it is to fall through. And nothing slows down the deal more than issues on valuation.

So be prepared to understand and work their "levers of success." Always be thinking on their side and how acquiring your venture will deliver value to their company. Your potential acquirer is working one of three key levers. One is efficiency, as they are looking to realize economies of scale and scope, and maximizing cost controls. The second is increasing their market leadership, as they are looking to enhance their company's brand reputation and securing technical knowledge of a competitor, or complementary venture. The third lever of success is reinvention. Their goal is not only changing their company, but also trying to tilt the entire industry in their favor.

Have a common sense approach to valuation and be prepared well in advance. Uncover "comparables" from looking at your direct competitors' business more closely. Examine S-1 Registration filings of companies in your space. Work with venture capitalists and investment bankers who have access to great valuation reports from research firms like Venture Economics. Research deals matching your industry, keywords, financing time period, stage of development, even geographical location. Develop a keen understanding in the valuation methodologies and pricing drivers that might be particular for your industry.

The successful closing of a sale may seem like the natural point in time to take a step back and relax. But working to ensure post-merger success is a major concern of the acquiring company. Most M&A failures are attributed to errors committed during the integration process. However, success stories can also be found. For example, Cisco claims a 94 percent retention rate of the key employees; all during the M&A process they gauge the chemistry, the culture, and the environment for entrepreneurial spirit that exists between them and the venture they are acquiring.[14]

In summary, ventures that integrate effectively and have a clear understanding of the M&A process are ready to implement an integration strategy from day one. It is important to realize that companies looking to acquire your venture want to see continued momentum and focusing throughout the integration process.

Making a Deal with Intel Capital

In 1988 Jeff Lawrence started Los Angeles-based Trillium Digital Systems after he was laid off. He says, "Getting laid off was the catalyst. Then it came down to assessing what I could do. I had knowledge in software development. And I figured if it didn't work out I still had the skills to go back and work for someone else."[15] Together with his partner Larisa Chistyakov, they pooled about $1,000 and started a company. After about five years, they went out and raised some $14 million from an investment bank and Intel Capital to fuel their growth strategy. In 2001 they sold their company to Intel for $300 million in cash and stock. Kirby Dyess, vice president and director of operations for Intel Capital, explains the first step in making a deal with Intel: "It's important that you really need a clear direction and strong sense of the value drivers before going into the deal."[16] And Lawrence found what he called a "great steward inside" Intel to help with the integration. They talked all the time, "even on Sundays when the deal was going sideways." Lawrence discovered that valuation was "more art than science" and that "it became a matter of opinion." His advice is that "to be successful you have to listen to people and be willing to change. You need to communicate with your people so they know what is going on. Encourage their input."

Setting Exit Goals and Triggering Events for Harvesting

A number of events may trigger a decision to sell your venture—since selling at the right time can provide substantial liquidity for you and your investors. And how important is the timing of the exit? Just like the window of opportunity for getting a venture launched, the window of opportunity for exiting and harvesting a venture opens and closes quickly as well. Inktomi illustrates when the timing is off. For example, it was valued at $23 billion in the eye of the Perfect Storm, with a price per share in March 2000 of $232. In December 2002, Yahoo eventually acquired them for $235 million, or $1.65 per share.

As Mark Heesen addressed in the Foreword to this book, venture capitalists and angel investors now share a long-term approach to their investing. According to Lawrence Mock, Jr., president of Pittsburgh-based Mellon Ventures, "It's more realistic to have an exit strategy of five to seven years, rather than what seemed like eighteen months in the late 1990s."[17] In addition to keeping a pulse on the IPO market conditions, venture capitalists also look at their ROI on each deal. So an exit could be triggered if the venture has reached point when the IRR is very favorable, industry valuation multiples are most favorable, and buyers are churning in the marketplace. The most common events that trigger an exit are listed in Figure 13-4.

Structuring the Transaction

There are many ways to structure a transaction and only three basic types of consideration. *Cash* is the least complex but it can be complicated by payment methods. For example, the buyer can put portions of it in escrow to offset against undisclosed liabilities and misrepresentations or breaches of warranties by the seller. The second type is *equities*. Common stock, if not publicly traded stock, will have problems in its valuation. Preferred stock is like a form of financing by the seller with the seller receiving regular dividends. The third type is *earn-outs* and *contingency payments*. These are post-closing payments based on the performance of the business after the closing. They are typically used when the buyer and seller are unable to agree on the value of the ven-

FIGURE 13-4. EVENTS THAT TRIGGER AN EXIT.

▲ **Macro-Environmental Issues.** Government, policy, and regulatory issues will make the venture unattractive in the near future.

▲ **Completion of Growth Strategy.** The transition from entrepreneurial management to professional management has been successful.

▲ **Product and Technology Lifecycles.** The core products or product platform has become a victim of commoditization and the market is squeezing the life out of profit margins.

▲ **Competitive Pressures.** Direct competitors, new entrants are threatening the venture's core competitive advantage.

▲ **Size of Company.** A preset valuation that matches the investors' ROI.

▲ **Revenue Model.** Top line sales revenues are firmly established for a period of time going into the future and/or bottom line profitability is proven.

▲ **Marquee Customers.** Certain customer contracts, orders, or large backlog guarantees strong revenues for a period of time.

▲ **Number of Employees.** Getting to a predetermined number, where it becomes "too large to manage" for the core venture team.

▲ **Diversification of Private Wealth.** The venture team's equity position is at nearly 100% of their net worth; they would like to get something out of their hard work.

▲ **Personal Issues.** Members of the venture team reached a certain age; just got married, have new kids, have grave health-related issues, or it is just time for a family transition in the business.

▲ **Attractive Opportunity.** Investment banks, brokers, and other companies have a deal in mind and are presenting letters of intent to purchase the company now.

ture, or when the buyer plans to retain the seller to manage the venture after the closing and wishes to provide a performance incentive. Earn-outs let the buyer commit a little money and then wait and see what the outcome is down the road. They are designed to help spread the risk in the deal and can last anywhere from eighteen months to about three years.

Seeing the Personal Side of Selling

It is important to keep your harvest options open and to think of harvesting as a vehicle for creating future entrepreneurial choices for you and your venture team. According to Herb Cohen, the author of *You Can Negotiate Anything,* "Although mentally exciting, in fact one of the most exciting moments in your business career, it is one of the most difficult decisions to make."[18] Follow his excellent advice and take comfort in knowing that you will grow and be part of something bigger rather than focusing on what you may have lost.

It is important to visualize the outcome of your life and work on creating a "win-win" scenario with all your venture's stakeholders. Cohen recommends seeking comfort with your peers and entrepreneurs, who have been successful in completing this final stage of the entrepreneurial life cycle. They can help you visualize and understand potential outcomes and stay emotionally detached from the process. They can also provide support and comfort during the transaction, especially since during the process of selling your venture you are likely to have at least one blow-up among the parties involved. Finally, once you have the process of selling your venture in play, consider what your life will be like post-transaction, and what a relief harvesting and closing the deal will be. Be sure to take a step back and let the investment bankers earn their fees.

PART V

Getting Your

Venture into Orbit

FOURTEEN

Putting It All Together and Getting Financed

Simplex veri sigillum
—Latin proverb for "Simplicity is the seal of truth."

If you can't describe what you are doing as a process, you don't know what you are doing.
—W. Edwards Deming

You can sometimes fool the fans, but you can never fool the players.
—**Jack Stack**, *The Great Game of Business*

Packaging: Preparing Your Quiver of Arrows

We now want to circle back to Chapter 12, "Financing the Emerging Growth Venture." To set the stage for this discussion, here is what Anita Roddick, founder of The Body Shop, once said: "There are only two ways of raising money: the hard way and the very hard way." As we said in the Introduction, the world of venture capitalism has its own language, its own process, and its own methods of communication between entrepreneurs and potential investors. All entrepreneurs must go through the formal venture drill when raising money from outside investors. The three steps to the drill are packaging, placing, and presenting. *Packaging* is researching and writing an effective business plan. *Placing* is skillfully introducing the opportunity before the best investors. *Presenting* is communicating and making the deal happen in a formal meeting at the investors' closing table.

What makes fund-raising so hard is not only understanding this process, but also at the same time putting your deal into a package that can be communicated and shared quickly and efficiently. Venture capitalists, especially those that focus on financing early stage ventures, get carpet-bombed with packages outlining business concepts at various stages of development. Facing such an information glut, venture capitalists have been conditioned to consume data at only two speeds. One is very slow, used when they are reviewing and editing investment agreements and the financials of deals before them. The other is very fast, as they become highly skilled at quickly sifting through slush piles of business plans and scanning thousands of e-mails. Therefore, your poten-

❖
Case in Point: Sun Microsystems Launches

No established company rode higher on the Information Technology wave than Santa Clara, California-based Sun Microsystems, whose sales nearly doubled, to $18 billion, in the three fiscal years that ended in June 2001. Stanford University graduates Scott McNealy, Bill Joy, Andy Bechtolsheim, and Vinod Khosla got together in 1982 to start SUN (Stanford University Network) Microsystems. Designed to be networked from the beginning, based on the fast-growing Ethernet, and running on the UNIX operating system, the SUN workstation began as a solution to the bottlenecks in the Stanford computer science department. It was perfect for the growing networking demands of engineers, researchers, and scientists around the world. By 1983, Kleiner Perkins was an investor, and the firm's partner, John Doerr, recruited Eric Schmidt to head up software operations. Later that year they launched operations in Europe.

Khosla, the founding chief executive officer, describes how he persuaded McNealy to join the start-up: "We used to say we own a great rocket ship but it doesn't matter how high it goes if it doesn't reach orbital velocity. If we're going to fail, we'll be a big splash. We'll go high and shoot for the moon and be the biggest belly flop ever, but our goal is truly to get in orbit." Along the way to orbital velocity and an IPO in 1986, Sun had revenues of $9 million the first year, $39 million the second year, $115 million the third year, $210 million the fourth year, and a "billion-something" the sixth year. In just over ten years, Sun reached an incredible milestone. They shipped one million systems and made their debut on the *Fortune 500*. They were the second-fastest computer company to ever reach $1 billion in annual sales, and had the fastest growth rate ever for a computer company with a direct sales force.

Sources: Sun Microsystems company Web site; Steve Lohr, "Sun, Again, Bets Against the Odds," *New York Times Online*, February 23, 2003; Stephen Segaller, *Nerds 2.0.1: A Brief History of the Internet* (New York: TV Books, 1999), pp. 228, 234; and Michael S. Malone, *Betting It All: The Entrepreneurs of Technology* (New York: John Wiley & Sons, 2002), p. 161.

tial investor is likely to make an instant judgment call just on the strength of the first few words you speak at a networking event, or the first few lines in your Executive Summary. We know of some VCs who consider the strength of the contents by looking only at the "Subject Box" of entrepreneurs' e-mails!

So how do you get around this communication problem? How do you get what you want said before the right person, at the right time, and in the right way? First you must "disambiguate" what you are attempting to communicate. Disambiguate, a word the Pentagon actually created, means to simplify and clarify. We help entrepreneurs disambiguate by having them create what we call a Quiver of Arrows. The arrows in your quiver are your Fast Pitch, Email Quickview, Executive Summary, PowerPoint Presentation, and Business Plan (see Figure 14-1). At the highest level of communication is your Fast Pitch. It is used verbally when meeting someone for the first time at a networking event or other business function. The next arrow is your Email Quickview. It is perfect for quickly following up with the folks you met. Its

FIGURE 14-1. QUIVER OF ARROWS.

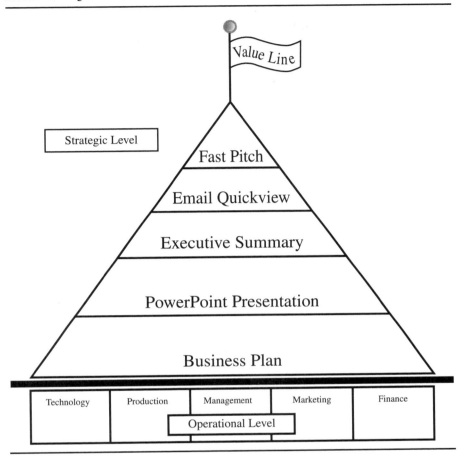

purpose is to get people hooked and interested in helping you. If the right person is targeted and is delivered a well-prepared Quickview, they will ask for more. Use your Executive Summary as a quick follow-up to the e-mails. Your PowerPoint Presentation and Business Plan are used only when you meet in face-to-face meetings with well-qualified senior partners at VC firms and other professionals.

Perfecting Your Fast Pitch

It is this simple: First moments matter most. The whole point of your Fast Pitch is to get investors interested enough in you to get their business cards and to agree to meet with you at a later date, or at least to get them to refer you to someone else who might be interested in your deal.[1] Jason Salfen, at MIT's Sloan School of Management Entrepreneurship Center, puts it succinctly: "You don't need to reel them in, it's just getting that initial hook." To help you get started with your Fast Pitch, see the Checklist in Figure 14-2. Investors know that the way you will engage your initial customer base is through a Fast Pitch. It is the same for attracting strategic partners and even recruiting executives, which means that in general, the investors know that entrepreneurs best suited for funding can usually articulate their venture's value proposition within a sentence or two. If it is more complicated than that to explain, it is probably not ready to be funded. So once you have your Fast Pitch down, be ready to catch the fruit as you shake the tree. Because a venture capitalist can call at any time after your first meeting, always be prepared to deliver a concise and compelling "Value Line" that succinctly illustrates your venture's key capabilities. Figure 14-3 lists examples of value lines of several popular companies.

Honing Your Email Quickview

Internet e-mail has become a key component of communication in the business world today. Think of your Email Quickview as the equivalent of tapping an investor on the shoulder at a networking event and saying, "Excuse me, but do you have a minute to talk?" If you are referred to investors by a colleague, or by an entrepreneur with whom they have invested, tell them this in the first line. Say "Referral from Dr. Smith" in the subject box of the e-mail

FIGURE 14-2. FAST PITCH CHECKLIST.

1. Who We Are. What stage are you at in the food chain? Describe your internal capabilities that no one else has. Were you founded by a serial entrepreneur, a domain expert, a mad scientist who is best in the field, or do you have a team led by a branded-CEO? Profile your external team's capabilities. You have assembled award-winning advisors, board of directors, and investors.

2. What We Got. Describe your opportunity, market need/pain, and solution. Specifically describe your traction in your market space, for example, letters of intent from marquee customers or recurring revenues.

3. Where We're Going. Overview of your growth benchmarks/milestones, discuss what is next in the product pipeline, describe where you see the sweet spot for your customers lie.

4. What We Need. Do not offer specific financial needs, especially in a public forum. Just be prepared to answer privately these questions, "How much do you guys need to launch this thing off?" and "What is your use of proceeds?"

5. Why Now. Get investors interested in following up with you immediately after you meet them. State what has changed in the world, like the inflection point that opens up the window to your particular opportunity.

6. What We Offer. Describe a basic understanding of how you will provide a return on investors' money.

7. Case Studies and References. It is very important to cite an example, preferably with a marquee customer, how you solved a particular pain. Also be prepared to have a viable list of references, personal and for the venture, to add credibility to your deal.

Figure 14-3. Great examples of values lines.

3M: "Leading Through Innovation."

Amgen: "Amgen Inc. is a global biotechnology company that discovers, develops, manufactures, and markets human therapeutics based on advances in cellular and molecular biology."

Cisco: "We network networks."

Emulex Corporation: "We network storage."

Home Depot: "We're the Sears & Roebuck's of the home-improvement industry."

Hewlett-Packard: "Hewlett-Packard designs, manufactures and services electronic products and systems for measurement, computation and communication."

IBM: "IBM creates, develops, manufactures and sells advanced information technologies, including computer systems, software, networking systems, storage devices and microelectronics."

Medtronic: "Medtronic, Inc. is a leader in producing therapeutic medical devices to improve the cardiovascular and neurological health of patients around the world."

Qualcomm: "We make wireless work wonders."

Yahoo!: "Yahoo! is the only place anyone has to go to find something, connect with someone, or buy something."

---

and be sure to "CC: Dr. Smith." This is not only a courtesy to Dr. Smith, but it also demonstrates that you have spoken with Dr. Smith, or better yet, know him well.

Prepare your Email Quickview by writing down what you are basically saying in your Fast Pitch. Close by stating something very positive and affirmative like, "Dr. Smith (your referral) was excited by our idea, I know you will be too. I look forward to hearing from your soon." Be sure to include your e-mail address and phone number. Printed out, your Email Quickview should not be much longer than one page. Be sure to Google the person that you are contacting. It is very important to learn as much as possible, and then try to personalize what you have learned when you write the e-mail. Remember that many investors will be reading their e-mail via a BlackBerry-type device, so make sure not to use any HTML, embedded net links, graphics, or attachments with your Email Quickview. Finally, do not sabotage yourself by letting your need for instant approval get the best of you. Do not call to follow up, because you will appear anxious and unprofessional. With a correctly prepared e-mail you have invited a response, so be patient and wait for it.

Nailing Down Your Executive Summary

If you have targeted the right investor at the right time, you will get an e-mail response asking for more information. Have your Executive Summary at the ready in your quiver for quickly following up. Once investors have your Executive Summary, you now have a reason to call them, politely saying something like this, "I'm calling to make sure you got our attachment OK." And you can add, "I'm following up to answer any questions you might have."

An effective Executive Summary succinctly highlights your Ten Value Drivers in three to five pages. It is best written in a word-processing application, like Microsoft Word. It should never include graphics, flying logos, HTML, or net links to special Web sites. If the Fast Pitch and Email Quickview are what get customers into the store from the streets, consider the Executive Summary as the brochure that prospective customers take home with them. A well-prepared Executive Summary will give you more than a mere advantage over the other deals on the desk of investors. It will invariably make the difference between success and failure.

Mastering Your Business Plan

As we first discussed in the Introduction to this book, business planning is the process of uncovering and identifying what creates and drives value in your business. The business plan is the document that communicates your value drivers, helps your team measure your progress, and as a roadmap communicates to all your stakeholders where you are going. The structure of a business plan is as important as its contents. It is important to keep the excitement, interest, and storyline going with your potential investors. You do not want to lose any momentum in the detailed or garbled writing of a business plan. Keep it very simple, and include an expanded discussion of your ten value drivers, the concise financials discussed in Chapter 12, and any supporting documents. A complete business plan outline is presented in Appendix A. Although some investors will request a complete business plan before committing to any formal meetings with senior partners, most will be satisfied with a well-prepared Executive Summary as the basis for an initial meeting over coffee or lunch. Try to limit the number of people who are reading your Business Plan at any one time. It should only be left behind with prequalified investors, such as after a formal PowerPoint presentation before senior partners at a reputable venture capital firm.

Placing: Targeting the Best Funding Sources and Getting Your Plan Placed

It is important to think of fund-raising as a process of *buying capital* rather than *selling equity*. This difference in mindset is subtle in the packaging, but very important with your placing efforts because venture capital is a commodity. Review the discussions in Chapter 12, prequalify a shortlist of VCs, and pitch only to senior partners. Do not waste your time with "tire-kickers," and be sure to protect your venture team from looters. Most importantly, do not download your hard-earned business intelligence on a VC firm if they are not truly qualified to take your meeting—you do not want them learning at your expense.

First-time entrepreneurs out raising money normally make one of two mistakes in approaching venture capitalists. They contact either too few, or too many. The typical first-time entrepreneur will carefully orchestrate an access point with a single investor. The VC will ask for the package and then the entrepreneur will wait patiently for a response. Then most often, in eagerness to please the one investor, the entrepreneur will eagerly hop into the teacup ride and whirl around, reworking not only the business plan, but also reconsidering the entire business model, strategy, and venture team in attempts to please this one investor. This teacup ride consumes a huge amount of time and critical resources, especially if the entrepreneur needs money pretty soon.

On the other hand, some entrepreneurs will go to the library and photocopy five-hundred names from a comprehensive reference like *Pratt's Guide to Venture Capital Sources*. Then they methodically prepare a nationwide "carpet-bombing" strategy in attempts to get the feeling that they are shopping it around.

It Is About Warm Body Referrals

According to Tom Clancy, a partner at Enterprise Capital, raising money for start-ups is probably more dependent on personal relationships than it is on the underlying potential and economics of the deal. Jesse Reyes, a researcher from Venture Economics, says that the best VCs only want qualified leads, adding that an introduction increases your odds of getting your foot in the door at least ten times. This "warm-body" referral is so important in the venture drill. Gary Rieschel, executive managing director at Mobius, agrees: "The reality is that there is no way any firm can respond to the flow of business plans it sees. You start to screen based on who is saying that this is a good deal."[2] As a result, VCs tell us that you need to work on a strategy for getting some kind of introduction.

Placing with angel investors is even more difficult. In their book, *Angel Investing: Matching Start-up Funds with Start-up Companies*, Mark Van Osnabrugge and Robert Robinson discuss why. First, there are no directories of angels; angels prefer anonymity to avoid being carpet bombed with business plans. The subject matter of angel investments is often private and personal; angels come from a population of wealthy individuals and want to avoid attention to their financial position. Finally, there are no public records of their investment transactions. As Gerald Benjamin and Joel Margulis point out in their book, *Angel Financing: How to Find and Invest in Private Equity*, 57 percent of angels receive their deals from a friend, family member, or co-worker, and 31 percent receive referrals from professionals. They found that only 12 percent of angel deals come from cold calls.

Placing a plan with an angel is a process of finding out who is who, and of networking around; we call it "triangulating." This triangulation process involves meeting with at least three individuals who can facilitate a warm-body referral to a particular angel or angel group. John Morris, a past-president of the Tech Coast Angels, one of the largest angel investment groups in the United States, told us that "what's gotten our interest in the past is that the entrepreneurs have done their homework on the process, in their space and on us—their investors."

So how do you get your first warm body referral? As Guy Kawasaki of Garage Technology Ventures says, "You have to be a part of the inner circle to get funding. You have to know someone on Sand Hill Road or at least play golf at the right place. Unless you're well-connected, it's difficult to get noticed."[3] We suggest that you begin when you first structure your organization. Review our discussions in Chapter 6. Work on getting the best professional service providers, advisors, and board members. You need to have a strong external team ready to go to bat for you. Here is an insider secret that one experienced venture capitalist shared with us: Do not forget that investors are humans too, which means that they do have to eat breakfast, lunch, and take coffee breaks—all of which present a great opportunity for an informal discussion. It can give you the chance to talk (they will be eating), and it is structured, meaning that it is not going to last much longer than forty-five minutes. Besides, you never know whom else you could meet while treating a well-known VC to a meal. Do not bring along your team, and do not expect to do a presentation on a laptop. Consider this an extended Fast Pitch opportunity and a one-on-one sales call.

If there is just one rule, one thing to remember about working with private equity investors, it is this: Their world is very connected—more connected than you could ever imagine. As Pierre Omidyar from eBay discovered, "The more VCs you talk to, the more chance you have to screw up your presentation, and then someone says, 'They really screwed up, they don't know what they're doing.'"[4] Investors know when a deal has made the rounds and they basically will shy away from the deal that has made the rounds. Remember that investors want to be on the creative edge of ideas and innovations, not the lagging edge. Plan on everyone in the VC community talking to each other, and even on their ganging together and completing one tough term sheet instead of two or three competing term sheets. They could basically tell you to take it or leave it. Finally, be careful about incorporating in your business plan and package any feedback, reviews, or key quotes from other investors you meet along the way. First, it can start the teacup ride; second, understand that for those who may get excited about seeing other names mentioned there may be an equal number who get turned off.

The Follow-Up

Since you are following the venture drill process, expect that just about every professional investor you contact will claim to be "interested," by responding with either an e-mail or a phone call. It is your job to follow up and get the investors on the phone, making sure they really have a strong interest in your deal. A good gauge is how quickly they arrange a meeting, whether a first-time informal meeting over coffee, or even better, an invitation for you to present before partners. In these early contacts, consider this: How is the chemistry between you and the investors? We have found that the importance of personal chemistry between the entrepreneur and the venture capital firm cannot be overemphasized. It lays the roots for success. It fertilizes the value-adding process. What is your attitude toward them as potential investors? What about having them in your board meetings? As Arthur Rock states, "I prefer someone who *wants* me to play a role in the enterprise's decision making."[5]

You will need to manage this relationship building with confidence, not desperation. Investors can, and will, smell desperation. Like with all champion golfers, you need to have the confidence to "play it where it lies." Confidence in golf comes from being well prepared and knowing what to do after each shot you make no matter where the ball lands. Be sure to ask questions. Find out issues that move investments along and what you can do to facilitate the process. Finally, the bandwidth of time is the most precious commodity of investors. Watch the fine line between persistence and annoyance. It is a fine line that entrepreneurs must learn to walk.

Dealing with NDAs

Do not get hung up on having every investor sign a nondisclosure agreement (NDA). Asking a formal private equity investor to sign an NDA, especially a venture capitalist, is a sign of an amateur. It will be an instant deal killer—you will never hear back nor have any discussions with that investor ever again about your particular deal. First, look at the NDA from the potential investor's viewpoint. They see thousands of business plans each year. How can they possibly track thousands of NDAs? It would be a legal and administrative nightmare. Second, venture capitalists are not in the business of stealing ideas and technologies. Third, maybe you are just too in love with your idea, and this demonstrates that you have not properly completed your due diligence.[6] Hisrich and Peters provide the best strategy in handling NDAs. They suggest that all readers of your business plan who are not representing a professional firm should sign a NDA. Those representing a professional firm (such as venture capitalists, law offices, or bankers) need not be asked to sign a NDA.[7]

Presenting: Perfecting Your Sales Pitch

If you have not already met for an initial informal meeting over coffee, after reading your Executive Summary the venture capitalist will normally telephone you to ask some basic questions and to see how you sound in real life. The VC will also go over your basic deal points and test the chemistry and the fit of your personalities. If all signs lead to a "Go" then the VC will invite you for a formal meeting at the firm's office before the partners. And congratulations—the odds are going in your favor, you made the first cut. Out of 1,000 business plans, maybe less than 100 are considered for a meeting, maybe less than twenty get to due diligence, and only about ten are actually funded.

Consider the VC's viewpoint of the meeting. As Art Rock says, "I don't talk much during these meetings; I'm there to listen. I want to hear what they've got to say and see how they think."[8] VCs want more information about your venture and how it will make them money. The meeting provides an opportunity to evaluate you, your team, and the organizational dynamics of the team. They are checking the "fit and finish" of your team. They are interested in laying the groundwork for getting a deal to the closing table. They are trying to determine how your deal fits with them, what obstacles there are, and what the probabilities are of it closing. This is ultimately what they are thinking, hanging on every word said by you and your team.

Presentation Pointers

First of all be prepared to energetically SELL, SELL, SELL!!! The first few minutes of your presentation are most critical. John Martinson, past-chairman of the NVCA and partner at Edison Venture Fund based in Lawrenceville, New Jersey, says that "the person giving the presentation must be engaging and convincing. They will have to sell their idea to many people in order for their company to succeed. So if their presentation is weak and uninspiring, one has to think how it will affect their customers and suppliers."[9]

Position your deal clearly and early on. Avoid using buzzwords. Be sure to just speak "English" and do not use "techie" jargon or fancy VC lingo. As Jesse Reyes of Venture Economics says, "Don't be cute. Everyone uses [buzzwords], and no one believes them, and what's worse, it speaks of hype." "We all come back to a common-sense litmus test," says Joe Aragona, general partner at Austin Ventures. "If in the first ten minutes or the first couple of slides you still don't know what this company is doing, the chances are you probably won't make an investment."[10] We know that writing a business plan is tough for everybody and creating a presentation that represents your best points is even more difficult. For suggestions and guidelines on preparing your presentation, review Appendix C, "PowerPoint Presentation Outline."

How to Get the Best Out of Your Meeting

Be sure to weave a great story. As Ann Winblad from Hummer-Winblad says, "Everybody needs to be a great storyteller."[11] Remember that investors are looking for reasons to believe you *and* they are looking for reasons to not believe you. Revisit this book's Introduction, where we first discuss effective storytelling. Through a well-practiced story you can be more comfortable to create a sense of energy, excitement, and commitment around your deal.

The lead entrepreneur/CEO will have about twenty minutes to describe strategy, business model, differentiation, size of the market potential, and how to execute and capture customers. The CFO will typically have about fifteen minutes to describe the financials from a "ground-up" approach: how the revenue model works, the performance metrics, and assumptions of the revenue drivers. To help you get ready for your first meeting, see Figure 14-4.

Following your presentation there will be a period of questions and answers. VCs spend their days asking entrepreneurs questions. You might get the feeling that VCs think of themselves as amateur psychologists attempting to discover "what makes you tick." Do not take any questions personal, do not give them vague answers, and do not lead them around in circles. It is far better to give an approximate answer to the right question, which is often vague, than an exact answer to the wrong question, which can also be vague. And never, ever, push against their suggestions, comments, and feedback. As Rock points out, "There's a thin line between refusing to accept criticism and sticking to your guns."

Be forewarned: there are really tough questions, and then there are the live hand grenades that will be rolled across the table to you. Andreas Stavropoulos from Draper Fisher Jurvetson, who likes to ask entrepreneurs hypothetical questions, says, "I'll even ask about scenarios that are extremely unlikely, just to see how entrepreneurs react to situations that they couldn't possibly have spent much time considering. What's most important is that you display adaptability, creativity, and intelligence. I don't want people just to tell me that the situation would never occur and leave it at that."[12]

Another VC puts it this way. "We ask a lot of peripheral questions. We might not want answers." Then why ask? They might be testing to see whether you are open to looking at things in different ways. They may want proof that you can respond articulately to unexpected questions and observations. And your answers may reveal an essential quality they need to see in a venture team: malleability.

Be sure to manage the closing of the presentation. You will be able to tell whether your presentation and your excitement and passion are communicated to the right investors at the right time. Consider their chemistry and feelings: If you have made an impression they will invite you back to meet with the other partners in the firm, or with other colleagues who are other experts in your space. If unsure, simply ask, "What should I tell my partners/venture team/board members that we accomplished today?" And if you have an insecure feeling, simply say something like this: "Let me get this straight— what I hear from you is that you are doubtful and need to see more information from us. So, if I complete the competitive landscape report you requested, are you going to fund our venture?"

Managing the Process

Sorry, just like in romance and dating, the answer is "No" until you hear a "Yes." Don't be shy, manage the relationship. Venture capitalists are very busy folks. They all have huge slush piles of unread business plans and unread

FIGURE 14-4. HOW TO GET THE MOST OUT OF YOUR MEETING WITH INVESTORS.

Target the right investors. Know your audience, who will be there, and why. Qualified investors are in a way cheering for you, that they have a sense of wanting you to succeed. They put their valuable time on the line to hear your presentation. The right investors want you to be comfortable and do well.

Prepare and rehearse. In a dress rehearsal, decide who is going to attend, who will talk about the business strategy, who will talk about the technology, and who will talk about the financials. VCs have deals and ideas pitched at them all day long. They remember human-interest stories; have a well-prepared storyline to share.

Change people's pulse with EXCITEMENT! Genuinely express yourself through your excitement and energy behind the deal. For example, feel free to jump up to use a whiteboard in the room. You are testing their openness and they are looking at your sales and communication skills. You must demonstrate confidence, not arrogance. You have the fearless courage to get it done.

Keep the positive chemistry going. Develop a rapport with the folks you just met, maintain eye contact with all. Describing your Eureka moment before your first PowerPoint slide is always the best way to break the ice. And explain how your venture team came together, why this problem you identified is so important to solve right now for your team. Be open for feedback, it is a sign of interest and buying. Do not bring a lawyer, accountant, or other advisors since there are no negotiations during the first meeting. This is a chance for the VCs to get to know you and your venture team without interference from others.

Manage their decision-making process. Take charge for your venture or no one else will! Be clear in what you want and expect from investors. If you cannot sell the venture, then they will assume that you cannot sell your product nor motivate your team. Ask questions about them and their deals, and investment process. Work toward setting up a strong, successful conclusion by identifying your "must remembers" and your takeaways. Go for a trial close.

Keep your finger on the pulse of the audience. Be prepared to keep notes, or better yet have someone there to help you keep notes—who and what they are asking, suggesting, and discussing. Not only so you can accurately follow up with them, but their feedback is golden—an extremely important part of getting successfully launched.

Have perfect leave-behinds. Such efficiency in both your package and presentation will create a favorable impression that is often an indication of how well you will run and manage a business. Bring completed detailed bios of executive team members with references so that they can feel comfortable about your backgrounds. Have copies of your slides and supporting documents for common questions; prepare a list of customer references in advance.

---

e-mails, and lots of board meetings to attend. It takes at least six calls or e-mails before they return one. If you presented at a meeting and feel that it was well received by the VCs then do not hesitate to follow up. Pick up the phone, send an e-mail or an express letter—do what you must to get a response. Although there is a fine line between being a tenacious entrepreneur and a pain-in-the-ass, work on maintaining the forward momentum. You are going against "pitch-decay," and a serious deal killer right now is an in-flight stall.[13] Be persistent and just get into the habit of validating your progress by asking, "Where does our deal stand right now? Are we likely to get an investment from you or not?"

Yes is great, No is OK, Maybe is the bad answer. First, if there is a Yes in the making you will hear it very quickly and early on. Very seldom will an investor say No. More than likely something in your plan needs to be either water-tested or retightened. It is not in their best interest to be saying No. They want you to feel that you do not have to go shopping elsewhere just in case you do get it tightened down and also in case you might have some other ideas.

Here is something that 99 out of 100 first-time entrepreneurs neglect: They do not ask for feedback. VCs love to provide advice. We found that the majority will provide honest, valuable feedback. These discussions can stimulate new ideas and new ways to rework your plan and deal. Soliciting feedback not only provides you an excuse to circle back to them, but it also presents a chance to place and present before other VCs. Ask them what other VCs might be interested in your deal. This is a chance to lobby hard with them, asking for names, e-mails, and phone numbers.

In research for their book, *Inside Secrets to Venture Capital*, Brian Hill and Dee Power found that 34 percent of the VC deals were referred by other VCs.[14] Most likely, after they realize they gave you some good names, they will say something like, "Be sure to circle back." Remember, they are in business to invest in new ventures like yours, and basically they say No because they are conditioned to safeguard their risks.

Work hard at learning from every No you hear. A No allows you to reposition your pitch for the next one and turn old weaknesses into new strengths. Each time you hear a No, do not walk away discouraged, and do not approach or counter the investors with an attitude that you can change their mind. Instead consider the fact that rejection is a tool you can use. In 1996, the co-founders of Hotmail were turned down by twenty-one VCs. The twenty-first VC referred them to Draper Fisher Jurvetson. DFJ provided almost $5 million in capital, and Microsoft acquired Hotmail in 1997 for $440 million, a sweet return for DFJ.

The only thing certain for one who quits is failure. Donald Valentine at Sequoia Capital was the seventy-seventh venture capitalist Sandy Lerner had approached to fund Cisco. Mike Medavoy, an entrepreneur who happens to do his thing in movie making, said that if he stopped at No the world would be without some of his hit movies, which include three Academy Award winners for Best Picture: "One Flew Over the Cuckoo's Nest," "Rocky," and "The Silence of the Lambs."[15] And as President Richard Nixon once said, "Defeat doesn't finish a man—quit does. A man is not finished when he's defeated. He's finished when he quits." Don't quit, the world may need your idea.

At the Closing Table and Beyond

Congratulations! Out of a thousand plans, maybe 100 or so get considered and only about twenty get to meeting—so you are on your way! As you get into the talking points of a deal, know that there is much you can control when negotiating with venture capitalists. In fact, far more is negotiable than you may think, it only depends on your negotiation skills and tactics. According to Richard Siegelman, general partner at Kleiner Perkins:

> A venture capitalist makes three decisions. First, to invest and how much. Second and third, with the rest of the board, to hire and fire a CEO. Everything else is cajoling, persuading, and presenting evidence."[16]

Intelligent negotiators are prepared, confident, and supremely effective. Herb Cohen, the author of *You Can Negotiate Anything*, defines negotiation as "a field of knowledge and endeavor that focuses on gaining the favor of people from whom we want things." Effective negotiators use information and power to affect behavior. Leigh Steinberg is a premier sports agent, and the movie "Jerry McGuire" is based on his success. He has negotiated more than $1 billion in salaries and bonuses. In *Winning with Integrity*, his guide to negotiation, he states, "Effective negotiation is about exhaustive preparation, utter clarity, heartfelt communication, and a sincere, demonstrated desire to fully understand not just your own needs but the needs of the other party."[17]

The negotiating techniques you select for your meeting with the investors will depend upon the particular situation, your personality, and the relative strengths on both sides of the closing table. But the ground you will inevitably cover includes stock restrictions, debt conversion, dilution protection, vesting, your ongoing commitment to the venture, downstream liquidity, directors, and price per share. The typical end product of this first round of negotiation is the term sheet that the venture capitalist prepares and presents to entrepreneurs. It specifies the key financial and legal terms of the investment and serves as a basis for the negotiation and preparation of the definitive legal documentation. The legal specialists that are working for your team should be very familiar with the many terms and restrictions that are typically found in such term sheets (see Appendix E for a sample term sheet).

Watch Out for Sand Traps, Land Mines, and Deal Killers

Imagine an inexperienced golfer, swinging and swinging away at a ball in a sand trap. Well, most venture capitalists will allow you to tee-up the ball and watch you take a swing. If you happen to land in a sand trap it demonstrates your competency (or really lack of) in the venture drill process. Missing some details, forgetting names and conversations from your last talks, is all part of the process. You will get a lot of room for making simple errors because they know that you are going into unknown territory.

Land mines, however, are a different story. Thomas Fuller, the English historian, once said, "Get the facts right, or the facts will get you." There are two types of land mines: an explosive that *you* will eventually stumble across, and an explosive that *VCs* will eventually stumble across. Venture capitalists evaluate business plans and presentations for a living. Remember everything you have said along the way because they will. And be very careful about what is projected or promised in your talks. Consider the fact that you will be held accountable for your projections and promises. Any deception in a plan or presentation will be caught right away and greatly lessens the possibility of an investment. Worse yet, having the VC step on a landmine in the due diligence process (something that should have been disclosed earlier) will probably permanently "disfigure" the deal and maybe damage some on the venture team as well.

Finally, there is the deal killer. Just like it sounds, it is something that will kill the deal instantly for that particular investor. Triggering any one of the deal killers listed in Figure 14-5 can be quite costly for you, especially when there is a limited number of venture firms you can approach.

The Closing

The objective is to obtain legal documents acceptable to the venture capitalists' legal team and to your venture team. But just this one step can seem to go on endlessly, as the legal drafts will get ping-ponged back and forth between the two teams of lawyers. As soon as a consensus is reached, you and the investors can sign the closing documents, and at that point you will get your check. Your role is to manage the process by being in touch with your lawyer, the VCs, their lawyers, and putting together all the required documents from your side. When problems arise you should be prepared to quickly be a part of the solution in order to keep the closing going. Finally, going to the VC's office to sign the legal documents and pick up the check is a very exciting moment for everyone involved. It will be very hectic and busy, so bring only the officers required to sign documents for your venture and your legal team. You will have to wade through piles of documents, and expect to sign your name no less than 100 times. Some of the documents you will sign to close the deal include:

❖ **Investment Agreement:** Details the terms of purchase and provision of the securities used.

❖ **Stockholders' Agreement:** Contains restrictions upon the transfer and voting of securities by your management team.

FIGURE 14-5. "DIRTY DOZEN DEAL KILLERS": THE TWELVE MOST COMMON REASONS WHY VENTURE
CAPITALISTS PASS ON DEALS.

1. Poor Presentation. Either an inability to be able to talk about what the venture does, or the presenter has no passion and/or no enthusiasm. If they cannot sell to the venture capitalists, how can they sell to hundreds of customers and recruit winning executives?

2. Push-Back. It is seen as "separating the dog from its bone" syndrome. VCs will tolerate a lot of unusual personality quirks in the pursuit of good deals; especially from high-tech mad scientists. But push-back and arrogance turns VCs off instantly. It demonstrates that the entrepreneurs are not malleable. VCs often say, "We don't require that the venture team be capable, just that they be coachable."

3. Family-Owned Business. Especially a man-wife team. To them, a family-controlled board triggers alarms, because it is perceived as impenetrable and stubborn. Plus there is almost always a disagreement of some sorts in a family business that distinguishes it from non-family businesses like a sibling rivalry or spouse-to-spouse conflict.

4. #*&%@$-Up Capitalization Table. They do not want to deal with a cap table that is messed up with investments from too many informal investors in the early rounds. Most often, these are shareholders that any professional investor would prefer not to deal with down the road. They also do not want to deal with unwinding shareholders' agreements that were written by Uncle Joe's law firm in exchange for equity on the deal.

5. A Lifestyle Business. There is no headroom in the marketplace, meaning it probably will not scale up and grow to a $50–100+ million business within 5–7 years.

6. Mine Detector Indicates Land Mines. Investors get an immediate sense of land mines, or the team appears disfigured from previous land mines.

7. Clingy CEO. Someone pushing a deal and investors too hard probably means that the venture is in a serious revenue crisis. It is probably flying on fumes and will have to ditch at sea unless it is funded right now.

8. Too Many Moving Parts. VCs just do not want to deal with too many steps on the path to profitability. They see many deals and may choose to just walk away—not having the patience to understand each deal in its entirety.

9. Stuck in the Valuation Trap. Entrepreneurs insisting on a certain valuation and not budging.

10. Saying "There Is No Competition." Simply consider the fact that the VCs have seen 10 similar deals, each business plan listing some five competitors. They know of at least 10–20 competitors in this space—so should you!

11. No Sales Traction. VCs do not want to be the first to buy into the deal. They want to hear from your marquee customer(s) how great the product works from them. Too often, entrepreneurs confuse first-mover with first-prover!

12. Too Much Time on the Deal. VCs will go onto the next deal if it sounds like it will take too much time for the entrepreneur to put it together or the entrepreneur takes too long to follow up with simple requests.

❖ **Employment and Confidentiality Agreement:** Assures the protection of intellectual property like valuable trade secrets and certain business rights.

❖ **Employee Stock Purchase or Stock Option Agreements:** Govern the current and future allocation of equity in the venture to executives and key employees to be hired.

❖ **Contingent Proxy:** Describes how voting rights will be transferred.

❖ **Registration Rights Agreement:** Describes how the preferred stock can be converted to common stock prior to an IPO.

❖ **Preferred Stock Resolution:** Only if applicable, used to amend corporate charters.

❖ **Warrant Agreement:** If applicable.

❖ **Debentures or Notes Agreement:** If applicable.

Depending on where you are on the entrepreneurial life cycle discussed in the Introduction, and on how quickly you can learn, the average time from when you start your fund-raising process till you get a check from the venture capitalists will be about nine to eighteen months. You will need about three to nine months for preparing your business plan and for early attempts at placing it. Then plan for another six to nine months once you have had your initial meetings with a venture capitalist. They need time to perform the due diligence, and most likely, they need time to put together a syndicated deal.

Beyond the Closing Table: Delivering the Value You Promised

You first objective after the closing should be to go out and build that great venture you promised. The last thing we want you to do is to be managed and controlled by fear. But you do need to understand this plain and simple cold-hard fact: You are dealing with professional investors. You will get only one chance to lead your venture to success. After the closing, your investors will be very busy managing other deals and portfolio companies. So it will be your responsibility to keep them informed about your business. You will be expected to communicate and work with your investors on a regular basis for the next two to seven years. Most VCs would prefer being e-mailed and called on a weekly basis, and most investment agreements will require you to submit monthly financial statements. VCs believe that no venture can be properly managed without accurate, timely, monthly financial statements. Be forewarned that to them, tardy and/or poorly prepared financials are red flags that most likely indicate a revenue crisis on the horizon.

Finally, expect to have quarterly board meetings at your location. You should be well prepared for these meetings. There should be an agenda, complete briefing books, and formal presentations, followed by walk-throughs to meet with key employees. Success comes to those who can form trusting relationships with their investors. Look at your investors as your best friends in the business world. On this matter, our best advice is for you to follow what Samuel Johnson once said, "There can be no friendship without confidence, and no confidence without integrity."

Reviewing the Four Cornerstones of Success

Try not to become a person of success but rather try to become a person of value.

—**Albert Einstein**

Failure is, in a sense, the highway to success, inasmuch as every discovery of what is false leads us to seek earnestly after what is true.

—**John Keats, English poet**

The dream of yesterday is the hope of today and the reality of tomorrow.
—**Robert H. Goddard, father of American rocketry**

Reviewing the Four Cornerstones of Success

In conclusion, we have found that on the road to entrepreneurial success there are no shortcuts. If you are bent on finding a shortcut—the easy way—you are not working hard enough on the fundamentals. As we witnessed in the Perfect Storm, some entrepreneurs may get away with it for a while, but there are no substitutes for the basics. And the first basic is good, old-fashioned hard work. Even with a lot of hard work, no business venture is going to grow unless it has a strong and sturdy foundation. With this in mind, let us review the four cornerstones to entrepreneurial success.

1. Commitment to the Opportunity

Commitment means being bound emotionally or intellectually to someone or something. In his book *Made in America*, Sam Walton advises: "Commit to your business. Believe in it more than anybody else. I think I overcame every single one of my personal shortcomings by the sheer passion I brought to my work. I don't know if you're born with this kind of passion, or if you can learn it. But I do know you need it. If you love your work, you'll be out there every day trying to do it the best you possibly can, and pretty soon everybody around will catch the passion from you—like a fever."[1]

Because of the risks, entrepreneurship is not for the faint of heart. Ron Margolis, the first angel investor in Starbucks, supports this by saying, "It appears to me that people who succeed have an incredible drive to do something. They spend the energy to take the gamble. In this world, relatively few people are willing to take a large gamble."[2] Len Bosack, co-founder of Cisco Systems, took a large gamble. His path to success was paved with endless hours of work. According to Bosack, "Sincerity begins at a little over 100 hours a week. You can probably get to 110 hours on a sustained basis, but it's hard. You have to get down to eating once a day and showering every other day, things of that sort to really get your life organized to work 110 hours."[3] It is only beyond 110 hours that one gets to what Len calls "commitment." To Dennis Conner, four-time winner of America's Cup, true commitment is a "commitment to the commitment"—focusing to the point of excluding all else.

2. Strategic Leadership

Leadership in fundamentally new business activities is a long-term risk that requires a long-term strategic vision. Leadership in a new industry is seldom built in anything less than ten to fifteen years of very hard committed work. Strategic leaders are expert risk-technicians. They are experts at identifying risks, knowing how to manage around risks, and becoming comfortable in high-risk environments. They know that developing an effective strategy for dealing with risk and uncertainty sets apart the winners from those lost at sea.

In the darkest of dark nights, for thousands of years, from anywhere in the world sailors could look to the North Star *Polaris* for guidance. Strategic leaders too have that long-term vision—they can always look to their North Star and get back on the heading toward success. Strategic leaders must also have the capacity to solve an enormous set of problems. In sum, they must know how to choose which mountains to climb and which seas to cross. They need to know how to inspire their team to keep going, even in the fog of war—and most importantly how to stay together all the way to success.

3. Organizational Capability

Planting the seeds for a sustainable competitive advantage means creating a common body of knowledge, organizational intelligence, domain expertise, and experience. Such organizational capability springs from three sources: *Financial capability* pertains to financial efficiencies—not just how to make a profit, but how to make wise investment decisions, and experience in providing a return to investors. *Marketing capability* pertains to building the right products, establishing a close relationship with customers, and having experience in effectively marketing products and services in the chosen industry. *Technological capability* pertains to technical innovation; R&D; being knowledgeable about new products, processes, and technologies; and experience in successfully bringing a new product to market.

4. Persistence

Steven Jobs, CEO and co-founder of Apple Computer, once proclaimed that "these overnight successes sure take a hell of a long time." Persistence means keep going even after setbacks, and converting the endless number of barriers and roadblocks into opportunities. Persistence is to an entrepreneur what courage is to warriors. It becomes an unprogrammable stick-to-itiveness that never ceases to end. Soichiro Honda once said that "success can be achieved only through repeated failure and introspection. In fact, success represents 1 percent of your work which results only from the 99 percent that is called failure."[4]

Truly an inspirational and engaging leader, John Wooden says that success is a marathon not a sprint. As a basketball coach for the UCLA Bruins, he won ten national championships, including seven in a row from 1967 through 1973. Only six other men's teams have won championships back to back, and none has managed three consecutively. But not many know that Wooden was at UCLA for thirteen years before he won his first NCAA college championship!

Dream It. Plan It. Do It.

We concur with James Collins, co-author of the bestseller *Built to Last,* who said that "entrepreneurship is becoming to the world what architecture is to the world of building buildings."[5] We feel that the true golden age of entrepreneurship is in front of us, not behind us. While the economy in general may still seem tough, we feel that there are many positive factors affecting entrepreneurs today. Today's creative disrupters will create new market opportunities and new groups of market leaders. We see that IT buyers are beginning to experiment with a range of new architectures and core technologies. Entrepreneurs can find and hire great people, and resources like real estate are plentiful. Business plans are more realistic and the best entrepreneurs are focusing, as they should, on true innovation and on creating sustainable long-term value.

Henry George, an American journalist, once said, "Whoever becomes imbued with a noble idea kindles a flame from which other torches are lit, and influences those with whom he may come in contact, be they few or many." We sincerely hope that this book has provided a flame from which *your* torch was lit and can now be used to illuminate your journey to success.

Business Plan Outline

Our outline simply follows the content and approach in this book. We recommend that the total length of your business plan be no more than 15 to 20 pages. Each value driver should be one page (10 total pages) with 3 to 5 paragraphs for each page. Your financial section should be limited to 3 to 5 pages (the notes and assumptions can be embedded on the spreadsheets) and your Executive Summary should also be 3 to 5 pages. Your Supporting Documents are discussed in Appendix B.

Executive Summary

Be sure to have all your key contact information listed here

Keep it brief (3–5 pages)

Highlight only the most important discussions of your business plan

I. **New Business Venture Opportunity and Analysis**

A. Opportunity Analysis and Opportunity Formation

1. Discuss your Eureka moment

2. Discuss the key strategic inflection point in your industry

3. What is the source of pain? Who says so?

4. What is your problem statement?

B. Industry Dynamics and Risk Analysis

1. Define your space

2. Describe competitor risk

3. Describe technology transition risk

4. Describe substitute risk

5. Describe customer risk

6. Describe resource risk

C. Discuss Your Work with Lead Users
1. Who has been integrated and why?
2. Discuss how you used lead user insights
3. Who can you sell to now?
D. Discuss Your Unique Solution
1. SWOT analysis
2. Competitor analysis
3. What is your solution statement?

II. Business Strategy and Competitive Advantage

A. Your Business Strategy
1. Discuss your approach to crafting one
2. Discuss your performance metrics
3. Define your core competencies
4. Describe your strategic vision
B. Your Competitive Advantage
1. Discuss how it was selected
2. Discuss how it is sustainable
C. Your Business Model
1. What company do you model and why?
D. Your Intellectual Property
1. What is your IP?
2. How you intend to manage IP?
3. How you intend to profit from IP?

III. Venture Team Development and Management

A. Discuss the Lead Entrepreneur and Founders
B. Discuss the Venture Team
1. How did it come together?
2. How is it structured?
3. How are the members compensated?
4. What are the gaps in the team?
5. How/when will the gaps be filled?
C. Venture Team Management Issues
1. Who makes the decisions?
2. How are they made?
3. How are conflicts handled?

    D. Legal Issues
       1. Describe the corporate structure
       2. Describe the capital structure
    E. Your External Team
       1. Discuss your professional service providers
       2. Discuss your board of advisors
       3. Discuss your board of directors

IV. Controlling and Allocating Critical Capital Resources
    A. Product Development Issues
       1. Technology strategy
       2. Product specifications
       3. Discuss your short-term objectives
    B. Resources Required to Launch
       1. Describe the exact resources required
       2. Define clear milestones
       3. Who is responsible for milestones and resources?
    C. Describe Financing Strategy to Date
       1. Bootstrapping and self-financing
       2. Early sales
       3. Strategic partnerships and alliances

V. Market Entry Strategy
    A. Discuss the Value Web in Your Industry
       1. Discuss your value chain link by link
    B. Your Market Entry Strategy
       1. How was it selected?
       2. What are others doing?
    C. Discuss Your Value Map
       1. Describe your traction
       2. Describe your barriers to entry

VI. Marketing and Sales Strategies
    A. Discuss Your Objectives
       1. Technical objectives
       2. Strategic objectives
       3. Financial objectives

B. Discuss Your Sales Crusader
1. If not the CEO, say why
2. Why selected?
3. How compensated?

C. Discuss Your Sales Tactics
1. Catalysis sales approach
2. Circling back to lead users

D. Your Revenue Model
1. Define and map out exactly when "the check clears"
2. Describe your sales titration process
3. Discuss your marketing and sales controls

VII. **Managing Rapid Growth**

A. Discuss Your Growth Strategy
1. Why and how selected?
2. Discuss examples, models of similar success stories

B. Discuss Your Transition to Professional Management Structure
1. What are the changes on the horizon and why?
2. When are the changes on the horizon?
3. What are the expected results?

C. Discuss Growth Wall
1. What is the typical growth wall in your industry?
2. How do companies overcome the growth wall?
3. What are you doing today to prevent this stall?

D. Managing in High-Growth Environment
1. Discuss how you will become a recruiting machine
2. Discuss your compensation and stock packages for recruits
3. Discuss ideas on how to manage in difficult times

VIII. **Managing the Networked Enterprise**

A. Discuss Your "Womb-to-Tomb" strategy of support
1. Enterprise specific
2. Customer specific
3. Strategic partner specific

B. Customer Collaboration
1. Discuss how you will collaborate via the Internet

C. Discuss Economics of Networking
1. Recurring revenues
2. Customer support
3. Time-to-market issues, new product development
4. Getting customer "lock-on"
D. Network Management
1. Discuss how it will be developed and maintained
2. Discuss objectives and milestones
3. Discuss costs and fees

IX. **Financing Strategy**
A. Describe Your Path
1. How much is needed?
2. When is it needed?
3. How will it be used?
4. Who is being targeted?
5. What do they get?
B. Pro Forma Income Statement
C. Pro Forma Balance Sheet
D. Statement of Stockholders' Equity
D. Capital Requirements
E. Assumptions and Notes to Financials
F. Discuss Your Valuation
1. Methodology used
2. Discuss comparables

X. **Exit Strategy and Exit Goals**
A. Describe Your Options
B. Discuss Initial Public Offering
1. Activity and comparables in your space
C. Discuss Merger & Acquisition
1. Activity and comparables in your space
D. Discuss Triggering Events for Exiting
1. What are the goals and expectations for the venture team?

Checklist for Supporting Documents

Do not include your supporting documents in any business plans you mail out. First, you do not want to be educating the investors on your dime. And this information should be considered very confidential and includes very personal matters. You can bring along a notebook binder with masters, or even with copies, to your face-to-face meetings with investors. That way, if you find that there is serious interest during the meeting, and the VCs begin to rattle off things they will need for due diligence, you have the documents ready to photocopy in their office.

We also found it very helpful to prepare a checklist of all the items you need to have at the ready. Create a simple Word document you can fax or send as an e-mail attachment before your meeting. In the instructions ask them to please indicate which documents they will need for the meeting and ask how many copies they will need. Keep in mind that every single item (and many more!) we list below will eventually come up in due diligence before any investment in made. You want to demonstrate that you are prepared for and knowledgeable about the venture drill process. And this step of having a checklist for supporting documents can be used as a screener, because they will ask for them only if they are really interested in investing in your venture.

- ❏ Resumes/references of key executives
- ❏ Resumes/references of key employees
- ❏ Board of advisors: CVs, backgrounders
- ❏ Board of directors: CVs, backgrounders
- ❏ Listing of professional service providers, consultants, and contact information
- ❏ Detailed financials, including monthly cash budget table and pro formas for five years out
- ❏ Any professionally audited or reviewed financials

❏ Information about suppliers and subcontractors

❏ Corporate data, bank account information, and contact(s)

❏ Articles of incorporation/chartering

❏ Bylaws and notes from board meetings

❏ Listing of marquee customers: key contact information, typical orders, how much they have ordered, volume, units, new orders, and when expected

❏ Letters of Intent to purchase products, purchase orders, details of orders in backlog

❏ Detailed product information: pictures of products, diagrams, exhibits, diagrams of architecture

❏ Copies of patent(s), patent-pending documents

❏ Information about any debts and their terms related to this venture, including debts of founders to the venture

❏ Tax returns, for at least the previous three years where applicable

❏ Market studies and marketing materials

❏ Questionnaires used to collect data as part of marketing research/product development

❏ Detailed results of marketing studies that support marketing, pricing assumptions

❏ Price list, literature, data sheets of direct, competing products

❏ Production and manufacturing details

❏ Current published information about the venture in magazines and research reports

❏ Current white papers published by the venture's executives or scientists

❏ Significant contracts: business agreements, business partnerships, and strategic alliances

❏ Investment agreements with prior investors

❏ Employee/executive stock option agreements

❏ Insurance documents, product liability, general liability, and directors and officers (D&O) liability insurance

❏ Non-compete agreements signed by the management team and key contributors, particularly if they play a key role in the invention or development of the product/technologies

❏ Organization chart, current and projected with new hires

❏ Regulatory forms, pertaining to EPA reports, SEC reports, etc.

❏ Information about the property leases, copies of each lease

PowerPoint Presentation Outline

For your presentation to investors, plan to have about 45 to 60 minutes. You will have about 15 to 25 minutes to make a formal presentation, followed by about 15 to 25 minutes of Questions and Answers. Generally, the Q&A is after you are finished making your formal presentation. Bring your own laptop; the investors will provide the LCD projector. Internet access may be available, but do not depend on it to make your presentation. Ask ahead and find out how many hard copies of your presentation you will need to bring to the meeting.

PowerPoint presentations with approximately 12 to 15 slides are generally most effective. It is best to use the limited time you have to emphasize the compelling factors about your investment opportunity and save unnecessary technology details for future meetings. A good approach is to put the substance on the pages in your business plan (see Appendix A for a business plan outline) and summarize each slide's most important talking points orally to the investors. Do not read the slides to your audience, as they will be following your presentation in their hard-copy handouts. Address only the key facts and conclusions you want investors to take from each slide.

Writing is tough for everybody, and making slides that represent what your deal is doubly tough. You want your listeners to be listening to your sales skills, not figuring out what you have on the slides, so keep it very simple and use only a 30-point font or larger on PowerPoint. Please note that the outline below simply follows the content and approach in our book.

1. Cover Slide
   This first slide and discussion should help position your venture so the investors have a framework for listening. Include the name of your venture, the presenter's name, and a one-sentence Value Line statement ("What we do").
2. New Business Venture Opportunity and Analysis

3. Business Strategy and Competitive Advantage

4. Venture Team Development and Management

5. Controlling and Allocating Critical Capital Resources

6. Market Entry Strategy

7. Marketing and Sales Strategies

8. Managing Rapid Growth

9. Managing the Networked Enterprise

10. Financing Strategy

11. Exit Strategy and Exit Goals

12. Conclusion Slide

Be sure to review what was discussed, and review what you want them to remember. Use the closing slide not only to close your presentation, but also to demonstrate your sales closing skills. Having a formal close is helpful for efficiently managing the follow-ups when you e-mail, call, and intercept investors at events, etc.

How to Prepare Your Financials

This appendix supports our discussion of this topic in Chapter 12. In a business plan, investors will expect to see the financial projections for 3 to 5 years out, which we discuss and present here.

Step 1. Begin where you left off with the cash budget table you prepared in Chapter 7. You will need to determine your top line sales revenues on a monthly basis for at least the next five years out. Stick to an actual cash/revenue received practice of accounting for your pro formas. Determine your costs of the goods that were sold in the period. Determine your overhead costs and determine your EBITDA. (Recall from our previous discussions that your EBITDA is "Earnings Before Interest, Taxes, Depreciation, and Amortization.")

Step 2. Determine how much money you will need to finance your growth strategy. Start by looking at the maximum cash shortfall and estimating the amount needed for working capital and contingencies. It will be important to go through many financial modeling exercises to determine the amounts. Your cumulative cash flow will incorporate your cash received from financing activities.

Step 3. Create your balance sheet. Determine your current assets, which should mostly comprise accounts receivables and some inventory. Cash is cash on hand at the end of the year. Very seldom will new business ventures require substantial fixed assets. Except for biotechnology ventures, most venture capitalists and angel investors will pass on capital-intensive investments.

Step 4. Prepare your Assumptions and Notes. The Assumptions and Notes act like a bridge between numbers that are standing alone in a spreadsheet and the written content in your business plan. You do not want an analyst reviewing your numbers to have to scour through your business plan to make decisions nor to retrieve information.

Step 5. Assemble the documents for the business plan. For our example using the Entrepreneur Bootcamp, we have prepared four documents: the Cash Budget Table (Year 1), Assumptions and Notes for Year 1, Financial Overview Years 1 to 5, and Assumptions and Notes for Years 1 to 5. Because our example only has two shareholders, we have a simplified Capitalization Table included on the Assumptions and Notes page. For the B Round, the venture in our example would most likely have to include a separate and more detailed Cap Table.

Storyline for our Example: Entrepreneur Bootcamp

The new business venture is an entrepreneurship bootcamp and consulting practice for corporate entrepreneurship. It will help entrepreneurs learn how to package, place, and present their businesses. These workshops will be held at convention centers, hotel banquet rooms around the country and on location at corporate clients. Current financing strategy—the two founders each contributed $45,000 in a Pre-Seed round for marketing and pricing studies, for paying a consultant to help with the business plan, and for legal expenses. By April the two partners decide to commit to the venture, and each pay $205,000 for their Seed Round. But this is just enough to get them started in building their venture, as our worksheet shows that the venture will be about $1 million short at the end of December. This is their AFN (additional funding needed). They determined that this A Round would need to be between $1.3 million and $1.5 million. They have a few options facing their impending cash crunch. They can speed up collections, they will have about $470,000 in accounts receivables by the end of the year (the difference between Total Sales and Total Cash Inflows). They could also work out the kinks in the inefficiencies in the SG&A, in order to get the overall cost per student down. They cannot increase the prices/adjust revenue model just yet because the marketing and pricing study they completed set a fixed pricing model for these first programs to be offered. They could work harder to get more sales, but this might come at more costs like hiring more people and consultants. Plus it will take away the founders' efforts in raising money too. They decide begin raise the AFN through private equity funding (angel investors, venture capitalists, and strategic partners).

ENTREPRENEUR BOOTCAMP: FINANCIAL OVERVIEW

	Year 1	Year 2	Year 3	Year 4	Year 5
Pro Forma Income Statement					
New Students	1,450	4,500	9,000	18,900	38,500
Total Number of Students	1,450	5,900	14,900	33,800	72,300
Average Price Paid	$880	$925	$980	$980	$1,050
Revenues ($000's)	$1,278	$4,271	$9,009	$19,184	$41,283
Gross Profit	599	2,285	4,920	11,542	24,934
Gross Margin (%)	47%	54%	55%	60%	60%
SG&A	2,086	2,951	4,377	7,072	12,105
EBITDA	(1,487)	(666)	543	4,470	12,829
Net Income	($1,454)	($645)	$587	$4,588	$13,169
Cash from Equity Financing					
Founders	500				
A Round	1,500				
B Round		2,500			
Total Financing	2,000	2,500			
Cumulative Cash Flow	$365	$657	$548	$363	$2,332
Pro Forma Balance Sheet					
Current Assets ($000's)					
Cash	$365	$657	$548	$363	$2,332
Accounts Receivables	467	2,361	3,464	8,297	17,744
Total Current Assets	832	3,018	4,012	8,660	20,076
Fixed Assets	53	88	133	215	324
Total Assets	$885	$3,106	$4,145	$8,875	$20,400
Short-Term Liabilities	315	631	1,007	2,197	5,407
Long-Term Liabilities	24	74	150	333	747
Total Liabilities	339	705	1,157	2,530	6,154
Equity					
Common Stock	500	500	500	500	500
Preferred Stock	1,500	4,000	4,000	4,000	4,000
Retained Earnings	(1,454)	(2,099)	(1,512)	1,845	9,746
Total Equity	546	2,401	2,988	6,345	14,246
Liabilities and Equity	$885	$3,106	$4,145	$8,875	$20,400

Assumptions and Notes For Year 1

1. Collections. Sales are made to individuals and corporations.

It is estimated that about 50–55% of the sales will be collected on a cash basis.

It is estimated that about 30–35% will be collected on a Net 30 basis.

The Company is budgeting about 10% of sales for overdue accounts.

Accounts receivables is forecasted to be around $470,000 by end of Year 1.

2. Direct Material Costs. These costs include notebooks, handouts, printing of case studies, and other printed materials. The Company will pay these costs on a cash basis.

In June the Company is budgeting around $1,200 for the creation of artwork for handouts etc.

3. SG&A. In April the Company plans to open up its first office location.

In August the rent and overhead will increase to about $9,000-$10,000 and remain fixed.

Additional expenses are budgeted for travel, curricula development, hiring of academic and sales team, and local marketing representatives. The balance is for banquets room rental and convention center expenses.

4. Outsourcing Expenses. These expenses include fees paid to guests speakers, lecturers, and adjunct instructors.

5. Start-Up Capital Expenses. These are combined with SG&A on the P&L.

These expenses include the consultant's fees for the preparation of a business plan, the fees for primary marketing research and pricing studies, the early development of the coursework and curricula, and legal expenses to incorporate the venture.

6. Debt Financing. The Company at this time does not plan to utilize any debt.

7. Equity Financing. The two founders each contributed $45,000 in the pre-seed round to conduct preliminary business investigation and to prepare a business plan.

In April the two founders each committed an additional $205,000 in the seed round to launch the business venture.

The total paid in equity by the founders is $500,000.

The Company needs to close an A Round of $1.3—$1.5 million by October.

Standard Term Sheet

Receiving a term sheet is a key turning point in getting financing from a venture capitalist or angel investor. Because they are very instrumental in negotiations at the closing table, term sheets are extremely confidential. Here we first define the term sheet and describe how it is used. We also share with you a term sheet that is used by one of the most successful venture capital firms in Silicon Valley.

Definition and Purpose

Once your venture team and the investors reach a verbal agreement as to the terms and condition of your relationship, you will want to get a nonbinding commitment letter, or what is known in the venture capital industry as a term sheet. The term sheet is for discussion purposes only. There is no obligation on the part of any negotiating party until all parties sign a definitive stock purchase agreement. The terms and conditions contemplated in the term sheet are subject to the satisfactory completion of due diligence and are designed to primarily protect investors. This document will be followed by legal documents, but the interim term sheet serves to put the agreement into writing. Some angel investors and VCs prefer not to issue term sheets because they view them as somewhat too binding. Nonetheless, we recommend you should always request some manner of written confirmation that will at least summarize the basic terms of your agreement. This can be used as a reference as you go into the legal realm of private securities and contract writings with your legal advisors.

Sale of Series A Preferred Stock
of
New Corporation

SUMMARY OF TERMS (00/00/03)

THIS TERM SHEET SUMMARIZES THE PRINCIPAL TERMS OF A PROPOSED PRIVATE PLACEMENT OF EQUITY SECURITIES OF New Corporation (the "Company"). THIS TERM SHEET IS FOR DISCUSSION PURPOSES ONLY; THERE IS NO OBLIGATION ON THE PART OF ANY NEGOTIATING PARTY UNTIL A DEFINITIVE STOCK PURCHASE AGREEMENT IS SIGNED BY ALL PARTIES. THIS TERM SHEET IS SUBJECT TO SATISFACTORY COMPLETION OF DUE DILIGENCE.

A. AMOUNT AND INVESTORS:

Venture Capital Fund, LP	$0,000,000
Venture Capital Partners, LLC	$0,000,000
	SUB-TOTAL

B. TYPE OF SECURITY:

Series A Preferred Stock.

C. PRICE PER SHARE:

$0.00 ["Series A Original Purchase Price"].

D. CAPITALIZATION:

0,000,000 total pre-financing fully-diluted Common shares and options issued, including:

Founders	0,000,000
Reserved for Employee Pool	0,000,000
SUB-TOTAL	0,000,000

This financing: 0,000,000 shares of Series A Preferred Stock issued as follows:

Venture Capital Fund, LP	0,000,000
Venture Capital Partners, LLC	0,000,000
SUB-TOTAL	0,000,000
GRAND TOTAL	00,000,000

Thus $0,000,000 buys 00% of the company.

E. VESTING SCHEDULE:

Unless the board determines otherwise, founders' and employees' Common stock shall vest 25% at the end of the first year of full-time employment, and at a rate of 1/48th per month thereafter, with respect to stock granted prior to an IPO. There shall be no accelerated vesting of Common stock in the event that the Company is acquired or merged.

F. COMPENSATION:

No Company employee shall receive annual compensation in excess of $100,000 (except those receiving commissions from approved comp plans) without consent of all of the directors until the company is merged, is sold, or completes an IPO.

G. DIVIDENDS:

The holders of Preferred shall be entitled to receive dividends at a rate of 8% per annum in preference to any dividend on Common Stock, whenever funds are legally available, when, if and as declared by the Board of Directors. Dividends shall be non-cumulative.

H. LIQUIDATION PREFERENCE:

In the event of any liquidation or winding up of the Company, the holders of Preferred A will be entitled to receive in preference to the holders of Common Stock an amount equal to their Original Purchase Price plus all declared but unpaid dividends (if any).

Preferred A will be participating so that after payment of the Original Purchase Price to the holders of Preferred A, the remaining assets shall be distributed pro-rata to all shareholders on a common equivalent basis.

A merger, acquisition or sale of substantially all of the assets of the Company in which the share-holders of the Company do not own a majority of the outstanding shares of the surviving corporation shall be deemed a liquidation.

I. CONVERSION:

1. The holders of Preferred will have the right to convert Preferred shares at the option of the holder, at any time, into shares of Common Stock at an initial conversion rate of 1-to-1. The conversion rate shall be subject from time to time to anti-dilution adjustments as described below.

2. Automatic Conversion: All Preferred shares will be automatically converted into Common upon (i) the closing of an underwritten public offering of shares of Common Stock of the Company at a public offering price per share (prior to under-writing commissions and expenses) that

values the Company at least $100 million in an offering of not less than $20 million, before deduction of underwriting discounts and registration expenses or (ii) approval of 50% of the Series A Preferred.

J. ANTIDILUTION:

Proportional antidilution protection for stock splits, stock dividends, combinations, recapitalizations, etc. The conversion price of the Preferred shall be subject to adjustment to prevent dilution, on a "weighted average" basis, in the event that the Company issues additional shares of Common or Common equivalents (other than reserved employee shares) at a purchase price less than the applicable conversion price.

K. VOTING RIGHTS:

The holders of a share of Preferred will have a right to that number of votes equal to the number of shares of Common Stock issuable upon conversion of Preferred.

L. REGISTRATION RIGHTS:

(1.) Demand Rights: If investors holding at least 40% of Preferred A (or Common issued upon conversion of the Preferred or a combination of such Common and Preferred) request that the Company file a Registration Statement for at least 20% of their shares (or any lesser percentage if the anticipated gross receipts from the offering exceed $2,000,000) the Company will use its best efforts to cause such shares to be registered; provided, however, that the Company shall not be obligated to effect any such registration prior to the earlier of (i) January 00, 2006, or (ii) within one year following the effective date of the company's initial public offering. The Company shall not be obligated to effect more than two registrations under these demand right provisions.

(2.) Company Registration: The Investors shall be entitled to "piggyback" registration rights on registrations of the company or on demand registrations of any later round investor subject to the right, however, of the Company and its under-writers to reduce the number of shares proposed to be registered pro rata in view of market conditions. No shareholder of the Company shall be granted piggyback registration rights superior to those of the Preferred A without the consent of the holders of at least 50% of the Series A Preferred (or Common issued upon conversion of the Series A Preferred or a combination of such Common and Preferred).

(3.) S-3 Rights: Investors shall be entitled to an unlimited number of demand registrations on form S-3 (if available to the Company) so long as such registration offerings are in excess of $500,000; provided, however, that the Company shall only be required to file two Form S-3 Registration Statements on demand of the Preferred every 12 months.

(4.) Expenses: The Company shall bear registration expenses (exclusive of underwriting discounts and commissions and special counsel of the selling shareholders) of all demands, piggy-backs, and S-3 registrations. The expenses in excess of $15,000 of any special audit required in connection with a demand registration shall be borne pro rata by the selling shareholders.

(5.) Transfer of Rights: The registration rights may be transferred provided that the Company is given written notice thereof and provided that the transfer (a) is in connection with a transfer of all securities of the transferor, (b) involves a transfer of at least 100,000 shares, or (c) is to constituent partners or shareholders who agree to act through a single representative.

(6.) Other Provisions: Other provisions shall be contained in the Purchase Agreement with respect to registration rights as are reasonable, including cross-indemnification, the period of time in which the Registration Statement shall be kept effective, standard standoff provisions, underwriting arrangements and the ability of the Company to delay demand registrations for up to 90 days (S-3 Registrations for up to 60 days).

M. BOARD OF DIRECTORS:

The Board of Directors will consist of five seats. The Series A Investors shall be entitled to elect two members of the Company's Board of Directors. The third director shall be the Company's Chief Executive Officer. The fourth and fifth directors (and any additional directors) will be elected by the Preferred Stock and Common Stock voting together as a class; these directors are also expected to be outside directors. Venture Capital Fund will also have board visitation rights for its other partners.

N. RIGHT OF FIRST OFFER:

The Preferred A Investors shall have the right in the event the Company proposes an equity offering of any amount to any person or entity (other than for a strategic corporate partner, employee stock grant, equipment financing, acquisition of another company, shares offered to the public pursuant to an underwritten public offering, or other conventional exclusion) to purchase up to a pro rata portion of such shares. If a Preferred A investor chooses not to exercise their right of first offer, the other Preferred A investors and/or their affiliated funds have the right to expand their investment to fill the gap.

The Company has an obligation to notify all Preferred Investors of any proposed equity offering of any amount.

If the affiliated groups of Preferred Investors do not respond within 15 days of being notified of such an offering, or decline to purchase all of such securities, then that portion which is not purchased may be offered to other parties on terms no less favorable to the Company for a period of 120 days. Such right of first offer will terminate upon an underwritten public offering of shares of the Company.

In addition, the Company will grant the Preferred shareholders any rights of first refusal or registration rights granted to subsequent purchasers of the Company's equity securities to the extent that such subsequent rights are superior, in good faith judgment of the Company's Board of Directors, to those granted in connection with this transaction.

O. CO-SALE:

The Company, the Series A Investors and the Founders will enter into a co-sale agreement pursuant to which any Founder who proposes to sell all or a portion of his shares to a third party, will offer the Series A Investors the right to participate in such sale on a pro rata basis or to exercise a right of first refusal on the same basis (subject to customary exclusions for up to 15% of the stock, gifts, pledges, etc.). The agreement will terminate on the earlier of an IPO or fifteen (15) years from the close of this financing.

P. RESTRICTIONS AND LIMITATIONS:

So long as Preferred A Stock remains outstanding, the Company shall not, without the vote or written consent of at least a majority of the Preferred A shareholders, authorize or issue any equity security senior to the Series A Preferred as to dividend rights or redemption rights or liquidation preferences. Furthermore, the Company shall not amend its Articles of Incorporation or By-laws in a manner that would alter or change the rights, preferences or privileges of any Preferred Stock without the approval of at least a majority of the Preferred shareholders. Written consent of a majority of the Series A shareholders shall be required for (a) any merger, consolidation, or other corporate reorganization, or (b) any transaction or series of transactions in which in excess of 50% of the Company's voting power is transferred or in which all or substantially all of the assets of the Company are sold.

Q. PROPRIETARY INFORMATION AND INVENTIONS AGREEMENT:

Each officer, director, and employee of the Company shall have entered into a proprietary information and inventions agreement in a form reasonably acceptable to the Company and the Investors. Each Founder and other key technical employees shall have executed an assignment of inventions acceptable to the Company and Investors.

R. PURCHASE AGREEMENT:

The investment shall be made pursuant to a Stock Purchase Agreement reasonably acceptable to the Company and the Investors, which agreement shall contain, among other things, appropriate representations and warranties of the Company, with respect to patents, litigation, previous employment, and outside activities, covenants of the Company reflecting the provisions set forth herein, and appropriate conditions of closing, including an opinion of the counsel for the Company.

S. LEGAL FEES & EXPENSES:

The Company shall pay the reasonable fees (not to exceed $5000) and expenses of counsel to the investors and the Company.

The foregoing Summary of Terms sets forth the good faith agreement of the parties set forth below. By accepting this term sheet, the Company agrees to refrain from solicitation, consideration or acceptance of alternative proposals to finance, recapitalize or sell the Company for a period of twenty-one (21) days from the date of the Company's signature below. This offer expires on Tuesday, January 11th, 2005 at 5 PM.

Venture Capital Fund   **New Corporation**

By:_____   By:_____

Date:_____   Date:_____

Notes

Preface

1. Reported in *The Global Entrepreneurship Monitor 2002*, an extensive survey of thirty-seven countries assessing entrepreneurial activity, prepared by Babson College, London Business School, and the Ewing Marion Kauffman Foundation.

2. Michael Dell, *Direct from Dell: Strategies That Revolutionized an Industry* (New York: HarperBusiness, 1999), p. 60.

3. Our definition of stakeholder for this book is based on Richard L. Daft, *Organization Theory and Design*, 4th ed. (Saint Paul, Minn.: West Publishing, 1992), p. 53.

Introduction

1. Diane Swonk, "United States: Getting the Engine Running Again." Presentation at the annual Milken Institute Global Conference, April 1, 2003, Los Angeles.

2. Alexis D. Gutzman, *Unforeseen Circumstances: Strategies and Technologies for Protecting Your Business and People in a Less Secure World* (New York: AMACOM, 2002), Preface.

3. Steve Forbes, "United States: Getting the Engine Running Again." Presentation at the annual Milken Institute Global Conference, April 1, 2003, Los Angeles.

4. Karen E. Klein, "Finding the Cash for Your Business," *BusinessWeek Online*, February 13, 2001.

5. Tony Perkins, "Leading the Flock," *Red Herring*, August 12, 2002.

6. Mark Boslet, "Tough Venture-Funding Pacts Turn Off Many Entrepreneurs," *Wall Street Journal Online*, March 6, 2002.

7. Robert D. Hisrich and Michael P. Peters, *Entrepreneurship*, 5th ed. (New York: McGraw-Hill, 2002), p. 57.

8. Peter F. Drucker, "Our Entrepreneurial Economy," *Harvard Business Review* (January 1984). In a discussion rich in historical examples of Edison, DuPont, 3M, IBM, and Motorola, this article demonstrates the role of foresight and discipline in professional management skills, ensuring lasting success.

9. Rhonda M. Abrams, *The Successful Business Plan: Secrets & Strategies* (Grants Pass, Ore.: The Oasis Press/PSI Research, 1993).

10. Peter F. Drucker, *Innovation and Entrepreneurship* (New York: HarperBusiness, 1985), p. 29.

11. D.C. Dension, "Author Finds a Hitch in Business Plan Tradition," *Boston Globe Online*, April 13, 2003.

12. Abrams, *The Successful Business Plan*.

13. Tom Copeland, Tim Koller, and Jack Murrin, *Valuation: Measuring and Managing the Value of Companies*, 3rd ed. (New York: John Wiley & Sons, 2000), pp. 17–45.

14. Abrams, *The Successful Business Plan*.

15. Andreas Stavropoulos, "What Top Venture Capitalists Look for in Internet Business Plans." See http://www.dfj.com.

16. Abrams, *The Successful Business Plan.*

17. David Berkus, "Business Plans That Get Funded." Presentation at the annual Harvard Business School Entrepreneurs Conference, May 14, 2001, Costa Mesa, Calif.

18. Bill Joos, "Perfecting Your Positioning and Pitching." Presentation at Garage Technology Venture's Startup Strategies workshop, June 25, 2002, Costa Mesa, Calif.

19. Tom Reamy, "Imparting Knowledge Through Storytelling," *Knowledge Management World* (July–August 2002), p. 12.

20. Disney Imagineers, *Walt Disney Imagineering: A Behind the Dreams Look at Making the Magic Real* (New York: Hyperion, 1996) p. 51.

21. Richard L. Daft, *Organization Theory and Design,* 4th ed. (Saint Paul, Minn.: West Publishing, 1992).

22. William A. Sahlman, "How to Write a Great Business Plan," *Harvard Business Review* (July–August 1997), pp. 98–108.

Chapter 1

1. Brenda L. Moore, "Changing Classes," *Wall Street Journal Online*, March 27, 2002.

2. Lester C. Thurow, "Building Wealth," *The Atlantic Monthly,* June 1999, pp. 57–69.

3. Bert F. Hoselitz, "The Early History of Entrepreneurial Theory." In *Essays in Economic Thought: Aristotle to Marshall,* 2nd ed., J.J. Spengler and W.R. Allen, editors (Chicago: Rand McNally, 1962), pp. 234–258.

4. Quoted in Leo Strauss and Joseph Cropsey, *History of Political Philosophy,* 3rd ed. (Chicago: University of Chicago Press, 1987), pp. 635–658.

5. Ibid, pp. 761–783.

6. Milton Friedman and Rose Friedman, *Free to Choose* (New York: Harcourt, 1980), p. 1.

7. Quoted in Andrew L. Zacharakis, William D. Bygrave, and Dean A. Sheppard, *Global Entrepreneurship Monitor: National Entrepreneurship Assessment of the United States of America, 2000 Executive Report,* Kauffman Center for Entrepreneurial Leadership (2000).

8. "Entrepreneurship Activity in the United States Declined Last Year," Kauffman Center for Entrepreneurship press release, May 14, 2002.

9. Detailed discussions on entrepreneurial activity can be found in Paul D. Reynolds, et al., *Global Entrepreneurship Monitor: 2000 Executive Report,* Kauffman Center for Entrepreneurial Leadership (2000).

10. Quoted from Alan Greenspan's testimony before the Committee on Banking and Financial Services, U.S. House of Representatives, February 17, 2000.

11. This section draws heavily on David Dary, *Entrepreneurs of the Old West* (Lawrence, Kans.: University Press of Kansas, 1997).

12. Margaret Milner Richardson and Kenneth C. Brown, "Taxes—A Cost or a Strategy and How to Manage." Presentation at the Ernst & Young Entrepreneur of the Year International Conference, November 12, 1998, Palm Desert, Calif. For this number they include small businesses, corporations with assets under $5 million, taxpayers filing Schedule C for business expenses or Schedule E for partnership and rental income, and partnerships and S Corporations.

13. T.P. Pare, "Passing on the Family Business" *Fortune* 121 (May 7, 1990), pp. 81–85.

14. See *Practical Accountant* (February 2002), p. 16.

15. Opening remarks by Gregory Ericksen at Ernst & Young Entrepreneur of the Year International Conference, November 10, 2000, Palm Desert, Calif. Ericksen is the global director for Ernst & Young's Entrepreneur of the Year awards program.

16. Michael R. Milken, *Fueling America's Growth: Education, Entrepreneurship, and Access to Capital* (Santa Monica, Calif.: Milken Institute, 1994).

17. Amar V. Bhide, *The Origin and Evolution of New Businesses* (New York: Oxford University Press, 2000), pp. 94–95.

18. This subject of retailing is discussed at length in Michael Levy and Barton A. Weitz, *Retailing Management* (Burr Ridge, Ill.: Irwin/McGraw-Hill, 1998).

19. Daniel Akst, "Pathos at the Muffler Shop," *Wall Street Journal Online*, June 18, 2002.

20. Levy and Weitz, *Retailing Management*.

21. Robert D. Atkinson and Randolph H. Court, "The New Economy Index: Understanding America's Economic Transformation." Published by Progressive Policy Institute (November 1998), p. 13.

22. See Deloitte & Touche Fast 500, "Highlights & Trends" (2002). http://www.deloitte.com

23. For a great article on how 3M grows through innovation, we refer you to Tim Studt, "3-M—Where Innovation Rules," *R&D Magazine*, April 2003, pp. 20–24.

24. See Bryon Acohido, "Will Microsoft's Xbox Hit the Spot?" *USA Today Online*, June 4, 2002; and Khanh T.L. Tran, "Microsoft to Spend $2 Billion on Xbox Videogame," *Wall Street Journal*, May 21, 2002.

25. Dean Takahashi, *Opening the Xbox: Inside Microsoft's Plan to Unleash an Entertainment Revolution* (Roseville, Calif.: Prima Publishing, 2002).

26. Marc Blaug, *Economic History and the History of Economics* (New York: New York University Press, 1986), p. 222.

27. For example, Brazilian Ayrton Senna is widely regarded as one of the greatest Formula-1 racecar drivers of all time. However, at the age of 34, he was killed on May 1, 1994, during lap seven of the San Marino, Italy, Grand Prix. See Christopher Hilton, *Ayrton Senna* (London: Patrick Stephen Limited/Haynes Publishing, 1994).

28. Brian O'Reilly, "What It Takes to Start a Startup," *Fortune*, June 7, 1999, pp. 135–140.

29. Gregory K. Ericksen, *The Ernst & Young Entrepreneur of the Year Award: Insights from the Winner's Circle* (Chicago: Dearborn Trade Publishing, 2002), p. 24.

30. There is an excellent discussion about intrinsic motivation in Teresa M. Amabile, "Motivating Creativity in Organizations: On Doing What You Love and Loving What You Do," *California Management Review* 40, 1 (Fall 1997), pp. 39–58.

31. Robert Mondavi, *Harvests of Joy* (New York: Harcourt Brace, 1998), pp. 24–25.

32. Richard Murphy, "Michael Dell," *Success*, January 1999, pp. 50–53.

33. An overview on the research by Roberts appears in George Gendron, "The Origin of the Entrepreneurial Species," *Inc.*, February 2000, pp. 105–113.

34. Joseph Schumpeter, *The Theory of Economic Development* (Cambridge, Mass.: Harvard University Press, 1949).

35. Charles Van Doren, *A History of Knowledge: Past, Present, and Future* (New York: Ballantine Books, 1991) p. 183.

36. Chris Murphy, "Taking the Leap," *Information Week*, June 26, 2000, pp. 19–22.

37. Meg Mitchell Moore, "Serial Entrepreneurs: Start Me Up," *Darwin*, June 2001, pp. 88–98.

38. Ibid.

39. Jason Pontin, "The Entrepreneur as Hero," *Red Herring*, September 2000, p. 552.

40. J.C. Weicher, "The Rich and the Poor: Demographics of the U.S. Wealth Distribution," *Review*, The Federal Reserve Bank of St. Louis (July 17, 1997), p. 25.

41. Howard Means, "The Man and His Money," *Upside*, June 2001, pp. 133–137.

42. Jeong H. Kim, presentation at the Ernst & Young Entrepreneur of the Year International Conference, November 13, 1998, Palm Desert, Calif.

43. Peter L. Bernstein, *Against the Gods: The Remarkable Story of Risk* (New York: John Wiley & Sons, 1998).

44. Jeffry A. Timmons, *New Venture Creation* (Chicago: Irwin/McGraw-Hill 1994), pp. 597–610. Readers interested in a more thorough analysis of the venture in financial trouble, creating a turnaround plan, and dealing with lenders during hard times are referred to Chapter 17 in Timmons, "The Entrepreneur and the Troubled Company."

45. William J. McDonough, "Issues in Corporate Governance," *Current Issues in Economics and Finance*, The Federal Reserve Bank of New York (September/October 2002).

46. John S. Taylor, "The State of the Private Equity Markets." Presentation at the annual Corporate Governance Conference, March 26, 2003, UCLA, Los Angeles. Taylor is the vice president of research at the National Venture Capital Association.

47. Michael S. Malone, *Betting It All: The Entrepreneurs of Technology* (New York: John Wiley & Sons, 2002), p. 57.

48. Russ Arensman, "Voices of Experience," *Electronic Business*, May 2002, pp. 49–54.

Chapter 2

1. Chris Freeman and Luc Soete, *The Economics of Industrial Innovations*, 3rd ed. (Cambridge, Mass.: The MIT Press, 1997), pp. 48–54.

2. Charles Van Doren, *A History of Knowledge: Past, Present, and Future* (New York: Ballantine Books, 1991).

3. Ibid, p. 264.

4. Ibid.

5. W. Devine, "From Shafts to Wires: Historical Perspective on Electrification," *Journal of Economic History* 43, 2 (1983).

6. Stephen S. Cohen, J. Bradford De Long, and John Zysman, "The Next Industrial Revolution?" *The Milken Institute Review* (first quarter 2000), pp. 16–22.

7. David L. Lewis, *The Public Image of Henry Ford: An American Folk Hero and His Company* (Detroit: Wayne State University Press, 1976), pp. 160–161.

8. For a more detailed discussion on the subject matter discussed in this section, see Michael R. Pakko, "The High-Tech Investment Book and Economic Growth in the 1990s: Accounting for Quality," *Review*, The Federal Reserve Bank of St. Louis (March–April 2002), pp. 3–18.

9. Thomas L. Mesenbourg, "Measuring Electronic Business," U.S. Bureau of the Census, August 2001.

10. Martin Baily, "Macroeconomic Implications of the New Economy." Paper presented at the annual symposium sponsored by The Federal Reserve Bank of Kansas City, August 30, 2001, Jackson Hole, Wyo.

11. Feldstein's comments can be found in Craig S. Hakkio, "Economic Policy for the Information Economy: A Summary of the Bank's 2001 Economic Symposium," *Economic Review*, The Federal Reserve Bank of Kansas City (fourth quarter 2001), pp. 5–24.

12. Michael R. Milken, *Fueling America's Growth: Education, Entrepreneurship, and Access to Capital* (Santa Monica, Calif.: Milken Institute, 1994).

13. Henry Mintzberg, *The Nature of Managerial Work* (New York: Harper & Row, 1972), p. 39.

14. Doug Bartholomew, "King of Customer," *Industry Week*, February 2002, pp. 40–44.

15. Alan Greenspan, "Job Insecurity and Technology," in *Technology and Growth*, Jeffrey C. Fuhrer and Jane Sneddon Little, editors. Conference Proceedings, The Federal Reserve Bank of Boston, Conference Series No. 40 (June 1996), pp. 173–181.

16. Michael Lewis, *The New New Thing* (New York: W.W. Norton & Company, 2000).

17. Everett M. Rogers, *Diffusion of Innovations* (New York: The Free Press, 1995). This classic on marketing and consumer behavior was first published in 1962 and is now in its 4th edition. See also C. Merle Crawford and C. Anthony Di Benedetto, *New Products Management*, 6th ed. (Burr Ridge, Ill.: Irwin/McGraw-Hill, 2000), pp. 367–368. Their discussion builds on Rogers's work.

18. Clayton Christensen, *The Innovator's Dilemma: When Technologies Cause Great Firms to Fail* (Boston: Harvard Business School Press, 1997), pp. 165–185.

19. David Packard, *The HP Way: How Bill Hewlett and I Built Our Company* (New York: HarperBusiness, 1995).

20. Nathan Rosenberg, "Uncertainty and Technological Change," in *Technology and Growth* (June 1996), pp. 91–110.

21. Our definition is influenced by these two sources: Stan Liebowitz, *Re-Thinking the Network Economy: The True Forces that Drive the Digital Marketplace* (New York: AMACOM, 2002), pp. 9–24; and Tim Berners-Lee, *Weaving the Web* (San Francisco: Harpers, 1999), pp. 211–219.

22. Leonard Kleinrock, "Beyond the Nether World of Cyberspace." Presentation at Anderson Forecast Conference, December 11, 2000, UCLA, Los Angeles. Also see Kleinrock's Web site at: http://www.lk.cs.ucla.edu.

23. For an account of these early years at Intel, see Kenneth A. Brown, *Inventors At Work: Interviews with 16 Notable American Inventors* (Redmond, Wash.: Tempus Books/Microsoft Press, 1988); and Steve Harmon, *Zero Gravity: Riding Venture Capital from High-Tech Start-Up to Breakout IPO* (Princeton, N.J.: Bloomberg Press, 1999), p. 74.

24. Gordon Moore is quoted in Jeff Papows, *Enterprise.com: Market Leadership in the Information Age* (New York: Perseus Books, 1998).

25. Berners-Lee, *Weaving the Web*, p. 36.

26. Robert H. Reid, *Architects of the Web: 1,000 Days that Built the Future of Business* (New York: John Wiley & Sons, 1997), Introduction.

27. John T. Wall, "The State of the World's Equity Markets." Presentation at the Fifth Annual Conference on Corporate Governance and Equity Offering, February 27, 2002, Los Angeles. Wall is president of NASDAQ International, Ltd.

28. Glenn Yago, Betsy Zeidman, and Bill Schmidt, *Creating Capital, Jobs and Wealth In Emerging Domestic Markets* (Santa Monica, Calif.: Milken Institute, 2003).

29. Wall, "The State of the World's Equity Markets."

30. Alice M. Rivlin, "Challenges of Modern Capitalism," The Federal Reserve Bank of Boston, *Regional Review* 12, 3 (2002), pp. 4–10.

31. Gene D'Avolio, Efi Gildor, and Andrei Shleifer, "The Financial Market Effects of the Information Economy." Paper presented at the annual symposium sponsored by The Federal Reserve Bank of Kansas City, August 30, 2001, Jackson Hole, Wyo.

32. Alfred R. Berkeley, III, "The State of the World's Equity Markets." Presentation at the annual Corporate Governance Conference, March 26, 2003, UCLA, Los Angeles. Berkeley is the past-president and now vice-chairman of the NASDAQ Stock Market.

33. Henry M. Paulson, Jr., "Good for All Americans," *Wall Street Journal Online*, March 19, 2003.

34. Berkeley, "The State of the World's Equity Markets."

35. Ken Gepfert, "Protracted Slump Would Slam Once Highflying Tech Regions," *Wall Street Journal Online*, July 29, 2002.

36. Ross Cockrell, presentation at VentureNet 2002, September 4, 2002, Dana Point, Calif. Cockrell is a general partner with Austin Ventures.

37. James Daly, "Five Questions with John Doerr," *Business 2.0*, April 17, 2001, p. 104.

38. Anthony B. Perkins and Michael C. Perkins, *The Internet Bubble* (New York: HarperBusiness, 1999), p. 92.

39. John A. Byrne, "Visionary vs. Visionary," *BusinessWeek*, August 28, 2000, pp. 210–214.

40. Lewis, *The New New Thing*.

41. "Information & Communications Technology Investment," Milken Institute 2002 Global Conference Briefing Book (2002), pp. III-8/9.

42. Regis McKenna, "The New Realities of Technology Marketing." Presentation at the Business of Technology: Perspectives, Problems, Profitability Conference, April 11, 2002, UCLA, Los Angeles.

43. Arthur B. Laffer, "A Buying Opportunity," *Wall Street Journal Online*, July 15, 2002.

44. See Perkins and Perkins, *The Internet Bubble*, pp. 187–188.

45. We got these numbers from Charles Phillips, "Stemming the Software Spending Spree," *Optimize Magazine*, April 2002, p. 57; and Mary Hayes, "A Delicate Balance," *Information Week*, April 22, 2002, pp. 38–49.

46. Mark G. Heesen, "Private Equity: State of the World." Presentation at the Fifth Annual Conference on Corporate Governance and Equity Offering, February 27, 2002, UCLA, Los Angeles.

47. National Venture Capital Association, *NVCA 2002 Yearbook* (Newark, N.J.: Thompson Financial Venture Economics, 2002), pp. 37–41.

48. John Taylor, "NVCA Confirms Increasing Levels of Venture Financing Available for Entrepreneurs," *AEEG Newsletter* (Spring 2000).

49. Brad Jones, presentation at VentureNet 2002, September 4, 2002, Dana Point, Calif.

50. *NVCA 2002 Yearbook*, p. 8; and Heesen, "Private Equity: State of the World."

51. Taylor, "NVCA Confirms Increasing Venture Financing."

52. Robert D. Hof, "Inside an Internet IPO," *BusinessWeek*, September 6, 1999, pp. 60–72.

53. Stan O'Neal, "Risky Business," *Wall Street Journal Online*, April 24, 2003. O'Neal is the CEO of Merrill Lynch.

54. Perkins and Perkins, *The Internet Bubble*, p. 197.

55. *NVCA 2002 Yearbook*, p. 21.

56. Frank A. Schmid, "Equity Financing of the Entrepreneurial Firm," *Review*, The Federal Reserve Bank of St. Louis (November–December 2001), p. 15–27.

57. Mark Veverka, "Pied Piper of the 'Net," *Barron's Online*, June 10, 2002.

58. Steve Hamm and Marcia Stepanek, "From Reengineering to E-Engineering," *BusinessWeek*, March 22, 1999, pp. EB14–EB18.

59. Perkins and Perkins, *The Internet Bubble*, p. 30; and Kevin Kelly, "The Web Runs on Love, Not Greed," *Wall Street Journal Online*, January 3, 2002.

60. The concept of doing business in "Internet Time" and the race to go public were first documented in Jim Clark, *Netscape Time: The Making of the Billion Dollar Start-Up That Took on Microsoft* (New York: St. Martin's Press, 1999).

61. Hof, "Inside an Internet IPO."

62. Bob Tedeschi, "Venture Capitalists Still on the Lookout for New Technologies," *New York Times Online*, May 27, 2002.

63. Jerry Borrell, "Seven Wise Men Speak," *Upside*, July 2002, pp. 42–48.

64. Bridget Karlin, "Early Stage Financings." Presentation at the Investment Capital Conference 2002, April 4, 2002, Los Angeles.

65. Stephen Segaller, *Nerds 2.0.1: A Brief History of the Internet* (New York: TV Books, 1999) p. 302.

66. Perkins and Perkins, *The Internet Bubble*, pp. 61–62.

67. Robert Dunn, "VC Garage Sale," *Corporate Board Member* (Autumn 2001), p. 19.

68. William Hearst, presentation at *Red Herring*, August 8, 1999, Los Angles.

Chapter 3

1. Udayan Gupta, "Once Upon a VC Time," *Upside*, November 2000, pp. 229–236.

2. Frank H. Knight, *Uncertainty and Profits* (Chicago: University of Chicago Press, 1972), pp. 310–311.

3. Alfred R. Berkeley, III, "The State of the World's Equity Markets." Presentation at the annual Corporate Governance Conference, March 26, 2003, UCLA, Los Angeles.

4. See Peter F. Drucker, "The Big Power of Little Ideas," *Harvard Business Review* (1964); and Peter F. Drucker, *Innovation and Entrepreneurship* (New York: Harper-Business, 1985), p. 12.

5. Chris Freeman and Luc Soete, *The Economics of Industrial Innovations*, 3rd ed. (Cambridge, Mass.: The MIT Press, 1997), p. 40.

6. Lester C. Thurow, "Building Wealth," *The Atlantic Monthly*, June 1999, pp. 57–69.

7. NVCA, "Three Decades of Venture Capital Investment Yields 7.6 Million Jobs and $1.3 Trillion in Revenue," press release, October 22, 2001.

8. Mark Heesen, "Unleashing the Power of Entrepreneurship: Stimulating Investment in America's Small Businesses." Presentation before U.S. Senate Committee on Small Business & Entrepreneurship, May 22, 2002.

9. John Taylor, "NVCA Confirms Increasing Levels of Venture Financing Available for Entrepreneurs," *AEEG Newsletter* (Spring 2000).

10. NVCA, "Three Decades of Venture Capital Investment."

11. Steve Jurvetson, "Changing Everything: The Internet Revolution and Silicon Valley," in *The Silicon Valley Edge: A Habitat for Innovation and Entrepreneurship*, Chong-Moon Lee, et al., editors (Stanford, Calif.: Stanford University Press, 2000), pp. 124–149.

12. Amy Cortese, "Venture Capital, Withering and Dying," *New York Times Online*, October 21, 2001. Khosla should know. He is often called the best venture capitalist on the planet today. A native of India, and armed with a Biomedical Engineering masters degree from Carnegie Mellon University in Pittsburgh, in the twenty-six years he has spent in the United States, he has helped to create forty ventures. These ventures have produced a total of $150 billion in market value.

13. William H. Payne, "What to Expect from Angel Networks," *entreworld.org*, April 2003. Payne has invested in some twenty-five ventures and is actively involved in Southern California's Tech Coast Angels, one of the largest formal angel networks in the United States.

14. Sohl's work is in "Business Angel Investing Groups Growing in North America," prepared by Ewing Marion Kauffman Foundation, October 2002. This report is the product of the first summit of organized angel groups, an April 2002 meeting with thirty representatives from eighteen groups.

15. Steve Harmon, *Zero Gravity: Riding Venture Capital from High-Tech Start-Up to Breakout IPO* (Princeton, N.J.: Bloomberg Press, 1999), p. 84.

16. Dan Bassett, presentation at Software Council of Southern California breakfast meeting, July 7, 2000, Costa Mesa, Calif.

17. See *NVCA 2002 Yearbook*, pp. 14 and 85–88; and *NVCA 2001 Yearbook*, pp. 83–85.

18. Suzanne McGee, "VCs Battle to Keep Portfolios Afloat," *Wall Street Journal Online*, January 2, 2002.

19. Bob Tedeschi, "Venture Capitalists Still on the Lookout for New Technologies," *New York Times Online*, May 27, 2002.

20. *NVCA 2002 Yearbook*, pp. 25–29. This research and discussion is based on an article by Jesse Reyes, vice president, Thompson Financial Venture Economics, and first appeared in the May 2002 edition of *Venture Capital Journal*.

21. John S. Taylor, "The State of the Private Equity Markets." Presentation at the annual Corporate Governance Conference, March 26, 2003, UCLA, Los Angeles.

22. R. Glenn Hubbard, "Global Perspectives: Sustaining Growth in an Interdepen-

dent World." Presentation at the annual Milken Institute Global Conference, April 23, 2002, Beverly Hills, Calif.

23. Vinod Khosla, "Funding the Storewidth Revolution." Presentation at Storewidth 2002, March 26, 2002, Dana Point, Calif.

24. McGee, "VCs Battle to Keep Portfolios Afloat."

25. Sarah Lacy, "VC Draper Still Rolling the Dice," *San Jose Business Journal Online*, March 4, 2002.

26. David R. Evanson, and Peter Kooiman, "Jackpot," *Entrepreneur*, July 2001, pp. 56–63.

Chapter 4

1. Peter F. Drucker, *Innovation and Entrepreneurship* (New York: HarperBusiness, 1985), pp. 130–132.

2. Lori Ioannou, "Make Your Company a Idea Factory," *Fortune Small Business*, May–June 2000, p. 122.

3. Clayton M. Christensen, "The Rules of Innovation," *Technology Review*, June 2002, pp. 33–38.

4. David P. Hamilton, "Inflection Point," *Wall Street Journal Online*, April 17, 2000.

5. Richard Murphy, "Michael Dell," *Success*, January 1999, pp. 50–53.

6. Karl H. Vesper, "New-Venture Ideas: Do Not Overlook Experience Factor," *Harvard Business Review* (May–June) 1979.

7. Amar Bhide, "How Entrepreneurs Craft Strategies That Work," *Harvard Business Review* (March–April 1994), pp. 150–161.

8. Michael Dell, *Direct from Dell: Strategies That Revolutionized an Industry* (New York: HarperBusiness, 1999), p. 12.

9. We refer to Michael E. Porter, "From Competitive Advantage to Corporate Strategy," *Harvard Business Review* (May–June 1987); and Michael E. Porter, *Competitive Strategy: Techniques for Analyzing Industries and Competitors* (New York: The Free Press, 1980), pp. 3–33.

10. Dawn Lepore, "Accelerating Change in the Information Economy." Conference at UCLA's Center for Management in the Information Economy, February 7, 2001, Los Angeles.

11. Marc Lautenbach, presentation at Association for Corporate Growth's M&A Conference, October 24, 2001, Beverly Hills, Calif.

12. Philip Kotler, *Marketing Management*, 10th ed. (Upper Saddle River, N.J.: Prentice-Hall, 1997), p. 131.

13. Kim B. Clark and Takahiro Fujimoto, *Product Development Performance: Strategy, Organization and Management in the World Auto Industry* (Boston: Harvard Business School Press, 1991).

14. Steve Lohr, "A Once and Present Innovator, Still Pushing Button," *New York Times Online*, May 6, 2003. See also Eric von Hippel, *The Sources of Innovation* (New York: Oxford University Press, 1988).

15. C. Merle Crawford, "When Using Qualitative Research to Generate New Product Ideas, Ask These Five Questions," *Marketing News*, May 14, 1982, p. 15.

16. Abbie Griffin and John R. Hauser, "The Voice of the Customer," *Marketing Science* 12, 1 (Winter 1993).

17. Bill Joos, "Perfecting Your Positioning and Pitching." Presentation at Garage Technology Venture's Startup Strategies workshop, June 25, 2002, Costa Mesa, Calif.

18. Larry Page, "Google's Parallel Universe." Presentation at Storewidth 2002, March 25, 2002, Dana Point, Calif.

19. Dan Bassett, presentation at Software Council of Southern California Program on Venture Capital, October 16, 2001, Costa Mesa, Calif.

20. Kotler, *Marketing Management*, p. 9.

21. Crawford, "When Using Qualitative Research."

22. Tim Koogle, presentation at The Business of Technology: Perspectives, Problems, Profitability Conference, April 11, 2002, UCLA, Los Angeles.

23. Peter F. Drucker, *The Essential Drucker: Selections from the Management Works of Peter F. Drucker* (New York: HarperBusiness, 2001).

Chapter 5

1. Lance Armstrong, *It's Not About the Bike* (New York: G.P. Putman's Sons, 2000). Armstrong won the Tour de France bicycle race five times: 2003, 2002, 2001, 2000, and 1999.

2. Michael E. Porter, *On Competition* (Boston: Harvard Business Review Books, 1996), p. 21.

3. *The Inc 500 Special Issue*, October 2002.

4. Jack Stack, *The Great Game of Business* (New York: Currency/Doubleday, 1992).

5. Charles H. House, and Raymond L. Price, "The Return Map: Tracking Product Teams," *Harvard Business Review* (January–February 1991), p. 93.

6. Gary Hamel and C.K. Prahalad, *Competing for the Future* (Boston: Harvard Business School Press, 1994), p. 135.

7. C.K. Prahalad and Gary Hamel, "The Core Competence of the Corporation," *Harvard Business Review* (May–June 1990), pp. 79–91. This article provides a detailed exposition of core competencies.

8. Karl Moore, Richard Sudek, and Kai Peters, "Ten Questions for a High-Tech Startup," *ZDNet Online*, April 3, 2003.

9. Howard Schultz, *Pour Your Heart Into It: How Starbucks Built a Company One Cup at a Time* (New York: Hyperion Books, 1997).

10. Moore, Sudek, and Peters, "Ten Questions for a High-Tech Startup."

11. Jeffrey Abrahams, *The Mission Statement Book: 301 Corporate Mission Statements from America's Top Companies* (Berkeley: Ten Speed Press, 1999). Contains many excellent suggestions on the characteristics and processes of producing outstanding mission statements.

12. Pat Riley, keynote presentation at the Mergers and Acquisition Finance Conference, Association for Corporate Growth, September 20, 2000, Beverly Hills, Calif.

13. We first came across these interesting comments in P. Boxall, "Placing HR Strategy at the Heart of Business Success," *Personnel Management* 26 (1994), p. 32.

14. Dr. Paul Jacobs, keynote presentation at *Red Herring* NDA, October 29, 2001, Dana Point, Calif.

15. Matt Hicks, "Scaling Toward the Petabyte," *eWeek*, June 17, 2002, p. 33.

16. Brian Sullivan and Michael Meehan, "Big Retailers Push Data Ties," *Computerworld Online*, June 10, 2002.

17. Megan Santousus, "Table Your Contents," *CIO*, May 15, 2003, p. 40.

18. For a detailed discussion on platform leaders, we suggest Annabelle Gawer and Michael A. Cusumano, *Platform Leadership: How Intel, Microsoft, and Cisco Drive Industry Innovation* (Boston: Harvard Business School Press, 2002).

19. Amar V. Bhide, *The Origin and Evolution of New Businesses* (New York: Oxford University Press, 2000), p. 296.

20. Regis McKenna, "The New Realities of Technology Marketing." Presentation at The Business of Technology: Perspectives, Problems, Profitability Conference, April 11, 2002, UCLA, Los Angeles.

21. Jennifer Maselli, "E-Ticketing Threatens Travel Agents," *Information Week*, March 25, 2002, p. 28.

22. Leonard Riggio, presentation at Milken Global Capital Conference, March 10, 2000, Beverly Hills, Calif.

23. Lea Goldman, "Machine Dreams," *Forbes*, May 27, 2002, pp. 149–150.

24. Erika Jonietz, "Economic Bust, Patent Boom," *Technology Review*, May 2002, pp. 71–77.

25. Eric W. Pfeiffer, "Setting Patent Traps," *Forbes ASAP*, June 24, 2002, p. 65.

26. Michael E. Porter, *Competitive Advantage: Creating and Sustaining Superior Performance* (New York: The Free Press, 1985), pp. 191–193.

Chapter 6

1. Jeffry A. Timmons, *New Venture Creation* (Chicago: Irwin/McGraw-Hill 1994), pp. 681–737. As Timmons points out in "Crafting a Personal Entrepreneurial Strategy," this process should be viewed as the personal equivalent of developing a business plan.

2. Gregory K. Ericksen, *The Ernst & Young Entrepreneur of the Year Award: Insights from the Winner's Circle* (Chicago: Dearborn Trade Publishing, 2002), p. 29.

3. Howard Anderson, "Not All VCs Are Created Equal," *MIT Sloan Management Review* (Summer 2001), pp. 88–92.

4. John Hamm, "Why Entrepreneurs Don't Scale," *Harvard Business Review* (December 2002), pp. 110–115.

5. Ericksen, *The Ernst & Young Entrepreneur of the Year Award*, p. 47.

6. John S. McClenahen, *Industry Week*, June 7, 1999, pp. 100–104.

7. Bill Reichert, "The Future of Venture Capital." Presentation at Los Angeles Venture Association (LAVA) conference, January 14, 2003, Pacific Palisades, Calif.

8. George Anders, "Marc Andreessen: Act II," *Fast Company Online*, February 2001.

9. David E. Gumpert and David P. Boyd, "The Loneliness of the Small-Business Owner," *Harvard Business Review* (November–December 1984).

10. A great source of stories about leading entrepreneurs is in *Forbes Great Minds of Business* (New York: John Wiley & Sons, 1997).

11. Arthur Rock, "Strategy vs. Tactics from a Venture Capitalist," *Harvard Business Review* (November 1987).

12. See Arnold C. Cooper and Catherine M. Daily, "Entrepreneurial Teams," *Entrepreneurship 2000* (1997), pp. 127–150; and Ilan Mochari, "The Numbers Game," *The Inc 500 Special Report, Inc.*, October 15, 2002. We looked over the data of the *Inc 500* winners from 1999 to 2002.

13. Gary S. Lynn and Richard R. Reilly, *Blockbusters: The Five Keys to Developing GREAT New Products* (New York: HarperBusiness 2002), pp. 149–173.

14. Larry Page, "Google's Parallel Universe." Presentation at Storewidth 2002, March 25, 2002, in Dana Point, Calif.

15. Timmons, *New Venture Creation*, pp. 253–281.

16. Tom Griesser, "BEA Systems, Inc.," *Entrepreneur of The Year 2001*, published by Ernst & Young (Fall 2001), pp. 30–31.

17. Richard Schulze, keynote presentation at Ernst & Young Entrepreneur of the Year International Conference, November 10, 2000, Palm Desert, Calif.

18. This interesting discussion was first introduced by Geert Hofstede, *Cultures and Organizations—Software of the Mind* (Maidenhead: McGraw-Hill Europe, 1991).

19. William A. Sahlman, "How to Write a Great Business Plan," *Harvard Business Review* (July–August 1997), pp. 98–108.

20. See Peter F. Drucker, "There's More Than One Kind of Team," *Wall Street Journal*, February 11, 1992, p. A16.

21. See *Fast Company*, November 2000, p. 382.

22. Richard Danzig, keynote presentation at *Red Herring* NDA, October 30, 2000, Carlsbad, Calif.

23. John Elway, keynote presentation at the Ernst & Young Entrepreneur of the Year International Conference, November 10, 2000, Palm Desert, Calif.

24. Steve Harmon, *Zero Gravity: Riding Venture Capital from High-Tech Start-Up to Breakout IPO* (Princeton, N.J.: Bloomberg Press, 1999), p. 84.

25. We picked this up from Kent V. Graham, partner, O'Melveny & Myers, LLP, "Sound Practices for Non-public Companies." Presentation at the annual Corporate Governance Conference, March 26, 2003, UCLA, Los Angeles.

26. For more information on this topic, see Susan F. Shultz, *The Board Book: Making Your Corporate Board a Strategic Force in Your Company's Success* (New York: AMACOM, 2001), pp. 7–8.

27. William J. McDonough, "Issues in Corporate Governance," *Current Issues in Economics and Finance*, The Federal Reserve Bank of New York (September/October 2002).

28. Jay W. Lorsch, "Roundtable discussion: Equity Markets and Governance." The Fifth Annual Conference on Corporate Governance and Equity Offering, February 27, 2002, UCLA, Los Angeles.

29. Catherine Fredman, "Michael Dell on How the Board Can Help," *Corporate Board Member* (January–February 2002), pp. 34–36.

30. For details on this deal, see Alison Bass, "Big Gene Machine," *CIO*, December 15, 2002, pp. 86–87.

31. John L. Nesheim, *High Tech Start Up* (New York: The Free Press, 2000).

32. Based on discussions with Richard D. Shuttleworth, senior vice president, Silicon Valley Bank, January 31, 2003, in Irvine, Calif.

33. Sharon Nelton, "Forging Advisors Into a Team," *Nation's Business*, December 1997, pp. 57–58.

Chapter 7

1. James Tobin, "To Fly!" *Smithsonian*, April 2003, pp. 50–62. Traces the Wright brothers's triumph over 100 years ago. From Orville Wright's comments about the first flight: "It was a flight very modest compared with that of birds but it was nevertheless the first in the history of the world in which a machine carrying a man had raised itself by its own power into the air in full flight, had sailed forward without reduction of speed, and had finally landed at a point as high as that from which it started."

2. Michael Dell, *Direct from Dell: Strategies That Revolutionized an Industry* (New York: HarperBusiness, 1999), p. 47.

3. Paul S. Adler, "Technology Strategy: A Guide to the Literatures," in *Research in Technological Innovation, Management, and Policy*, Vol. 4, Richard S. Rosenbloom, editor (Greenwich, Conn.: JAI Press, 1989), p. 26.

4. Stacy Forster, "New Ventures Meet the Challenges of a Struggling Start-Up Climate," *Wall Street Journal Online*, March 27, 2002.

5. Discussions with George Abe, June 8, 2001, in Irvine, Calif.

6. Tobin, "To Fly!"

7. James Tobin, *To Conquer The Air: The Wright Brothers and the Great Race for Flight* (New York: Free Press, 2003), pp. 55–56, 124–125. Wilbur Wright conceived the theory of wing-warping—a method of steering that is still used today, with elevators and rudders on the wings and tails of airplanes—by twisting an empty bicycle tube box one day at their bicycle shop in Dayton, Ohio.

8. Friedrich A. von Hayek, *Individualism and Economic Order* (Chicago: University of Chicago Press, 1969), p. 203.

9. Dr. Paul Jacobs, keynote presentation at *Red Herring* NDA, October 29, 2001, Dana Point, Calif.

10. Ross Cockrell, presentation at VentureNet 2002, September 4, 2002, Dana Point, Calif. Cockrell is a general partner with Austin Ventures.

11. Jerry Borrell, "Computer Graphics & Imaging," *Upside*, October 2001, pp. 116–120.

12. Ibid.

13. Based on discussions with Richard D. Shuttleworth, senior vice president, Silicon Valley Bank, January 31, 2003, Irvine, Calif.

14. Michael S. Malone, *Betting It All: The Entrepreneurs of Technology* (New York: John Wiley & Sons, 2002), p. 83.

15. Joshua Hyatt and Robert A. Mamis, "Profile of a Bootstrapper," *Inc.*, August 1997, pp. 61–63.

16. See *Inc.*, October 19, 1999, p. 22.

17. Ilan Mochari, "The Numbers Game," *The Inc 500 Special Report*, October 15, 2002.

18. Susan Greco, "A Little Goes A Long Way," *The Inc 500 Special Report*, October 15, 2002.

19. Ibid.

20. See *Practical Accountant*, February 2001, p. 6; and Jan Norman, "Business Notes," *The Orange County Register*, March 5, 2001.

Chapter 8

1. Ian Mount, and Brian Caufield, "The Missing Link: What You Need to Know About Supply Chain Technology," *eCompany*, May 2001, pp. 82–88.

2. For more on this interesting discussion, see Milton Friedman and Rose Friedman, *Free To Choose* (New York: Harcourt, 1980), pp. 11–13.

3. Bruce D. Henderson, "The Origin of Strategy," *Harvard Business Review* (November–December 1989).

4. Arlene Weintraub, "In Hot Pursuit of the Wi-Fi Wave," *BusinessWeek*, April 29, 2002, p. 106.

5. Clayton M. Christensen, "The Rules of Innovation," *Technology Review*, June 2002, pp. 33–38.

6. Timothy M. Laseter, et al., "Amazon Your Industry: Extracting Value From the Value Chain," *Strategy & Business* (first quarter 2000), pp. 94–105.

7. Clayton Christensen, "The Innovator's Solution." Presentation at the 3rd Annual Gilder/Forbes Storewidth Conference, March 25, 2003, Dana Point, Calif.

8. B.R. Schlender, "How Sony Keeps the Magic Going," *Fortune*, February 24, 1992, p. 23.

9. Victoria Murphy, "Day of Reckoning," *Forbes*, June 10, 2002, pp. 98–100.

10. See Richard Evans, "On the Fast Track," *Context*, June/July 2001, pp. 34–38; and John Tagliabue, "How Ducati Roared Onto the Internet," *New York Times Online*, April 18, 2001.

11. R. David Thomas, *Dave's Way* (New York: Berkley Books, 1992).

12. Charles R. Fellers, "Inside Intel Capital," *Venture Capital Journal Online*, April 1, 2002.

13. John Markoff, "Technologist Question IBM Move," *New York Times Online*, April 29, 2002.

14. For the discussion about substitutes, see Michael E. Porter, *Competitive Strategy: Techniques for Analyzing Industries and Competitors* (New York: The Free Press, 1980), p. 23; and Michael E. Porter, *Competitive Advantage: Creating and Sustaining Superior Performance* (New York: The Free Press, 1985), pp. 273–314.

15. Steve Lohr, "As Linux Nips at Microsoft, Its Advocates Talk Numbers," *New York Times Online*, January 20, 2003.

15. Bill Roberts, "Funding Grind," *Electronic Business*, May 2002, p. 24.

Chapter 9

1. Steve Wynn, "Branding: Players and Positioning." Presentation at the annual Milken Institute Global Conference, April 23, 2002, Beverly Hills, Calif.

2. Edward Iacobucci, keynote presentation at the Ernst & Young Entrepreneur of the Year International Conference, November 12, 1999, Palm Desert, Calif.

3. Chong-Moon Lee, et al., *The Silicon Valley Edge: A Habitat for Innovation and Entrepreneurship* (Stanford, Calif: Stanford University Press, 2000), pp. 1–15.

4. Amar V. Bhide, *The Origin and Evolution of New Businesses* (New York: Oxford University Press, 2000), pp. 108–110.

5. Ed Sperling, "It's All in the Statistics," *Electronic News*, May 14, 2003. Sperling notes that the average cost of a sales call in the high-tech electronics world has risen from $128 in 1980 to about $350 in 2003.

6. William H. Davidow, *Marketing High Technology: An Insider's View* (New York: The Free Press, 1986), pp. 118–132.

7. Amy Cortese, "Start-Ups No Longer Shout from the Rooftops," *New York Times Online*, January 20, 2002.

8. Tony Perkins, "Leading the Flock," *Red Herring*, August 12, 2002.

9. William A. Sahlman, "How to Write a Great Business Plan," *Harvard Business Review* (July–August 1997), pp. 98–108.

10. Stephen Segaller, *Nerds 2.0.1: A Brief History of the Internet* (New York: TV Books, 1999), pp. 177–181.

11. This example is presented in Joel Dreyfuss, "Reinventing IBM," *Fortune*, August 14, 1989, p. 35.

12. Julie Bort, *Network World 200*, April 29, 2002, pp. 50–56.

13. Kim Cross, "Does Your Team Measure Up?" *Business 2.0*, June 12, 2001, pp. 22–28.

Chapter 10

1. See *The Inc 500 Special Issue*, October 2002. This annual edition contains many interesting facts and data about some of America's fastest-growing private ventures.

2. Martha E. Mangelsdorf, "The Startling Truth About Growth Companies," *Inc.*, May 15, 1996, pp. 85–92.

3. Tom Griesser, "BEA Systems, Inc.," *Entrepreneur of the Year 2001*, published by Ernst & Young (Fall 2001), pp. 30–31.

4. T. G. Belden and M. R. Belden, *The Lengthening Shadow: The Life of Thomas J. Watson* (Boston: Little, Brown, 1962), p. 100.

5. Michael Dell, *Direct from Dell: Strategies That Revolutionized an Industry* (New York: HarperBusiness, 1999), p. 18.

6. Amar V. Bhide, *The Origin and Evolution of New Businesses* (New York: Oxford University Press, 2000), p. 252.

7. Adam Cohen, *The Perfect Store: Inside eBay* (New York: Little, Brown, 2002), p. 110.

8. Carole Matthews, "Founding CEOs Versus Second CEOs," *Inc. Online*, May 20, 2002.

9. Michael J. Roberts, "Managing Growth," in *New Business Venture and the Entrepreneur*, Stevenson, et al., editors (Burr Ridge, Ill: Irwin/McGraw-Hill, 1999), pp. 460–464.

10. Stephanie Gruner, "Death by Unnatural Causes," *Inc. 500*, 1997, pp. 60–65.

11. Dell, *Direct from Dell*, pp. 35–36.

12. David Packard, *The HP Way: How Bill Hewlett and I Built Our Company* (New York: HarperBusiness, 1995).

13. Eric Wahlgren, "Passing the Baton Peacefully," *BusinessWeek*, March 5, 2001.

14. Cohen, *The Perfect Store*, p. 73.

15. George Anders, "The Auctioneer: Margaret Whitman, the CEO of eBay, talks about the Company's Rapid Growth—and Heady Ambitions," *Wall Street Journal Online*, November 22, 1999.

16. Michael E. Porter, *On Competition* (Boston: Harvard Business Review Books, 1996), p. 68.

17. Julia Lawlor, "Alan Patricof as Entrepreneurial Curmudgeon," *Red Herring*, September 1, 2001, pp. 38–40.

18. Bhide, *The Origin and Evolution of New Businesses*, p. 208.

19. John Diebold, *The Innovators: The Discoveries, Inventions, and Breakthroughs of Our Time* (New York: Truman Talley Books, 1990), pp. 25–44. Diebold presents an excellent overview of how Federal Express was created and also discusses the innovators behind the transistor, the laser, and fiber optics.

20. David Packard, *The HP Way: How Bill Hewlett and I Built Our Company* (New York: HarperBusiness, 1995), pp. 163–164.

21. Dell, *Direct from Dell*, p. 109.

22. "Staffing Performance Report," *Darwin Magazine*, March 2002, p. 18. Staffing .org surveyed 679 companies in thirteen different business sectors about the number of hires, total compensation, and staffing costs. The cost per hire for firms with fewer than 100 employees is $7,122; for 100 to 499 employees, $7,155; and for 500 to 999 employees, $8,210.

23. Dell, *Direct from Dell*, p. 29.

24. William A. Sahlman, "How to Write a Great Business Plan," *Harvard Business Review* (July–August 1997), pp. 98–108.

25. S. Michael Camp, Larry W. Cox, and Barbara Kotalik, *2001 Survey of Innovative Practices: Hallmarks of Entrepreneurial Excellence*, Kauffman Center for Entrepreneurial Leadership (2001).

26. T. J. Rogers, "Options Aren't Optional in Silicon Valley," *Wall Street Journal Online*, March 4, 2002.

Chapter 11

1. Denise Benou Stires, "Branding: Players and Positioning." Presentation at the annual Milken Institute Global Conference, April 23, 2002, Beverly Hills, Calif.

2. Ravi S. Achrol and Philip Kotler, "Marketing in the Network Economy," *Journal of Marketing* 63 (1999), pp. 146–163.

3. Rosabeth Moss Kanter, "Change is Everyone's Job: Managing the Extended Enterprise in a Globally Connected World," *Organizational Dynamics* (Summer 1999), pp. 7–23.

4. Michael Harris, "Defining: Col-labo-ra-tive Com-merce," *EAI Journal* (March 2002), pp. 41–42.

5. Thomas M. Siebel, *Taking Care of eBusiness* (New York: Doubleday, 2001), pp. 25–29.

6. Larry W. Cox and S. Michael Camp, *International Survey of Entrepreneurs: 2001 Executive Report*, published by the Kauffman Center for Entrepreneurial Leadership (2001). This is research conducted in conjunction with Ernst & Young's global Entrepreneur of the Year (EOY) program. It is a most comprehensive study of the world's premier entrepreneurs, many of whom are finalists from the EOY program.

7. Ginger Conlon, "Customers Really Matter," *Customer Relationship Management*, August 2002, pp. 32.

8. Michael Dell, *Direct from Dell: Strategies That Revolutionized an Industry* (New York: HarperBusiness, 1999), p. 39.

9. Nikki Goth Itoi, "Metamorphosis of the Middleman," *Industry Week*, September 2001, p. 28.

10. William A. Sahlman, "How to Write a Great Business Plan," *Harvard Business Review* (July–August 1997), pp. 98–108.

11. Hans Hinterhuber and Andreas Hirsch, "Starting Up a Strategic Network," *Thunderbird International Business Review* 40, 3 (May–June 1998), pp. 185–207.

12. Bill Robinson, "Q&A with Ingram Micro's Guy Ambro: Making Business Global," March/April 2001, *iQ Magazine*, pp. 76–80.

13. Abbie Lundberg, "The I.T. Inside the World's Biggest Company," *CIO*, July 1, 2002, p. 68.

14. Leonard Kleinrock, "Beyond the Nether World of Cyberspace." Presentation at Anderson Forecast Conference, December 11, 2000, UCLA, Los Angeles. Also see Kleinrock's Web site at: http://www.lk.cs.ucla.edu.

15. Rob Norton, "How to Build a Great Website." *Corporate Board Member*, March/April 2002, pp. 58–63.

Chapter 12

1. Tony Perkins, "The Angler: VCs Must Learn from the Past," *Red Herring Online*, October 28, 2002.

2. Ilan Mochari, "The Numbers Game," *The Inc 500 Special Report*, October 15, 2002.

3. Bill Roberts, "Finding Funds," *Electronic Business*, October 2002, pp. 27–32.

4. Bill Roberts, "Funding Grind," *Electronic Business*, May 2002, p. 24.

5. John L. Nesheim, *High Tech Start Up* (New York: The Free Press, 2000).

6. "Venture Capitalists: More Caution, More Due Diligence, More Diversity." *Knowledge@ Wharton Online*, August 8, 2000.

7. Desh Deshpande, "Entrepreneur in Residence: In Pursuit of Venture Capital," *Red Herring*, January 2, 2001, p. 128.

8. James M. Stancill, "How Much Money Does Your New Venture Need?" *Harvard Business Review* (May–June 1986).

9. William A. Sahlman, "Aspects of Financial Contracting in Venture Capital," *Harvard Business Review* (1988).

10. Frank M. Singer, *How to Value a Business* (1999). Singer is a member of the Tech Coast Angels based in Southern California. This self-published 28-page booklet is actually available on Amazon.com.

11. Shannon P. Pratt, Robert F. Reilly, and Robert P. Schweihs, *Valuing a Business: The Analysis and Appraisal of Closely Held Companies*, 3rd ed. (Chicago: Irwin Professional, 1996), p. 36. Pratt's book is one of the most valuable books that investors can own.

12. This list is based on Karl T. Ulrich and Steven D. Eppinger, *Instructor's Manual to Accompany Product Design and Development* (New York: McGraw-Hill, 1995), p. 118.

13. Pratt, Reilly, and Schweihs, *Valuing a Business,* pp. 161–165. For readers who want to learn how to create their own formulas, this book provides the most comprehensive information on estimating the discount rate.

14. S.N. Kaplan and R.S. Ruback, "The Market Pricing of Cash Flow Forecasts: Discounted Cash Flows versus the Method of Comparables," *Journal of Applied Corporate Finance* 8, 4 (1996), pp. 45–60.

15. Michael Peltz, "High Tech's Premier Venture Capitalist," *Institutional Investor*, June 1996, pp. 89–98.

16. William D. Bygrave and Jeffry A. Timmons, *Venture Capital at the Crossroads* (Boston: Harvard Business School Press, 1992), pp. 149–165. Chapter 6, "Performance of Venture Capital Funds: Rates of Returns," provides an excellent summary on how the venture capital industry began using the IRR method for measuring return on investments.

17. In addition to discussions we had with leading angel investors and venture capitalists, we reviewed the following literature: R.B. Carter and H.E. Van Auken, "Venture Capital Firms' Preferences for Projects in Particular Stages of Development," *Journal of Small Business Management* (January 1994), pp. 60–73; A.V. Bruno and T.T. Tyebjee, "The Entrepreneur's Search for Capital," *Journal for Business Venturing* 2 (1985), pp. 64–74; and J. Freear, J.E. Sohl, and W.E. Wetzel, "Angels: Personal Investors in the Venture Capital Market," *Entrepreneurship & Regional Development* (1995), pp. 85–94.

18. Anthony Effinger and Ashley Gross, "Siebel: System Error," *Bloomberg Markets*, April 2003, pp. 57–62. Siebel issued 21 percent; Cisco, 3.8 percent; Intel, 3.5 percent; Oracle, 1.1 percent; and Microsoft, 0.7 percent. It is interesting to note that Tom Sie-

bel, Siebel Systems' founder and the biggest shareholder with a 10.7 percent stake in the company, has sold $959 million worth of Siebel stock.

19. To simplify our sector-by-sector analysis of first-round investment activity, we pared down the seventeen sectors we discussed in Chapter 4 to nine in this section. For the Communications sector, we combined the data of Telecommunications and Networking and Equipment sectors. For the analysis, Retailing & Media, Retailing & Distribution, Consumer Products & Services, and Media & Entertainment sectors were all combined. Computer Software was not combined with any other. For Computer Hardware & Services, we examined the combined data of Computers & Peripherals, and IT Services. Biotechnology was not combined with any other. For Healthcare Related, we examined the combined data of Medical Devices & Equipment, and of Healthcare Services. For Semiconductors & Electronics, we examined the combined data of Semiconductors, and of Electronics & Instrumentation. For Business & Financial, we examined the combined data of Business Products & Services, and of Financial Services. And for Industrial & Energy, we examined the combined data of Industrial/Energy and all other investment activity.

20. John Markoff and Matt Richtel, "Signs of Rebound Appear in the High-Tech Heartland," New York Times Online, January 14, 2002.

21. Brad Jones, presentation at VentureNet 2002, September 4, 2002, Dana Point, Calif.

22. Bill Stensrud, presentation at the annual Investment Capital Conference 2001, March 14, 2001, Los Angeles.

23. D. G. Smith, "How Early Stage Entrepreneurs Evaluate Venture Capitalists." Paper presented at the Babson College-Kauffman Foundation Research Conference, University of South Carolina, May 12, 1999. Smith's study looked at entrepreneurs who received venture capital: 71 percent received more than one offer to invest, and 54 percent received three or more offers. In choosing their VCs, the entrepreneurs spent on the average forty hours, with 29 percent spending more than one hundred hours. They relied on other entrepreneurs, on other VCs, and on their own collective insights and experience.

24. Brian Bedol, presentation at Eventure Forum, June 27, 2000, Los Angeles.

25. Kenneth W. Rind, "Dealing with the Corporate Strategic Investor," in Pratt's Guide to Venture Capital Sources (New York: Securities Data Publishing, 1999), pp. 93–96. Provides an excellent briefing on the background of corporate investing, problems, and selecting investors.

26. Howard Anderson, "Not All VCs Are Created Equal," MIT Sloan Management Review, (Summer 2001), pp. 88–92.

27. Shannon Henry, "With Venture Funds Scarce, Start-Up Firms Turn to U.S." Washington Post Online, October 29, 2002.

28. "New Private Placements: Funds Raised, 2002," Milken Institute 2003 Global Conference Briefing Book (2003), p. II–11.

29. For example, see Michael N. Brette, Raising Capital For Your Business: Through the Use of Private Placement Offerings, Direct Public Offerings, & Small Corporate Offerings (Torrance, Calif.: Griffin Publishing Group, 1998). Brette has prepared a great how-to workbook that focuses on using private placement under Regulation D Securities Act of 1933, also Regulation A, and details the process behind a Small Corporate Offering Registration (SCOR) with the completion of the U-7 Form.

30. Joanne Sammer, "A Fresh Look at Asset-Based Lending," Business Finance, July 2002, p. 54.

31. Ilan Mochari, "The Numbers Game," The Inc 500 Special Report, October 15, 2002.

32. Alec R. Levenson and Kristen L. Willard, "Do Firms Get the Financing They Want? Measuring Credit Constraints Among Small Businesses in the United States." Working paper published by the Milken Institute (June 1997). This paper measures credit constraints for small businesses in the United States in the late 1980s. They found that only 2.1 percent of small businesses were directly credit-constrained in 1987–1988. Another 2.2 percent may have faced some short-run constraints on invest-

ment. Finally, an additional 4.2 percent were indirectly constrained, discouraged from applying because of expected denial.

33. As quoted in Jeffry A. Timmons, *New Venture Creation* (Chicago: Irwin/Mc-Graw-Hill 1994), p. 543.

Chapter 13

1. William D. Bygrave and Jeffry A. Timmons, *Venture Capital at the Crossroads* (Boston: Harvard Business School Press, 1992), p. 167.

2. J. William Petty, "Harvesting Firm Value: Process and Results," in *Entrepreneurship 2000*, Donald L. Sexton and Raymond W. Smilor, editors (Chicago: Upstart Publishing, 1997), pp. 71–94.

3. William J. Link, "Identify All Possible Exits," *entreworld.org*, November 2002.

4. See *NVCA 2002 Yearbook*, p. 79.

5. S. Holmberg, "Value Creation and Capture: Entrepreneurship Harvest and IPO Strategies," in *Frontiers of Entrepreneurship Research,* Neil C. Churchill, et al., editors (Wellesley, Mass.: Babson College, 1991), pp. 191–204.

6. Alix Nyberg, "The Tough Go Shopping," *CFO*, January 2001, pp. 89–93.

7. Richard H. Gamble, "The IPO Brass Ring," *Controller Magazine*, December 1997, pp. 24–29.

8. L. Brokaw, "The First Day of the Rest of Your Life." *Inc.* 15 (1993), p. 144.

9. *Solving the Merger Mystery: Maximizing the Payoff of Mergers and Acquisitions*, a report published by Deloitte Consulting LLC (2001).

10. The information in this passage is from Steve Cadigan, acquisition integration specialist, Cisco Corporation. Presentation at the 2000 Middle Market Conference Mergers Acquisition & Finance, September 20, 2000, Beverly Hills, Calif.

11. Heesen is quoted in "Venture Capitalists Utilize M&A Market to Compensate for Weak IPO Market in 2001," NVCA press release, February 13, 2002.

12. See *NVCA 2002 Yearbook*, pp. 81–83.

13. Ammar Hanafi (director of acquisitions, Cisco Corporation). Keynote presentation at the 2000 Middle Market Conference Mergers Acquisition & Finance, September 20, 2000, in Beverly Hills, Calif.

14. Ibid.

15. Jeff Lawrence (Trillium Digital Systems), "Mergers and Acquisitions—The Transactions." Presentation at the Software Council of Southern California Program on M&A, October 4, 2001, Santa Monica, Calif.

16. Kirby Dyess (vice president, director, new business development, Intel), "Strategic Buyers." Presentation at the 2000 Middle Market Conference Mergers Acquisition & Finance, September 20, 2000, Beverly Hills, Calif.

17. "Venture Capitalists: More Caution, More Due Diligence, More Diversity." *Knowledge@ Wharton Online*, August 8, 2000.

18. Herb Cohen, keynote presentation at the 1999 Middle Market Conference Mergers Acquisition & Finance, September 22, 1999, Beverly Hills, Calif.

Chapter 14

1. Hal Lancaster, "The Art of the Pitch, And How to Craft It," *Wall Street Journal Online* (2001). Jonathan Seelig, one of the co-founders of Akami Technologies, learned how to perfect his Fast Pitch the hard way—nobody was listening, and worse yet, nobody was investing. His first pitch was too technologically focused. He learned that investors were more interested in hearing how their customers would use their technology instead. His painful lesson, as he said, "turned us into a more market-focused group" and by the time the venture team was ready to seek funds seriously, their Fast Pitch focused on defining their market, their service, and customer demand.

2. Meredith Trueblood, "The Accidental Venture Capitalist," *Upside*, June 2000, p. 60.

3. Daryl Savage, "Weathering the Storm," *Palo Alto Weekly Online*, October 19, 2001.

4. We found this great quote in Adam Cohen, *The Perfect Store: Inside eBay* (New York: Little, Brown, 2002), p. 73.

5. Arthur Rock, "Strategy vs. Tactics from a Venture Capitalist," *Harvard Business Review* (November 1987).

6. Rob Adams, *A Good Hard Kick in the Ass: Basic Training for Entrepreneurs* (New York: Crown Business, 2002), p. 18; and Jim Clark, *Netscape Time: The Making of the Billion Dollar Start-Up That Took on Microsoft* (New York: St. Martin's Press, 1999), p. 20. Jim Clark of Netscape fame calls it the "fox-and-hedgehog" theory. The fox knows a lot of things. The hedgehog knows only one big thing. Most high-tech entrepreneurs are hedgehogs. And if the idea looks to be a success, the hedgehog is determined to hold onto the idea "tenaciously."

7. Robert D. Hisrich and Michael P. Peters, *Entrepreneurship*, 5th ed. (New York: McGraw-Hill, 2002), p. 227.

8. Rock, "Strategy vs. Tactics from a Venture Capitalist."

9. Nora Macaluso, "Raising Capital: Dos and Don'ts for Small E-Businesses," *e-Commerce Times Online*, November 20, 2001.

10. David Armstrong, "The VC Game," *Wall Street Journal Online*, October 15, 2001.

11. Ann Winblad, presentation at UCLA Women's Business Conference, March 3, 2000, Los Angeles, Calif.

12. Andreas Stavropoulos, "What Top Venture Capitalists Look for in Internet Business Plans." See http://www.dfj.com.

13. Bill Joos, "Perfecting Your Positioning and Pitching." Presentation at Garage Technology Venture's Startup Strategies workshop, June 25, 2002, Costa Mesa, Calif. Joos, vice president of entrepreneur development at Garage Technology Ventures, has heard some 100,000 pitches since the beginning of Garage. According to him, "pitch-decay" means that listeners can remember only 50 percent after one hour or so and not much more than 10 percent in one week. In their follow-up call, entrepreneurs need to provide some context and content about their presentation. For example, they should say, "Here's when and where we talked/met. Here's what we talked about. Here's what you suggested me to do. I did it and I'm calling you back."

14. Brian E. Hill and Dee Power, *Inside Secrets to Venture Capital* (New York: John Wiley & Sons, 2001). In research for their book, they asked VCs: "What's the most common way you have found the companies you have actually invested in?" Answers: For 34 percent, another VC referred the deal; for 30 percent, the VC was directly contacted by the entrepreneur; for 17 percent, intermediary consultants placed the deal; and for 21 percent, the deal came through others, such as attorneys and accountant, or through business events.

15. Mike Medavoy, chairman and CEO, Phoenix Studios, "Entertainment—How Does California Maintain Its Competitive Edge?" Presentation at the Milken Institute State of the State Conference, November 6, 2001, Santa Monica, Calif.

16. Howard Anderson, "Not All VCs Are Created Equal," *MIT Sloan Management Review* (Summer 2001), pp. 88–92.

17. Leigh Steinberg, *Winning with Integrity: Getting What You're Worth Without Selling Your Soul* (New York: Times Business, 1998), p. 14.

Afterword

1. Sam Walton, *Sam Walton: Made in America* (New York: Doubleday, 1992).

2. Howard Schultz, *Pour Your Heart into It: How Starbucks Built a Company One Cup at a Time* (New York: Hyperion Books, 1997).

3. Stephen Segaller, *Nerds 2.0.1: A Brief History of the Internet* (New York: TV Books, 1999).

4. William Davis, *The Innovators: The Essential Guide to Business Thinkers, Achievers and Entrepreneurs* (New York: AMACOM, 1987).

5. Jerry Useem, "The March of Progress: Entrepreneurship," *Business 2* (August 2001), p. 81.

Index